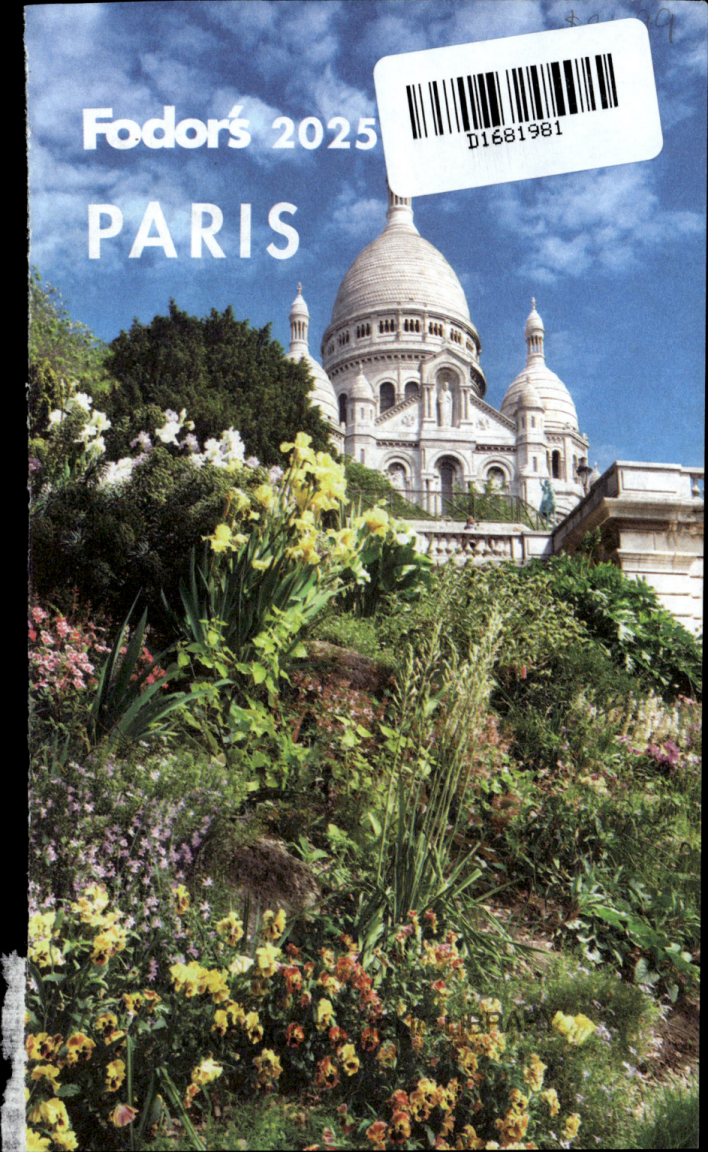

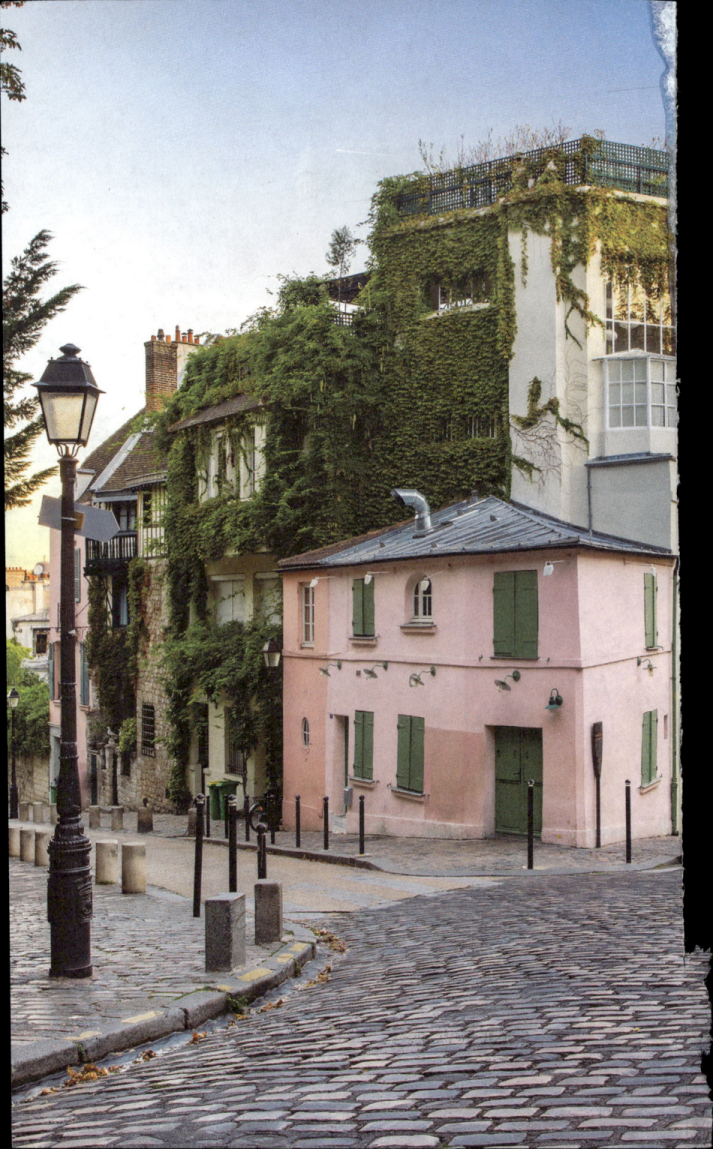

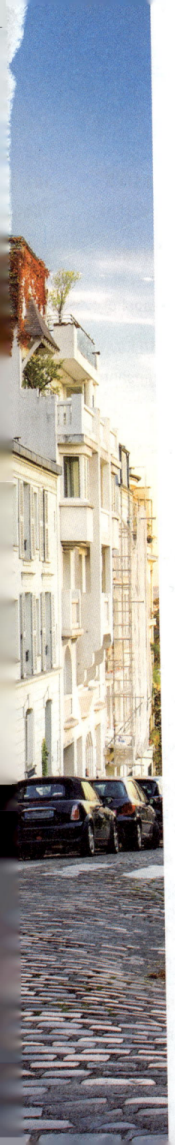

Welcome to Paris

Paris is one of the most beautiful cities on earth, a truth easily appreciated on a stroll that could yield one stunning vista after another, from the epic Eiffel Tower to the regal Jardin des Tuileries to the petite cafés bursting onto the sidewalks. Beyond the city's visual appeal, the cultural riches of the French capital are unsurpassed. Whether you opt to explore the historic, fashion-conscious, bourgeois, or bohemian and arty sides of Paris, one thing is certain: the City of Light will always enthrall. As you plan your upcoming travels to Paris, please confirm that places are still open and let us know when we need to make updates by writing to us at editors@fodors.com.

TOP REASONS TO GO

★ **Iconic landmarks:** From the Eiffel Tower to the Arc de Triomphe, Paris dazzles.

★ **Chic shopping:** The Champs-Élysées and Rue St-Honoré are the ultimate shopaholic high.

★ **Heavenly food:** Whether it's haute cuisine or baguettes, locals know how to eat.

★ **The Seine:** The river's bridges and islands reward exploration by foot or boat.

★ **Grand museums:** From the mammoth Louvre to the petite Musée Rodin, art abounds.

★ **Majestic churches:** Notre-Dame and Sacré-Coeur boldly mark the city's skyline.

Contents

1 EXPERIENCE PARIS 6

20 Ultimate Experiences 8

What's Where 16

Paris Today.................... 18

What to Eat and Drink in Paris.. 20

What to Buy in Paris........... 22

Best Museums in Paris 24

Best Churches in Paris......... 26

Best Parks and Gardens in Paris 28

Under-the-Radar Paris 30

An Art Lover's Guide to Paris... 32

Paris with Kids 34

What to Read and Watch....... 36

2 TRAVEL SMART 39

Know Before You Go........... 40

Getting Here and Around....... 42

Essentials 51

Best Tours in Paris............. 59

Helpful French Phrases 60

On the Calendar 62

Great Itineraries............... 66

Contacts 68

3 ÎLE DE LA CITÉ AND ÎLE ST-LOUIS 69

Neighborhood Snapshot 70

Île de la Cité................... 71

Île St-Louis.................... 79

4 AROUND THE EIFFEL TOWER.. 81

Neighborhood Snapshot 82

5 THE CHAMPS-ÉLYSÉES 103

Neighborhood Snapshot 104

6 AROUND THE LOUVRE AND LES HALLES 129

Neighborhood Snapshot 130

7 LES GRANDS BOULEVARDS .. 171

Neighborhood Snapshot 172

8 MONTMARTRE............... 199

Neighborhood Snapshot 200

9 THE MARAIS 217

Neighborhood Snapshot 218

10 EASTERN PARIS 247

Neighborhood Snapshot 248

Bastille, Bercy, Nation, and Around 250

Oberkampf and Charonne 260

Canal St-Martin and République............... 268

Belleville to La Villette 277

11 THE LATIN QUARTER......... 281

Neighborhood Snapshot 282

12 ST-GERMAIN-DES-PRÉS 297

Neighborhood Snapshot 298

13 MONTPARNASSE 323

Neighborhood Snapshot 324

14 WESTERN PARIS............. 335

Neighborhood Snapshot 336

15. SIDE TRIPS FROM PARIS 345

Welcome to
Side Trips from Paris.......... 346
Planning 349
Versailles 351
Rambouillet 366
Chartres 367
Giverny 370
St-Germain-en-Laye 373
Rueil-Malmaison 374
Suresnes..................... 375
Auvers-sur-Oise 376
Chantilly 378
Senlis........................ 379
Compiègne 382
Disneyland Paris 383
Château de Vaux-le-Vicomte .. 385
Barbizon 386
Courances 387
Fontainebleau 388

INDEX........................ 390

ABOUT OUR WRITERS........ 399

Fodor's *Features*

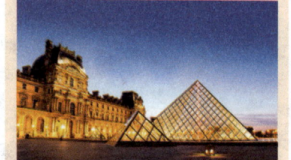

Musée du Louvre.................. 138
Versailles 354

MAPS

Ile de la Cité and
Ile St-Louis................ 74–75
Around the Eiffel Tower 84–85
The Champs-Élysées..... 106–107
Around the Louvre....... 132–133
The 2nd Arrondissement .. 174–175
Outside of the
2nd Arrondissement 192–193
Montmartre 204–205
The Marais............... 222–223
Bastille, Bercy, Nation,
Oberkampf, and Charonne .. 252–253
Canal St-Martin, République, and
Belleville to La Villette 270-271
The Latin Quarter 286–287
St-Germain-des-Prés 302
Montparnasse................ 328
Western Paris 340
Western Île-de-France........ 352
Eastern Ile-de-France......... 380

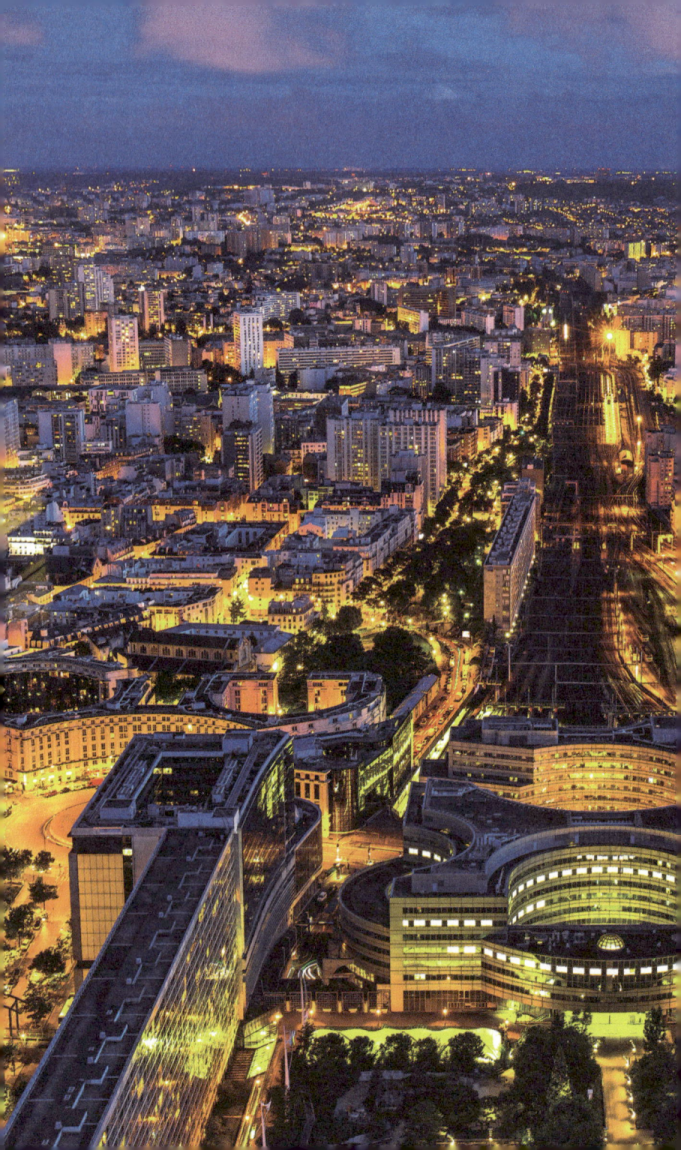

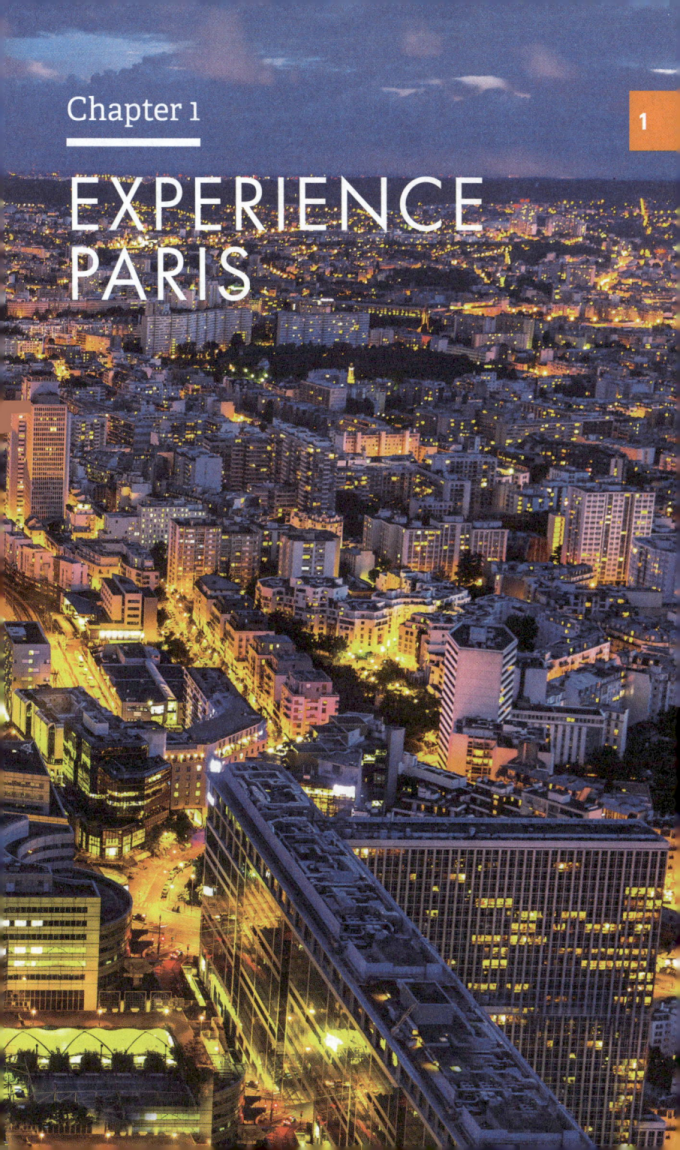

Chapter 1

EXPERIENCE PARIS

20 ULTIMATE EXPERIENCES

Paris offers terrific experiences that should be on every traveler's list. Here are Fodor's top picks for a memorable trip.

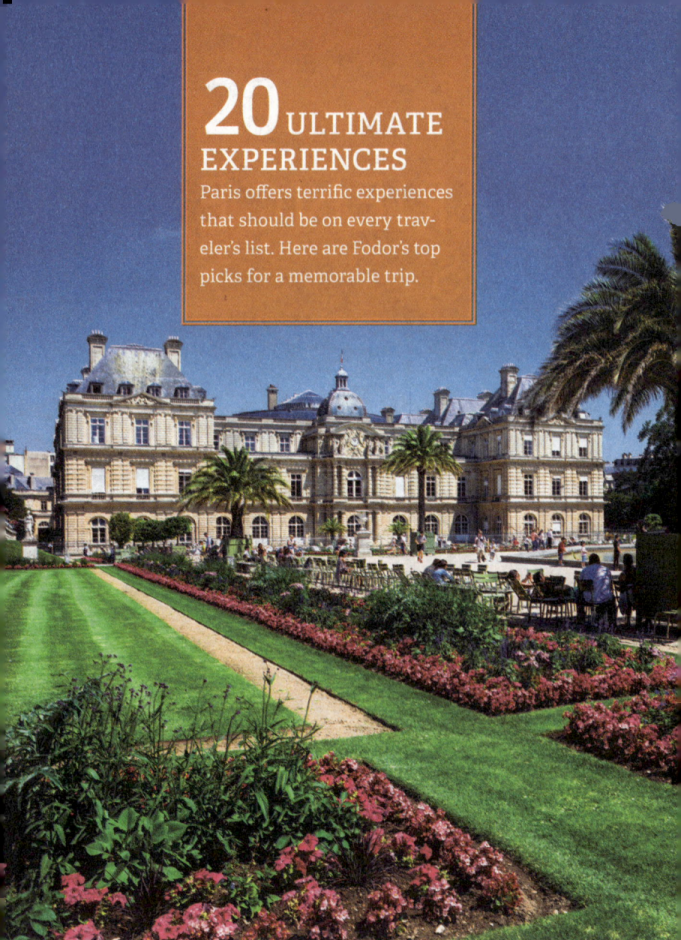

1 Luxembourg Gardens

Bordered by St-Germain-des-Prés and the Latin Quarter, these charming gardens are the definition of a true Parisian park. Here, you can relax on a lawn chair in the sunshine or enjoy an impromptu picnic. *(Ch. 12)*

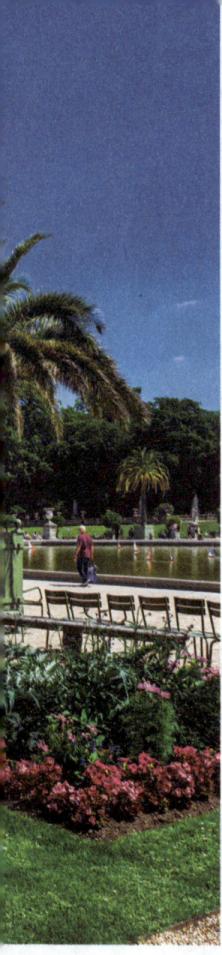

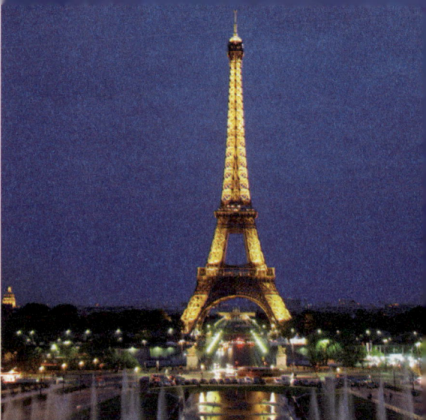

2 Eiffel Tower

Whether you head to the top or pose for a selfie in front, the breathtaking Eiffel Tower is the ultimate symbol of Paris for most visitors. (Ch. 4)

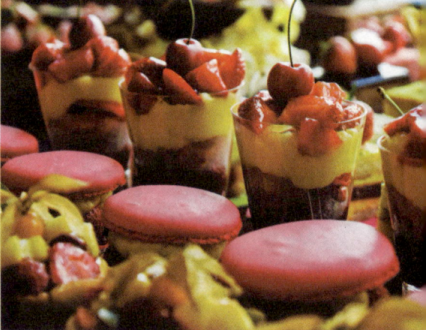

3 Parisian Cuisine

From pastries and macarons to baguettes and crêpes, food in Paris is nothing short of sublime. (Ch. 3–14)

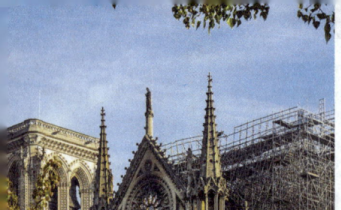

4 Notre-Dame

Everyone in Paris is eagerly awaiting the December 2024 reopening of this cathedral that is the symbolic heart of the city and, for many, of France itself. *(Ch. 3)*

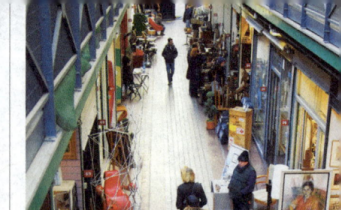

5 Marché aux Puces St-Ouen

The 150-year-old market is the world's largest and maybe most famous flea market, selling everything from vintage couture to gilded mirrors and burnished silver. *(Ch. 8)*

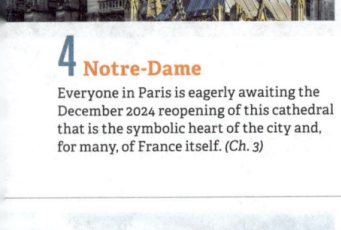

6 The Seine

There's nothing like seeing Paris via a walk or boat trip on its main waterway. Along the tranquil Seine, historic bridges connect the city's most famous landmarks. *(Ch. 3)*

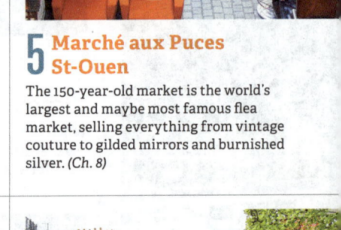

7 Champs-Élysées

A mecca for shoppers (both locals and visitors alike), the Champs-Élysées remains the most famous avenue in Paris—and, perhaps, the world. *(Ch. 5)*

8 Parisian Cafés

Still the center of social life for many Parisians, neighborhood cafés offer great food and coffee, and better people-watching. *(Ch. 3–14)*

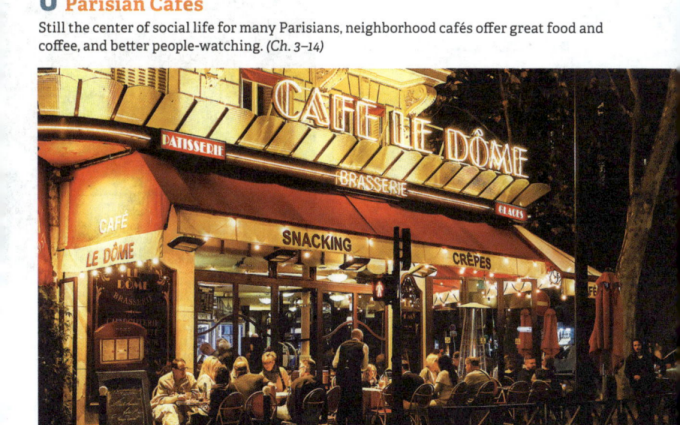

9 Montmartre

Montmartre, and other neighborhoods like Canal St-Martin and the Latin Quarter, are like charming villages filled with shops, eateries, and cobblestone streets. *(Ch. 8)*

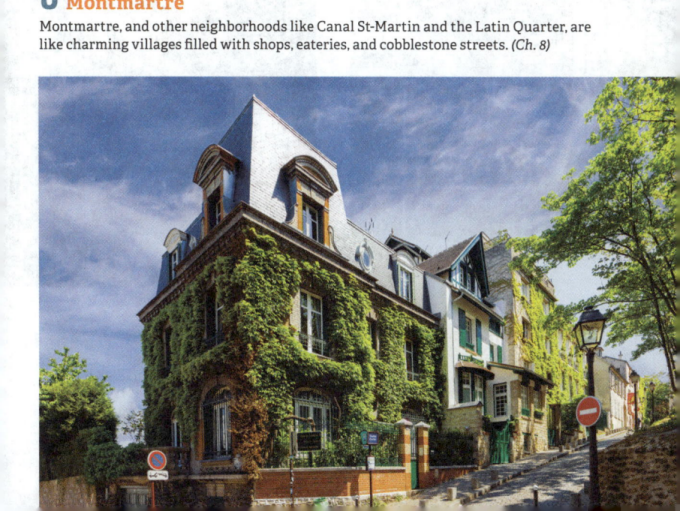

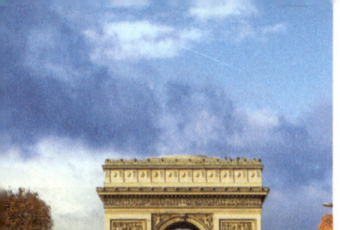

10 *Arc de Triomphe*

This colossal monument to military victory is a major landmark of the city, with excellent views from the top of all of Paris. *(Ch. 5)*

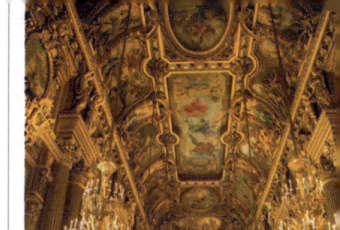

11 *Opéra Garnier*

Home of *The Phantom of the Opera* and the inspiration for Edgar Degas's dancer paintings, the dazzling Palais Garnier is one location of the National Opera of Paris. *(Ch. 7)*

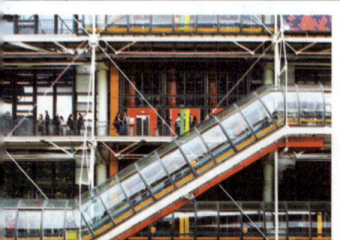

12 *Centre Pompidou*

One of modern Paris's more controversial buildings when it was built in 1977, this art complex now houses the city's modern art museum. *(Ch. 9)*

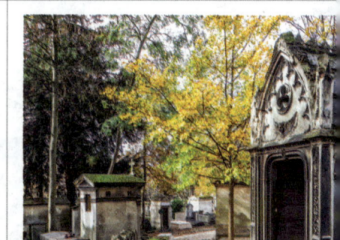

13 *Cimetière du Père-Lachaise*

Perhaps the world's most famous cemetery, this oasis is the final resting place for notable figures like Marcel Proust, Oscar Wilde, Jim Morrison, and Gertrude Stein. *(Ch. 10)*

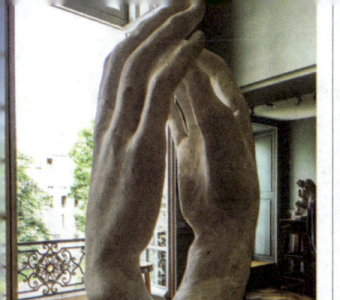

14 Musée Rodin

Once the sculptor's studio, this stately 18th-century mansion contains more than 6,000 sculptures, including Rodin's masterpieces *The Thinker* and *The Kiss.* (Ch. 4)

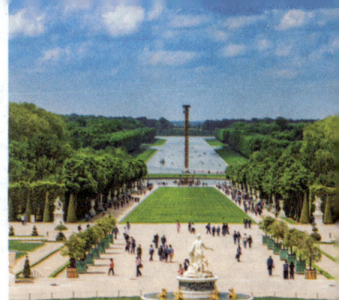

15 Versailles

The famous château was home to Louis XIV and Marie-Antoinette and remains the grandest palace in France, from its dazzling Hall of Mirrors to its landscaped gardens. (Ch. 15)

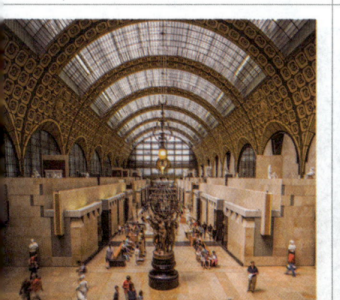

16 Musée D'Orsay

Under the soaring roof of one of Paris's grand Beaux-Arts railway stations, the Musée d'Orsay contains the world's largest collection of impressionist masterpieces. (Ch. 12)

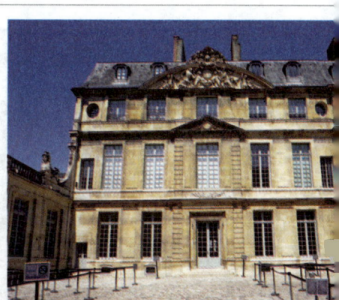

17 Musée Picasso

Home to the world's largest public collection of Pablo Picasso works, the paintings, sculptures, and drawings here span the artist's entire career. (Ch. 9)

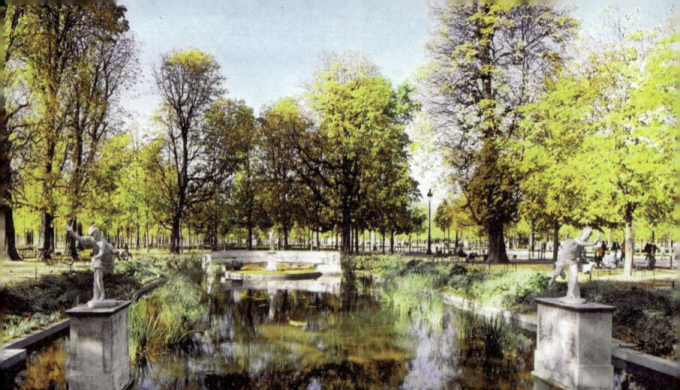

18 Jardin des Tuileries

This quintessential French garden was once where Paris's wealthiest came to stroll, and today is still one of the city's best walks. *(Ch. 6)*

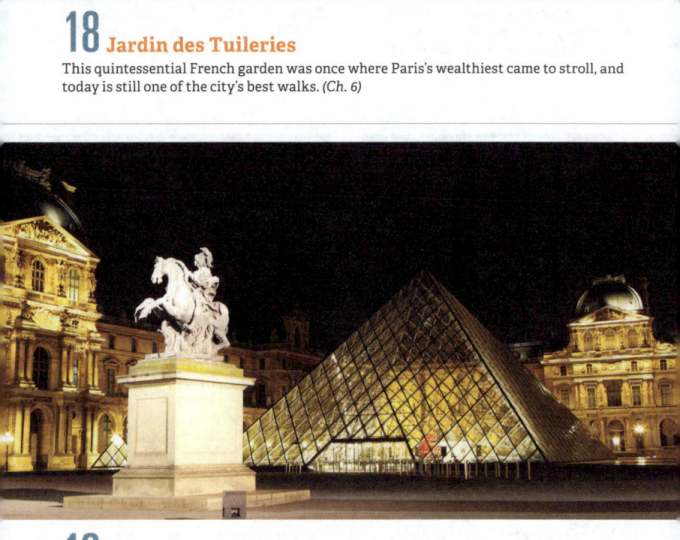

19 The Louvre

The world's greatest art museum—and the largest, with works from almost every civilization on earth—houses masterpieces like the *Mona Lisa* and the *Venus de Milo*. *(Ch. 6)*

20 Basilique du Sacré-Coeur

It's hard not to feel as though you're climbing up to heaven when you visit Sacred Heart Basilica, the white castle in the sky perched atop the city. (Ch. 8)

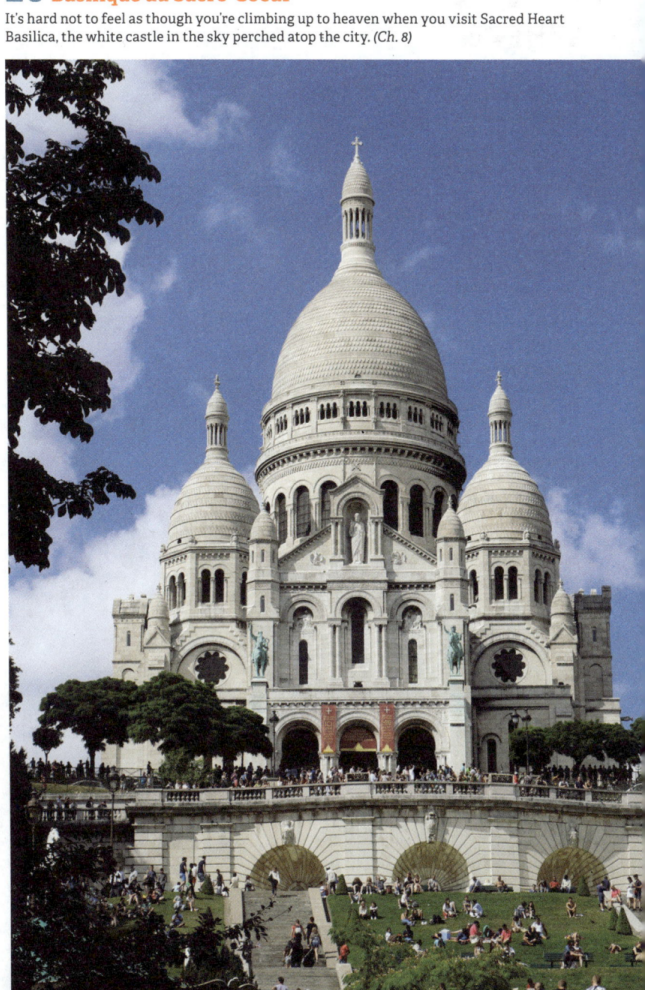

WHAT'S WHERE

1 Île de la Cité and Île St-Louis. Just a few steps from the "mainland," these small islands in the Seine are the heart of Paris.

2 Around the Eiffel Tower. With the Champ de Mars, Les Invalides, and the Seine nearby, many lovely strolls give you camera-ready views of Paris's ultimate monument.

3 Champs-Élysées. The Champs-Élysées and Arc de Triomphe are obvious stops for visitors, but several excellent museums here are also well worth checking out.

4 Around the Louvre. This neighborhood is paved with chic streets and *passages couverts* that attract shoppers as well as art lovers.

5 Les Grands Boulevards. Use the Palais Garnier as your landmark as you set out to do some power shopping.

6 Montmartre. Montmartre feels separate from the rest of Paris—but it's prime tourist territory, with Sacré-Coeur as its main attraction.

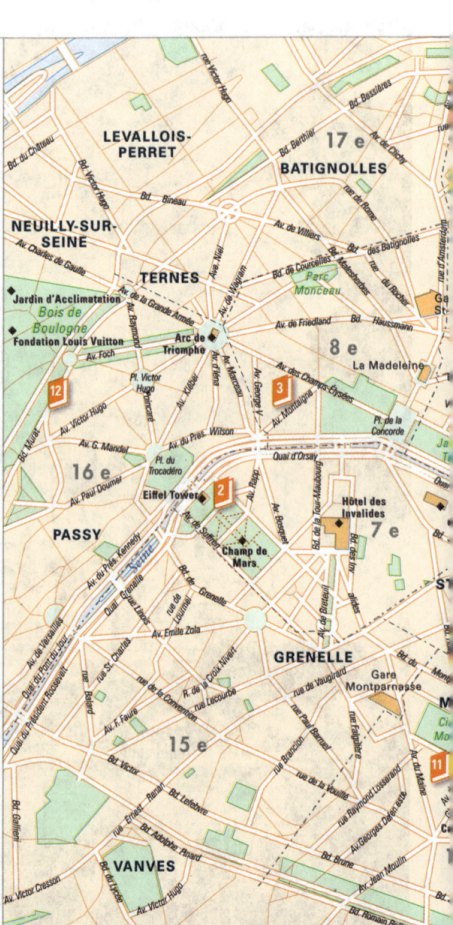

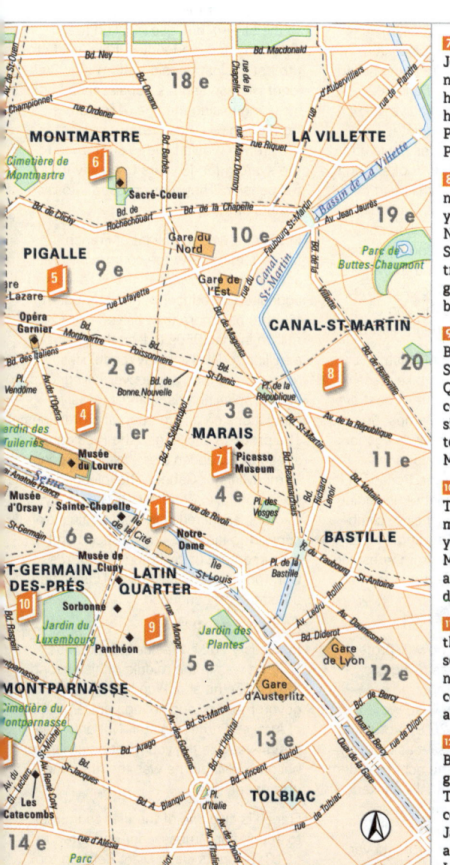

7 Le Marais. Paris's old Jewish neighborhood is now one of the city's hippest hoods. While here, visit the Musée Picasso and linger at Place des Vosges.

8 Eastern Paris. If it's new and happening, you'll find it out here. Neighborhoods like Canal St-Martin overflow with trendy eateries, funky galleries, and edgy boutiques.

9 The Latin Quarter. Built around the fabled Sorbonne, the Latin Quarter has been the center of student life since 1257. It's also home to the Panthéon and Musée de Cluny.

10 St-Germain-des-Prés. The Musée d'Orsay is a must-see, but make sure you leave time for the Musée Delacroix or an amble through the Jardin du Luxembourg.

11 Montparnasse. Once the haunt of creative souls, Montparnasse is now known for its contemporary-art scene, as well as the Catacombs.

12 Western Paris. The Bois de Boulogne is one great reason to trek here. The popular park contains the kid-friendly Jardin d'Acclimatation and art-filled Fondation Louis Vuitton.

Paris Today

PARIS POST-OLYMPICS

For the last few years, Paris has been all about the 2024 Summer Olympic Games, which finally took place July 26 through August 11. Despite being hailed as the "Games for all" by Paris 2024 chief Tony Estanguet, expensive ticket prices were criticized by athletes who wondered how their families could afford to attend. The city used 95% of existing or temporary venues but still went over the €3.35-billion budget earmarked for construction and the €3.9-billion budget for the event itself. The grand total rang in at €8 billion but compared to the €12.2 billion spent for the 2020 Tokyo games or €11.8 billion for the 2016 Rio games, the Paris games looked downright affordable.

For the first time in Olympic history, the opening ceremony did not take place in the main stadium; it was the largest ever held in the history of the Games. Some 10,500 athletes and national delegations were paraded for 4 miles along the Seine, ending in front of the Trocadéro for the final show. Competitions—including four new events: break dancing, climbing, skateboarding, and surfing—were scattered across the city, from wrestling in front of the Eiffel Tower to equestrian matches at Versailles.

PROTESTS

The city of Paris knows how to protest. At the end of 2018, it was rising gas prices at the pump that spurred on the *gilets jaunes* (yellow vest) wave of demonstrations across 2019, protesting what the working class saw as a government primarily serving the rich. President Emmanuel Macron eventually backed down from further fuel tax increases, but the French continued to hit the streets every weekend in protest over his general economic policies until the coronavirus pandemic threw the country into lockdown in March 2020.

Then, in January 2023, workers and unions across the country not only took to the streets but also blocked fuel deliveries and randomly cut electricity to protest against pension reforms by President Macron and his Renaissance Party, including raising the age of retirement from 62 to 64. These reforms meant that the French would have to contribute to the system for 43 years to qualify for a full pension. They were passed into law in April of that year.

In 2024, it was the plight of French farmers that threw the country into yet another crisis. France is the EU's leading agricultural producer but its number of farmers has more than halved from 2½ million in the 1950s to less than half a million today. Highway roadblocks represented their anger over falling food prices, spiraling costs, and excessive regulations on environmental protections. The protests challenged the President ahead of European elections but French Prime Minister Gabriel Attal pledged a freeze on taxes for diesel fuel used by tractors, an increase in existing financial support to farmers, and to speed up the disbursement of cash under the EU's Common Agricultural Policy. Unsatisfied, the stand-off continued.

LGBTQ+ RIGHTS

In January 2024, President Emmanuel Macron was in the middle of his second term when he shook up his unpopular government by appointing Parisian Gabriel Attal as Prime Minister. Not only was the 34-year-old the youngest politician to become PM, but he was the first who was openly gay.

France is also one of the first countries to appoint an Ambassador dedicated to LGBTQ+ rights (Jean-Marc Berthon took on the role in 2022) and to dedicate a €2 million fund through its embassies "to support those who are defending LGBTQ rights on a daily basis around the world, sometimes at risk to their lives."

Paris continues to rank high as one of the best cities in the world for LGBTQ+ travel. City Hall organizes an annual "14th Pride" (a reference to its location in the 14th arrondissement), a two-week festival to raise public awareness of the fight against LGBTQ+ discrimination with 20 events and cultural activities, most of which are free.

CITY DEVELOPMENTS

The good news is that Notre Dame Cathedral is on track to reopen in December 2024, five years after a fire nearly destroyed it. The bad news is that the Centre Pompidou, Paris's museum of modern and contemporary art, will soon close to the public for a five-year €200 million renovation until 2030. Still, some of its work will be temporarily housed in the Louvre and Grand Palais, among other sites. Not to fret, to celebrate its 40-year anniversary, the Cartier Foundation moves from the 14th arrondissement to the Louvre des Antiquaires. The 14,000-square-meter space redesigned by Jean Nouvel includes 6,000 square meters of exhibitions, permanent collections, and cinema, making it the largest private art center in Paris.

Finally, the southern section of Paris *métro* line 15 from Pont de Sèvres to Noisy-Champs is scheduled to open in 2025, with the entire automated line running by the early 2030s. As one of four Grand Paris Express lines, it will connect the suburbs of Paris (Hauts-de-Seine, Val-de-Marne, and Seine-St-Denis) and become the world's longest underground rapid tunnel for passenger traffic.

SWIMMING IN THE SEINE

One of the most famous rivers on the planet, the Seine runs 775 kilometers (481 miles) from Burgundy in east-central France through Paris and northwest to the sea in Normandy. For many, the Seine turned out to be the biggest winner at the 2024 Paris Olympics. Swimming in it had been banned since 1923, and the river was declared biologically dead in the 1960s. It was resurrected as a venue for open-water marathons and triathlons during the Games and was made swimmable after nearly a hundred years to the tune of €1.4 billion. The city is hoping that access to open-air swimming areas will draw 7 million tourists a year and, more importantly, provide Parisians respite from the suffocating *canicule*, the heatwave that hits anytime from June to September. Paris Mayor Anne Hidalgo announced Bras Marie, Bras de Grenelle, and Bercy as the first swimming spots along the Seine with quayside access.

What to Eat and Drink in Paris

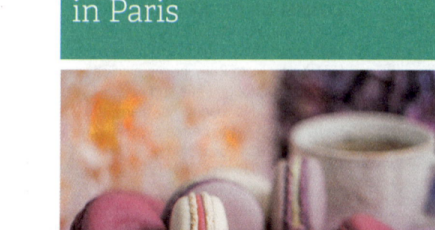

MACARONS

The French luxe variation of an Oreo cookie consists of flavored buttercream or ganache sandwiched between two gravity-defying soft-meringue shells. France's most popular cookie tends to be expensive thanks to the ingredients and the persnickety prep required.

BAGUETTES

Biting off the end of a baguette as you leave a bakery is one of the rare times it's acceptable to eat and walk at the same time in this country. Seriously though, is there anything better than oven-fresh French bread, especially when you can buy it for an average of just one euro? *Une baguette traditionnelle* is more expensive and, by law, can only be made from flour, water, leaven, and salt. If you prefer a softer baguette, order *pas trop cuite* or if you like it crunchy, *trop cuite*. It's hard for any true French bakery to make a bad baguette, but every Parisian has their favorite.

COCKTAILS

Paris nightlife can mean a lot of different things, but if you want to get a taste of how Parisians party, you need to check out the city's cocktail scene. Over the last few years, bars here have seen a surge of mixologists take over drink menus, creating unique and impressive concoctions from a wide range of ingredients. Some of the city's most famed bars have gotten in on the action, too.

CROISSANTS

There might not be any French food more iconic than a simple croissant. Originally shaped to symbolize the Ottoman flag ensign, these days a moon-shape croissant means it's made with margarine and, by law, must be tucked in on the ends. But between the price of butter and flour skyrocketing and industrial-made croissants with loads of preservatives finding their way into local bakeries, the buttery Gallic icon is currently in crisis. Fortunately, this is Paris, where baked-on-the-premises goods are usually available by 9 am.

WINE

From Bordeaux and Burgundy to Alsace and Beaujolais, tasting wine in Paris is a given, but *vin naturel* is de rigueur. Natural wines are considered a step up from organic, usually with low or no sulfites added. The supply of wine bars here is endless, so be sure to spend some time at one (or several) to discover how to drink like a Parisian.

COFFEE

This is how every Parisian morning should be spent: tasting glorious coffee roasts at a classic café. Coffee culture is pretty serious business in Paris, and it involves sitting or standing—not walking or driving. Most French drink *un petit café* (an espresso), but if that's too strong, order a diluted version: *un café allongé* (or *un café serré* if you need a jolt). A *café crème* is made with steamed milk, and you can sprinkle a little chocolate to make a cappuccino. A *noisette* is an espresso-size café crème. And, an "American" is a larger cup of brewed coffee (*café dilute*).

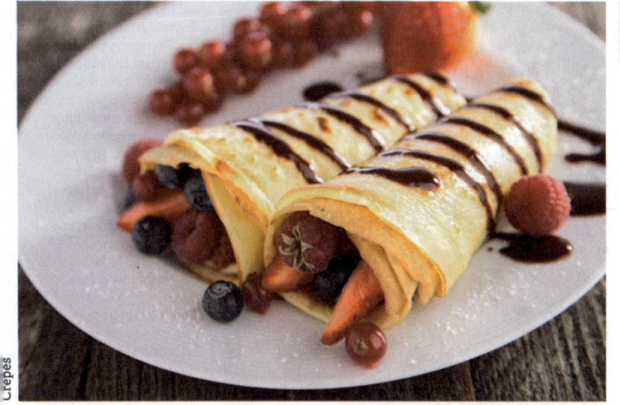

Crêpes

PASTRIES

While you're here, throw away the Fitbit and focus on the task at hand: enjoying melt-in-your-mouth traditional pastries that you can find only in Paris. Nearly any pastry shop or bakery you visit will include typical French classics, like madeleines, *pain au chocolat,* éclairs, and profiteroles. But more unique options include *puits d'amour* ("well of love"), a puff pastry with bourbon-vanilla cream glazed with caramel, or Paris-Brest, circular cream puffs filled with praline cream and topped with hazelnuts.

HAUTE GASTRONOMY

While eating in Paris on a budget is possible, it's also very, very easy to spend a small (or large) fortune on dining here, thanks to some of the world's most extravagant, well-reviewed, and yes, expensive restaurants. Before you head off all Michelin-starry-eyed to indulge in haute cuisine, remember that the "best" restaurants in Paris can be uncomfortably ceremonious—think ornate purse stools, price-less menus, and waiters hovering to decrumb the table at every bite. There are currently nine three-Michelin-starred restaurants in Paris, none of which could be called affordable, but all offer a level of fine dining that is hard to match anywhere else in the world.

CRÊPES

Crêpes are an essential part of French culture. You've probably heard of Pancake Tuesday, but what about Crêpe Chandeleur? A Groundhog Day–esque holiday, La Chandeleur takes place on February 2 each year; if it rains, expect another 40 days of winter. The French are superstitious about La Chandeleur; they hold a coin in their writing hand while flipping crêpes with the other. But, of course, you can enjoy crêpes at any time of the year here. The golden *sucré* crêpe is wheat-based and topped with sweet ingredients, while the darker galette crêpe is made from gluten-free buckwheat and is a base for savory combinations.

STEAK FRITES

Dig into a French brasserie classic dish: steak and fries. On a menu, it could be *entrecôte* (rib eye) or *faux filet* (strip steak), and restaurants will even list where the beef is sourced. There's usually a choice of accompanying sauce (which sometimes costs extra) like béarnaise, Roquefort, or peppercorn—or just go for au naturel. Americans have a tendency to overcook meat (*bien cuit*), but if you can't stomach *saignant* (rare), go for *moyen* (medium).

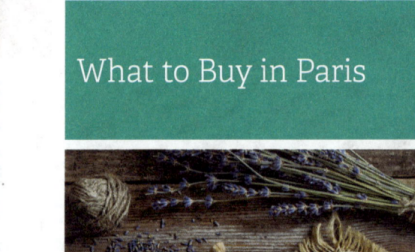

TEA AND COFFEE

With 800 varieties from 36 countries, French tea, including the famed Mariage Frères gourmet loose-leaf tea, has been exported globally. For coffee lovers, Café Verlet has been roasting since 1880, and large sacks of coffee beans greet you as you enter.

ARTWORK

Buying art in Paris requires confidence on two fronts: to get past the judgmental looks when you walk into a gallery and to not be bullied into buying something that's not a *coup de coeur.* Located atop Paris's tallest hill, Place du Tertre has attracted local artists for a century, although for Picasso, Renoir, and van Gogh, it may have been due to Montmartre's tax-exempt wine laws. Tertre may be touristy, but what a great backdrop for your street-art caricature. Marché de la Création is an open-air art market that takes place every Sunday (10 am to 7 pm) where you can meet the artists in person. For French vintage posters, head to Marché aux Puces de St-Ouen, the world's largest antique and secondhand market.

MARINIÈRE BRETON SWEATER

You can thank Coco Chanel for this French fashion staple (and for making the suntan "a new precedent of beauty" in the 1920s). The *marinière* striped pullover can be credited to 19th-century sailors in Brittany (aka Bretagne) who wore a layer of wool as protection from the harsh weather. But it didn't truly become part of French DNA until 1858, when the wool-knit striped *chandail* became the official naval uniform by decree: 21 white stripes (20 millimeters wide) and 21 blue stripes (10 millimeters wide), 15 white stripes and 14 or 15 blue stripes on the sleeve.

According to boutique shop Saint James, which has been making marinières for 130 years, the number 21 was meant to represent the naval victories of Napoléon's fleet against the British.

FRENCH WINE

French wine is sold throughout the world, and while there's nothing like actually visiting the vineyards in Bordeaux and Burgundy, the truth is that in Paris, you're going to see a lot of what you can find at home, unless you know where to look. A good place to stock up on unique wines and rosé is Lavinia, the city's largest wine shop.

MACARONS

Take a bite of this chewy soft-meringue cookie and you'll understand why it's France's best-selling biscuit. Its origins date back to 1533 Italy, but it didn't become a sandwich—two shells with flavored ganache in between—until a century ago. Not to be confused with coconut macaroons, these delicacies made of sugar, egg white, and almond flour can be sweet (salted caramel), savory (foie gras), fruity (raspberry rose), nutty (pistachio), or exotic (wasabi).

JEWELRY

Go big or go home sums up the Paris jewelry scene these days. That's not to say you need to over-accessorize—"less is more," as the fashion advice says. Named as one of the coolest jewelers by *Vogue*, Ana Khouri creates responsibly sourced rings and ear pieces to be "worn in an un-black-tie kind of way"; you can find her creations in the boutique shop WHITEbIRD. At the concept store Passage Doré, each collection by Louise Damas is named after a woman, because "wearing jewelry, each woman has her own story." Her exquisite bracelets, earrings, and necklaces are superfeminine and affordable.

PERFUME

Many of the perfumes you'll find in Paris have "Grasse roots." That means they're from the microclimate town of Grasse, located north of Cannes and known as the perfume capital of the world. This status is thanks to Jean de Galimard, who first invented fashionable perfumed gloves to cover the nauseating smell of tanners (workers who used to tan leather and hides). Some 250 years later, the global perfume industry is a $40 billion business with scents that go for $4,200 per ounce (that would be Chanel's Grand Extrait).

ANTIQUES AND VINTAGE CLOTHING

Three words that get French shoppers' hearts beating: *Grande Braderie*, which means "giant sale,"

and *brocante*, a second-hand market (not to be confused with *Dépôts-ventes*, or consignment stores). Marché aux Puces de St-Ouen is the mother of all flea markets with 1,500 high-end antiques dealers and 15 markets sprawling across almost 750,000 square feet. As the only market in central Paris, Marché aux Puces de la Porte de Vanves has 400 stalls with furniture, paintings, and jewelry. For the thrift-hearted, Les Puces de Montreuil is all about vintage clothes, toys, LPs, comics, and furniture. The Marché du Livre Ancien et d'Occasion at Parc de Georges Brassens attracts a European crowd for its books, old documents, vinyl records, and photos.

DESIGNER CLOTHING

Rule number one for dressing like a Parisian: learn to mix casual and dressy, and it doesn't have to be haute couture expensive. The moderately priced Sessùn sells eclectic and flowing designs that will earn you compliments back home for your unique style. Of course, if you really want to break the bank, you'll have plenty of flagship stores from world-famous designers to browse. Create your own Paris Fashion Week by checking out the haute couture at stores like Chanel, Dior, Saint Laurent, and Hermès. If you prefer one-stop shopping, the LVMH-owned department store La Samaritaine is home to 600 brands, so there's little chance you will leave without purchases in hand.

BERET

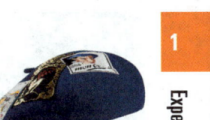

The one question on all our minds: can you pull off a beret if you're not actually French? The only thing we know for sure is that you should definitely try. The French couture designer Laulhère has been making the quintessential disc-shape hats since 1840. Stop by the boutique to pick up a unisex merino wool Genuine Beret (*Béret Véritable*), a steal at €79.

LINGERIE

The French are known for being a little more liberal than Americans when it comes to all things sex, so it makes sense that lingerie shops abound in Paris. And we're not talking Victoria's Secret; these are high-fashion, custom-made pieces that are nothing short of works of art. And there are options if you're looking for something provocative and seductive but a little more affordable.

Best Museums in Paris

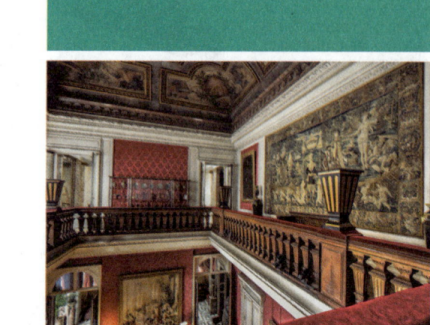

MUSÉE JACQUEMART-ANDRÉ

This museum was created from the private home—and private collections—of 19th-century Parisians Edouard André and Nélie Jacquemart and is as much a reflection of the lifestyle of the 19th-century Parisian bourgeoisie as it is of the art housed within it.

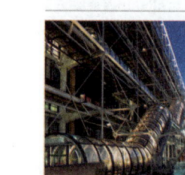

CENTRE POMPIDOU

Home to the largest modern art museum in Europe, the Pompidou Center is known for its extensive temporary exhibits, often devoted entirely to the work of just one artist. The center itself is a true work of art as well.

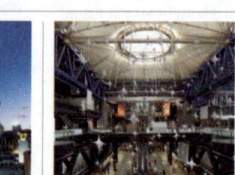

CITÉ DES SCIENCES ET DE L'INDUSTRIE

The City of Science and Industry is the largest science museum in Europe, located within the expansive Villette Park in Paris's 19e arrondissement. Particularly popular among children, the Cité des Sciences is home to a planetarium, IMAX theater, and greenhouse spaces.

MUSÉE RODIN

Auguste Rodin is one of France's most well-known sculptors, and this museum, located in the artist's former home not far from Les Invalides, contains one of the most extensive collections of his work. The museum's collections are displayed both within the house and in the expansive private garden outside; there is also a room devoted to the work of Camille Claudel, Rodin's lover and coworker.

PICASSO MUSEUM

Housed within a former private mansion, the collection here includes more than 5,000 of Picasso's works, including many of his larger sculptures. The museum also features pieces from Picasso's own art collection, including works by Cézanne, Degas, and Matisse.

MUSÉE DE L'ORANGERIE

This small museum within the Tuileries Gardens is a former orangery—or citrus greenhouse—transformed into an art gallery devoted to Impressionist and Postimpressionist paintings. The jewel of these collections is the series of eight water lily paintings by Claude Monet: the massive paintings have been permanently glued to the walls of the oval rooms specifically designed to house them.

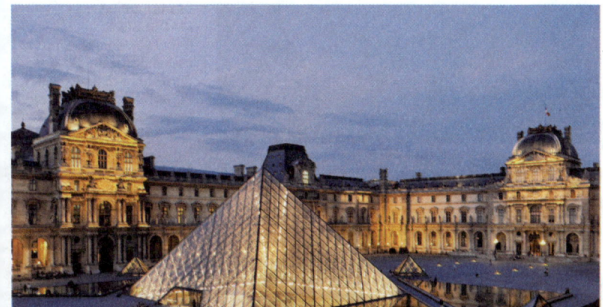

MUSÉE DE CLUNY

The Musée de Cluny, also known as the Musée National du Moyen Age, is a museum devoted to medieval history and art. Housed within the medieval Hôtel de Cluny and sitting atop the remnants of third-century Gallo-Roman baths, the building itself is as historic as its collections.

THE LOUVRE

Housed within the former royal palace of France's royalty is the Louvre Museum, a collection of more than 380,000 works of art from all over the world. Its most famous pieces include Leonardo da Vinci's *Mona Lisa* and the Venus de Milo.

MEMORIAL DE LA SHOAH

Paris's Marais has long been the Jewish quarter of Paris, so it's only appropriate that it be home to this memorial and museum to Jewish life during World War II. Opened by President Jacques Chirac, the first French president to publicly apologize for the acts of the French government contributing to the Holocaust, the memorial notably features a wall listing the names of the approximately 76,000 French Jews who were deported and murdered during the Shoah.

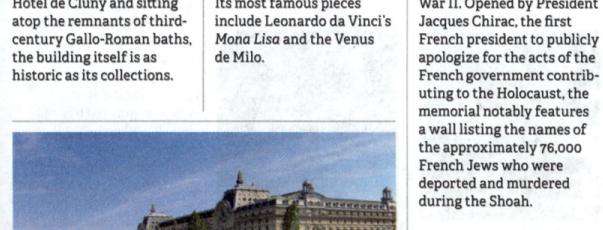

MUSÉE D'ORSAY

The Musée d'Orsay houses mostly French works dating from 1848 to 1914 within a former railway station, the Gare d'Orsay. The most famous works here are the pieces that make up the extensive Impressionist collections.

Best Churches in Paris

ÉGLISE DE LA MADELEINE

Built between 1754 and 1842 and surrounded by 52 Corinthian columns standing 65 feet tall, Église de la Madeleine was intended to be a temple of glory to honor Napoléon's Great Army. In 1806, Napoléon brought architect Pierre-Alexandre Vignon onboard, who drew inspiration from the Temple of Olympian Zeus in Athens to create the Madeleine we know today. After Napoléon's fall, King Louis XVIII ordered the neoclassical building to serve as a functioning church.

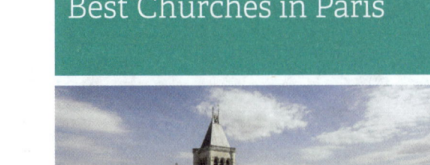

SAINT DENIS BASILICA AND ROYAL NECROPOLIS

From 987 to 1789, the kings and queens of France knew where they would end up: a distinguished burial at Saint Denis Basilica. The birthplace of Gothic art, the basilica, 5 km (3 miles) north of Paris, boasts the first cross-ribbed vault ever built in France.

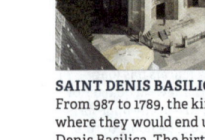

SACRÉ-COEUR BASILICA

Some 10 million tourists trek up to Montmartre every year (either via the 222 stairs or by funicular) to visit the Sacred Heart of Paris. Unlike other churches in Paris, the basilica features Romanesque-Byzantine architecture, similar to San Marco in Venice.

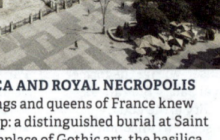

LA SAINTE-CHAPELLE

You are here for the magnificent medieval stained glass, all 1,113 panes depicting stories from both the New and Old Testaments. La Sainte-Chapelle was built between 1242 and 1248 to accommodate the Passion relics that were purchased by King Louis IX in 1239.

SAINT-EUSTACHE PARISH

At 346 feet in length, the dimensionally impressive Saint-Eustache in Les Halles features a range of architectural styles due to being built in 1532 (Louis XIV received communion here) and then restored in 1840. Saint-Eustache's central Chapel of the Blessed Virgin, with its marble Pigalle statue, was inaugurated by Pope Pius VII when he was in town for Napoléon's coronation. Music is a key element of the church's history. Mozart attended his mother's funeral at Saint-Eustache, and in 1855, Berlioz first conducted "Te Deum" with some 900 performers.

SAINT-ÉTIENNE-DU-MONT

Behind the Panthéon in the Latin Quarter, you'll find Saint-Étienne-du-Mont and, within it, Paris's last Renaissance rood screen.

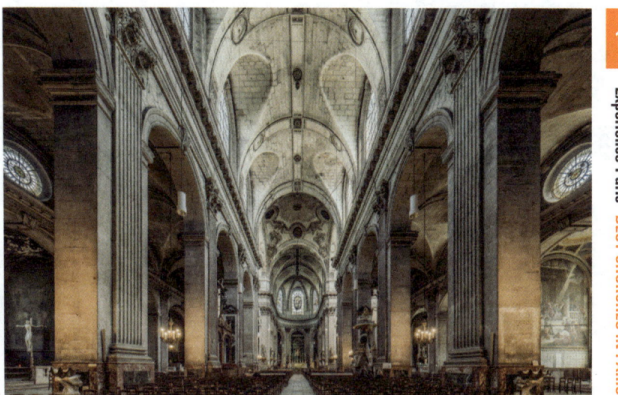

The finely carved stone structure spans the entire width of the nave between the north and south walls. Built in the 1530s, the church contains a mix of Gothic and Renaissance artwork and houses the remains of Genevieve, a patron saint of Paris.

ÉGLISE SAINT-SULPICE

The second-tallest church in Paris is famous for its gnomon, which played a role (although factually inaccurate) in the book and film *The Da Vinci Code*. The Église Saint-Sulpice was also where writer Victor Hugo was married. Building started on the Baroque church and its two distinctive mismatched towers in 1646, but it would take almost 100 years to complete. Today it features three paintings by Delacroix in the Chapelle des Anges to the right of the entrance.

CHAPELLE EXPIATOIRE

Built at the request of Louis XVIII to expiate his brother, this neoclassical chapel is where Louis XVI and Marie-Antoinette were buried after their 1793 execution (eventually their remains were moved to the Basilica of Saint-Denis). Constructed between 1816 and 1826, the Chapelle Expiatoire is a small historic monument with not much to see besides the crypt and a marble sculpture of Louis XVI and Marie-Antoinette. What makes it fascinating is the 2018 discovery that this was the site of the cemetery where 3,000 bodies were thrown after being guillotined at the Place de la Concorde.

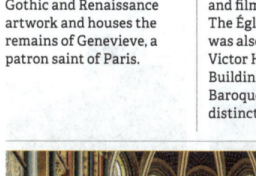

ÉGLISE ST-GERMAIN-DES-PRÉS

Originally an abbey founded in 543 dating back to the first kings of France, the oldest church in Paris is one of the city's first examples of Gothic architecture. Église St-Germain-des-Prés has witnessed everything from Viking ransacks to the manslaughter of monks.

Best Parks and Gardens in Paris

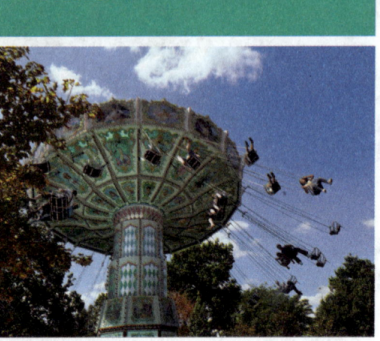

BOIS DE BOULOGNE

Paris's second-largest park used to be a hunting ground for kings of France, but now it mostly attracts art lovers (courtesy of the acclaimed Fondation Louis Vuitton located in the northern part of the park) and nature lovers (thanks to the bridle paths and cycling routes throughout).

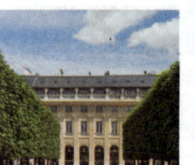

PALAIS-ROYAL

Across from the Louvre, the Palais-Royal, with its three magnificent arcades, is the only garden in Paris with the distinction of "Remarkable Garden" by the French Ministry of Culture. Not solely a favorite spot for locals and tourists to hang out, many movies have been filmed here, too, including *The Da Vinci Code* and *Interview with the Vampire*.

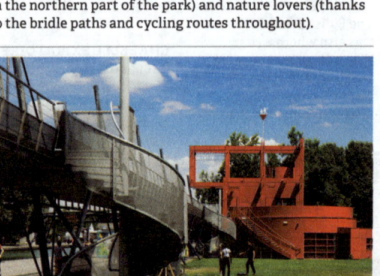

PARC DE LA VILLETTE

At 135 acres, Parc de la Villette is the largest in Paris. It boasts not only 35 green spaces, including several theme gardens like the bamboo garden, the garden of mirrors, and the dragon's garden, but also several art spaces, like the Geode cinema, the Zenith concert hall, and the Paris Philharmonic.

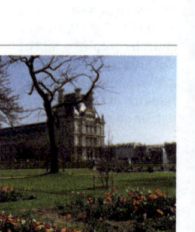

JARDIN DES TUILERIES

Nestled between the Louvre and Place de la Concorde, the Tuileries Garden was actually the site of an old tile (*tuile*) factory before the Palais des Tuileries was built in 1564. A century later, King Louis XIV's gardener designed it in the style of a formal French garden, but it wouldn't be until after the French Revolution that it became a public park.

BEST PARKS AND GARDENS IN PARIS

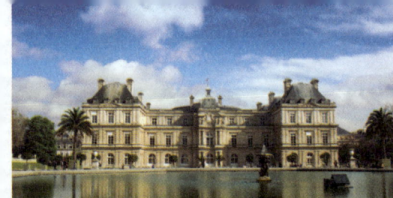

LUXEMBOURG GARDENS

Once upon a time, this 62-acre garden on the Left Bank was the pride of Luxembourg Palace. A central pond divides the space into the geometrically correct French garden and the charming English garden with its 106 statues, apple orchard, and apiary.

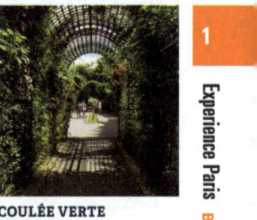

COULÉE VERTE

The former railroad line taking well-to-do Parisians to the Vincennes woods has been closed to trains and opened to pedestrians: bit by bit, the city is turning these former tracks into parks, one of the most beautiful of which is located near Bastille.

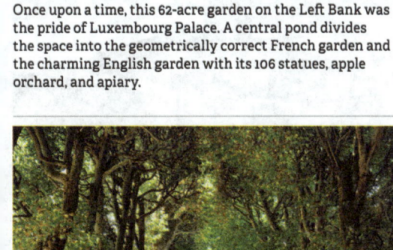

JARDIN DES PLANTES

This 400-year-old botanical garden dedicated to scientific research is located in front of the Grande Galerie de l'Evolution, one of three buildings that make up the National Museum of Natural History in the heart of the city.

CHAMP DE MARS

Forget the long lines at the Eiffel Tower and head to nearby Champ de Mars, one of the largest outdoor green spaces in Paris. Picnic on the vast lawns or stroll in the gardens and enjoy the Iron Lady like a Parisian. Even better, come after sunset and watch from a perfect perch as the tower's 20,000 lights sparkle for five minutes, every hour on the hour.

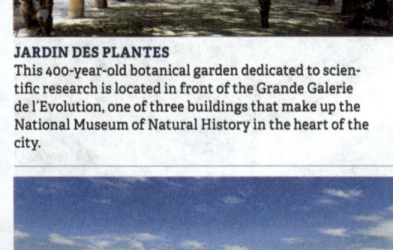

PARC MONCEAU

Dating back to the 17th century, this could well be the most elegant garden in Paris. Wrought-iron gates adorned in gold, a Renaissance archway, gorgeous statues, and magnificent trees are all here.

PARC DES BUTTES-CHAUMONT

The typical guinguette of the Camargue in Southern France has been transported to Paris with Rosa Bonheur, a café and wine bar located within the Parc des Buttes-Chaumont. This 19e arrondissement park, a local favorite, is home to one of the highest hills in the city.

Under-the-Radar Paris

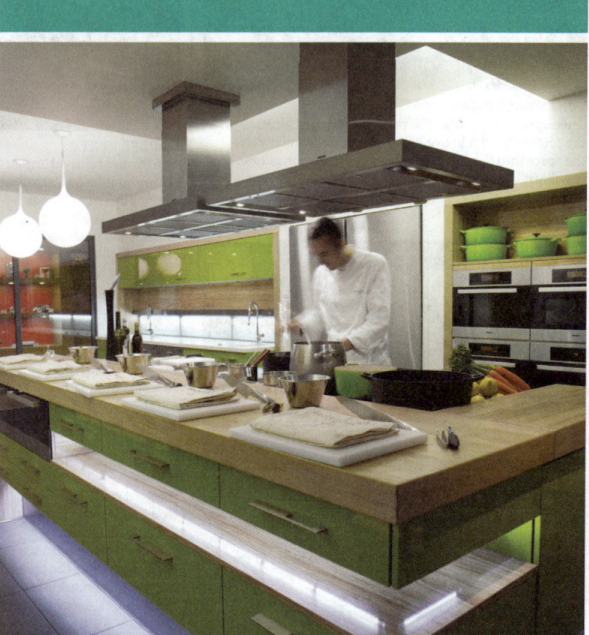

École de Cuisine Alain Ducasse

GO SWIMMING
Opened in 1924, all three pools of the picturesque indoor-outdoor Butte-aux-Cailles complex are fed by an underground spring. Care to swim in the Seine? The city invested €1.4 billion to clean up the river for the 2024 Olympic Games with the promise that three spots—Bras Marie (Parc des Rives de Seine, Right Bank); Bras de Grenelle (the banks of Île aux Cygnes (15th);

and the Passerelle Simone de Beauvoir, below Bercy Park (12th)—will be open for public swimming the following year. Afloat on the river (but not in it), the popular Piscine Joséphine Baker is the next best thing, with a retractable roof that keeps sunbathers happy. The Piscine Molitor is open to guests at the MGallery Hotel only, but it may be worth the splurge for a dip in Paris's most glamorous pool.

TAKE A COOKING CLASS
Whether it's a featherweight soufflé or buttery croissant, after a few hours at Le Foodist, you'll be ready to impress your friends with culinary skills acquired firsthand in Paris. At the École de Cuisine Alain Ducasse you can learn (in English) how to make chou pastry or the secrets of haute cuisine. Though pricier, the classes are also taught in English

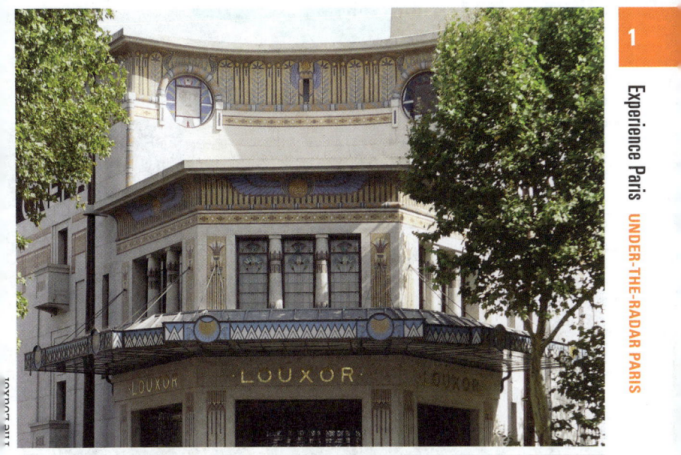

and are backed by a name synonymous with French cooking.

WATCH A FILM AT A HISTORIC MOVIE THEATER

The Louxor cinema, a masterpiece of Egyptian-inspired Art Deco architecture, is a designated historic monument situated in the scruffy but up-and-coming Pigalle neighborhood. Dating from 1932, the illustrious Grand Rex on Grands Boulevards boasts Europe's largest screening room with 2,800 seats and baroque-inspired decor. For English-only speakers, the company Lost in Frenchlation holds screenings of the latest French films with English subtitles at independent cinemas in Paris.

DANCE THE NIGHT AWAY

To celebrate Bastille Day, two nights a year—July 13 and 14—every city hall in Paris and its suburbs hosts a *bal des pompiers* (firemen's ball), starting at 9 pm and lasting into the wee hours of the morning. Once a month at the marvelous 104 Centquatre-Paris, one of the city's reigning contemporary arts centers, locals gather under garlands of lights to dance to live music. The *bals pop* are free and have a different theme each month, listed on the Centquatre website.

EXPLORE AN ABANDONED RAILWAY

Part of a huge, many-year restoration project spearheaded by Paris City Hall, La Petite Ceinture (Little Belt), a 30-km-long (19-mile-long) abandoned railway that rings the city, is Paris's final green frontier. The

newest portion of the park, referred to as the "green lung," is located in the 20e arrondissement from Rue de la Mare and Rue Ménilmontant. Adventurers can hop in anywhere along the line to find the favorite lairs of Paris graffiti artists and hidden entrances to the Catacombs.

VISIT A VILLAGE WITHIN THE CITY

On any sunny day in the Mouzaïa (also known as the Quartier d'Amérique), the sound of birdsong fills the air as residents tend their luxuriant gardens. A slice of the countryside in Paris, this is one of the city's last hidden neighborhoods, where nearly 300 unique cottages, dating from the late 19th and early 20th centuries, were built over Paris's old gypsum quarries.

An Art Lover's Guide to Paris

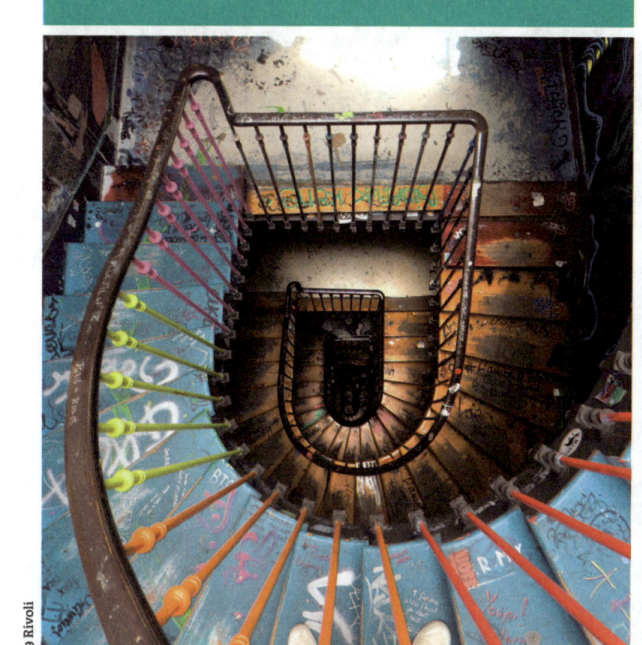

59 RIVOLI
For years, artists were illegally squatting in an abandoned bank building located at 59 rue de Rivoli, but their work attracted 40,000 visitors in 2001 alone, which made it the third-most visited center for contemporary art in Paris. The city bought the building in 2006 and reopened it three years later, renting 30 studios to artists who pay minimal rent.

LE 104
Centquatre-Paris is a cultural arts center in the 19e arrondissement that was converted from a former municipal morgue around 1905. The monumental, open steel-and-glass space covers 420,000 square feet, more than enough for its countless concerts and exhibits.

STREET ART ON RUE ST-MAUR
The 2½-km (1½-mile) stretch along Rue St-Maur in the 10e and 11e arrondissements offers an insider's view of Parisian street art. The street is lined by a variety of art, from popular female artist Kashink to portraits by Shepard Fairey, the graphic designer behind former President Obama's now-iconic "Hope" campaign posters.

Experience Paris AN ART LOVER'S GUIDE TO PARIS

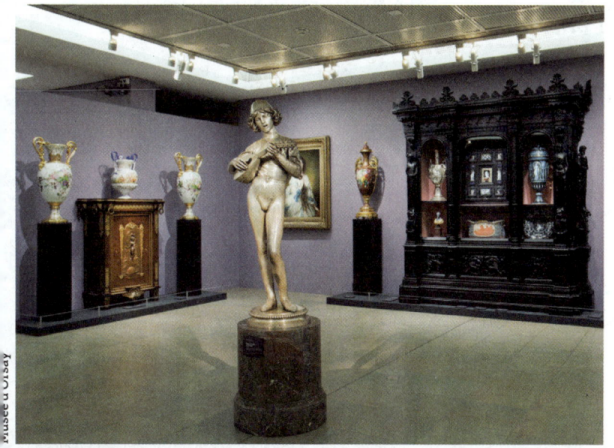

THE BIG FOUR OF MUSEUMS

No art lover should miss the usual suspects for art in Paris—the Louvre, Musée d'Orsay, Centre Pompidou, and Musée de l'Orangerie—but you should recognize that they come at a cost: crowds. Look for temporary exhibits and book tickets online in advance.

HAUT MARAIS

The tiny streets that run from the Musée Picasso to the Place de la République make up the golden triangle of Paris's coolest designer district, Haut Marais. For a long time, the area was an unexceptional working-class neighborhood. But that changed in 2009 when Marie-France Cohen converted an old wallpaper factory into her fashion and decor shop, Merci. Since then the NoMa, as Haut Marais is called, has exploded with sophisticated bistros, Made in Paris designer shops, and contemporary art galleries.

ARTIST-FOCUSED MUSEUMS

At Musée Rodin, Dalí Paris, Musée Gustave Moreau, and Musée Marmottan Monet, you'll get a deep dive into one particular artist. In many cases, the mansions they're housed in are as intriguing as the art collections themselves.

FONDATION LE CORBUSIER

The apartment-studio where this Swiss-French designer lived with his wife for more than three decades makes for a fascinating visit for art lovers. The modern building, "Immeuble Molitor," was designed by Le Corbusier himself in the 1930s and today is a UNESCO World Heritage site.

L'ATELIER DES LUMIÈRES

Paris's first digital art museum, the Atelier des Lumières uses 140 laser video projectors to create an immersive, three-dimensional, floor-to-ceiling art experience across 30-foot-high walls.

PALAIS DE TOKYO

Steps from the Eiffel Tower, the Palais de Tokyo is the largest center of contemporary art in Europe. The original Palais de Tokyo was built for the 1937 International Exposition of Art and Technology in Modern Life.

Paris with Kids

Paris may be an adult playground, but there's no shortage of children's activities to keep the young ones busy—many of the city's top attractions have carousels parked outside them in summer.

MUSEUMS

Paris has a number of museums that cater to the young and young at heart. They're great places to occupy restless minds, especially if the weather is unfavorable. The Parc de la Villette's **Cité des Sciences et de l'Industrie** is an enormous science center with a kids' area that's divided into two main sections: one for 2- to 7-year-olds, another for the 5-to-12 set. Interactive exhibits let inquisitive young visitors do everything from building a house to learning about communications through the ages. The **Cité de la Musique**, also in the Parc de la Villette, will appeal to more arts-minded children, while the **Palais de la Découverte** has high-definition, 3-D exhibits covering subjects like chemistry, biology, meteorology, and physics along with the chance to participate in scientific experiments and laboratories. Many of the displays are in French, but that doesn't stop most kids from having a blast—the choice between this and the Louvre is a no-brainer. The **Musée de l'Homme** was previously an anthropological museum but now it's supremely kid-friendly, where little ones can shake hands with a Neanderthal man, sample some of 7,000 languages, enjoy plenty of interactive exhibits, and, on Sundays, play "Little Researcher." For more interactive fun, the privately owned museum **Choco Story de Paris** is a crowd-pleaser with 450 pounds of chocolate monuments; visits include tastings, of course.

ZOOS

Visiting a zoo is usually a good way to get kids' attention, although you might want to keep in mind that most European ones aren't as spacious as their American counterparts. As part of the **Muséum National d'Histoire Naturelle** (with its own exceptional butterfly collection and Gallery of Paleontology and Comparative Anatomy with too many bones on display to count), the **Ménagerie** at the Jardin des Plantes is an urban zoo dating from 1794 and is home to more than 200 mammals, nearly 300 birds, 200 reptiles, and 300 insects. The **Parc Zoologique** in the city's largest park, Bois de Vincennes, lets you observe animals in realistic habitats. The **Musée de la Chasse et de la Nature** in the Marais is another place to get up close and personal with ferocious lions, tigers, and one in-your-face polar bear—the only catch being that these aren't alive. The impressive collection of taxidermy trophies takes children on a safari to discover man's relationship with animals.

SHOWS

What child could pass up the circus? There are several in the city, including perennial favorites **Espace Chapiteaux** at the Parc de la Villette and **Cirque d'Hiver de Bouglione** near Place de la République. For traditional entertainment, try **Les Guignols**, French puppet shows. The original Guignol was a marionette character created by Laurent Mourguet, supposedly in his own likeness, celebrating life, love, and wine. Today, shows are primarily aimed at children and are found in open-air theaters throughout the city in the warmer months. Check out the Marionettes at Champ de Mars, Parc Montsouris, Parc des Buttes-Chaumont, Jardin du Luxembourg, and the Parc Floral in the Bois de Vincennes. Even if they don't understand French, kids are usually riveted.

UNDERGROUND PARIS

There's something about exploring underground that seems to fascinate kids, at least the older ones. **Les Égouts** allows a peek into the storied Paris sewer tunnels that harbored revolutionaries on the run throughout the ages. At the redesigned **Catacombs,** in Montparnasse, dark tunnels filled with skulls and skeletons of 6 million Parisians are spookily titillating—provided you're not prone to nightmares. For some cheap underground entertainment without the ick factor, the métro itself can be its own sort of adventure, complete with fascinating station art such as the submarine decor at Arts-et-Métiers, the colorful Parisian timeline murals at Tuileries, or the Egyptian statues of the Louvre–Rivoli station. ■ **TIP→ Métro line 4 features driverless trains that let you sit at the very front, and kids love the sensation that they're the conductor.**

ACTIVE OPTIONS

Many kids are oddly thrilled at the prospect of climbing countless stairs just to get a cool view. The **Eiffel Tower** is the quintessential Paris climb (especially now that the first level boasts a dizzying glass floor), and the **Arc de Triomphe** is a good bet, since it's at the end of the Champs-Élysées. Parks offer other opportunities for expending energy. In summer, kids can work off steam on trampolines or ride ponies at the **Jardin des Tuileries**; the **Jardin du Luxembourg** has a playground and a pond where they can rent miniature boats; and the **Bois de Boulogne** has real rowboats, bumper cars, and lots of wide-open spaces. For rainy day rescues, the **Paris Aquarium,** across the river from the Eiffel Tower, is open 24/7 with 13,000 fish, including 38 large sharks, 700 coral colonies, and the largest jellyfish exhibition in Europe with 25 tanks. In winter, consider ice-skating.

From mid-December through January several outdoor sites (including one in front of the Eiffel Tower) transform into spectacular rinks with twinkling lights, music, and rental skates available.

SWEET TREATS

All that activity will no doubt make kids hungry, and luckily there's no shortage of special places to stop for a snack. Crêperies always aim to please, and you'll find plenty along the main tourist streets. Also be on the lookout for hot chocolate—the French puddinglike version is deliciously rich and thick, unlike what American children are usually used to. You'll also find plenty of places offering decadent ice cream. French children adore the pastel clouds of meringue that decorate almost every pâtisserie window—and, when in need, a chocolate croissant is never hard to find. After filling up, you can cap the day with perhaps the best treat of all, a **boat ride on the Seine.** It's the perfect way to see the sights while resting weary feet.

What to Read and Watch

AMÉLIE

Nominated for five Academy Awards, this 2001 French romantic comedy is perhaps the best-known cinematic export to many Americans. The film tells the story of a shy waitress, played by Audrey Tautou, who decides to make the lives of those around her better while trying to cope with her own isolation. The movie spotlights the colorful Montmartre neighborhood where Amélie lives; her place of work, Cafe de 2 Moulins, is a real place, too, but don't expect any of the waitresses there to change your life.

A MOVEABLE FEAST BY ERNEST HEMINGWAY

This memoir was first published in 1964, three years after Hemingway died by suicide. His series of vignettes set in Paris in the early 1920s is so perfect, many consider it one of the best books about Paris ever written. With specific addresses of cafés, bars, and places he lived, you can retrace the journey of one of the most prolific writers of the 20th century, who captured the directionless wanderings of the lost generation so well.

THE AUTOBIOGRAPHY OF ALICE B. TOKLAS BY GERTRUDE STEIN

Gertrude Stein admitted to writing this book in six weeks to make a quick buck, and Alice B. Toklas, Stein's life partner, didn't think the story would be a success. Nevertheless, Modern Library has ranked it as one of the 20 greatest nonfiction books of the 20th century. Narrated by Toklas, the book describes the couple's life together in Paris at 27 rue de Fleurus as they rub elbows with some of Paris's great artistic elites and live through WWI while volunteering for the war effort.

THE ELEGANCE OF THE HEDGEHOG BY MURIEL BARBERY

First released in 2006, Muriel Barbery's book became an instant success in France and has been translated into more than 40 languages. It's the story of a concierge at 7 rue de Grenelle in Paris who keeps her intelligence concealed until the 12-year-old daughter of rich upper-class tenants uncovers her aptitude. The events and ideas of the novel touch on philosophy, personal conflict, and class-consciousness through the thoughts and reactions of the two main characters.

EMILY IN PARIS

This Netflix series starring Lily Collins (daughter of rocker dad Phil) had Parisians up in arms over its portrayal of French stereotypes. Created by Darren Star of *Sex and the City* fame, the show follows Chicagoan Emily Cooper, who lands her dream job at a French luxury marketing company in the City of Light. The questionably fashioned millennial believes that her American work ethic and can-do smile will win over the office, but by season three, her save-the-day ad pitches grow a little tiresome.

GIOVANNI'S ROOM BY JAMES BALDWIN

Baldwin moved to Paris in 1948 and eight years later, at age 32, he published this controversial second novel, a fictional story with what many called explicit homoerotic content. Narrated by an American expat living in Paris, the main character, David, struggles with his sexuality and his internalized shame. He succumbs to social pressure and proposes to Hella, but when she goes away on a trip, David starts a tormented affair with Giovanni, an Italian bartender. Repressing his homosexuality, he leaves

Giovanni for Hella until she discovers his secret. Baldwin always maintained a connection to France. In 1970, he moved to the artistic enclave Saint-Paul-de-Vence in the south of France.

GIGI

Remember "Thank Heaven for Little Girls"? This is the movie that song comes from. Perhaps Maurice Chevalier's most celebrated song, this musical follows the story of Gigi, who is sent to live with her aunt to learn the ways of high French society. Although the infamous song does not stand the test of time and seems quite creepy now, watch the movie if only to see the sparkling charm of Maurice Chevalier and what the Paris of the elites would have looked like at the turn of the century.

GIRLHOOD

This 2014 drama shows a side of Paris far from the Arc de Triomphe and Louvre. Directed by Celine Sciamma, *Girlhood* is a coming-of-age film that tells the story of Marieme, a young Black girl who lives in a rough suburb of Paris. It discusses the perceptions of race, gender, and class that all of France and Europe at large are experiencing now.

LA VIE EN ROSE

It's hard to think of any unofficial anthem for Paris other than the song "La Vie en Rose." The opening notes from the accordion are as emblematic of the city as a beret and baguette. In 2007, Olivier Dahan wrote and directed this stunning biopic on one of France's storied singers, Edith Piaf. Piaf did not live a charmed life: she grew up a street urchin in Paris, lived through the Nazi occupation, and her love life was heartbreaking, as was her eventual death. Marion Cotillard won an Oscar for her performance in the title role.

LES MISÉRABLES BY VICTOR HUGO

Victor Hugo's novel is widely considered one of the greatest novels of the 19th century, a love story that has been adapted to stage, television, and film. Forget reality TV, this storyline includes lies, theft, pregnancy, justice, and lots of secrets. Set against the backdrop of the June Rebellion of 1832, this is the story of Jean Valjean, who agrees to care for a factory worker's daughter while being hunted down by a policeman named Javert over the course of several decades.

MOULIN ROUGE!

Paris's most famous nightclub and its racy cancan dancers have symbolized a frenzied vision of turn-of-the-century Paris that endures to this day. Baz Luhrmann's 2001 splashy and colorful jukebox musical brings the decadence of the club back to life. Starring Ewan McGregor as a young English poet who falls for cabaret performer and courtesan Nicole Kidman, the film is a whirlwind of boy meets girl and then desperately tries to hold on to that girl.

PARIS STORIES BY MAVIS GALLANT

Celebrated Canadian writer and *New Yorker* contributor Mavis Gallant, who died in 2014 at age 91, spent most of her life in Paris. This series of short stories, selected by Michael Ondaatje, another feted Canadian author, are her most memorable and run the gamut from mysterious to funny as they weave together a tale of the city through the eyes of expats, exiles, children, and wayward saints. The stories form a literary mosaic of a dynamic city in modern times.

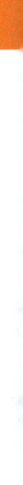

Experience Paris WHAT TO READ AND WATCH

PARISIANS: AN ADVENTURE HISTORY OF PARIS BY GRAHAM ROBB

You could spend a lifetime trying to study the history of Paris, but Graham Robb tries to do it through a series of engaging factual stories of various characters who lived in the city. Adulterers, policemen, murderers, prostitutes, and revolutionaries all get a turn as Robb spans the centuries, from 1750 to the present day. The end result not only shows the varied personalities of the City of Light, but also the many events that shaped the city, from the Terror to the May '68 revolt, which took the country to the brink of civil war.

PARIS, JE T'AIME

A city like Paris has a thousand stories. The 2006 movie *Paris, je t'aime* contains 18 of them. This anthology film was originally meant to have 20 stories, one for each arrondissement in Paris, but the 15e and 11e arrondissement shorts could not be integrated into the final film. The plots are as eclectic as the different writers and directors who were selected for each vignette. From the Coen brothers to Japanese director Nobuhiro Suwa, each little film within this big film paints a distinct portrait of Paris.

THE PARIS WIFE BY PAULA MCLAIN

While a great writer, Ernest Hemingway was a poor boxer and an even worse husband. Paula McLain's 2011 best seller is a fictionalized account of Hemingway's first marriage to Hadley Richardson. The narrator is Richardson, who describes her marriage and life in Paris in the early 1920s. Eventually their nuptials fall apart when Hemingway has an affair with her friend, but along the way, they meet famous expats like Gertrude Stein, F. Scott Fitzgerald, and James Joyce.

RATATOUILLE

This 2007 Pixar animated film tells the story of a gastronomically talented rat who stumbles into the path of Linguini, a young man working in one of Paris's fanciest restaurants. While hiding under Linguini's hat, Remy the rat pulls the strings leading to eventual haute cuisine success. Prior to filming, the director and several crew members spent a week in Paris eating at several top restaurants. Sadly, they did not interview any Parisian rats while there.

THE RED BALLOON

If you've taken a high school French class then you have seen *The Red Balloon*. This 1956 French fantasy/comedy/drama follows the adventures of a young boy who one day finds a sentient, mute red balloon. Writer and director Albert Lamorisse cast his own children as the two main protagonists. It was filmed in the Belleville area of Paris, but much of what you see no longer exists thanks to the city's effort to rebuild the once-decaying neighborhood.

Chapter 2

TRAVEL SMART

Updated by Nancy Heslin

★ **CAPITAL:** Paris	🏢 **COUNTRY CODE:** 33	⏰ **TIME:** 6 hours ahead of New York
# POPULATION: 2.1 million	⚠ **EMERGENCIES:** 112	🌐 **WEB RESOURCES:** www.parisjetaime.com/eng www.visitparisregion.com/en www.paris.fr www.france.fr/en/paris
💬 **LANGUAGE:** French	🚗 **DRIVING:** On the right side of the road	
$ CURRENCY: Euro	⚡ **ELECTRICITY:** 220 v/50 cycles; Continental-type plugs, with two round prongs	

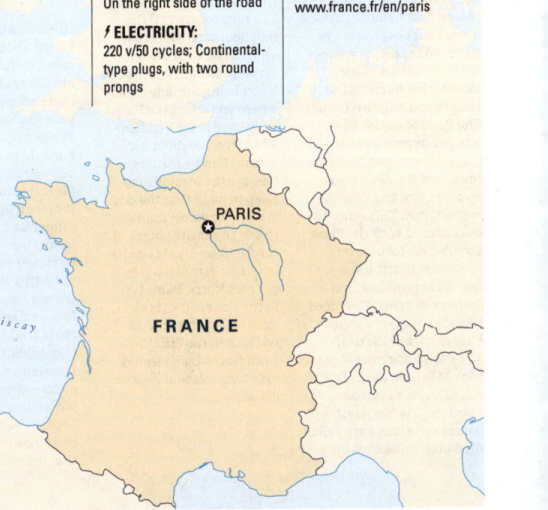

your no wheat, no dairy, no fat diet, and forget ordering off menu. You can ask for dairy-free sauce, but regardless what the server says, you could likely be served the same sauce from the same pot as everyone else. This can be a serious issue for those with severe food allergies; even if you're able to articulate your issue in French, not all places take allergies as seriously as they do in the United States. People with severe food allergies are better off preparing their meals at their lodging or eating at vegan or organic shops and bakeries; these eateries tend to be more upfront with their ingredients, and their staff are more in tune with health concerns.

Also, eat slowly—there are only two services for dinner so there's lots of time—and don't be embarrassed to order tap water (*une carafe d'eau*) instead of forking out for the bottled stuff. Earn brownie points by ordering the plat du jour and break off an extra piece of bread to wipe the plate clean (but never butter your bread!) Also, and this is a biggie, don't do work when you're eating a meal. And to really blend in, make sure you order your tea or coffee after your dessert. Typically, tipping is included with a meal's price and is not an incentive for better service. Feel free to leave 5%–10% if the service is excellent. But here's the biggest tip: dress nicely, and if you are with your kids, don't let them run wild.

CLOSURES

Paris is by no means a 24/7 city, so planning your days beforehand can save you some aggravation. Museums are closed one day a week (usually Monday or Tuesday), and most stay open late at least one night each week, which is also the least crowded time to visit. Store hours are generally 9:30 or 10 am to 7 or 8 pm, Monday through Saturday, although post offices, banks, and smaller shops may close for several hours during the afternoon. Department stores—including Galeries Lafayette and Printemps Haussmann—are open on Sunday, and along the Champs-Élysées, the Marais, Montmartre, and the Latin Quarter, you'll find shops that usually open between 1 to 3 pm on Sunday.

In France, summertime (particularly August) is when many businesses shut down for their monthlong *fermeture annuelle*, or annual holiday, and residents escape to the countryside. Museums, monuments, and attractions operate as usual, but if there's a certain restaurant you've been dying to try, it's best to confirm in advance it's open. There are also 11 national holidays throughout the year. In May there's a holiday nearly every week, so be prepared for stores, banks, and post offices to shut their doors for days at a time. If a holiday falls on a Tuesday or Thursday, many businesses close on the bridging Monday or Friday as well. Bastille Day (July 14) is still observed in true French form. Celebrations begin on the evening of the 13th, when some city firefighters open the doors to their stations, often classed as historical monuments, to host their much-acclaimed all-night balls and finish the next day with the annual military parade and air show.

THE MÉTRO

The *métro* is a practical and often economical way to travel around a city that battles traffic and congestion. The walking distance to the next métro is never more than a quarter mile, and it will get you just about anywhere you want to go for €2.15 a ride (the famed carnet, or "pack" of 10 paper tickets, was phased out in 2022 and replaced with contactless tickets, 10 for €17.95); tickets also work on buses, trams, and the RER train line within Paris. Trains start running at 5:30 am with the last train pulling into the station at around 1:15 am weekdays (and 2:15 am on weekends). Tickets can be purchased at the green machines in stations with cash and chip-based credit cards or use the Bonjour RATP app. Remember to validate your ticket at the turnstile and hold on to it in case an inspector asks to see it; otherwise you could be fined. Except for new trains, you'll have to open the doors by button or handle. Use the train number as your guide, not the color. And no matter how you choose to get around Paris, the airports, SNCF train service, métro, and most taxis and boat rides all have apps to give you real-time schedules and traffic info.

Getting Here and Around

Addresses in Paris are fairly straightforward: there's the number, the street name, and the zip code designating one of Paris's 20 *arrondissements* (districts); for instance, in Paris 75010, the last two digits ("10") indicate that the address is in the 10e. The large 16e arrondissement has two numbers assigned to it: 75016 and 75116.

The arrondissements are laid out in a spiral, beginning from the area around the Louvre (1er arrondissement), then moving clockwise through the Marais, the Latin Quarter, St-Germain, and then out from the city center to the outskirts to Ménilmontant/Père Lachaise (20e arrondissement). Occasionally you may see an address with a number plus *bis*—for instance, 20 bis, rue Vavin. This indicates the next entrance or door down from 20 rue Vavin. Note that in France you enter a building on the ground floor, or *rez-de-chaussée* (RC or 0), and go up one floor to the first floor, or *premier étage*. General address terms used in this book are *av.* (avenue), *bd.* (boulevard), *carrefour* (crossway), *cours* (promenade), *passage* (passageway), *pl.* (place), *quai* (quay/wharf/pier), *rue* (street), and *sq.* (square).

 Air

Flying time to Paris is about 7 hours from New York, 8 hours from Chicago, and 11 hours from Los Angeles. Flying time from London to Paris is 1½ hours.

The French are notoriously stringent about security, particularly for international flights. Don't be surprised by the armed security officers and military patrolling the airports, and be prepared for very long check-in, security, and passport control lines. Peak travel times in France are between mid-July and

September, during the Christmas–New Year's holidays in late December and early January, and during the February school break. Through these periods airports are especially crowded, so allow plenty of extra time. Never leave your luggage unattended, even for a moment, as it will be considered a security risk and may be destroyed.

AIRPORTS

The major airports are Charles de Gaulle (CDG, also known as Roissy), 26 km (16 miles) northeast of Paris, and Orly (ORY), 16 km (10 miles) south of Paris. Both are easily accessible from the city. Whether you take a car, bus, or ride-share to travel from Paris to the airport on your departure, always allot an extra hour because of the often horrendous traffic tie-ups in the airports themselves (especially in peak seasons and at peak times). Free light-rail connections (Orlyval and CDGval), available between the major terminals, are one option for avoiding some of the traffic mess, but still give yourself enough time to navigate these busy airports.

GROUND TRANSPORTATION

By bus from CDG/Roissy: Roissybus, operated by the RATP (Paris Transit Authority), runs between Charles de Gaulle (all terminals) and the Opéra every 15 minutes (though the wait can be far longer) from 6 am to 8:45 pm and then every 20 minutes until 12:30 am; the cost is €16.60, and tickets can be purchased directly from the driver. The trip takes about 60 minutes in regular traffic, about 90 minutes at rush hour.

By taxi from CDG/Roissy: Taxis are the most convenient way into Paris but certainly not the fastest during peak times. At best, the ride takes 30 minutes, but it can hit 90 minutes during rush hour. The fares are fixed by the government in either direction; count on a flat rate of €62 (Left Bank) and €55 (Right Bank). Taxis G7 has a real-time app and offers Familycabs (baby car seat and two boosters) and English-speaking drivers. Only take an official taxi from designated areas outside the terminal; they will have an illuminated roof sign and a meter. Uber, Marcel, and other ride-hailing apps service CDG and are marginally cheaper.

By train from CDG/Roissy: The cheapest—and often the fastest—way into Paris from CDG is via the RER-B Line, the hybrid rapid transit–suburban train, which runs from 5 am to 11 pm daily. The free CDGVal light-rail connects each airport terminal (except 2G) to the Roissypôle RER station in six minutes. For Terminal 2G, take the free N2 "navette" shuttle bus outside Terminal 2F. Trains to central Paris (Les Halles, Gare du Nord, St-Michel, Luxembourg, Palais-Royal) depart every 10 to 15 minutes on weekdays. The fare (including métro connection) is €11.80, and the journey time is about 35 minutes to Les Halles. △ **Until 2025, there is major work being done on the RER-B Line and in some cases, you may have to take a replacement bus provided by SNCF. Stay updated with the RER-B Blog www.rerb-leblog.fr/travaux.**

By bus from Orly: RATP's Orlybus leaves every 10 to 15 minutes for the Denfert-Rochereau métro station in Montparnasse from Exit L in Orly South and Exit D in Orly West. The cost is €11.20. The cheapest bus is the RATP city bus 183, which shuttles you from métro Porte de Choisy (Line 7) to Orly South (Exit L, stop 4) for just €2.15. (Tram 9 also gets you to Porte de Choisy to catch the 183.) The bus departs every 15 minutes from 6 am to 12:20 am (frequency may be reduced on Sunday and holidays); travel time is about 45 to 60 minutes.

By taxi from Orly: You'll find taxi stands at Orly South at Exit L and at Orly West at Exit B (look for signs). A cab to Paris costs a flat rate in either direction of €35 (Left Bank) and €41 (Right Bank); plan on 25–40 minutes in normal traffic. Uber and other ride-hailing apps service Orly.

By train from Orly: Bus 183 has replaced the Go C Paris shuttle bus ("*Paris par le train*") to the train station RER-C Pont de Rungis–Aéroport d'Orly. Trains to Paris leave every 15 minutes. Buy tickets at the automatic machines; the combined fare is €6.40 and journey time is about 50 minutes. Another slightly faster option is to take the Orlyval monorail, which runs from both Orly terminals to the Antony RER-B daily every four to seven minutes from 6 am to 11:35 pm. Passengers arriving in the South Terminal should use the automatic machines or Orlyval counter at Exit K; take Exit A if you've arrived in the West Terminal. The fare to Paris is €14.50 including the RER transfer.

A Paris-Visite travel pass allows unlimited public transportation over one, two, three, or five consecutive days. Prices start at €14.90 with airport travel, and the pass can be purchased online at ® *www.parisjetaime.com.*

TRANSFERS BETWEEN AIRPORTS

To travel between Paris's airports, there are several options. The RER-B goes from CDG to Paris St-Michel–Notre-Dame (€11.45) where you transfer to the RER-C to Orly West (€6.40). Total transit time is about 60 to 80 minutes. Taxis are available but expensive: from €80 to €100, depending on traffic.

 **Bicycle**

With an extensive system of dedicated bike lanes, cycling in Paris has never been easier. There are many bike-rental services and tours available, including Vélib' Métropole city bikes. For those

Getting Here and Around

too tired to pedal, 40% of the bikes have an electric option (they are aqua blue; regular bikes are light green) clocking a top speed of 25 kph (15 mph). While you may occasionally see a Vélib' with a deliberately punctured tire or a seat twisted off, city cyclists and visitors alike have embraced this service, copied in many cities worldwide, as a hassle-free alternative to public transportation. There are two ways to rent a Vélib': sign up on the website or buy a ticket from a machine at each docking station (major credit cards accepted). First, select the amount of time you wish to rent (the €3 Ticket-V, 24-hour pass Classic €5 or Electric €10 pass, or €20 3-Day Pass), then tap the code you're given on the bike's keypad to unlock it. The idea is to take short rides; depending on the Pass and whether you choose an electric bike, the first 30- to 60 minutes are free, then it's €1 or €2 for every 30 minutes. If you're staying in Paris for more than a week, check out the subscription options on the app.

 Boat

Ferries linking France and the United Kingdom cross the Channel in about 90 minutes; popular routes connect Boulogne and Folkestone, Le Havre, and Portsmouth, and—the most booked passage—Calais and Dover. P&O European Ferries alone has 11 sailings a day for this crossing. A company called Direct Ferries groups the websites for several operators to make reservations more streamlined.

The driving distance from Calais to Paris is 290 km (180 miles). The fastest routes to Paris from each port are via N43, A26, and A1 from Calais and the Channel Tunnel; and via N1 from Boulogne.

Several boat-tour companies operate Seine cruises that include sightseeing and, in some cases, dining. Tickets are typically a few Euros cheaper online. Batobus offers a convenient way to travel between all major sights along the river, including Notre-Dame, the Louvre, and the Eiffel Tower. A ticket for one day of unlimited hop-on/hop-off travel costs €23. One-hour Bateaux Parisiens sightseeing trips start from €7 online and depart from the Eiffel Tower every 60 minutes from 10:30 am to 10 pm (times may vary in high season); theme brunch, lunch and dinner cruises start from €45.50. Canauxrama organizes leisurely tours year-round in flat-bottom barges along the Seine and the Canal St-Martin in eastern Paris. There are about five departures throughout the week from April to October (less during the rest of the year); trips cost €23 and last about 2½ hours, with commentary in French and English. Bateaux-Mouches runs a tight ship 12 months of the year. Tickets for the 70-minute Seine tour cost €15; brunch cruises are from €59 and dinner cruises start at €85. Other year-round operators include Paris Canal, which offers 2½-hour trips with live bilingual commentary between the Musée d'Orsay and the Parc de La Villette (€23; €90 lunch cruise).

 Bus

ARRIVING AND DEPARTING PARIS

The excellent national train service in France means that long-distance bus transportation in the country is practically nonexistent; regional buses are found where train service is spotty. Local bus information to the rare rural areas where trains do not go can be obtained from the SNCF.

The largest international bus operator here is FlixBus, whose main terminal is in the Parisian suburb of Bagnolet (a ½-hour métro ride from central Paris, at the end of métro Line 3). It runs to more than 170 cities in France and more than 3,000 cities in Europe with fares as cheap as €5, so if you have the time and the energy, this is a good way to cut the cost of travel.

IN PARIS

With dedicated bus lanes now in place throughout the city—allowing buses and taxis to whiz past other traffic mired in tedious jams—taking the bus is an appealing option. Although nothing can beat the métro for speed, buses—eco-friendly electric and diesel-electric hybrids—offer great city views, and air-conditioning is a nice perk on sweltering August days.

Paris buses are green and white; the route number and destination are marked in front, and major stopping places are noted along the sides. Glass-covered bus shelters contain timetables and route maps (as well as the vital USB plug to recharge your phone), and most have electronic boards telling you how long you'll wait for your ride; note that buses at stops servicing multiple lines must be hailed. Less frequented stops are designated simply by a pole bearing bus numbers. Today 346 bus lines thread Paris, reaching virtually every neighborhood and city outskirt. On weekdays and Saturday, buses run every 5 to 10 minutes, but you'll have to wait 15 to 20 minutes on Sunday and holidays. One ticket will take you anywhere within the city and is valid for one bus transfer within 90 minutes. Remember to validate the ticket when you board.

Most routes operate from 5:15 am to 12:30 am. From that point, you'll have to take either the métro—which shuts down at 12:45 am Sunday through Thursday and 1:45 am on Friday, Saturday, and on major holidays—or one of the Noctilien lines, indicated by a separate signal at bus stops. Using the same tickets as the métro and regular buses, 32 Noctilien buses operate every 15 to 60 minutes (11:45 pm–6 am) between Châtelet, major train stations, and various nearby suburbs; you can hail them at any point on their route. The N01 and N02 loop around the city's main train stations in opposite directions and are particularly popular with tourists. You can buy a ticket onboard for €2.50, but note you'll have to buy a new ticket when transferring between Noctilien buses.

A map of the bus system is on the flip side of every métro map, in all métro stations, and at all bus stops. Maps are also found in each bus; a free map is available at RER stations and tourist offices, or download the Bonjour RATP app on iTunes, GooglePlay, or @ *www.ratp.fr.* An onboard electronic display announces the name of the next stop. To get off, press one of the red buttons mounted on the silver poles that run the length of the bus, and the *arrêt demandé* (stop requested) light directly behind the driver will light up. Use the middle or rear door to exit.

Trams and buses take the same tickets as the métro. A single ticket can be bought onboard for €2.50 (exact change appreciated) or for €2.15 in advance. Contactless ticket packs of 10 (€17.35) have replaced the paper 10-ticket *carnet.* If you have individual tickets or Paris-Visite passes, you should be prepared to validate your ticket in the gray machines at the entrance of the vehicle. You can also buy tickets in some newsstands and bar-tabac cafés, but this is being phased out in favor of purchasing directly from the Bonjour RATP app.

Getting Here and Around

 Car

It can't be said enough: unless you have a special, compelling reason, do yourself a favor and **avoid driving in Paris.** But if you've decided to do it anyway, there are some things to know. France's roads are classified into five types, which are numbered and have letter prefixes: *A* (*autoroute,* expressways), *N* (*route nationale*), *D* (*route départmentale*), and the smaller *C* or *V.* There are excellent links between Paris and most French cities. When trying to get around Île-de-France, it's often difficult to avoid Paris—just try to steer clear of rush hours (7–9:30 and 4:30–7:30). A *péage* (toll) must be paid on most expressways outside Île-de-France: the rate varies but can be steep. Certain booths allow you to pay with a credit card.

The major ring road encircling Paris is called the *périphérique,* with the *périphérique intérieur* going counterclockwise around the city, and the *périphérique extérieur,* or the outside ring, going clockwise; maximum speed, for the time being, is still 70 kph (43 mph). Up to five lanes wide, the périphérique is a major highway from which 30 *portes* (gates) connect Paris to the major highways of France. The names of these highways function on the same principle as the métro, with the final destination as the determining point in the direction you must take.

Heading north, look for Porte de la Chapelle (direction Lille and Charles de Gaulle Airport); east, for Porte de Bagnolet (direction Metz and Nancy); south, for Porte d'Orléans (direction Lyon and Bordeaux); and west, for Porte d'Auteuil (direction Rouen and Chartres) or Porte de St-Cloud (Boulogne-Billancourt).

PARKING

Finding parking in Paris is tough. If you must have a car, at least paying to park it is easy, if expensive. You have to pay for metered parking from Monday to Saturday from 9 am to 8 pm. You can park for up to six consecutive hours in the same place but can only pay for a maximum two hours at one time, which in the capital costs €4 to €6 for the first hour, depending on whether you're in arrondissements 1e–11e or 12e–20e. However, the rate jumps for the third hour and you'll be paying €50 to €75 for the full six hours. Look for the nearest dark green ticket machine *horodateur* and choose English. Enter your license plate number to begin, then choose the amount of time you want, and insert your card (no cash or coins). Place the green receipt on the passenger side of the dashboard. The Indio Neo app (@ *www.indigoneo.fr*) not only lets you book a parking spot in advance and extend the meter remotely, but also pay in actual time. You can also download the PayByPhone, ParkNow, and Flowbird apps, all verified by City Hall, and pay on your phone. Parking tickets are expensive, and there's no shortage of blue-uniformed parking police doling them out. An often cheaper alternative is finding a lot or underground garage—look for the blue signs with a white "P"; rates in the city center start at about €3.50 an hour, or €20 per day, while outside of the center you'll pay €10 to €15 per day. Parkings de Paris (@ *www.parclick.fr*) lets you reserve and prepay a spot in around 150 city car parks while BePark (@ *www.bepark.eu*) has the added bonus of opening the parking lot door via your cell phone. Happily, you can park for free on Sunday and national holidays; sadly, the city stopped the popular practice of free street parking in August.

ROAD CONDITIONS

Chaotic traffic is a way of life in Paris. Some streets in the city center can seem impossibly narrow; street signs are often hard to spot; jaded city drivers often make erratic, last-minute maneuvers without signaling; and motorcycles weave around traffic, often in the oncoming traffic lane. Priority is given to drivers coming from the right, so watch for drivers barreling out of small streets on your right. A move by City Hall cutting the speed limit in much of the capital to 30 kph (18.6 mph) drew scoffs from annoyed drivers, but since 2020 some 85% of city streets have been subject to the lower limit. Watch out for cyclists in 30 kph zones; they are permitted to pedal against traffic on one-way streets. Traffic lights are placed to the left and right of crosswalks, not above, so they may be blocked from view by vehicles ahead of you. And remember, you cannot turn right on a red light.

There are a few major roundabouts at the most congested intersections, notably at L'Étoile (around the Arc de Triomphe), Place de la Bastille, and Place de la Concorde; stick to the outer lane to make your exit. The périphériques (ring roads) are generally easier to use. Quays that parallel the Seine are no longer open to cars, causing even more traffic jams on the roads above. Electronic signs on the périphériques and highways post traffic conditions: *fluide* (clear) or *bouchon* (jammed). And to further complicate matters, many roads, including the Champs-Élysées, are designated car-free the first Sunday of every month from midmorning to early evening, depending on the time of year.

Some important traffic terms and signs to note: *sortie* (exit), *sens unique* (one way), *stationnement interdit* (no parking),

impasse (dead end). Blue rectangular signs indicate a highway; triangles carry illustrations of a particular traffic hazard; speed limits are indicated in a circle, with the maximum speed circled in red.

 Métro

Taking the métro is the most efficient way to get around Paris. Métro stations are recognizable either by a large yellow "M" within a circle or by the distinctive curly green Art Nouveau railings and archway bearing the full title (*Métropolitain*).

Sixteen métro and five RER (Réseau Express Régional, or the Regional Express Network) lines crisscross Paris and the suburbs to take you to 300 stations, and you are seldom more than 500 yards from the nearest one. The métro network, which is divided into five pricing zones, connects at several points in Paris with the RER, the commuter trains that go from the city center to the suburbs. RER trains crossing Paris on their way from suburb to suburb can be great time-savers because they make only a few stops in the city (you can use the same tickets for the métro and the RER within Paris).

It's essential to know the name of the last station on the line you take, as this name appears on all signs. A connection (you can make as many as you like on one ticket) is called a *correspondance*. At junction stations, illuminated orange signs bearing the name of the line terminus appear over the correct corridors for each correspondence. Illuminated blue signs marked *sortie* indicate the station exit. Note that tickets are valid only inside the gates, or *limites*. Access to métro and RER platforms is through an automatic ticket barrier. Slide your ticket

Getting Here and Around

in and pick it up as it pops out. Keep your ticket during your journey; you'll need it to leave the RER system and in case you run into any green-clad ticket inspectors, who will impose a hefty fine if you can't produce your ticket (they even accept credit cards).

Métro service starts at 5:30 am and continues until the last trains reach their terminus at 1:15 am Sunday through Thursday, and until 2:15 am on Friday, Saturday, and some national holidays. Some lines and stations in Paris can be dodgy late at night, in particular Lines 2 and 13, and the mazelike stations at Les Halles and République, so don't travel alone. But in general, the biggest risk on the métro is posed by the nimble Parisian pickpockets, so keep an eye on your wallet and pricey gadgets.

All métro tickets and passes are valid not only for the métro but also for all RER, tram, and bus travel within Paris. Métro tickets cost €2.15 each; a 10-ticket "carnet" for €17.35 is a better value. The *Carte Navigo* system is the daily, monthly, and weekly subscription plan, with reusable cards available at automatic ticket machines and ticket windows. (Note that at many stations your only option is to use the machines; they accept bills or cards with electronic chips.) For unlimited travel, get a Paris Visite pass for 1, 2, 3, or 5 days (€13.95 to €44.45). There's also the Forfait Navigo card for one day (€8.65), one week (€30.75), or one month (€86.40, beginning the first of the month), plus a €5 fee for the card. Be sure to sign your name and immediately attach a passport-size photo (there are photo booths in larger métro stations). The card allows you to swipe through the turnstiles and can be kept for years; just recharge it at any purple kiosk in the métro stations.

Ticket/Pass	Price
Single fare	€2.15
Paris-Visite one-day pass	€13.95
10 paperless tickets	€17.35
Paris-Visite two-day pass	€22.65
Paris-Visite three-day pass	€30.90
Paris-Visite five-day pass	€44.45
Pass Navigo Découverte weekly	€30.75
Pass Navigo Découverte monthly	€86.40

■ **TIP→ For itineraries, maps, and real-time tips on delays and closings, download the RATP transit system's Vianavigo, Moovit, or Citymapper for a trove of handy info like which end of the métro platform gets you closest to your exit on the other end of your journey.**

 Taxi

Taxi rates are based on location and time. Monday to Saturday, the daytime rate (10 am–5 pm) within Paris is €1.14 per km (½ mile); the nighttime rate (7 pm–midnight) is €1.53 per km. On Sunday, you'll pay €1.70 per km from midnight to 7 am and €1.53 from 7 am to midnight within Paris. Thanks to competition from ride-hailing services like Uber, the once unpredictable rates that official taxis charged to and from the airports into Paris are now fixed, and drivers are obligated to accept credit cards—and most cab companies now have an app. Pay a flat €55 to and from Charles de Gaulle/Roissy for the Right Bank, €62 for the Left Bank; to and from Orly, pay €35 for Left Bank and €41 for Right Bank. There's a basic pick-up charge of €2.60 for all rides (excluding flat fares and taxis reserved in advance), and a minimum fare of €7.30. It's customary, but not obligatory, to tip up to 5%. Waiting time is charged at €36.02 per hour. The easiest way to get a taxi is to ask your hotel or a restaurant to call one for you (a reservation supplement of €7 could apply). Order one yourself with the handy app by Taxi G7, or find a taxi stand, which is marked by a square, dark-blue sign with a white "T" in the middle.

 Train

The SNCF, France's rail system, is fast, reasonably punctual, comfortable, and comprehensive—when it's not on strike. There are various options: local trains, overnight trains with sleeping accommodations, and the high-speed TGVs (or Trains à Grande Vitesse), which average 320 kph.

The TGVs, the fastest way to get around the country, operate between Paris and Lille/Calais, Paris and Lyon/Switzerland/ Provence, Paris and Angers/Nantes, Paris and Tours/Poitiers/Bordeaux, Paris and Brussels, and Paris and Amsterdam. TGVs also go direct to Avignon, Marseille, and Nice.

Paris has six international rail stations: Gare du Nord (northern France, northern Europe, and England via Calais or Boulogne); Gare St-Lazare (Normandy, and England via Dieppe); Gare de l'Est (Strasbourg, Luxembourg, Basel, southern Germany, and central Europe); Gare de Lyon (Lyon, Marseille, Provence, Geneva, and Italy); Gare d'Austerlitz (Loire Valley, central France, and overnight to Nice and Spain); and Gare Montparnasse (Brittany, Aquitaine, TGV-Atlantique service to the west and southwest of France, Spain). Smoking is prohibited on all trains in France.

The country has two classes of train service: *première* (first class) or *deuxième* (second). First-class seats have 50% more legroom and nicer upholstery than those in second class, and the first-class cars tend to be quieter. First-class seats on the TGV also have the all-important power sockets for computer connections and individual reading lights, but fares can cost nearly twice as much as those for second-class seats. As part of first-class, Business Premier passengers have access to a lounge, fast-track boarding, and a free newspaper and beverage.

Fares are cheaper if you avoid traveling at peak times of day (and around holidays and weekends) and purchase tickets at least 15 days to three months in advance; for the best prices check the SNCF website for deals. Reserving online is the easiest way to book your trip, but you can call for train information or reserve tickets in any Paris station, irrespective of destination, and you can access the multilingual computerized schedule information network at any Paris station, and buy your tickets there. Go to the Grandes Lignes counter for travel within France and to the Billets Internationaux desk if you're heading out of the country.

Seat reservations are required on TGVs, but not on the regional TER network. So if you're traveling by TER, be sure to board early during busy travel periods, especially in July and August, to ensure you get a seat; otherwise, it is standing-room only. The trains are notoriously overbooked, and even a first-class ticket may not guarantee you a seat. Note that you need a reservation for sleeping accommodations.

Getting Here and Around

France is one of 33 European countries where you can use Eurail passes, which provide unlimited train travel for a set amount of time. If you plan to travel outside Paris by train, consider purchasing a Eurail One Country Pass; it allows for one, two, three, four, five, six, seven, or eight days of unlimited train travel in one country within one-month from your start date. If you travel solo in France for up to eight days in one month, it will cost $412 and $324 in first and second class respectively. If you plan to rack up the miles, get a Eurail Global Pass; it's valid for rail travel in first or second class in two or more of the participating nations. Costs for first-class range from the minimum four-day option at $299 to $1,011 for three months.

■ TIP→ The Eurail Mobile Pass applies to both the Eurail One Country and Eurail Global options, allowing you to purchase your pass up to 11 months before traveling without having to select a start date. The paperless ticket is added immediately to the app and replaced for free should you lose your phone.

THE CHANNEL TUNNEL

Short of flying, taking the Channel Tunnel is the fastest way to cross the English Channel: 35 minutes from Folkestone to Calais, 60 minutes from motorway to motorway, or two hours and 15 minutes from London's St. Pancras Station to Paris's Gare du Nord, with stops in Ebbsfleet (UK), Ashford (UK), Calais, and Lille. The Belgian border is just a short drive northeast of Calais. High-speed Eurostar trains use the same tunnels to connect London's St. Pancras Station directly with Midi Station in Brussels in around two hours.

There are three categories of travel and a vast range of prices for Eurostar—round-trip tickets range from €632 for business class (with access to the Philippe Starck–designed Première Class lounge, free cancellations, unlimited ticket exchanges, and a three-course Raymond Blanc meal) to €44 for the most basic return ticket. Booking early can save you a bundle. Last-minute tickets can cost more than flying.

It's a good idea to make a reservation with Eurotunnel's Le Shuttle if you're traveling with your car on a Chunnel train; vehicles without reservations, if they can get on at all, are charged a higher fare.

Essentials

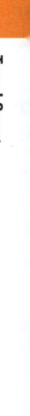

 Dining

A new wave of culinary confidence has been running through one of the world's greatest food cities and spilling over both banks of the Seine. And Paris chefs—established and up-and-coming, native and foreign—are proving that there is more to a menu than *Emily in Paris's* bloody steak and *frites*.

The sustainable trend of fresh and local has not gone anywhere, but in the post-pandemic world, food fusion has been replaced with chef collaborations (like at Bistrot Tontine) and the quiet *table pour deux* replaced with community seating and background beats (at Doublevie, steps from Sacré-Coeur). Oh, and reservations? Now it's all about living—or, in this case, eating—in the moment and you'll find some restaurants dropping their formerly stiff policies.

"World food" options are everywhere in Paris, from cocktail bars like Bar Principal to the Thai, Spanish, Italian, Korean, or burger food trucks in the business district, La Defense. But don't panic, the bistro classics are better than ever, as proven by the newly opened Géosmine (11e) and Les Parcelles (3e).

For those who are not overly adventurous, note that all establishments must post menus outside so they're available to look over before you enter. Most have two basic types of menu: à la carte and fixed price (*prix fixe, le menu*, or *la formule*). Although it limits your choices, the prix fixe is usually the best value. If you feel like indulging, the *menu dégustation* (tasting menu), consisting of numerous small courses, lets you sample the chef's offerings.

According to French law, prices must include tax and tip (*service compris* or *prix nets*), but pocket change left on the

table in cafés, or an additional 5% in better restaurants, is always appreciated. Beware of bills stamped "Service Not Included" in English or restaurants slyly using American-style credit-card slips, hoping that you'll be confused and add the habitual 15% tip.

HOURS

Paris restaurants generally serve food from noon to 2 pm and from 7:30 or 8 pm to about 11 pm. Brasseries have longer hours and often serve all day and late into the evening; some are open 24 hours. Surprisingly, many restaurants close on Sunday and Monday, while annual *fermetures* are typically several weeks in July and August, as well as a week in February, around Easter, or at Christmas.

RESERVATIONS

Restaurant staff will nearly always greet you with the phrase "*Avez-vous réservé?*" (Have you reserved?), and a confident "*Oui*" is the best answer, even in a neighborhood bistro. Although some wine bars do not take reservations—or take them online only—many do, so call and check.

☆ *Price per person for a main course at dinner, or if dinner is not served, at lunch, including tax (10%) and service.*

What It Costs in Euros

$	$$	$$$	$$$$
AT DINNER			
under €18	€18–€24	€25–€32	over €32

 Lodging

If your Parisian fantasy involves romantic evenings in a historic grand-dame or a chic boutique hotel that pampers you in

Essentials

high style, here's some good news: you don't have to be wealthy to make your dreams come true. With some 1,600 hotels, the City of Light gives visitors swanky options in all price ranges, and a place with plenty of charm is practically a given, especially with the new generation of hotels popping up in the Right Bank (in neighborhoods like Pigalle, Ménilmontant, République, and Bastille) catering to style and affordability.

In terms of location and price, there are more hotels on the *Rive Droite* (the Right Bank) offering formal luxury with premium service than on the *Rive Gauche* (the Left Bank), where the hotels are frequently smaller though richer in charm. The Rive Droite's 1er, 8e, and 16e arrondissements are still the most exclusive, and their prices reflect that. Paris's famed "Palace" hotels—12 hotels in the city that are considered better than a five-star—charge more than €1,000 a night for a standard room, and the high-end competition is heating up. On both sides of the Seine, Paris is in the throes of a lodging renaissance in both established and up-and-coming neighborhoods, with everything from chic new boutique hotels to deluxe five-star dwellings.

But those on a budget should fear not, because less expensive alternatives can be found in the fashionable Marais (the 3e and 4e arrondissements), as well as the Latin Quarter (5e arrondissement), along with a slew of newcomers that have laid their cornerstones in the newly chic 2e (Sentier). The Rive Gauche's 6e arrondissement (St-Germain) is another hotbed for stylish hotels, and choices on all budgets are available in the 5e and 7e. Everything from excellent budget deals to splendid designer spaces can also be found slightly off-the-beaten track in the 10e, 13e, and 20e arrondissements.

Wherever possible, in the more expensive neighborhoods we've located budget hotels—check out the handful of budget-priced sleeps in the shadow of Notre-Dame, St-Germain-des-Prés, and the Louvre.

These days, nearly every hotel offers free Wi-Fi (although reception in an 18th-century building is another conversation), international TV channels (meaning CNN and BBC News in English), high-definition screens, free coffee and tea, minibars, and in-room safes. Another recent change is the increasing availability of air-conditioning in both hotels and restaurants—a godsend in the *canicules* (dog days) of July and August. One thing that hasn't changed, however, is the lack of elbow room. Indoor spaces—from bedrooms and bathrooms to elevators—may feel cramped to those not used to life on a European scale. If you're flush and looking for enough room to spread out multiple suitcases, be sure to book a suite.

Almost all Parisian hotels charge extra for breakfast, with per-person prices ranging from €12 to more than €50. If you decide to eat elsewhere (and with so many cafés around that's often a better value), inform the staff so breakfast won't be charged to your bill. Occasionally, a continental breakfast—coffee, baguette, croissant, jam, and butter—will be included in the room rate, especially with an online booking directly from the hotel.

In France, the "first floor" is the floor above the ground floor (*rez-de-chaussée*). The number of rooms listed at the end of each review reflects those with private bathroom (which means they have a shower or a tub, but not necessarily both). In budget hotels, cube-size "tubs" don't always have fixed curtains or shower heads; how the French rinse themselves with the handheld nozzle

Where Should I Stay?

	NEIGHBORHOOD VIBE	PROS	CONS
St-Germain and Montparnasse (6e,14e, 15e)	The center of café culture and the emblem of the Rive Gauche.	A safe, historic area with boutiques, famous cafés and brasseries, and lovely side streets; always lively.	Overdeveloped. Noisy along main streets; the busy commercial area is devoid of charm.
The Latin Quarter (5e, 6e)	The historic student quarter of the Rive Gauche. Full of narrow, winding streets, major parks, and sights.	Plenty of cheap eats and sleeps; safe area for walks day and night.	Lacking in métro stations around the Panthéon; can be noisy in summer; hotel rooms tend to be smaller.
Marais and Bastille (3e, 4e, 11e)	Museums, chic shops, and bustling cafés line the narrow streets. Farther east are stylish bars and boutiques.	Excellent shopping, museum-going, and café culture in active Marais; bargains aplenty at Bastille hotels.	Overcrowded. Rooms don't always come cheap; always noisy around the boulevards of Place de la Bastille.
Montmartre and northeast Paris (18e, 19e, 20e)	The Rive Droite's hilltop district is known for winding streets leading up to the stark-white Sacre-Coeur.	Amazing views of Paris; romantic cobblestone streets; easy access to Roissy-Charles de Gaulle airport.	Inconvenient. Steep staircases can be challenging; few métro stations; Pigalle and Barbès area can be unsafe.
Champs-Élysées and Western Paris (8e, 16e, 17e)	The Triangle D'Or (Golden Triangle) and famous avenues are lively 24/7 with nightclubs, cinemas, and shops.	Home to many of the city's famous palace and five-star hotels, with no shortage of luxury and designer goods.	Expensive. Sky-high prices and commercial, touristy vibe.
Around the Eiffel Tower (7e, 15e)	The impressive Eiffel Tower and sweeping Champ de Mars sit next to the Seine River.	Safe and quiet, this Rive Gauche area of Paris has picture-perfect views at every turn.	Residential. With fewer shops and restaurants, this district is quiet at night; longer distances between métro stations.
Louvre, Les Halles, Île de la Cité (1er, 2e, 8e)	This central district is known for sightseeing and shopping; Les Halles is a buzzing commercial hub.	Excellent for getting around Paris on foot, bus, or métro. Safe district close to the Seine and major museums.	Noisy. The main artery of Rue de Rivoli can be loud with traffic; restaurants cater to tourists.
Grands Boulevards (9e, 10e)	The newly chic historic district is popular for its lively streets and important sights.	Perfect for walking tours, the area has unique finds and distinct neighborhoods.	Crowded. Tourists and locals keep districts full of cars, buses, trucks, taxis, and scooters.

Essentials

without flooding the entire bathroom remains a cultural mystery. Moderately priced places that expect guests to share toilets or bathrooms are pretty much extinct, but be sure you know what facilities you are getting when you book at an economy hotel.

⇨ *Prices in the reviews are the lowest cost of a double standard room in high season.*

What It Costs in Euros

$	$$	$$$	$$$$
FOR TWO PEOPLE			
under €200	€200–€350	€351–€500	over €500

Nightlife

You haven't seen the City of Light until you've seen the city at night. Crowds pour into popular streets, on weekends and weeknights, late and early, filling the air with the melody of engaged conversation and clinking glasses. This is when locals let down their hair and reveal their true bonhomie, laughing and dancing, flirting and talking. Parisians love to savor life together: they dine out, sip wine, offer innumerable toasts, and are often so reluctant to separate that they party all night.

Paris bars include everything from the toniest hotel lounge to the tiniest neighborhood *troquet*, where old-timers gather for a chat over their morning *petit blanc*. Hotel bars were once considered the aristocrats of the genre, but these days even the palaces are seeking a more modern edge. A few still represent the chicest spots for high-roller visitors to Paris, but breathtaking prices and stiff competition from the rival cocktail bar

scene means a hotel bar had better be special to be worth the price (and many are: the Hemingway Bar at the Ritz and Les Ambassadeurs at Hôtel de Crillon are two of the city's best).

Parisian cocktail bars focus on mixed drinks—although most offer everything from locally crafted beer to small-producer Champagnes—and run the gamut from dauntingly elegant hotel lounges to designer dives, attracting a diverse crowd willing to shell out anywhere from €7 to €25 a libation. Once called barmen, the new curators of cocktails are "mixologists" whose drinks are crafted, ingredients are sourced, booze is barrel-aged or infused, syrups are house-made, and ice is artisanal. Beyond beverages, cocktail bars are also giving wine bars a run for their money by offering food options, from small bites to mouthwatering dinners.

Wine bars (*caves à manger*) are different from regular bars in that they also serve food, from simple snacks like cheese and charcuterie to full meals, plus handpicked wines that are often "natural" or *biodynamique*. Wine bars keep mealtime hours and close earlier than proper bars—somewhere between 11 and midnight. Be warned, though: many establishments calling themselves *bars à vins* are in fact full-fledged restaurants, with no bar to speak of.

Paris's cabarets range from vintage venues once haunted by Picasso and Piaf to those sinful showplaces where *tableaux vivants* offer acres of bare flesh. Some of these places, like the Lido, are more Vegas than the petticoat vision re-created by Hollywood in Baz Luhrmann's *Moulin Rouge*—but the rebirth of burlesque is making some of the old-school venues and racier versions like the lascivious Crazy Horse more popular. Although you can dine at many cabarets, food isn't the attraction. Prices range from about €75 (admission only) to more than €180 (dinner plus a show) and can go as high as €360 for the works. At all but a handful of specific cabarets on specific nights, the clientele tends overwhelmingly to be visitors, middle-age and older, from either the French countryside or abroad.

Paris's hyped *boîtes de nuit* (nightclubs)—commonly referred to as simply *boîtes*—tend to be expensive and exclusive. If you're friends with a regular or relatively famous (or if you're a group of women), you'll have an easier time getting through the door. Cover charges at some can be upward of €25, with drinks at the bar starting at €10 for a beer. Others are free to enter, but you'll pay a fortune inside. Locals looking to dance generally stick to the more laid-back clubs, where the cover ranges from free (usually on slower weekdays) to €20, and the emphasis is on the dancing, music, and offbeat atmosphere (think on a barge or under a bridge). Club popularity depends on the night or event, as Parisians are more loyal to certain DJs than venues and often hit two or three spots before ending up at one of the many after-parties, which can last until noon the next day. It's best to avoid the overpriced Champs-Élysées neighborhood.

The LGBTQ+ nightlife scene is mostly concentrated in the Marais and Les Halles, but, unlike the legendary La Mutinerie on Rue St-Martin, many of these spots fall in and out of favor at lightning speed. Pick up a copy of the leading LGBTQ+ magazine *Têtu* (available at newsstands and online at *www.tetu.com*), or check out ParisGayVillage (*www.parisgayvillage.com*) to see a What's On guide. The Pride en France site (*www.gaypride.fr*)is also super-informative.

Wherever you end up, know that most bars stay open until between midnight and 2 am, with no specific last call; however, wine bars and hotel bars tend to close earlier. Clubs usually stay open until 5 am, although more dance clubs are staying open until dawn or beyond (some even serve breakfast). Many drinking establishments are closed Sunday night, so check before heading out on the town. If you want to hit bars at a relatively quiet hour, go for an *apéro* around 6 pm, and take advantage of the terrace if weather permits.

The métro runs until 1:15 am Sunday through Thursday; however, there is service on Friday night, Saturday night, and nights before holidays until 2:15 am, when the last train on each line reaches its terminus. After that, you can try a cab, but it can be extremely difficult to find one after midnight (or anytime there's a chance of rain), or Uber. Another alternative is the Noctilien, the sometimes rowdy night bus system. And if you're having a lot of fun, you can always stay out until the métro starts running again at 5:30 am.

 Performing Arts

The performing arts scene in Paris runs the gamut from highbrow to lowbrow, cheap (or even free) to break-the-bank expensive. Venues are indoors and outdoors, opulent or spartan, and dress codes vary accordingly. Regardless of the performance you choose, it's probably unlike anything you've seen before. Parisians have an audacious sense of artistic adventure and a stunning eye for scene and staging. An added bonus in this city of classic beauty is that many of the venues themselves—from the opulent interiors of the Opéra Garnier and the Opéra Royal de Versailles to the Art Deco

Essentials

splendor of the Théâtre des Champs-Élysées—are as wonderfully dramatic as the scenes on stage.

One thing that sets Paris apart in the arts world is the active participation of the Ministry of Culture, which sponsors numerous concert halls and theaters, like the Comédie Française, that tend to present less commercial, though artistically captivating, productions. Other venues with broader appeal are known for sold-out shows and decade-long runs. Most performances are in French, although you can find English theater productions. English-language movies are often presented in *version original*, with subtitles and Lost in Frenchlation (@ *www.lostin frenchlation.com*) regularly shows French films with English subtitles. Of course, you don't need to speak the language to enjoy opera, classical music, dance, or the circus.

Detailed entertainment listings can be found online in English at@ *www.sorti-raparis.com/en*and the superb *ParisVoice* (@ *www.parisvoice.com*) or in French from the weekly magazine*L'Officiel des Spectacles* in the Wednesday entertainment insert *Figaroscope* in the *Figaro* newspaper (@ *evene.lefigaro.fr*). Most performing arts venues also have their own websites, and many include listings as well as other helpful information in English. The website of the Paris Tourist Office (@ *parisjetaime.com/eng*) has theater and music listings in English.

Safety

Paris is as safe as any big city can be, but you should always be streetwise and alert. Certain neighborhoods are more seedy than dangerous, thanks to the night trade that goes on around Les Halles, Gare du Nord/Gare de l'Est, and St-Denis and on Boulevard de Clichy in Pigalle. Some off-the-beaten-path neighborhoods (particularly the outlying suburban communities) may warrant extra precaution and small streets, while charming, should be avoided after hours. And, as elsewhere, you could be subjected to bag checks when entering public buildings.

The métro is quite safe overall, though some lines and stations, in particular Lines 2 and 13, get dodgy late at night, so try not to travel alone, memorize the time of the last métro train to your station, ride in the first car by the conductor, and just use common sense. If you're worried, spend the money on a taxi or Uber. Pickpocketing is the main problem, day or night. It goes without saying: best not to tempt sticky fingers by putting your phone or tablet on a café table.

Scarcely a week goes by without some kind of demonstration or public gathering in Paris, and although most are peaceful, it's usually best for tourists to avoid them. The CRS (French riot police) carefully guard all major protests, directing traffic and preventing violence as they are armed and use tear gas when and if they see fit.

Shopping

Nothing, but nothing, can push you into the current of Parisian life faster than a few hours of shopping. Follow the lead of locals, who slow to a crawl as their eyes lock on a tempting display. Window-shopping is one of this city's greatest spectator sports; the French call it *lèche-vitrine*—literally, "licking the windows"—which is fitting because many of the displays look good enough to eat.

Store owners here play to sophisticated audiences with voracious appetites for everything from spangly flagship stores to minimalist boutiques to under-the-radar spots in 19th-century glass-roofed *passages*. Parisians know that shopping isn't about the kill, it's about the chase: walking down cobblestone streets looking for items they didn't know they wanted, they're casual yet quick to pounce. Watching them shop can be almost as much fun as shopping yourself, but remember that here, they ain't charging it: the French do not have credit cards like most Western countries; they might have cards that say Visa or Mastercard, but they are actually debit cards.

As for what to buy, the sky's the limit in terms of choices, but if you shop in January or July, you'll likely come across the six-week official sales periods—aka *les soldes d'hiver* and *les soldes d'été*—as designated by the government. If your funds aren't limitless, take comfort in knowing that treasures can be found on a budget.

Store hours can be tricky in Paris. Aside from department stores, which keep slightly longer hours and usually shut their doors late on Thursday, shops tend to open around 10 am and close around 7 pm. It's not unusual to find a "back at 3" sign taped on the doors of smaller boutiques at lunchtime. Plan to do most of your foraging between Tuesday and Saturday, as the majority of shops, excluding the two major department stores, Printemps and Galeries Lafayette, are closed Sunday and some on Monday as well. You can find areas—particularly the Marais and tourist-oriented Champs-Élysées—where stores are open on Sunday. However, if you're making a special trip somewhere, it's wise to check hours online or call ahead because in France, Sundays are still cherished days off.

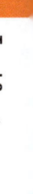

Tipping Guidelines for Paris

Bellhop	€1–€2, depending on the level of the hotel
Hotel concierge	€5–€20 if they perform a service for you
Hotel doorman	€1–€2 if they help you get a cab
Housekeeper	€1–€2 a day (either daily or at the end of your stay, in cash)
Hotel room-service waiter	€1–€2 per delivery, even if a service charge has been added
Tour guide	10% of the cost of the tour (but museum guides, €1–€1.50 after a tour)
Valet parking attendant	€1–€2, but only when you get your car
Waiter	Round up for small bills, €1–€3 for meals, 5%–10% in expensive restaurants
Restroom attendant	Restroom attendants in more expensive restaurants expect small change or €1

 Tipping

In France, tipping is not a cultural norm. Bills in bars and restaurants must by law include service (despite what entrepreneurial servers may tell you), so tipping isn't required. Waiters are paid well; it is polite, however, to round your bill with small change unless you're dissatisfied. The amount varies—from €0.20 for a beer to €1–€3 after a meal. In expensive restaurants, it's common to leave an additional 5%–10% on the table.

In some theaters and hotels cloakroom attendants may expect nothing (watch for signs that say *pourboire*

Essentials

interdit—tipping forbidden; otherwise, give them €1). If you stay more than two or three days in a hotel, leave something for the housekeeper—about €1–€2 per day. Expect to pay €2 (€1 in a moderately priced hotel) to the person who carries your bags or hails a taxi for you. In hotels providing room service, give €1–€2 to the waiter (unless breakfast is routinely served in your room). If the concierge has been helpful, leave a tip of €5–€20 depending on the service. Museum guides should get €1–€1.50 after a tour. For other kinds of tours, tip the guide or leader 10% of the tour cost. It's standard practice to tip long-distance bus drivers about €2 after an excursion, too. Taxi drivers usually aren't tipped, but if you're one of the few people paying cash, round up to the nearest euro.

Just note that the program's implementation has been delayed several times, so be sure to confirm in advance that ETIAS-registration is required at the time of your trip.

 Visas

Starting in mid-2025, France and other European Union countries will implement an electronic visa waiver program designed for foreign visitors to the EU from countries that don't require a visa to visit. If you are a citizen of one of these 60 or so non-EU countries (this includes the United States and the United Kingdom), this means you will now have to "pre-register" your trip through a simple online process that costs €7; this pre-registration covers multiple trips of up to 90 days in any 180-day period and lasts three years or until your passport expires—whichever comes first. Visit the official ETIAS website at *https://travel-europe.europa.eu/etias_en* to apply. The vast majority of applications should be approved within minutes, but it's still smart to not book flights or hotels until your application is approved. For more information, visit *www.etias.com*.

 When to Go

Although the City of Light is magical all year round, summer is the most popular (and priciest) time to go. It used to be that Paris was largely deserted in August when locals fled to the coast or countryside, leaving a wake of closed shops and restaurants. But today it remains very much alive throughout the summer, with outdoor music festivals, open-air movie screenings, and convivial activities available at the popular Paris Plages, the "beaches" on the Right Bank of the Seine and along the upper Canal St-Martin.

Nevertheless, the city is perhaps most appealing in late spring and early fall. June, when long, warm days translate into extended hours of sightseeing (the sun doesn't set until 10 pm), is particularly gorgeous. Ditto for September, which tends to have more temperate weather, saner rates, and cultural events timed for the *rentrée* (or return), signifying the end of summer vacation. In the third weekend in September, scores of national buildings that are normally closed to the public open for visits during the annual Journées du Patrimoine (Patrimony Days).

Winter can be dark and cold, but it's also the best time to find cheap airfares and hotel deals. Spring tends to remain damp and chilly into May, when prices start rising in sync with the mercury in local thermometers.

Best Tours in Paris

Sometimes a guided tour is the way to go, even if you usually prefer to fly solo while traveling. Tours can provide an insider's perspective on where locals eat and play, and to learn about interesting aspects of the city's history, inhabitants, or architecture. Whether you want a boat tour along the Seine or a more personal, interest-specific walk, you'll find it here.

BOAT TOURS

Batobus. Hop on and off at one of Batobus's nine stops, which include the Eiffel Tower, Musée d'Orsay, and the Champs-Élysées. A one-day pass for unlimited travel—boats are heated and have panoramic views but offer no commentary—is €23; a two-day pass is only €27. ✉ *Port de la Bourdonnais* ☎ *01–76–64–79–12* ⊕ *www.batobus.com* 💰 *From €23.*

Green River Cruises. Whether it's an hour-long Sunday cruise or a three-hour candlelight stroll along the Seine, the boat outings offered by Green River Cruises are limited to 12 people maximum, providing a more intimate tour of the city. Champagne is included in some options, but you are welcome to bring your own wine and snacks. Four boats are electric, and the company plans to be emissions-free by 2025. ✉ *Bateau Play Time, 66 Quai d'Austerlitz* ☎ *06–50–22–90–65* ⊕ *www.greenriverparis.fr* 💰 *From €55 per person.*

WALKING TOURS

Sight Seeker's Delight. This company's unique two- or three-hour walking tours, from "Pièce De Résistance" to "Tickling Your Tastebuds," bring the city's various quarters to life with engaging information and personal insight from English-speaking guides. ☎ *06–22–52–57–90* ⊕ *www.sightseekersdelight.com* 💰 *From €20.*

Wego Walking Paris. These 3½-hour walking tours in English begin next to Notre-Dame and end at the Eiffel Tower, covering 20 attractions with lots of history and fun anecdotes in between. Often called the most entertaining tour in Paris, it's pay what you wish, or more accurately, you pay your guide what you think they deserve. Due to popularity, it's best to reserve or get on a waiting list by credit card beforehand, but remember that if you're a no-show or cancel less than 48 hours before the tour, there's a charge of €20. ✉ *1 Pont au Double* ⊕ *www.wegowalking.com.*

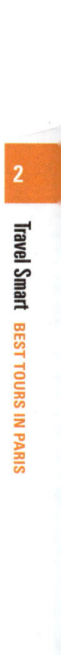

SPECIALTY TOURS

Eating Europe. It will be hard for epicureans to choose between the Paris food tours offered by this company: daytime in Montmartre or a night out in Le Marais? But the three-hour Julia Childs–inspired walk, that has you discovering St-Germain and the Left Bank, may just redefine food history for you. ⊕ *www.eatingeurope.com/paris* 💰 *From €114.*

Midnight In Paris On Wheels. Take in the city's main monuments on a two- or three-hour nocturnal escapade in a classic 2CV car. The tour guide will tailor the ride to your tastes, whether it be history or a desire to discover new areas. A bottle of bubbly is provided, too. ☎ *06–51–19–24–88* ⊕ *www.midnightinparisonwheels.com* 💰 *From €120.*

Helpful French Phrases

BASICS

English	Pronunciation	French
Yes/no	wee/nohn	Oui/non
Please	seel voo play	S'il vous plaît
Thank you	mair- **see**	Merci
You're welcome	deh ree- **ehn**	De rien
Excuse me, sorry	pahr- **don**	Pardon
Good morning/ afternoon	bohn- **zhoor**	Bonjour
Good evening	bohn- **swahr**	Bonsoir
Good-bye	o ruh- **vwahr**	Au revoir
Mr. (Sir)	muh- **syuh**	Monsieur
Mrs. (Ma'am)	ma- **dam**	Madame
Miss	mad-mwa- **zel**	Mademoiselle
Pleased to meet you	ohn-shahn- **tay**	Enchanté(e)
How are you?	kuh-mahn-tahl- ay **voo**	Comment allez-vous?
Very well, thanks	tray bee-ehn, mair- **see**	Très bien, merci
And you?	ay voo?	Et vous?

NUMBERS

English	Pronunciation	French
one	uhn	un
two	deuh	deux
three	twah	trois
four	**kaht**-ruh	quatre
five	sank	cinq
six	seess	six
seven	set	sept
eight	wheat	huit
nine	nuf	neuf
ten	deess	dix
eleven	ohnz	onze
twelve	dooz	douze
thirteen	trehz	treize
fourteen	kah- **torz**	quatorze
fifteen	kanz	quinze
sixteen	sez	seize
seventeen	deez- **set**	dix-sept
eighteen	deez- **wheat**	dix-huit
nineteen	deez- **nuf**	dix-neuf
twenty	vehn	vingt
twenty-one	vehnt-ay- **uhn**	vingt-et-un
thirty	trahnt	trente
forty	ka- **rahnt**	quarante
fifty	sang- **kahnt**	cinquante
sixty	swa- **sahnt**	soixante
seventy	swa-sahnt- **deess**	soixante-dix
eighty	kaht-ruh- **vehn**	quatre-vingts
ninety	kaht-ruh-vehn- **deess**	quatre-vingt-dix
one hundred	sahn	cent
one thousand	meel	mille

COLORS

English	Pronunciation	French
black	nwahr	noir
blue	bleuh	bleu
brown	bruhn/mar- **rohn**	brun/marron
green	vair	vert
orange	o- **rahnj**	orange
pink	rose	rose
red	rouge	rouge
violet	vee-o- **let**	violette
white	blahnk	blanc
yellow	zhone	jaune

DAYS OF THE WEEK

Sunday	dee- **mahnsh**	dimanche
Monday	luhn- **dee**	lundi
Tuesday	mahr- **dee**	mardi
Wednesday	mair-kruh- **dee**	mercredi
Thursday	zhuh- **dee**	jeudi
Friday	vawn-druh- **dee**	vendredi
Saturday	sahm- **dee**	samedi

MONTHS

English	Pronunciation	French
January	zhahn-vee- **ay**	janvier
February	feh-vree- **ay**	février
March	marce	mars
April	a- **vreel**	avril
May	meh	mai
June	zhwehn	juin
July	zhwee- **ay**	juillet
August	ah- **oo**	août
September	sep- **tahm**-bruh	septembre
October	awk- **to**-bruh	octobre
November	no- **vahm**-bruh	novembre
December	day- **sahm**-bruh	décembre

USEFUL PHRASES

English	Pronunciation	French
Do you speak English?	par-lay **voo** ahn- **glay**	Parlez-vous anglais?
I don't speak ...	zhuh nuh parl pah ...	Je ne parle pas ...
French	frahn- **say**	français
I don't understand	zhuh nuh kohm- **prahn** pah	Je ne comprends pas
I understand	zhuh kohm- **prahn**	Je comprends
I don't know	zhuh nuh say **pah**	Je ne sais pas
I'm American/ British	zhuh sweez a-may-ree- **kehn** / ahn- **glay**	Je suis américain/ anglais
What's your name?	ko-mahn vooz a-pell-ay- **voo**	Comment vous appelez-vous?
My name is ...	zhuh ma- **pell** ...	Je m'appelle ...
What time is it?	kel air eh- **teel**	Quelle heure est-il?
How?	ko- **mahn**	Comment?
When?	kahn	Quand?
Yesterday	yair	Hier
Today	o-zhoor- **dwee**	Aujourd'hui

Tomorrow	duh- **mehn**	Demain
Tonight	suh **swahr**	Ce soir
What?	kwah	Quoi?
What is it?	kess-kuh- **say**	Qu'est-ce que c'est?
Why?	poor- **kwa**	Pourquoi?
Who?	kee	Qui?
Where is ...	oo ay	Où est ...
the train station?	la gar	la gare?
the subway station?	la sta- **syon** duh may- **tro**	la station de métro?
the bus stop?	la-ray duh booss	l'arrêt de bus?
the post office?	la post	la poste?
the bank?	la bahnk	la banque?
the ... hotel?	lo- **tel**	l'hôtel ...?
the store?	luh ma-ga- **zehn**	le magasin?
the cashier?	la **kess**	la caisse?
the ... museum?	luh mew- **zay**	le musée ...?
the hospital?	lo-pee- **tahl**	l'hôpital?
the elevator?	la-sahn- **seuhr**	l'ascenseur?
the telephone?	luh tay-lay- **phone**	le téléphone?
Where are the ...	oo sohn lay	Où sont les ...
restrooms?	twah- **let**	toilettes?
(men/women)	(**oh**-mm/ **fah**-mm)	(hommes/femmes)
Here/there	ee- **see** /la	Ici/là
Left/right	a goash/a draht	A gauche/à droite
Straight ahead	too drwah	Tout droit
Is it near/far?	say pray/lwehn	C'est près/loin?
I'd like ...	zhuh voo- **dray**	Je voudrais ...
a room	ewn **shahm**-bruh	une chambre
the key	la clay	la clé
a newspaper	uhn zhoor- **nahl**	un journal
a stamp	uhn **tam**-bruh	un timbre
I'd like to buy ...	zhuh voo- **dray ahsh-tay**	Je voudrais acheter ...
cigarettes	day see-ga- **ret**	des cigarettes
matches	days a-loo- **met**	des allumettes
soap	dew sah- **vohn**	du savon
city map	uhn plahn de **veel**	un plan de ville
road map	ewn cart roo-tee- **air**	une carte routière
magazine	ewn reh- **vu**	une revue
envelopes	dayz ahn-veh- **lope**	des enveloppes
writing paper	dew pa-pee- **ay** a **let**-ruh	du papier à lettres
postcard	ewn cart pos- **tal**	une carte postale
How much is it?	say comb-bee- **ehn**	C'est combien?
A little/a lot	uhn peuh/bo- **koo**	Un peu/beaucoup
More/less	plu/mwehn	Plus/moins
Enough/too (much)	a-say/tro	Assez/trop
I am ill/sick	zhuh swee ma- **lahd**	Je suis malade
Call a ...	a-play uhn	Appelez un ...
doctor	dohk- **tehr**	docteur
Help!	o suh- **koor**	Au secours!

Stop!	a-reh- **tay**	Arrêtez!
Fire!	o fuh	Au feu!
Caution!/Look out!	a-tahn-see- **ohn**	Attention!

DINING OUT

A bottle of ...	ewn boo- **tay** duh	une bouteille de ...
A cup of ...	ewn tass duh	une tasse de ...
A glass of ...	uhn vair duh	un verre de ...
Bill/check	la-dee-see- **ohn**	l'addition
Bread	dew panh	du pain
Breakfast	luh puh- **tee** day-zhuh- **nay**	le petit-déjeuner
Butter	dew burr	du beurre
Cheers!	ah vo-truh sahn- **tay**	A votre santé!
Cocktail/aperitif	uhn ah-pay-ree- **teef**	un apéritif
Dinner	luh dee- **nay**	le dîner
Dish of the day	luh plah dew **zhoor**	le plat du jour
Enjoy!	bohn a-pay- **tee**	Bon appétit!
Fixed-price menu	luh may- **new**	le menu
Fork	ewn four- **shet**	une fourchette
I am diabetic	zhuh swee dee-ah-bay- **teek**	Je suis diabétique
I am vegetarian	zhuh swee vay-zhay-ta-ree- **en**	Je suis végétarien(ne)
I cannot eat ...	zhuh nuh puh pah mahn- **jay** deh	Je ne peux pas manger de ...
I'd like to order	zhuh voo- **dray** ko-mahn- **day**	Je voudrais commander
Is service/the tip included?	ess kuh luh sair- **veess** ay comb- **pree**	Est-ce que le service est compris?
It's good/bad	say bohn/mo- **vay**	C'est bon/mauvais
It's hot/cold	say sho/frwah	C'est chaud/froid
Knife	uhn koo- **toe**	un couteau
Lunch	luh day-zhuh- **nay**	le déjeuner
Menu	la cart	la carte
Napkin	ewn sair-vee- **et**	une serviette
Pepper	dew **pwah**-vruh	du poivre
Plate	ewn a-see- **et**	une assiette
Please give me ...	doe-nay- **mwah**	Donnez-moi ...
Salt	dew sell	du sel
Spoon	ewn kwee- **air**	une cuillère
Sugar	dew **sook**-ruh	du sucre
Waiter!/Waitress!	muh- **syuh** / mad-mwa- **zel**	Monsieur!/ Mademoiselle!
Wine list	la cart day vehn	la carte des vins

On the Calendar

January

Paris Fashion Week. The first Paris Fashion Week (PFW) in November 1973 was a fundraiser at Versailles to help cover the palace's $60 million renovation. Its success launched a catwalk rivalry for industry insiders, but the French public would have to wait until 1984 when Thierry Mugler became the first fashion designer to offer paid access to one of his fashion shows. Since then, PFW has become one of the world's leading fashion events, after New York, London, and Milan Weeks. Men and Haute Couture shows are typically in January and June/July, while women's ready-to-wear are in March and September/October. ⊕ *www.fhcm.paris/en/the-events-of-fhcm.*

The Grand Prix d'Amérique. Held every year on the last Sunday of January since 1920, the Grand Prix d'Amérique at the Vincennes hippodrome is the most prestigious harness race in the world. ⊕ *www.prixdameriqueraces.com.*

February

Carnaval de Paris. The Paris Carnival takes place every year on the Sunday before Mardi Gras. A parade with musical performances starts at 2 pm at Place Gambetta (20e) and ends at the Place de la République around 5 pm, followed by a party. A month later the Carnaval des Femmes (Women's Carnival) kicks off in Place du Châtelet (4e). Both events are free. ⊕ *www.carnaval-paris.org.*

April

Goût de France/Good France. In 2010, the "gastronomic meal of the French" was officially acknowledged as part of humanity's intangible cultural heritage by UNESCO. The organization said the meal "emphasizes togetherness, the pleasure of taste, and the balance between human beings and the products of nature." Over four days in April, food lovers can take part in the Goût de France/Good France (formerly the Fête de la Gastronomie) with events across Paris, including a *dîner à la française* at one of 2,000 restaurants around the world celebrating French gastronomy.

Paris Marathon. What better way to see all the city's major landmarks than running 42.195 km with a Marathon de Paris souvenir T-shirt at the finish? On a Sunday in April, some 60,000 runners from 140 countries depart from the Champs-Élysées, and pass by the Louvre, the Bastille, Notre-Dame Cathedral, and the Eiffel Tower before a photo finish on Avenue Foch near the Arc de Triomphe. If you're not up for running the marathon yourself, join the crowds along the route cheering on the runners. ⊕ *www.schneiderelectricparismarathon.com.*

May

Nuit des Musées. You won't see Ben Stiller, but this cultural event gives the public free access to Paris museums on a Saturday in May, from 7 pm to 1 am. ⊕ *nuitdesmusees.culture.gouv.fr.*

The French Open. Held over two weeks at the end of May through early June, the French Open, or Roland Garros as it's also known, is one of the four Grand Slam tennis tournaments. The big-name matches are played on the Philippe Chatrier court, and while tickets for the public go on sale in early March, Experience Packages are available two weeks earlier. And in case you're wondering, Roland Garros was not a famous French tennis player but a fighter pilot during World War I. ⊕ *www.rolandgarros.com/en-us.*

June

Orangerie du Parc de Bagatelle Festivals. The Chopin Festival and the Solistes Festival strike musical high notes in the Orangerie du Parc de Bagatelle, one of Paris's most beautiful gardens. The former runs from mid-June through mid-July, while the latter is held on three consecutive weekends in September or October. Tickets will set you back €21 to €35. ⊕ *ars-mobilis.fr.*

Fête de la Musique. Also known as World Music Day, Fête de la Musique is an international festival founded in 1981 by French minister of culture Jack Lang. On June 21 (the summer solstice), free concerts by amateurs and professionals alike are performed on city streets and in village squares throughout France. In Paris, it's an all-night party (literally, noise regulations are overlooked) and a great opportunity to hear some music and blend in like a Parisian. ⊕ *fetedelamusique.culture.gouv.fr.*

Paris Pride March. Pride parades in France have taken place on a national level since 1993. Every June, Paris Pride—or the Marche des Fiertés LGBTQ+—brings together some 60 LGBTQ+ associations to fight against sexual orientation and gender identity discrimination. The

carnival procession unites hundreds of thousands of supporters and ends usually at Place de la Bastille or Place de la République followed by a free concert. Celebrations eventually spill over to nightclubs and bars around the city. ⊕ *www.inter-lgbt.org.*

July

Days Off Festival. Held over 10 days in early July at the Philharmonie de Paris, this festival focuses on pop-rock, with some jazz and electro thrown in for good measure. Headliners like Rufus Wainwright and Blur frontman Damon Albarn lure Parisians away from their offices. Tickets are from €35. ⊕ *www.daysoff.fr.*

Bastille Day. You won't want to miss France's national holiday celebrations on July 14, especially the military parade along the Champs-Élysées in the morning. There is a free symphony Concert de Paris outside the Eiffel Tower followed by fireworks at 11 pm. In between, the Louvre gives you something to smile about as its permanent collection, which includes the Mona Lisa, is free to visit on Bastille Day.

Tour de France. If Lycra is your thing, head to the Champs-Élysées on the final day of the Tour de France. Cyclists, who have just completed some 3,500 kilometers over 23 days (with two days off for rest), arrive in central Paris and follow the Rue de Rivoli on to the Place de la Concorde before entering the Champs-Élysées to the Finish. ⊕ *www.letour.fr/en.*

Paris Summer Festival. The three-week Paris Festival l'Eté offers artistic events, from theater and dance to circus and plastic installations, with the goal of

On the Calendar

making art and culture available to all. Free and paid performances draw 100,000 spectators to 30 (mostly) outdoor venues across Paris, including national monuments, gardens, swimming pools, and churches. ® *www.parislete.fr.*

Paris Plages. You might not think of Paris as a beach destination, yet for six weeks every summer the Seine riverbanks and Villette canal basin offer everything you need to beat the summer heat— free sun umbrellas, deck chairs, palm trees, sports activities, and swimming. ® *en.parisinfo.com/discovering-paris/major-events/paris-plages.*

August

Cinéma en Plein Air. The free open-air summer cinema at the Parc de la Villette is the largest in Paris, showing around 30 new and old releases—both French and *version originale* (VO) foreign films with subtitles. Screenings start at 9:30 or 10:30 pm, and some are accessible for those who are hard of hearing. ® *lavillette.com/programmation.*

Classique au Vert Festival. For free outdoor classical concerts, the Classique au Vert Festival is staged on weekends at 4 pm from August to mid-September, drawing fans to the Parc Floral in Bois de Vincennes. This is also the spot that hosts the Paris Jazz Festival each weekend in June and July. ® *festivalsduparcfloral.paris/programmation/classique-au-vert.*

Rock en Seine. This rock music festival on the outskirts of Paris is one of the largest of its kind in France. Past headliners include the Cure, Lana Del Rey, Arcade Fire, Cypress Hill, and the Foo Fighters. A four-day pass is €219. ® *www.rockenseine.com.*

September

Paris Beer Festival. France is home to more than 1,500 microbreweries, the most in Europe, according to Statista. And although wine is still the favorite drink, beer is the most consumed alcoholic beverage per capita. Paris Beer Week brings together 50 craft microbreweries with beer enthusiasts in various locations in Paris over four days in September. ® *parisbeerfestival.fr/en.*

Jazz à la Villette. The annual Jazz à la Villette Festival is held at various Parc de La Villette venues, including the Philharmonie de Paris and Trabendo, over 10 days in early September. Tickets range from €26 to €43. ® *www.jazzalavillette.com/fr.*

Festival d'Automne à Paris. Since 1972, the Paris Autumn Festival has featured a packed program that includes contemporary dance, theater, music, visual arts, and film. From September to December, 100,000 fans attend 50 productions from more than a dozen countries at various venues in and around the city. ® *www.festival-automne.com.*

October

Nuit Blanche. Don't expect to get too much sleep the first Saturday in October. A contemporary all-night art festival, the Nuit Blanche lets you attend installations, concerts, and artistic performances at museums, cultural institutions, and other public and private spots across the city. And it is all free. ⊕ *www.facebook.com/NBParis.*

Fête des Vendanges de Montmartre. Picasso, Renoir, and van Gogh were inspired by Montmartre's hilltop and its tax-exempt wine laws. That is no longer the case, but locals have been celebrating the Grape Harvest Festival and the arrival of cuvées from Clos Montmartre since 1934 with wine tastings, a wine auction, and lots of live music over a weekend in early October. ⊕ *www.fetedesvendang-esdemontmartre.com.*

Salon du Chocolat. Chocoholics will want to head to Porte de Versailles for the world's largest event dedicated to everything chocolate and cocoa. Over five days in October, you can take part in tastings, workshops, and exhibits with the planet's biggest names in chocolate and pastries. There's also a dedicated area for kids. ⊕ *www.salon-du-chocolat.com.*

November

Paris Cheese and Wine Week. Uncorked in 2021, some 80 eclectic cheesemakers, wine merchants, restaurants, bistros, hotels, and bakers offer tastings and events across the city each November. ⊕ *parischeeseandwineweek.com.*

Fête du Beaujolais Nouveau. The third Thursday of November is all about this popular *vin primeur.* While the small Beaujolais wine region in eastern France produces reds, whites, and rosés, it's well known around the globe for its red Beaujolais Nouveau that untypically needs to be consumed within weeks of harvest. The taste can vary from year to year, and wine bars, bistros, and restaurants across Paris wait, corkscrew in hand, for its annual arrival.

December

Christmas Markets. It would not be Christmas in Paris without the Marchés de Noël. Around 15 Christmas markets pop up around the city four Sundays before Christmas. The most popular can be found in Tuileries Garden, next to the Louvre. The amusement park rides and traditional chalets attract about 13 million visitors every season.

Great Itineraries

Paris is a treasure of neighborhoods and history, and a visit to this glorious city is never quite as simple as a quick look at a few landmarks. But if you have only a day to take it all in, there are some icons that you just can't miss. Over five days, you'll have the luxury to truly take in the sights and museums while leaving time for random exploring, including sampling the foods and beverages that have put the capital on the gastronomic world map.

Paris in 1 Day

Begin your day at the Trocadéro métro, where you can get the best views of the **Eiffel Tower** from the esplanade of the Palais de Chaillot. If you want to ride to the top, now is the best time to get in line (it opens at 9:30 am year-round). Afterward, take a walk along the Seine, stopping to visit the sculpture gardens of the **Musée Rodin** (be sure to stop at the café L'Augustine for a coffee), and continuing on to the **Musée d'Orsay** to tackle the late-19th-century works of art and admire the gorgeous former train station. Steps from here you can visit the city's newest cultural institution, Maison Gainsbourg, with its 25,000 items that belonged to the singer Serge Gainsbourg.

If your feet are still happy, cross the gilded Pont Tsar Alexandre III to the **Champs-Élysées**, passing the Belle Époque art palaces known as the **Grand Palais** and **Petit Palais**. You can take Bus 73 from the **Assemblée Nationale** across the bridge to **Place de la Concorde** and all the way up **Avenue des Champs-Élysées** to the **Arc de Triomphe**. Open until 10:30 or 11 pm, its panoramic viewing platform is ideal for admiring the City of Light.

Next, head to the most famous art museum in the world, the **Louvre**. With just one day in the city, you'll have to limit your time here, but grab a museum guide and hit up the Big Three: the *Mona Lisa*, *Venus de Milo*, and *Winged Victory of Samothrace*. There should still be time to get a glimpse of the exterior of **Notre-Dame Cathedral**, which still stands proud and mighty even after the 2019 fire that almost destroyed the interior; currently, there are plans for it to finally reopen in December 2024.

Paris in 5 Days

DAY 1: NOTRE-DAME AND THE LATIN QUARTER

Start your day at Pont Neuf for excellent views off the western tip of Île de la Cité, then explore the island's magnificent architectural heritage, including the **Conciergerie**, **Sainte-Chapelle**, and **Notre-Dame**.

Take a detour to neighboring Île St-Louis for lunch before heading into the medieval labyrinth of the **Latin Quarter**; its most valuable treasures are preserved in the **Musée de Cluny**, including the reconstructed ruins of 2nd-century Gallo-Roman steam baths. At the summit of the hill above the Sorbonne University is the imposing **Panthéon**, a monument (and mausoleum) of French heroes. Follow Rue Descartes to Rue Mouffetard for a café crème on one of the oldest market streets in Paris.

DAY 2: JARDIN DES TUILERIES, THE LOUVRE, AND THE MUSÉE D'ORSAY

Begin at **Place de la Concorde**, where an Egyptian obelisk replaces the guillotine where Louis XVI and Marie-Antoinette met their bloody fate during the French Revolution, then escape the traffic in the formal **Jardin des Tuileries**, which once belonged to the 16th-century Tuileries Palace, destroyed during the Paris Commune of 1871. Pass through the small

Arc du Carrousel to the modern glass pyramid that serves as the main entrance to the **Louvre**, the world's grandest museum, once a 12th-century fortress. You'll never be able to see it all, but take a few hours to explore and make sure you hit up all the essentials.

The **Musée d'Orsay** merits an afternoon gander. The short post-Louvre stroll to this museum on the Left Bank is just long enough to get some fresh air before feasting your eyes on the world's biggest collection of Impressionist and Postimpressionist masterpieces, housed in a building that's equally visually magnificent.

DAY 3: EIFFEL TOWER, CHAMPS-ÉLYSÉES, AND ARC DE TRIOMPHE

Begin your day at the Trocadéro métro, where you can get the best views of the **Eiffel Tower** from the esplanade of the Palais de Chaillot. Visit the **Musée de l'Homme**, with 63 mummies and 700,000 prehistoric artifacts and fossils, and take advantage of the spectacular selfie ops of both the Tour Eiffel and the Seine.

Then meander over to Quai d'Orsay, near Invalides, stopping for a *plat du jour* along the way before crossing the Alexandre III bridge to the Grand Palais, where you can now sneak some rooftop peeks, and then visit its sister, the Petit Palais. From here, you can walk all the way up **Avenue des Champs-Élysées** (focus on the prize and not the chain stores that line the avenue) to the **Arc de Triomphe**. Open until 10:30 or 11 pm, its panoramic viewing platform is ideal for admiring the City of Light.

DAY 4: THE MARAIS

In the 4e arrondissement, the hip Marais district just keeps getting hipper and is the perfect neighborhood to spend a relaxing day filled with culture, food, and fashion. To the south you can find the **Hôtel de Sens**, home to King Henry IV's feisty ex-wife Queen Marguerite, and one of the few surviving examples of late-medieval architecture. Around the corner on Rue Charlemagne is a preserved section of the city's 12th-century fortifications built by King Philippe-Augustus. Cross busy Rue St-Antoine to Le Marais and enter the **Hôtel de Sully**, a fine example of the elegant private mansions built here by aristocrats in the early 17th century. Stop by any of the old aristocratic mansions in Le Marais that have been turned into museums, including the **Musée Picasso** and the offbeat **Musée de la Chasse et de la Nature**.

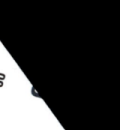

DAY 5: VERSAILLES

On Day 5, head 20 km (12½ miles) southwest of Paris to the gilded palace and reminder of pre-Revolution indulgence that is **Versailles**. The estate is divided into four sections: the Palace with the King's Grand Apartments and the famous Hall of Mirrors, the Grand Trianon, Marie-Antoinette's Estate, and, of course, the spectacular gardens. Book an English tour, which includes the King's Apartments, Royal Chapel, and Opera, and make sure you get there by 9 am so you can be sure to see everything. The easiest (and least expensive) way to visit Versailles is by the 40-minute Paris RER train serviced from St-Michel-Notre-Dame, Musée d'Orsay, Invalides, and Tour Eiffel stations. Buy tickets (destination: Versailles Rive G) directly from the automatic ticket machines or from the booth.

ontacts

 Air

AIRPORT INFORMATION Charles de Gaulle/Roissy and Orly. ☎ 3950 (press "0" for service in English) €0.35 per minute, 0033/1-70-36-39-50 outside of France ⊕ www.parisaeroport.fr.

 Bicycle

BICYCLE Vélib'. ☎ 01-76-49-12-34 ⊕ www.velib-metropole.fr.

 Boat and Ferry

BOAT Bateaux Parisiens. ✉ Port de la Bourdonnais, 7e ☎ 01-76-64-14-45 ⊕ www.bateauxparisiens.com. **Batobus.** ✉ Port de la Bourdonnais, 7e ☎ 01-76-64-79-12 ⊕ www.batobus.com. **Canauxrama.** ✉ Bassin de la Villette, 13 quai de la Loire, 19e ☎ 01-42-39-15-00 ⊕ www.canauxrama.com. **Compagnie des Bateaux-Mouches.** ✉ Port de la Conférence, 8e ☎ 01-42-25-96-10 ⊕ www.bateaux-mouches.fr. **Paris Canal.** ✉ Paris Canal, Bassin de la Villette, 21 quai de la Loire, 19e ☎ 01-42-40-29-00 ⊕ www.pariscanal.com.

FERRY Direct Ferries. ⊕ www.directferries.fr. **P&O European Ferries.** ☎ 03-66-74-03-25 ⊕ www.poferries.com.

 Bus

BUS INFORMATION Flixbus. ⊕ global.flixbus.com. **RATP.** ☎ 3424 ⊕ www.ratp.fr.

 Metro

MÉTRO INFORMATION RATP. ☎ 3424 ⊕ www.ratp.fr.

 Taxi

COMPANIES Alpha Taxis. ☎ 01-45-85-85-85 ⊕ www.alphataxis.fr. **Taxis G7.** ☎ 3607 €0.45/min, 01-41-27-66-99 for service in English ⊕ www.g7.fr.

 Train

TRAIN INFORMATION Eurail. ⊕ www.eurail.com. **SNCF.** ☎ 3635 ⊕ www.sncf-connect.com. **TGV.** ☎ 3635 ⊕ www.sncf-connect.com/tgv.

CHANNEL TUNNEL INFORMATION Eurostar. ☎ 01-70-70-60-88 in France ⊕ www.eurostar.com. **Eurotunnel.** ☎ 08-10-63-03-04 €0.06/min ⊕ www.eurotunnel.com.

Chapter 3

ÎLE DE LA CITÉ AND ÎLE ST-LOUIS

Updated by Jack Vermee

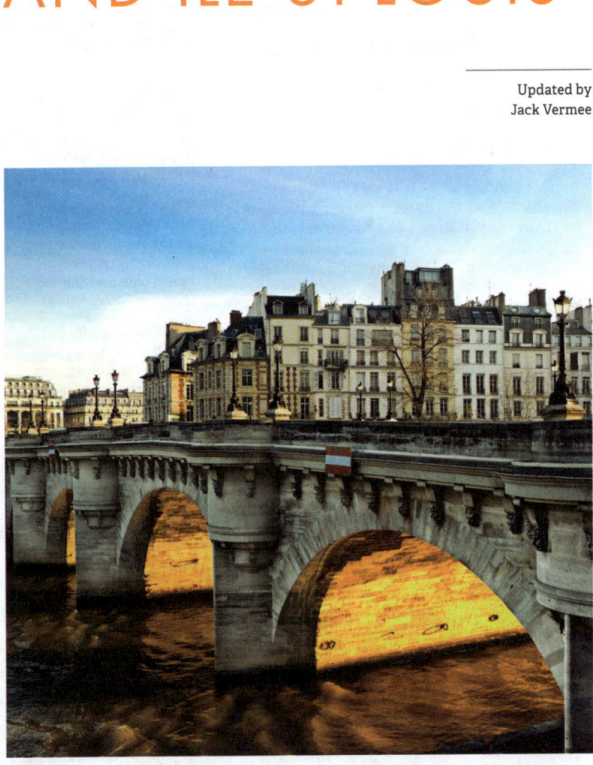

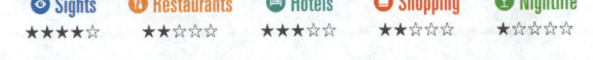

NEIGHBORHOOD SNAPSHOT

MAKING THE MOST OF YOUR TIME

This little area of Paris is easily walkable and packed with sights and stunning views, so give yourself as much time as possible to explore. With Notre-Dame, the Conciergerie, and Sainte-Chapelle, you could spend a day wandering, but the islands are easily combined with the St-Germain quarter. On warmer days, Rue de Buci is an ideal place to pick up a picnic lunch to enjoy in leafy Square du Vert-Galant at the tip of Île de la Cité. If you have limited time in the area, survey the ongoing reconstruction of Notre-Dame and go for a stroll.

GETTING HERE

Île de la Cité and Île St-Louis are in the 1er and 4e arrondissements (Boulevard du Palais is the dividing line between the 1er and 4e arrondissements on Île de la Cité). If you're too far away to get here on foot, take the *métro* to St-Michel station or Cité.

PAUSE HERE

At the western tip of Île de la Cité, the Square du Vert-Galant is a favorite spot for local picnickers. The garden is a peaceful oasis in the very heart of the city. Take métro Line 7 to Pont Neuf, cross the famous bridge, nod to the statue of Henri IV on horseback, and then relax.

TOP REASONS TO GO

■ **Notre-Dame.** This gorgeous Gothic cathedral has welcomed visitors to Paris for centuries. While you currently cannot visit inside due to the tragic 2019 fire that nearly destroyed the entire church, the imposing edifice and famed towers still remain a must-see from the outside (and the cathedral currently has plans to reopen in December 2024).

■ **Sainte-Chapelle.** Visit on a sunny day to best appreciate the exquisite stained glass in this 13th-century chapel built for King Louis IX.

■ **La Conciergerie.** Constructed in the late 13th and early 14th centuries as part of the original palace of the kings of France, in 1391 this striking building became a prison. During the French Revolution, Marie-Antoinette languished 76 days here awaiting her execution.

■ **Strolling the Islands.** Île de la Cité is where Paris began. Start with the city's oldest bridge, the Pont Neuf (incongruously called the "new bridge") and give a nod to the statue of Henry IV, who once proudly said, "I make love, I make war, and I build." From here, cross to Place Dauphine and make your way to Île St-Louis, one of the city's most exclusive enclaves.

At the heart of Paris, linked to the banks of the Seine by a series of bridges, are two small islands: Île St-Louis and Île de la Cité. They're the perfect places to begin your visit, with postcard-worthy views all around. The Île de la Cité is anchored by mighty Notre-Dame, badly damaged by the 2019 fire but scheduled to reopen in December 2024; farther east, the atmospheric Île St-Louis is dotted with charming hotels, cozy restaurants, and small specialty shops.

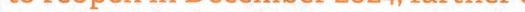

Île de la Cité

At the western tip of Île de la Cité is regal **Place Dauphine**, one of Paris's oldest squares. The impressive **Palais de Justice** (courthouse) sits between **Sainte-Chapelle**, the exquisite medieval chapel of saintly King Louis IX, and the **Conciergerie**, the prison where Marie-Antoinette and other bluebloods awaited their slice of history at the guillotine.

The Gothic powerhouse that is **Notre-Dame** originally loomed over a medieval huddle of buildings that were later ordered razed by Baron Georges-Eugène Haussmann, the 19th-century urban planner who transformed Paris into the city we see today. In front of the cathedral is **Place du Parvis**, the point from which all roads in France are measured. On the north side of the square is the **Hôtel-Dieu** (roughly translated as "general hospital"); it was immortalized by 19th-century author Honoré de Balzac as the squalid last stop for the city's most unfortunate, but today it houses a modern hospital. Just behind the cathedral lies Rue du Cloître-Notre-Dame, which cuts through the **Ancien Cloître Quartier**, on whose narrow streets you can imagine the medieval quarter as it once was, densely packed and teeming with activity. At 9–11 quai aux Fleurs, a plaque commemorates the abode that was the setting of the tragic 12th-century love affair between the philosopher Peter Abélard and his young student, Héloïse.

At the eastern tip of Île de la Cité is the **Mémorial des Martyrs de la Déportation**, all but hidden in a pocket-size park. A set of stairs leads down to this impressive and moving memorial, which honors the French citizens who died in Nazi concentration camps.

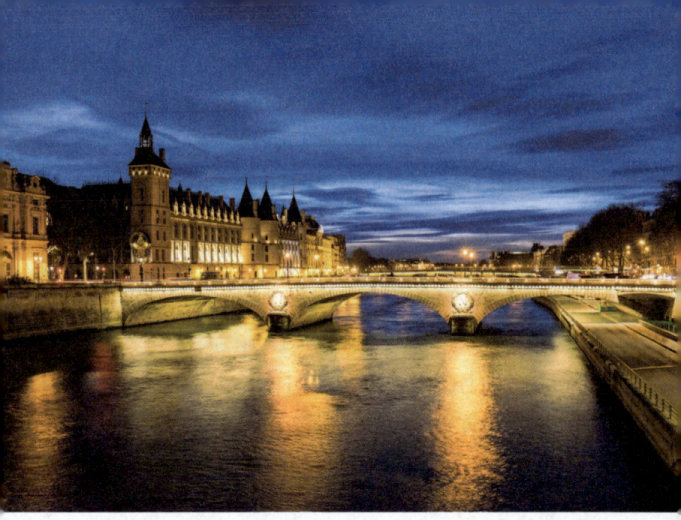

The Île de la Cité is perhaps most charming at night, when its embankments along the Seine are illuminated by street and bridge lights.

⊙ Sights

Ancien Cloître Quartier

NEIGHBORHOOD | Hidden in the shadows of Notre-Dame is an evocative, often-overlooked tangle of medieval streets. Through the years lucky folks, including Ludwig Bemelmans (who created the beloved *Madeleine* books) and the Aga Khan, have called this area home, but back in the Middle Ages it was the domain of cathedral seminary students. One of them was the celebrated Peter Abélard (1079–1142)—philosopher, questioner of the faith, and renowned declaimer of love poems. Abélard boarded with Notre-Dame's clergyman, Fulbert, whose 17-year-old niece, Héloïse, was seduced by the compelling Abélard, 39 years her senior. She became pregnant, and the vengeful clergyman had Abélard castrated; amazingly, he survived and fled to a monastery, while Héloïse took refuge in a nunnery. The poetic, passionate letters between the two cemented their fame as thwarted lovers, and their story inspired a devoted following during the romantic 19th century. They still draw admirers to the Père-Lachaise Cemetery, where they're interred *ensemble*. The clergyman's house at 10 rue Chanoinesse was redone in 1849; a plaque at the back of the building at 9–11 quai aux Fleurs commemorates the lovers. ✉ *Rue du Cloître-Notre-Dame north to Quai des Fleurs, 4e, Ile de la Cité* Ⓜ *Cité*.

★ Cathédrale Notre-Dame de Paris

CHURCH | Looming above Place du Parvis, this Gothic sanctuary is the symbolic heart of Paris and, for many, of France itself, now more than ever. A heartbreaking 2019 fire almost destroyed the entire cathedral. The roof was devastated, and the 300-foot spire collapsed, but after the fire was extinguished, the building was deemed structurally sound, and most of its priceless relics and articles survived, including the famed rose windows, the crown of thorns said to have been worn by Jesus Christ, the 800-year-old organ, and numerous pieces of classic artwork.

Many of these items sustained some damage that required extensive restoration work—a projected partial reopening is expected to coincide with the opening of the Paris Olympic Games in July 2024 while completion is currently scheduled for December 2024. Although visitors have not been able to go inside for quite some time, the towers outside still stand as testaments to the power, history, and meaning of Notre-Dame. Napoléon was crowned here, and kings and queens exchanged marriage vows before its altar. Begun in 1163, completed in 1345, badly damaged during the Revolution, and restored in the 19th century by Eugène Viollet-le-Duc, Notre-Dame may not be the country's oldest or largest cathedral, but in beauty and architectural harmony it has few peers. ☒ *6 parvis Notre-Dame–Pl. Jean-Paul II, 4e, Ile de la Cité* ☎ *01–42–34–56–10* ⊕ *www.notredamedeparis.fr* Ⓜ *Cité.*

Conciergerie

NOTABLE BUILDING | FAMILY | Most of Île de la Cité's medieval structures fell victim to wunderkind urban planner Baron Haussmann's ambitious rebuilding program of the 1860s. Among the rare survivors are the jewel-like Sainte-Chapelle, a vision of shimmering stained glass, and the Conciergerie, the cavernous former prison where Marie-Antoinette and other victims of the French Revolution spent their final days.

Constructed by Philip IV in the late 13th and early 14th centuries, the Conciergerie—which takes its name from the building's concierge or keeper—was part of the original palace of the kings of France before the royals moved into the Louvre around 1364. In 1391, it became a prison. During the French Revolution, Marie-Antoinette languished 76 days here awaiting her date with the guillotine. There is a re-creation of the doomed queen's sad little cell—plus others that are far smaller—complete with wax figures behind bars. In the chapel, stained

> ## Monsieur Guillotin
>
>
> **Beheading by means of an axe or sword was a popular form of punishment long before the French Revolution, but it was Dr. Joseph-Ignace Guillotin who suggested there was a more humane way of decapitating prisoners. Not surprisingly, Dr. Guillotin's descendants changed their surname.**

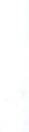

glass, commissioned after the queen's death by her daughter, is emblazoned with the initials *M.A.* Outside you can see the small courtyard where women prisoners took meals and washed their clothes in the fountain (men enjoyed no similar respite). Well-done temporary exhibitions on the ground floor aim to please kids and adults alike; themes have included enchanted forests and Gothic castles. There are free guided tours (in French only) most days at 11 and 3. Pick up a free English guide at reception and ask for a "Histopad" (also free), an "augmented reality" tablet that allows you to go back in time and view 30 reconstructions. ☒ *2 bd. du Palais, 4e, Ile de la Cité* ☎ *01–53–40–60–80* ⊕ *www.paris-conciergerie.fr* ✉ *€13; €20 with joint ticket to Sainte-Chapelle* ⚐ *Reservation required* Ⓜ *Cité.*

Mémorial des Martyrs de la Déportation

(*Memorial of the Deportation*)

MONUMENT | On the east end of Île de la Cité lies this stark monument to the more than 200,000 French men, women, and children who died in Nazi concentration camps during World War II. The evocative memorial, inaugurated by Charles de Gaulle in 1962, was intentionally designed to be claustrophobic. Concrete blocks mark the narrow entrance to the crypt, which contains the tomb of an unknown deportee killed at the

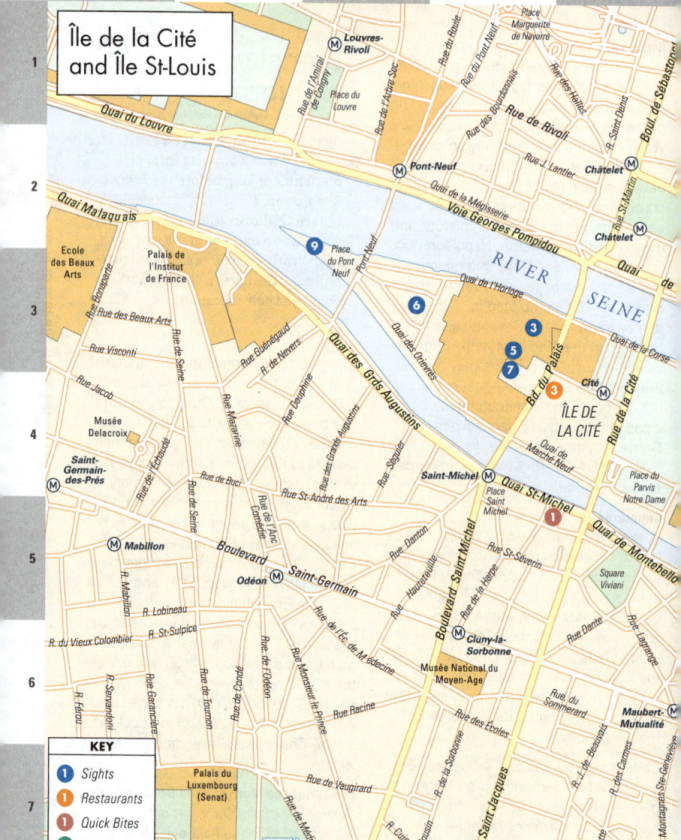

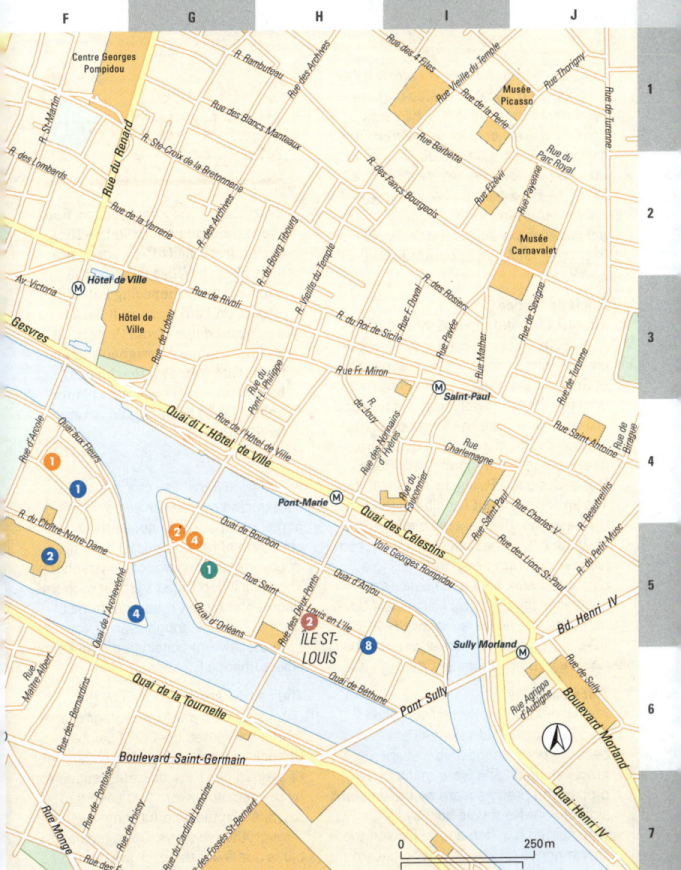

Hotels

1	Hôtel Saint-Louis en l'Isle	G5

Neustadt camp. A dimly lit narrow gallery studded with 200,000 pieces of glass symbolizes the lives lost, while urns at the lateral ends contain ashes from the camps. ✉ *Square de l'Île-de-France, 7 quai de l'Archevêché, 4e, Ile de la Cité* ☎ 06-14-67-54-98 🌐 www.onac-vg.fr/hauts-lieux-memoire-necropoles/memorial-des-martyrs-de-la-deportation ✉ *Free* ⊘ *Closed 1st Mon. of month* Ⓜ *Cité, St-Michel.*

Palais de Justice

NOTABLE BUILDING | This 19th-century, neoclassical courthouse complex occupies the site of the former royal palace of St-Louis that later housed Parliament until the French Revolution. It is recognizable from afar with the tower of Sainte-Chapelle, tucked inside the courtyard, peeking out. Although the new Renzo Piano–designed Palais de Justice in the 17e arrondissement handles the bulk of the caseload, this venerable edifice is now the court of appeals. Black-frocked judges can often be spotted taking a cigarette break on the majestic rear staircase facing Rue du Harlay. ✉ *4 bd. du Palais, 4e, Ile de la Cité* ☎ 01-44-32-52-52 🌐 *www.cours-appel.justice.fr/paris* ✉ *Free* ⊘ *Closed Sun.* Ⓜ *Cité.*

Place Dauphine

PLAZA/SQUARE | The Surrealists called Place Dauphine "le sexe de Paris" because of its suggestive V shape; however, its origins were much more proper. The pretty square on the western side of Pont Neuf was built by Henry IV, who named it in homage to his son the crown prince (or *dauphin*) who became Louis XIII when Henry was assassinated. In warm weather, treat yourself to a romantic meal on a restaurant terrace here—the square is one of the best places in Paris to dine *en plein air.* ✉ *4e, Ile de la Cité* Ⓜ *Cité.*

★ Sainte-Chapelle

CHURCH | Built by the obsessively pious Louis IX (1214–70), this Gothic jewel is home to the oldest stained-glass

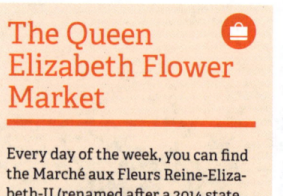

windows in Paris. The chapel was constructed over seven years, at phenomenal expense, to house the king's collection of relics acquired from the impoverished emperor of Constantinople. These included Christ's crown of thorns, fragments of the Cross, and drops of Christ's blood—though even in Louis's time these were considered of questionable authenticity.

The narrow spiral staircase by the entrance takes you to the upper chapel where the famed beauty of Sainte-Chapelle comes alive: 6,458 square feet of stained glass are delicately supported by painted stonework that seems to disappear in the colorful light streaming through the windows. Deep reds and blues dominate the background, noticeably different from later, lighter medieval styles such as those of Notre-Dame's rose windows.

The chapel is essentially an enormous magic lantern illuminating 1,130 biblical figures. Besides the dazzling glass, observe the detailed carvings on the columns and the statues of the apostles. The lower chapel is gloomy and plain, but take note of the low, vaulted ceiling

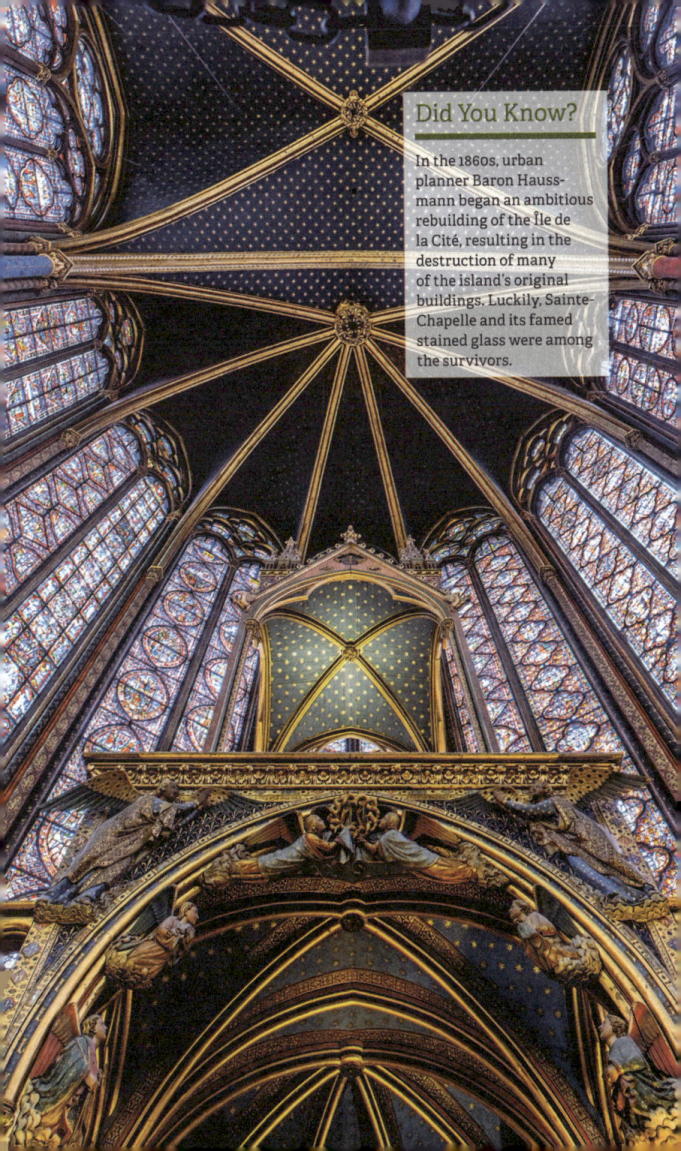

Did You Know?

In the 1860s, urban planner Baron Haussmann began an ambitious rebuilding of the Île de la Cité, resulting in the destruction of many of the island's original buildings. Luckily, Sainte-Chapelle and its famed stained glass were among the survivors.

decorated with fleurs-de-lis and cleverly arranged Ls for "Louis." Audioguides (€3) are available, or you can download a phone app focusing on the church's stained glass windows.

Sunset is the optimal time to see the rose window; however, to avoid waiting in killer lines, plan your visit for a weekday morning, the earlier the better. Come on a sunny day to appreciate the full effect of the light filtering through all that glorious stained glass. You can buy a joint ticket with the Conciergerie: lines are shorter if you purchase it there or online. The chapel makes a divine setting for classical concerts; check the schedule at www.classictic.com. ✉ 4 bd. du Palais, 4e, Ile de la Cité ☎ 01–53–40–60–80 🌐 www.sainte-chapelle.fr ✉ €13; €20 with joint ticket to Conciergerie ⚠ Reservation required Ⓜ Cité.

Square du Vert-Galant

PLAZA/SQUARE | The equestrian statue of the Vert Galant himself—amorous adventurer Henry IV—keeps a vigilant watch over this leafy square at the western end of Île de la Cité. The dashing but ruthless Henry, king of France from 1589 until his assassination in 1610, was a stern upholder of the absolute rights of monarchy and a notorious womanizer. He is probably best remembered for his cynical remark that *"Paris vaut bien une messe"* ("Paris is worth a Mass"), a reference to his readiness to renounce Protestantism to gain the throne of predominantly Catholic France. To ease his conscience, he issued the Edict of Nantes in 1598, according French Protestants (almost) equal rights with their Catholic countrymen. The square is a great place for a quay-side picnic. It's also the departure point for Vedette Pont Neuf tour boats (at the bottom of the steps to the right). ✉ 4e, Ile de la Cité Ⓜ Pont Neuf.

Restaurants

Île de la Cité and Île St-Louis are great for sightseeing, which is why much of the dining scene on these islands revolves around fast food and tourist traps. Luckily, a few long-established brasseries and inspired bistros on elegant Île St-Louis—not to mention the legendary Berthillon, the city's great *glacier* (ice-cream maker)—more than compensate. Among the shops, épiceries, and ancient bookstores of Rue St-Louis-en-l'Île, the island's central spine, you'll find enough quality dining to keep you satisfied at any time of the day.

Au Vieux Paris d'Arcole

$$$ | **FRENCH** | Built in 1512 as a residence for the Canon of Notre-Dame, Au Vieux Paris d'Arcole was converted into a wine bar in 1723, making it one of the city's oldest restaurants. It specializes in dishes from the Aveyron region in the southwest (if it's on the menu, try the *coufidou d'Aubrac*, a rich beef stew made with Marcillac wine) and serves everything in plush red-velvet-and-antiques dining areas that are a treat for the eyes. **Known for:** quirky antique decor; quiet setting; lovely terrace. **§** *Average main: €27* ✉ *24 rue Chanoinesse, 4e, Île Saint-Louis* ☎ *01–40–51–78–52* 🌐 *www.restaurantauvieuxparis.fr* Ⓜ Cité.

Brasserie Les Deux Palais

$$ | **BRASSERIE** | Set in the shadow of Sainte-Chapelle's spire, this bright and friendly brasserie has been serving classic fare—*tartare de boeuf, cuisse du canard confit*—to the lawyers and judges of the Palais du Justice across the street since 1930. Take some time to admire the 19th-century light fixtures and lovely tiled floor. **Known for:** striking historical decor; friendly service; good value. **§** *Average main: €20* ✉ *3 bd. du Palais, 4e, Île Saint-Louis* ☎ *01–43–54–20–86* 🌐 *www.brasserielesdeuxpalais.fr* Ⓜ Cité.

Île St-Louis

Nearby Pont St-Louis, which always seems to be occupied by street performers, leads to Île St-Louis, one of the city's best places to wander. There are no cultural hot spots, just a few narrow streets that comprise one of the most privileged areas in Paris. Small hotels, eateries, art galleries, and shops selling everything from chocolate and cheese to silk scarves line the main street, Rue St-Louis-en-L'Île. There were once two islands here, Île Notre-Dame and Île aux Vaches ("Cow Island," an erstwhile grazing pasture), both owned by the Church. Speculators bought the islands, joined them, and sold the plots to builders who created what is today some of the city's most elegant and expensive real estate. Baroque architect Louis Le Vau (who later worked on Versailles) designed fabulous private mansions for aristocrats, including the majestic Hôtel de Lauzun on lovely Quai d'Anjou.

 Sights

St-Louis-en-L'Île

CHURCH | You can't miss the unusual lacy spire of this church as you approach Île St-Louis; it's the only church on the island and there are no other steeples to compete with it. It was built from 1664 to 1726 according to the Baroque designs of architect François Le Vau, brother of the more famous Louis, who designed several mansions nearby—as well as the Palace of Versailles. Saint-Louis's interior was essentially stripped during the Revolution, as were so many French churches, but look for the odd outdoor iron clock, which dates from 1741. Check the church website for upcoming classical music events. ✉ *19 bis, rue St-Louis-en-L'Île, Île Saint-Louis* ☎ *01–46–34–11–60* ⊕ *www.saintlouisenlile.catholique.fr* Ⓜ *Pont Marie.*

 Restaurants

Brasserie de l'Isle Saint-Louis

$$$ | **BRASSERIE** | With its dream location on the tip of Île St-Louis overlooking the Seine and Notre-Dame, you'd think this charming brasserie, like so many before it, would have succumbed to its own success. Yet it remains exactly what a decent neighborhood brasserie should be, with authentic decor, efficiently friendly service, and reliably good food. **Known for:** fantastic views of Notre-Dame; coveted outdoor terrace by the Seine; decent prices, considering the location. [$] *Average main: €28* ✉ *55 quai de Bourbon, 4e, Île Saint-Louis* ☎ *01–43–54–02–59* ⊕ *www.labrasserie-isl.fr* ♡ *Closed Wed.* Ⓜ *Pont Marie, Maubert-Mutualité, Sully-Morland.*

Le Saint-Régis

$$$ | **BISTRO** | Wondering where locals drink their coffee on touristy Île St-Louis? Try this old-time café that also features a menu of classic French dishes—it's open until 2 am daily. **Known for:** interesting people-watching; perfect eggs Benedict; beef tartare du St-Regis. [$] *Average main: €26* ✉ *6 rue Jean du Bellay, 4e, Île Saint-Louis* ☎ *01–43–54–59–41* ⊕ *www.lesaintregis-paris.com* Ⓜ *Pont Marie.*

 Coffee and Quick Bites

Amorino

$ | **ICE CREAM** | **FAMILY** | Popping up all over—and winning converts faster than you can finish a double scoop—is the Amorino chain of gelaterias, which serves inventive frozen concoctions in the shape of flower blossoms. Popular flavors include rich *bacio* (dark chocolate with hazelnuts) and mascarpone with figs. **Known for:** Italian gelato with a French twist; sweet crêpes and macarons; Italian coffee, tea, and hot chocolate. [$] *Average main: €6* ✉ *47 rue St-Louis-en-l'Île, 4e, Île Saint-Louis* ☎ *01–44–07–48–08* ⊕ *www.amorino.com* Ⓜ *Pont Marie.*

★ **Berthillon**

$ | **ICE CREAM** | Parisian ice cream is served at cafés all over town, but it's worth making the pilgrimage to this mecca of artisanal *crèmes glacées* to understand what all the fuss is about. The family-owned Berthillon shop features more than 30 flavors that change with the seasons, from mouth-puckering *cassis* (black currant) in summer to nutty *marron* (candied chestnut) in winter. **Known for:** delicious ice cream with natural ingredients; long lines; classic tearoom atmosphere. ⓘ *Average main: €8* ✉ *31 rue St-Louis-en-l'Île, 4e, Île Saint-Louis* ☎ *01-43-54-31-61* ⊕ *www.berthillon.fr* ◎ *Closed Mon. and Tues.* Ⓜ *Pont Marie.*

 Hotels

Hôtel Saint-Louis en l'Isle

$$ | **HOTEL** | The location on the exceptionally charming Île St-Louis is the real draw of this five-story hotel, which retains many of its original 17th-century stone walls and wooden beams. **Pros:** romantic location; ancient architectural details; friendly staff. **Cons:** location is a bit far from the sights; métro stations are not so convenient; small rooms. ⓘ *Rooms from: €315* ✉ *75 rue St-Louis-en-l'Île, 4e, Île Saint-Louis* ☎ *01-46-34-04-80* ⊕ *www.saintlouisenlisle.com* ↜ *20 rooms* ✪ *No Meals* Ⓜ *Pont Marie.*

 Shopping

Although Île de la Cité is so dominated by Notre-Dame, the Palais du Justice, and the Conciergerie that shopping for anything other than tourist trinkets is impossible, Île St-Louis offers visitors a small collection of designer shops and art galleries, nearly all of which are located on Rue St-Louis-en-l'Île, the main street that bisects the island.

Bamyan

CLOTHING | A shopping destination since 1986, this stylish purveyor of "ethnic chic" showcases the work of talented young Indian and Middle Eastern designers whose multicolored creations range from silk-brocaded saris and stunningly embroidered coats to pashmina scarves and leather handbags. ✉ *72 rue St-Louis-en-l'Île, 4e, Île Saint-Louis* ☎ *01-43-29-39-50* ⊕ *www.bamyanparis.com* Ⓜ *Pont Marie.*

Céline Wright

HOUSEWARES | Poetically binding thousands of strips of *washi* (Japanese paper) into handcrafted, one-of-a-kind lighting fixtures has made Céline Wright a familiar name in Paris's art and design community. Her famous "cocoon" lamps reflect artisanal, eco-friendly traditions while evincing a thoroughly modern sensibility. ✉ *56 rue St-Louis-en-l'Île, 4e, Île Saint-Louis* ☎ *01-43-29-33-93* ⊕ *www.celinewright.com* Ⓜ *Pont Marie.*

Clair de Rêve

TOYS | Stepping into the pleasantly cluttered shop of this maker of marionettes and restorer of automata is like time-traveling to the Belle Époque. Music boxes and wind-up toys are also for sale. ✉ *35 rue St-Louis-en-l'Île, 4e, Île Saint-Louis* ☎ *01-43-81-11-37* ⊕ *www.clairdereve.com* Ⓜ *Pont Marie.*

Les sacs de Louise

HANDBAGS | A warm welcome is guaranteed at this appealing little boutique, which specializes in a well-curated selection of designer handbags and other leather goods. ✉ *56 rue St-Louis-en-l'Île, 4e, Île Saint-Louis* ☎ *06-19-51-47-31* Ⓜ *Pont Marie.*

Chapter 4

AROUND THE EIFFEL TOWER

Updated by
Jennifer Ladonne

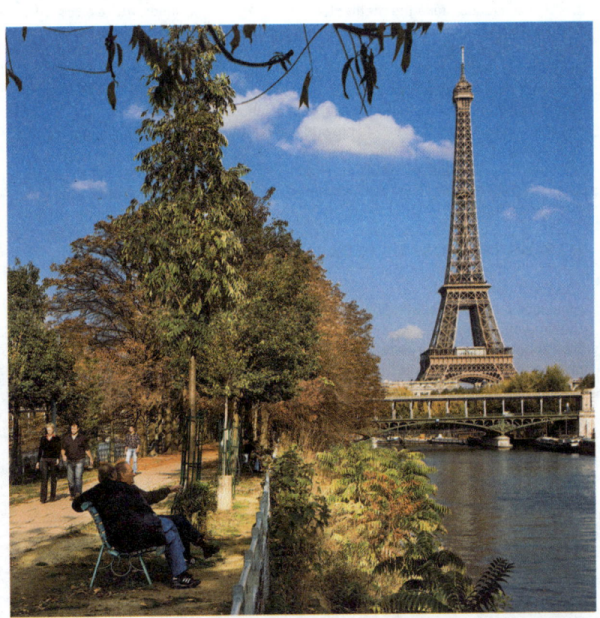

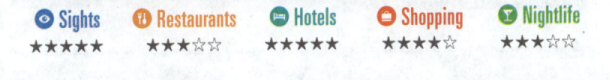

GHBORHOOD SNAPSHOT

GETTING HERE

This neighborhood includes the 7e, 15e, and 16e arrondissements. The most romantic way to reach the Eiffel Tower is via Bateau Mouche boat or the Batobus, which stops at the foot of the tower. Alternatively, you can head for RER C: Champ de Mars/ Tour Eiffel. But for the best views, you have some options: get off at the marvelous Bir-Hakeim *métro* stop (Line 6), one of the few elevated stations left in Paris, then take the Allée de Cygnes walkway to get a glimpse of the spectacular views and a replica of the Statue of Liberty (the original was a gift to the United States from France; this one was a gift from the U.S. to France); take the métro stop Alma Marceau (Line 9) for views from the Pont de l'Alma; or use the métro stop Trocadéro (Line 9 or 6) for the majestic panorama of Place de Trocadéro and make the short walk over the Pont d'Iéna to the tower (you'll be skirting crowds unless you opt for a school day in the off-season; if there are crowds, be vigilant of pickpockets). For the Musée Rodin, get off at Varenne (Line 13). Use this same stop or La Tour-Maubourg (Line 8) for Hôtel des Invalides, home to Napoléon's Tomb.

MAKING THE MOST OF YOUR TIME

This neighborhood is home to one of the world's most iconic sights, the Eiffel Tower. Depending on the time of year, you can wait hours to ascend La Tour (it helps to buy your ticket online—come at night when lines are shorter, join a tour that skirts the line, or, best of all, reserve a spot at Madame Brasserie, the Jules Verne restaurant, or the tower's Champagne Bar for access to the VIP elevator). But even if you stay firmly on the ground, it's worth a trip to see the landmark up close. Afterwards, explore Rue St-Dominique's shops, bakeries, and cafés. If you have a morning or afternoon to spare, do not miss the Musée Rodin. From here, it's a short walk to Napoléon's over-the-top tomb at the Hôtel des Invalides, which also houses the Musée de l'Armée devoted to military history. To appreciate art from Asia, Africa, and Oceania, spend an hour or two in the Musée du Quai Branly.

TOP REASONS TO GO

■ **Eiffel Tower.** Without a question, the ultimate symbol of France is worth a visit at least once in your life.

■ **Musée Rodin.** A must-see for fans of the master sculptor, this 18th-century *hôtel particulier* (private mansion) was Rodin's former workshop. The stunning grounds, with a rose garden and a reflecting pool, are the perfect setting for his timeless works, and the indoor-outdoor garden café is lovely.

■ **Napoléon's Tomb.** The golden-domed Hôtel des Invalides is a fitting place for the grandiose emperor's remains. Military history buffs will appreciate the impressive display of weaponry and armor in the adjoining Musée de l'Armée.

■ **Palais de Chaillot.** A favorite of tourists and fashion photographers, this statue-lined plaza-terrace at Place du Trocadéro has the city's best view of the Eiffel Tower.

■ **A boat ride.** Whether by a guided Bateaux Mouches tour or a trip on the Batobus (water bus), cruising the Seine is a relaxing way to see city highlights without traffic or crowds. Book a ride after dark when Paris is aglow.

The posh 7e arrondissement (where nearly every block affords a view of the Eiffel Tower) is home to the French *bourgeoisie* and well-heeled expats. Commanding the southwestern end of Paris, the Eiffel Tower was considered an iron-latticed monstrosity when it opened in 1889. Today, it is a beloved icon, especially after sundown, when thousands of twinkling lights sparkle for five minutes at the top of every hour.

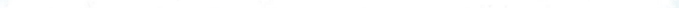

There are other monumental sights here too, notably the **Hôtel des Invalides,** a sprawling neo-Baroque complex with a towering golden dome under which lies the grandiose tomb of Napoléon. Along the river, there is the Palais Bourbon, seat of the French Parliament, which is an 18th-century homage to ancient Greek architecture. Other imposing government buildings are housed in elegant mansions in this area. Nearby is the modern **Musée du Quai Branly,** built by star architect Jean Nouvel. Don't miss the **Musée Rodin,** where the master's sculptures ooze sensuality both outside in the garden and inside the elegant Hôtel Biron. Around Trocadéro, north of the Eiffel Tower, the **Palais de Chaillot complex** includes the Cité de l'Architecture et du Patrimoine, a must for architecture buffs, along with the anthropology-oriented Musée de l'Homme and the newly restored Musée National de la Marine, documenting maritime life in France.

From the Eiffel Tower east, the walkway along the Seine will take you past **Les**

Égouts (where you can embark on a subterranean tour of actual working sewers) and the **American Church.** For one of the best views in Paris, cross Pont Alexandre III, the city's most ornate bridge spanning the Seine, from Invalides to the Grand Palais. Named for the Russian czar to celebrate Franco–Russian friendship, the bridge was built between 1896 and 1900 and is bedecked with gilded sculptures, cherubs, and romantic Art Nouveau lamps.

 Sights

American Church

CHURCH | Not to be confused with the American Cathedral across the river at 23 avenue George V, this pretty, neo-Gothic, Protestant church was built between 1927 and 1931. It features a pair of Tiffany stained-glass windows—a rare find in Europe. Besides ecumenical services, the church hosts architectural tours, free classical and acoustic concerts, and lectures and workshops on well-being

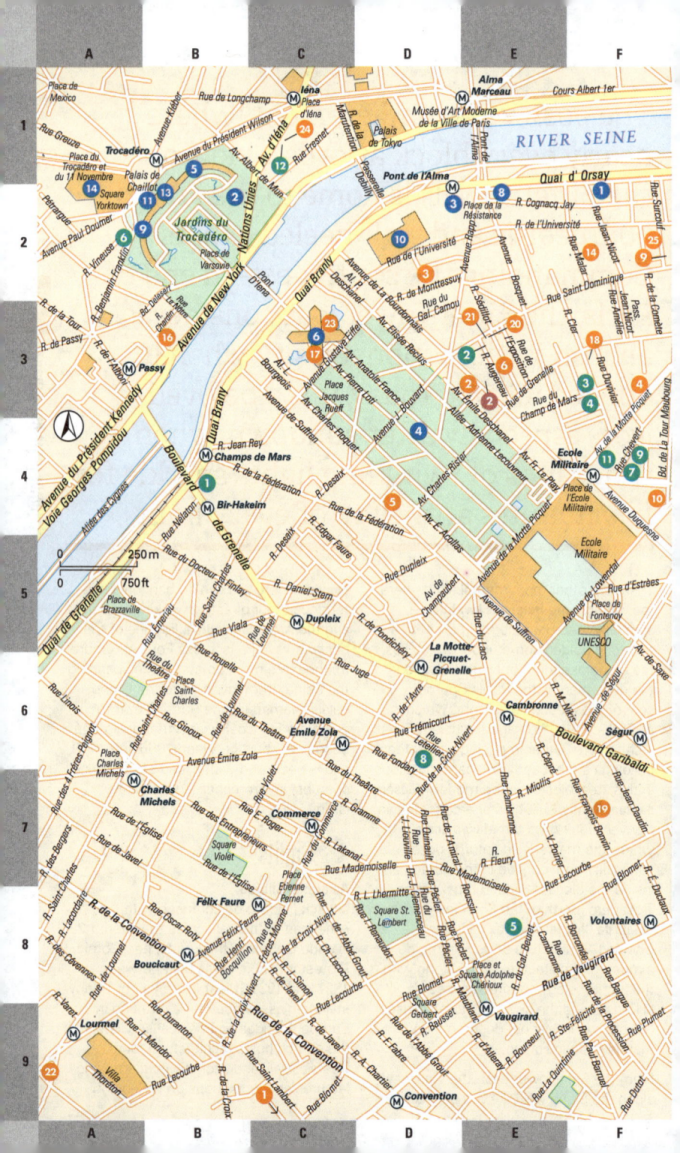

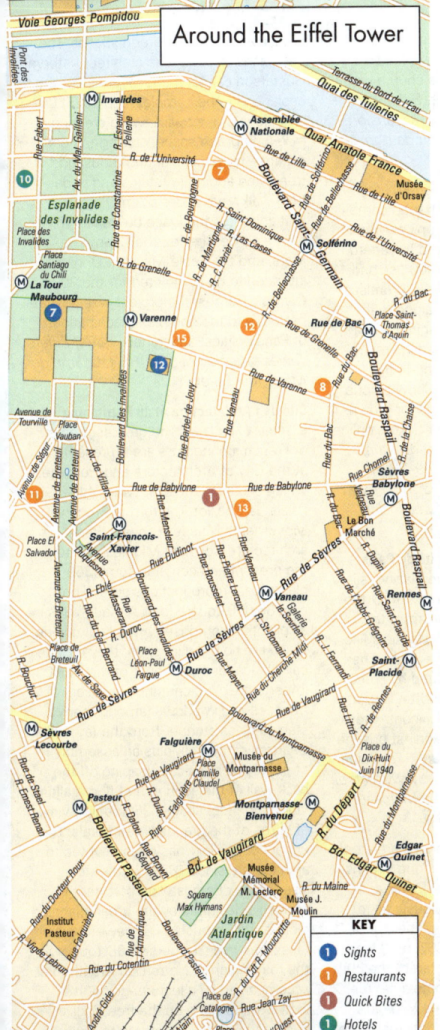

Sights

#	Name	Grid
1	American Church	F2
2	Aquarium de Paris	B2
3	Cathédrale de la Sainte-Trinité de Paris	D2
4	Champ de Mars	D4
5	Cité de l'Architecture et du Patrimoine	B1
6	Eiffel Tower	C3
7	Hôtel des Invalides	G3
8	Les Égouts	E2
9	Musée de l'Homme	B2
10	Musée du Quai Branly – Jacques Chirac	D2
11	Musée National de la Marine	B2
12	Musée Rodin	H4
13	Palais de Chaillot	B2
14	Passy Cemetery	A2

Restaurants

#	Name	Grid
1	Afaria	C9
2	Arnaud Nicolas	E3
3	Au Bon Accueil	D2
4	Auberge Bressane	F3
5	Aux Cerises	D4
6	Café de Mars	E3
7	Café des Ministères	I2
8	Café Varenne	I4
9	David Toutain	F2
10	D'Chez Eux	F4
11	Gémellus	G5
12	La Laiterie Sainte Clotilde	I3
13	La Table d'Aki	I5
14	L'Ami Jean	F2
15	L'Arpège	H3
16	L'Astrance	B3
17	Le Jules Verne	C3
18	Le Petit Cler	F3
19	Le Troquet	F7
20	Le Violon d'Ingres	E3
21	Les Cocottes de Christian Constant	E3
22	L'Os à Moelle	A9
23	Madame Brasserie	C3
24	Shang Palace	C1
25	Tomy & Co.	F2

Quick Bites

#	Name	Grid
1	Café Coutume	H5
2	Terres de Café	E3

Hotels

#	Name	Grid
1	Eiffel Seine Hôtel	B4
2	Hôtel de Londres Eiffel	E3
3	Hôtel du Cadran	F3
4	Hôtel du Champ de Mars	F3
5	Hotel Eiffel Blomet	E8
6	Hôtel Eiffel Trocadéro	A2
7	Hôtel Le Tourville	F4
8	Hôtel Wallace	D6
9	Le Cinq Codet	F4
10	Le Narcisse Blanc	G2
11	Le Walt	F4
12	Shangri-La Paris Hotel	C1

and topics of current interest. You can check event listings and download a self-guided PDF tour at the church website. ✉ *65 quai d'Orsay, 7e, Eiffel Tower* ☎ *01–40–62–05–00* ⊕ *www.acparis.org* Ⓜ *Alma-Marceau; RER: Pont de l'Alma.*

Aquarium de Paris

AQUARIUM | FAMILY | An aquarium and cinema may seem like a strange combination, but the two coexist nicely in this attractive space beneath the Trocadéro gardens. In addition to 10,000 fish and a giant tank of small sharks, it promises puppet and magic shows, along with workshops for children in animation, art, and dance (these are offered in French, but the staff speaks English). In the cinema, kid-oriented films show on one big screen, and feature films for grownups play on a second. Book tickets online to avoid lines. ✉ *5 av. Albert de Mun, 16e, Eiffel Tower* ☎ *01–40–69–23–23* ⊕ *www.aquariumdeparis.com* ✈ *From €21* ☞ *Last entry 1 hr before closing* Ⓜ *Trocadéro.*

Cathédrale de la Sainte-Trinité de Paris

CHURCH | At first glance, the blazing, silvery onion domes of this Russian Orthodox cathedral, an easy walk from the Eiffel Tower and Quai Branly, appear like a mirage of Moscow on the Seine. The ultramodern edifice, designed by French architect Jean-Michel Wilmotte, is worth a quick peek for its graceful icons, mosaics, and colorful frescoes against pristine marble walls. ✉ *1 Quai Branly, 7e, Eiffel Tower* ☎ *07–67–09–81–01* ⊕ *www.cathedrale-sainte-trinite.fr* Ⓜ *Alma-Marceau.*

Champ de Mars

CITY PARK | FAMILY | Big changes are afoot for the tree-lined paths and long expanse of grass between the Eiffel Tower and École Militaire. It was previously used as a parade ground and was the site of the world exhibitions in 1867, 1889, and 1900. Landscaped at the start of the 20th century, the park has become a centerpiece of current mayor Anne Hildago's plan to reduce pollution and increase the

city's pedestrian and green spaces. The new plans by American architect Kathryn Gustafson call for a total overhaul of the esplanade to be completed in 2025. The ambitious project will involve creating a mile-long green space, closing the entire expanse to traffic, planting thousands of trees, and adding fountains and pedestrian walkways under a "unifying axis" that connects the Place du Trocadéro, the Palais de Chaillot, the Champ de Mars, and the École Militaire. Originally intended to be completed for the 2024 Olympic Games, the project was pushed back due to the complex machinations of Paris politics: stay tuned. ✉ *7e, Eiffel Tower* Ⓜ *École Militaire; RER: Champ de Mars–Tour Eiffel.*

Cité de l'Architecture et du Patrimoine

SPECIALTY MUSEUM | The greatest gems of French architecture are represented at the City of Architecture and Heritage, which occupies the east wing of the Palais de Chaillot. The former French Monuments Museum covers French architecture from the Middle Ages to the present and contains some 350 plaster-cast reproductions spread out over 86,000 square feet. Although this is a collection comprised entirely of copies, these are no ordinary ones: they include partial facades from some of the most important Gothic churches, a gallery of frescoes and windows (among them a stained-glass stunner from the famous Chartres cathedral), plus an assembly of gargoyles practically leaping off the back wall of the soaring first-floor gallery. Video monitors allow a 360-degree view of some of the grandest cathedrals. The upper-floor gallery has been devoted to architecture since 1851, with a life-size replica of a postwar apartment in Marseille designed by the urban-planning pioneer Le Corbusier. The newest exhibit takes you on an immersive 3D tour of the restoration of Notre-Dame Cathedral, accompanied by a lecturer-guide. It's well worth picking up the free English audiovisual guide. When you're ready

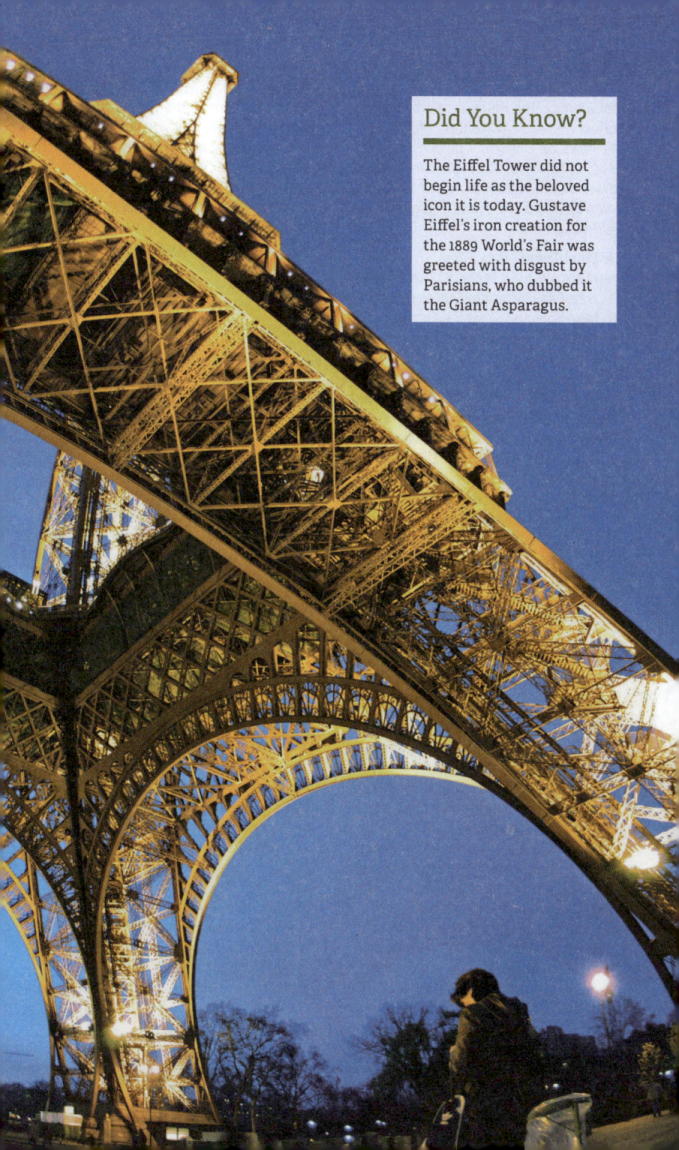

Did You Know?

The Eiffel Tower did not begin life as the beloved icon it is today. Gustave Eiffel's iron creation for the 1889 World's Fair was greeted with disgust by Parisians, who dubbed it the Giant Asparagus.

for a break, the museum's small café offers a great view of the Eiffel Tower. ✉ *Palais de Chaillot, 1 pl. du Trocadéro, 16e, Eiffel Tower* ☎ *01–58–51–52–00* ⊕ *www.citedelarchitecture.fr* ✈ *€9; €12 with temporary exhibits* ♡ *Closed Tues.* Ⓜ *Trocadéro.*

★ Eiffel Tower (*Tour Eiffel*)

NOTABLE BUILDING | FAMILY | The Eiffel Tower is to Paris what the Statue of Liberty is to New York and what Big Ben is to London: the ultimate civic emblem. French engineer Gustave Eiffel spent two years working to erect this iconic monument for the World Exhibition of 1889. Because its colossal bulk exudes such a feeling of permanence, it's hard to believe that the tower nearly became 7,000 tons of scrap when the concession expired in 1909. Only its potential use as a radio antenna saved the day. Though many prominent Parisians derided it at first, the tower gradually became part of the city's topography. It's most breathtaking at night, when every girder is highlighted in a glittering show of 20,000 golden lights for five minutes every hour on the hour from nightfall until 11:45 pm (until 1 am in summer).

More recent enhancements include a renovation of the first level that added a vertigo-inducing "transparent" floor 187 feet above the esplanade as well as a miniturbine plant, four vertical turbine windmills, and eco-friendly solar panels to minimize the tower's carbon footprint over time. You can stride up 704 steps as far as the second level, but only the elevator goes to the top. The view of the flat sweep of Paris at 1,000 feet is sublime—especially if you come in the late evening, after the crowds have dispersed. Beat the crushing lines by reserving your ticket online, or book a skip-the-line guided tour offered by many companies (from €45). Better yet, ride up the private elevator to chef Frédérick Anton's Jules Verne restaurant—with its Michelin star—on the tower's second

floor. It's about as dramatic a lunch or dinner spot as you'll find, apart from Madame Brasserie, a chic sit-down bistro helmed by Michelin-starred chef Thierry Marx on the first floor (online reservations for both restaurants are a must). Or you can watch the glimmering lights from the top of the tower over a glass of bubbly or a nonalcoholic drink at the Bar à Champagne. There are also small "buffet" snack shops on the esplanade and the first and second floors.

At the tower's tippy top is Gustave Eiffel's "secret apartment," which he used as his office, including wax mannequins of Eiffel in conversation with Thomas Edison; the blonde woman in the background represents Claire, Eiffel's oldest daughter, with whom he was very close. You'll also hear actual recordings of Eiffel's voice. ✉ *Quai Branly, 7e, Eiffel Tower* ☎ *08–92–70–12–39 costs €0.35 per min* ⊕ *www.toureiffel.paris* ✈ *By elevator from €19; by stairs from €12* ♡ *Stairs close at 6 pm in off-season (Oct.–June). Closed last 2 wks in Jan. for annual maintenance* Ⓜ *Trocadéro, Bir-Hakeim, École Militaire; RER: Champ de Mars–Tour Eiffel.*

★ Hôtel des Invalides

HISTORIC SIGHT | The Baroque complex known as Les Invalides (pronounced lehz-ahn-vah- *leed*) is the eternal home of Napoléon Bonaparte (1769–1821) or, more precisely, his remains, which lie entombed under the golden dome. Louis XIV ordered the facility to be built in 1670 to house disabled soldiers (hence the name), and, at one time, 4,000 military men lived here. Today, a portion still serves as a veterans' residence and hospital. The Musée de l'Armée, containing an exhaustive collection of military artifacts from antique armor to weapons, is also here.

If you see only a single sight, make it the Église du Dome (one of the two churches here) at the back of the complex. Napoléon's tomb was moved here in

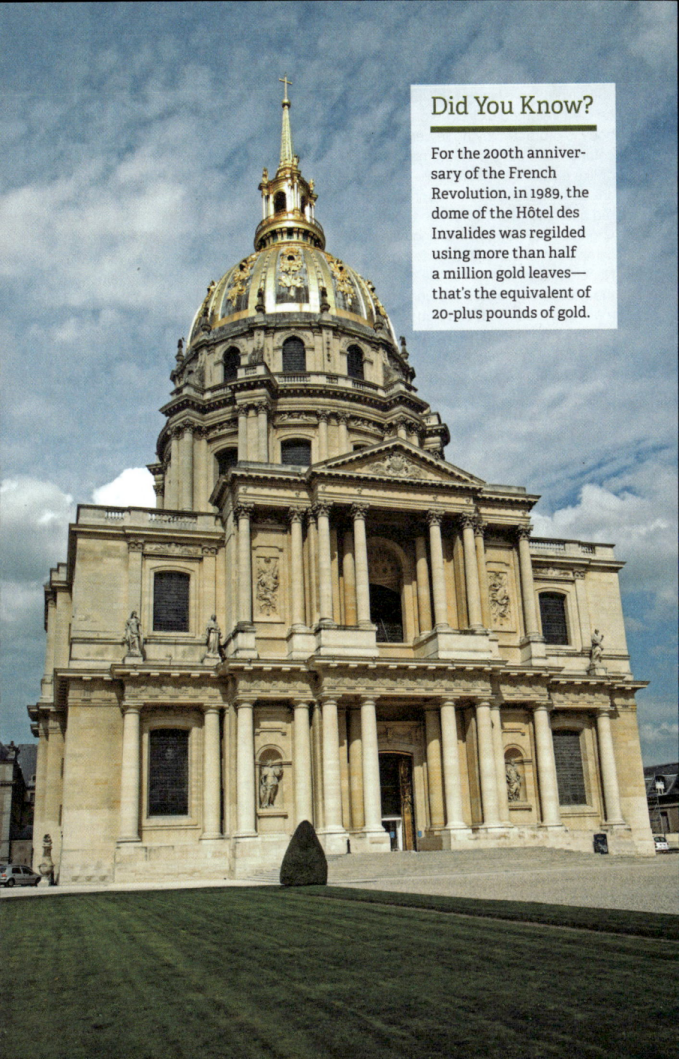

Did You Know?

For the 200th anniversary of the French Revolution, in 1989, the dome of the Hôtel des Invalides was regilded using more than half a million gold leaves—that's the equivalent of 20-plus pounds of gold.

1840 from the island of St-Helena, where he died in forced exile. The emperor's body is protected by no fewer than six coffins—one set inside the next, sort of like a Russian nesting doll—which are then encased in a sarcophagus of red quartzite. The bombastic tribute is ringed by statues symbolizing Napoléon's campaigns of conquest. To see more Napoléoniana, check out the collection in the Musée de l'Armée featuring his trademark gray frock coat and huge bicorne hat. Look for the figurines reenacting the famous coronation scene when Napoléon crowns his empress, Josephine. You can see a grander version of this scene by the painter David hanging in the Louvre.

The best entrance is at the southern end, on Place Vauban (Avenue de Tourville); the ticket office is here, as is Napoléon's tomb. There are automatic ticket machines at the main entrance on Place des Invalides. ✉ *Pl. des Invalides, 7e, Eiffel Tower* ☎ *01–44–42–38–77* 🌐 *www.musee-armee.fr* 💰 *€15 with temporary exhibitions* ⏰ *Last admission 30 mins before closing* Ⓜ *La Tour-Maubourg, Varenne.*

Les Égouts (*The Sewers*)

HISTORIC SIGHT | FAMILY | Leave it to the French to make even sewers seem romantic. Part exhibit but mostly, well, sewer, the 1,640-foot stretch of tunnels provides a fascinating—and not too smelly—look at the underbelly of Paris. You can stroll the so-called galleries of this city beneath the city, which comes complete with street signs mirroring those aboveground. Walkways flank tunnels of whooshing wastewater wide enough to allow narrow barges to dredge sand and sediment. Lighted panels, photos, and explanations in English detail the workings of the system. Immortalized as the escape routes of the Phantom of the Opera and Jean Valjean in *Les Misérables*, the 19th-century sewers have a florid real-life history. Since Napoléon

ordered the underground network built to clean up the squalid streets, they have played a role in every war, secreting revolutionaries and spies and their stockpiles of weapons. Grenades from World War II were recovered not far from where the gift shop now sits. The display cases of stuffed toy rats and "Eau de Paris" glass carafes fold into the walls when the water rises after heavy rains. Buy your ticket at the kiosk on the Left Bank side of the Pont de l'Alma. Guided one-hour tours by friendly *égoutiers* (sewer workers) are available in French only; call or email ahead for details. ✉ *Opposite 93 quai d'Orsay, 7e, Eiffel Tower* ☎ *01–53–68–27–81* 🌐 *musee-egouts.paris.fr/en* 💰 *€9* ⏰ *Closed Mon.* Ⓜ *Alma-Marceau; RER: Pont de l'Alma.*

Musée de l'Homme

HISTORY MUSEUM | FAMILY | When President Jacques Chirac's legacy project (the Musée du Quai Branly, dedicated to the world's indigenous arts and cultures) pilfered half of this museum's pieces, few thought the rest of Paris's storied anthropology museum would survive, but it has come roaring back to life. Focused on "science and human societies," the Musée de l'Homme has 33,368 square feet of sparkling exhibition space in the west wing of the Palais de Chaillot, where it displays more than 700,000 prehistoric artifacts and art objects. It now uses the most modern museum tricks—including interactive displays, 3D projections, and educational games—to help visitors understand the history of the human species. While you're admiring the 25,000-year-old Venus of Lespugue or comparing the skull of Cro-Magnon man with that of René Descartes, don't forget to look out the window: the view from the upper floors across to the Eiffel Tower and southern Paris is spectacular. ✉ *Palais de Chaillot, 17 pl. du Trocadéro, 16e, Eiffel Tower* ☎ *01–44–05–72–72* 🌐 *www.museedelhomme.fr* 💰 *€13* ⏰ *Closed Tues.* Ⓜ *Trocadéro.*

Musée du Quai Branly – Jacques Chirac

ART MUSEUM | FAMILY | This eye-catching museum overlooking the Seine was designed by architect Jean Nouvel to house the state-owned collection of "non-Western" art, culled from the Musée National des Arts d'Afrique et d'Océanie and the Musée de l'Homme. Exhibits mix artifacts from antiquity to the modern age, such as funeral masks from Melanesia, Siberian shaman drums, Indonesian textiles, and African statuary. A corkscrew ramp leads from the lobby to a cavernous exhibition space, which is color coded to designate sections from Asia, Africa, and Oceania. The lighting is dim—sometimes too dim to read the information panels (which makes investing in the €5 audioguide a good idea).

Renowned for his bold modern designs, Nouvel has said he wanted the museum to follow no rules; however, many critics gave his vision a thumbs-down when the museum opened in 2006. The exterior resembles a massive, rust-color rectangle suspended on stilts, with geometric shapes cantilevered to the facade facing the Seine and louvered panels on the opposite side. The colors (dark reds, oranges, and yellows) are meant to evoke the tribal art within. A "living wall" composed of some 150 species of exotic plants grows on the exterior, which is surrounded by a wild jungle garden with swampy patches—an impressive sight after dark when scores of cylindrical colored lights are illuminated. The trendy Les Ombres restaurant on the museum's fifth floor (separate entrance) has prime views of the Eiffel Tower—and prices to match. The budget-conscious can enjoy the garden at Le Café Branly on the ground floor. ✉ *37 quai Branly, 7e, Eiffel Tower* ☎ *01–56–61–70–00* ⊕ *www.quaibranly.fr* ✈ *From €14 (free 1st Sun. of month)* ⊘ *Closed Mon.* ☞ *Ticket office closes 1 hr before museum* Ⓜ *Alma-Marceau.*

★ Musée National de la Marine (*National Maritime Museum*)

SPECIALTY MUSEUM | FAMILY | After a six-year, state-of-the-art restoration, this once-underappreciated museum in the west wing of the Palais de Chaillot reopened in late 2023 to enthusiastic fanfare. One of five national museums dedicated to all things nautical (other locations are in Brest, Port-Louis, Rochefort, and Toulon), the Paris branch is the country's foremost treasure trove of art and artifacts documenting maritime development pertinent to France over the centuries. The sparkling new design includes impressive special effects, interactive features, and games for adults and kids. Exhibits highlight an notable collection of models of vessels, from 17th-century flagships to modern warships. Kids can climb a step to get a closer look at a model aircraft carrier or a nuclear submarine cut in half to expose their decks. The main gallery displays several figureheads recovered from sunken ships, including a giant Henri IV, miraculously saved from a shipwreck in 1854 during the Crimean War. An enormous representation of Napoléon, in his favored guise as a Roman emperor, was taken from the prow of the frigate in 1846. There is also a sinister-looking metal diving suit from 1882 and the menu from a 1935 voyage of the SS cruise ship. The café-restaurant offers snacks and warm meals along with views of the Eiffel Tower, and the shop stocks original sea-themed artworks, chic clothing, and toys. Free English audioguides are available. ✉ *Palais de Chaillot, 17 pl. du Trocadéro, Eiffel Tower* ☎ *01–53–65–69–53* ⊕ *www.musee-marine.fr* ✈ *€11; €15 with temporary exhibits* ⊘ *Closed Tues.* Ⓜ *Trocadéro.*

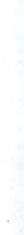

★ Musée Rodin

ART MUSEUM | FAMILY | Sculptor Auguste Rodin (1840–1917) briefly made his home and studio in the Hôtel Biron, a magnificent 18th-century mansion that now houses this museum dedicated to his work. He died rich and famous, but many of the works that earned him a place in art history were originally greeted with contempt by the general public, which was unprepared for his powerful brand of sexuality and raw physicality.

Most of Rodin's best-known sculptures are in the gardens. The front one is dominated by *The Gates of Hell* (circa 1880), which illustrates stories from Dante's *Divine Comedy*. Rodin worked on the sculpture for more than 30 years, and it served as a "sketch pad" for many of his later works: you can see miniature versions of *The Kiss* (bottom right), *The Thinker* (top center), and *The Three Shades* (top center). The museum also showcases long-neglected models, plasters, and paintings, which offer insight into Rodin's creative process. Pieces by other artists from his personal collection are on display as well—including paintings by van Gogh, Renoir, and Monet. A room is devoted to works by Camille Claudel (1864–1943), his student and longtime lover, herself a widely acclaimed sculptor. An English audioguide (€6.50) is available for the permanent collection and for temporary exhibitions.

■ **TIP→ Tickets can be purchased online for priority access.** If you wish to linger, L'Augustine café serves meals and snacks indoors or outdoors under the garden's linden trees. The fine museum boutique sells quality gifts and objects d'art, such as reproductions of some of the master's most famous sculptures made from the original molds. ✉ *77 rue de Varenne, 7e, Eiffel Tower* ☎ *01–44–18–61–10* ⊕ *www.musee-rodin.fr* ✉ *€14 (free 1st Sun. of month); €25 combined ticket with Musée d'Orsay* ⊘ *Closed Mon.* Ⓜ *Varenne.*

★ Palais de Chaillot

NOTABLE BUILDING | FAMILY | Home to four major cultural centers, this honey-colored Art Deco structure on Place du Trocadéro was built in the 1930s to replace a Moorish-style building constructed for the 1878 World's Fair. Its esplanade is also a top draw for camera-toting visitors intent on snapping the perfect shot of the Eiffel Tower. Facing the building from the Place du Trocadéro, to the left are the Cité de l'Architecture et du Patrimoine—billed as the world's largest architectural museum —and the Théâtre National de Chaillot, one of the city's major dance and performance venues, which occasionally stages plays in English. The twin building to the right contains the Musée de l'Homme, a thoroughly modern anthropology museum, and the marvelous Musée National de la Marine, reopened in 2023 after a six-year restoration. Sculptures and fountains adorn the garden leading to the Seine. ✉ *Pl. du Trocadéro, 16e, Eiffel Tower* Ⓜ *Trocadéro.*

★ Passy Cemetery

CEMETERY | Visiting graveyards in Paris can become addictive. Less well known than Montparnasse or Père Lachaise, Passy Cemetery, which dates from 1821, is raised high above Place du Trocadéro behind towering walls so that passersby hardly know it's there. Here under the chestnut trees are the tombstones of famous aristocrats and artists, such as composer Claude Debussy, Impressionist painters Édouard Manet and Berthe Morisot, and fashion designer Hubert de Givenchy, all with superb, and eternal, views of the Eiffel Tower. ✉ *2 rue du Commandant Schloesing, 16e, Eiffel Tower* ☎ *01–47–27–51–42* ⊕ *www.cimetiere-de-passy.com* Ⓜ *Trocadéro.*

🍴 Restaurants

Afaria

$$ | BISTRO | The otherwise unexciting 15e arrondissement is home to much-lauded chef Ludivine Merlin and her Basque-inspired recipes. Basque cooking is known for its bold flavors and generosity, and the choices at Afaria are no exception. **Known for:** laid-back, classic bistro atmosphere; artichoke terrine with smoked bacon and aged Comté cheese; hazelnut soufflé with homemade dark-chocolate sorbet for dessert. **§** *Average main: €23*

The Best Dining Experience on the Seine

French gastronomy meets all the magic and romance of Paris on the capital's only Michelin-starred Seine River cruise. Arrive at Port Debilly at 7:45 pm to sip a glass of Champagne on deck before stepping into the historic *Don Juan II* yacht's intimate mahogany-paneled dining room, with glimmering silver and crystal on snowy linens and a fireplace in winter. The exceptional five-course menu is everything you'd expect from Michelin-star chef Frédéric Anton (of three-star Pré Catelan and the Eiffel Tower's one-star Jules Verne). You might start with exquisite fennel cream with dashi flan and caviar, followed by crab in an ethereal cloud of Granny Smith apple-infused foam, delicate langoustine raviolis, and melt-in-your-mouth lamb—all paired with superlative wines—all while cruising past Paris's iconic bridges and monuments. You'll savor your last bites of soufflé facing a glittering Eiffel Tower to top off an unforgettable Paris evening worth every cent of the €240 ticket (drinks not included; cruise departs at 8:15 pm and returns at 10:15 pm). Be sure to reserve online in advance. ☎ 01–83–77–44–40 ⊕ donjuan2.yachtsdeparis.fr/en.

✉ 15 rue Desnoüettes, 15e, Eiffel Tower ☎ 01–48–42–95–90 ⊕ www.restaurant-afaria.fr ♡ Closed Sun., Mon., and 2 wks at Christmas Ⓜ Convention.

Arnaud Nicolas

$$$ | **FRENCH** | This "best craftsman of France" revives the gastronomic art of French charcuterie in dishes like dreamy foie gras and succulent slabs of country terrine enrobed in a golden buttery crust. The small-but-choice menu also highlights specialties from the sea: shellfish soufflé or delicate fish quenelles (a specialty of Lyon, France's charcuterie capital). **Known for:** high-quality meats; shop on premises; smallish menu. **$** *Average main: €29* ✉ *46 av. de la Bourdonnais, 7e, Eiffel Tower* ☎ *01–45–55–59–59* ⊕ *arnaudnicolas.paris* ♡ *Closed Sun. and Mon.* Ⓜ *École Militaire.*

Auberge Bressane

$$$ | **FRENCH** | Parisian gastronomic extravagance has largely disappeared in favor of leaner fare. But that is not the case at this beloved stalwart, where you can revel in such Gallic classics as towering soufflés, buttery frogs' legs, or a hearty steak smothered in sauce béarnaise.

Known for: classics done right; traditional Parisian charm; cozy spot. **$** *Average main: €27* ✉ *16 av. de la Motte-Picquet, 7e, Eiffel Tower* ☎ *01–47–05–98–37* ⊕ *www.auberge-bressane.com* ♡ *No lunch Sat.* Ⓜ *La Tour-Maubourg, École Militaire.*

Au Bon Accueil

$$$ | **BISTRO** | To see what well-heeled Parisians eat these days, book a table at this chic little bistro run by Jacques Lacipière as soon as you get to town. The contemporary dining room is unusually comfortable, but it's the excellent, well-priced *cuisine du marché* that has made this spot a hit. **Known for:** good value three-course menus; excellent price-to-quality ratio means reservations are essential; scintillating views of the Eiffel Tower from the charming sidewalk terrace. **$** *Average main: €28* ✉ *14 rue de Monttessuy, 7e, Eiffel Tower* ☎ *01–47–05–46–11* ⊕ *www.aubonaccueilparis.com* ♡ *Closed weekends and 3 wks in Aug.* Ⓜ *Métro or RER: Pont de l'Alma.*

 Aux Cerises

$ | **CAFÉ** | Don't expect to be mobbed by tourists at this casual, bright café two minutes from the Champ de Mars. Locals love it for the sidewalk terrace and garden seating in the back—not to mention the good coffee, tea, and stellar brunch. **Known for:** superb brunch or lunch served seven days a week; reservations a good idea on weekends; minutes from the Eiffel Tower. **$** *Average main: €16* ✉ *47 av. de Suffren, 7e, Eiffel Tower* ☎ *01–42–73–92–97* 🌐 *www.auxcerises.fr/en* ♡ *No dinner* Ⓜ *Dupleix, La Motte–Picquet Grenelle.*

★ Café de Mars

$$ | **BISTRO** | California-born chef Gina McLintock's elegant-cozy interiors perfectly echo her scrumptious gourmet bistro fare with an Asian twist. Crowd-pleasers include dishes like delicate pumpkin beignets, rib-eye steak, and a juicy bacon burger. **Known for:** great value; located near Eiffel Tower; live jazz on Saturday. **$** *Average main: €23* ✉ *11 rue Augereau, 7e, Eiffel Tower* ☎ *01–45–50–10–90* 🌐 *instagram.com/cafe_de_mars/?hl=en* ♡ *No dinner Mon.* Ⓜ *École Militaire.*

★ Café des Ministères

$$$ | **FRENCH** | **FAMILY** | Don't let its veneer of a mere neighborhood café mislead you—this is one of the most sought-after tables in the 7e arrondissement and a great option after a visit to the Musée d'Orsay just a few steps away. Jean and Roxane Sévegnès have transformed it into a restaurant Parisians adore, focused on seasonal dishes with a southwest flair that mix traditional recipes, like tripe, *tête de veau* (veal brains), or that hard-to-find favorite *vol au vent* (truffled sweetbreads with chicken and spinach in puff pastry) with a contemporary touch. A list of well-chosen wines, including natural and organic choices, and gentle prices for the quality make this a good choice, whether you happen to be in the neighborhood or not. **Known for:** quality ingredients and curated wine list; gracious service and good prices make this popular; pleasant atmosphere. **$** *Average main: €26* ✉ *83 rue de l'Université, 7e, Eiffel Tower*

☎ *01–45–33–73–34* 🌐 *www.cafedesministeres.fr* ♡ *Closed weekends. No lunch Mon.* Ⓜ *Assemblée Nationale.*

Café Varenne

$$ | **BISTRO** | **FAMILY** | Giant mirrors, red leatherette banquettes, vintage posters, and checker-tile floors add up to a '60s movie set of a Parisian bistro. But the menu of delicious comfort food—made with top-quality artisanal ingredients and the best produce from throughout France—is delightfully real. **Known for:** well-priced and reliably good food and wine; open all afternoon and until late; charm galore. **$** *Average main: €24* ✉ *36 rue de Varenne, 7e, Eiffel Tower* ☎ *01–45–48–62–72* 🌐 *instagram.com/cafevarenne/?hl=en* ♡ *Closed Sun.* Ⓜ *Frankin D. Roosevelt.*

★ David Toutain

$$$$ | **FRENCH FUSION** | Although two-Michelin-star chef David Toutain's approach may be exasperatingly conceptual for some, others find his earthy, surprising, and inspired concoctions, served in a sleek modern space, utterly thrilling. Each dish is a lesson in contrasts—of temperature, texture, and flavor—as well as a feat of composition: briny oysters, brussels sprouts, and foie gras in a warm potato consommé; creamy raw oysters with tart kiwi and yuzu; crispy pork chips alongside velvety smoked potato puree. **Known for:** equally wonderful choices for vegetarians and carnivores; reservations essential for this epitome of "seasonal" cuisine; prix-fixe menus only, with plenty of avant-garde thrills. **$** *Average main: €248* ✉ *29 rue Surcouf, 7e, Eiffel Tower* ☎ *01–45–50–11–10* 🌐 *www.davidtoutain.com* ♡ *Closed weekends. No lunch Wed.* Ⓜ *Invalides, La Tour-Maubourg.*

D'Chez Eux

$$$ | **BISTRO** | The red-checked tablecloths and the jovial maître d' at this authentic southwestern French bistro near the Invalides might seem like a tourist trap until you realize that it's just as popular with food-loving locals and top French politicians as it is with foreigners. Everything on the menu is hearty and delicious, if not especially refined—don't miss the gooey help-yourself chocolate mousse. **Known for:** spacious sidewalk terrace; famous "house-made" charcuterie; extremely generous portions. **$** *Average main: €32* ✉ *2 av. de Lowendal, 7e, Eiffel Tower* ☎ *01–47–05–52–55* ⊕ *www.chezeux.com* ♡ *Closed Mon. and Tues.* Ⓜ *Varenne, École Militaire.*

★ Géméllus

$$$$ | **MODERN FRENCH** | Elegant and relaxed don't usually come together so seamlessly in this upscale neighborhood, but this beautiful, cozy dining room—luminous in the daytime and romantic at night—is the perfect setting for a meal that's ambitious without being pretentious or fussy. Chef Maxime Le Meur, finally on his own after stints in top Parisian kitchens, crafts beautiful dishes with surprising pairings that combine meat and fish, but can be tailored to your desires: tuna ceviche and foie gras with apple, grapefruit, and a vibrant watercress sauce; or velvety veal on a bed of salsify with sweet burnt onion and shaved black truffle. **Known for:** warm and attentive service; chef who will tailor menus according to dietary needs; pretty location, especially when outdoor terrace is open in warm weather. **$** *Average main: €80* ✉ *37 av. Duquesne, 7e, Eiffel Tower* ☎ *01–45–55–87–57* ⊕ *www.gemellus-restaurant.fr/en* Ⓜ *Saint-François-Xavier.*

La Laiterie Sainte Clotilde

$$$ | **FRENCH** | It's not just this contemporary bistro's chic black storefront and floor-to-ceiling windows that stand out among the elegant neighborhood's pale sandstone buildings and pricey dining. A frisson of excitement in fresh, imaginative, and unfussy dishes paired with small-producer wines brings a breath of fresh air. **Known for:** chic crowd; lively atmosphere; quality ingredients. **$** *Average main: €29* ✉ *64 rue de*

Bellechasse, 7e, Eiffel Tower ☎ *01–45–51–74–61* ⊕ *www.lalaiteriesainteclotilde.fr* ♡ *Closed Sun.* Ⓜ *Varenne, Rue du Bac.*

L'Ami Jean

$$$$ | **BASQUE** | If you love Yves Camdeborde's southwestern France–inflected cooking at Le Comptoir but can't get a table for dinner, head to this tavernlike Basque restaurant run by his longtime second-in-command, Stéphane Jégo. Jégo's style is remarkably similar to Camdeborde's because he uses the same suppliers and shares his knack for injecting basic ingredients with sophistication reminiscent of haute cuisine. You can go hearty with Spanish *piquillo* peppers stuffed with salt-cod paste or *poulet Basquaise* (chicken stewed with peppers), or lighter with seasonal dishes that change weekly. **Known for:** convivial atmosphere (especially when rugby is on); popularity with locals means reservations are essential; seasonal, market-driven menu. **$** *Average main: €40* ✉ *27 rue Malar, 7e, Eiffel Tower* ☎ *01–47–05–86–89* ⊕ *lamijean.fr* ♡ *Closed Sun., Mon., and Aug.* Ⓜ *Invalides.*

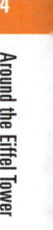

★ L'Arpège

$$$$ | **MODERN FRENCH** | Breton-born Alain Passard, one of the most respected chefs in Paris, famously shocked the French culinary world by declaring that he was bored with meat. Though his vegetarianism is more lofty than practical—L'Arpège still caters to fish and poultry eaters—he does cultivate his own vegetables outside Paris, and his dishes elevate the humblest produce to sublime heights. **Known for:** legendary Paris chef and one of Paris's rare three-star restaurants; redefining what a cook can do with simple vegetables; remarkably expensive main courses. **$** *Average main: €210* ✉ *84 rue de Varenne, 7e, Eiffel Tower* ☎ *01–47–05–09–06* ⊕ *www.alain-passard.com* ♡ *Closed weekends* Ⓜ *Varenne.*

★ L'Astrance

$$$$ | MODERN FRENCH | Pascal Barbot, who rose to fame at his Rue Beethoven digs (where he earned three Michelin stars), recently reopened in a larger, more luminous dining room. Though he lost a star in 2019, his cuisine remains resolutely haute (and his clientele just as loyal), with dishes that often draw on Asian ingredients, as in black-curry roasted pigeon or suckling lamb in a date and ginger sauce followed by a palate-cleansing white sorbet spiked with chili pepper and lemongrass. **Known for:** set menus that change daily (though there are à la carte options); space seats only 26 lucky diners a night, so reserve well ahead; extraordinary wine list. **◻** *Average main: €85* ✉ *32 rue de Longchamp, 16e, Eiffel Tower* ☎ *01–40–50–84–40* 🌐 *www.astranceparis.fr* ⊘ *Closed weekends and Aug.* Ⓜ *Iéna.*

La Table d'Aki

$$$$ | MODERN FRENCH | Set in a quiet, aristocratic *quartier* near the Musée Rodin, postage stamp-size La Table d'Aki features cuisine centered on the sea. Chef Akihiro Horikoshi works all alone in an open kitchen while 16 lucky diners await the next course: lush, simple dishes like plump langoustine shimmering in a silky shallot-fennel sauce or delicate medallions of sole in a mellow red-wine-and-leek reduction. **Known for:** small, cozy space; perfectly prepared fish; reservations essential for this small space. **◻** *Average main: €45* ✉ *49 rue Vaneau, 7e, Eiffel Tower* ☎ *01–45–44–43–48* ⊘ *Closed Sun., Mon., 2 wks in Feb., and Aug.* Ⓜ *St-François-Xavier.*

★ Le Jules Verne

$$$$ | MODERN FRENCH | In a highly publicized battle, the prestigious helm of Paris's most *haute* (literally; it's in the Eiffel Tower) restaurant was wrested from Alain Ducasse by three-star chef Frédéric Anton of the prestigious Le Pré Catelan in the Bois de Boulogne, with Anton's "zero waste" approach and his idea to

serve less complicated fare, focusing on French meats and vegetables produced by smaller French artisanal farms and regional delicacies, winning out. Though not cheap (tasting menus from €255), winning a Michelin star in 2020 clinched the restaurant's standing as one of Paris's top splurge-worthy dining rooms. **Known for:** famous Eiffel Tower dining (with accompanying views); lavishly priced set-price menus are the only option; advance reservations a must. **◻** *Average main: €255* ✉ *Tour Eiffel, south pillar, Av. Gustave Eiffel, 7e, Eiffel Tower* ☎ *01–83–77–34–34* 🌐 *www.restaurants-toureiffel.com* 👔 *Jacket and tie* Ⓜ *Bir-Hakeim.*

Le Petit Cler

$ | CAFÉ | From a wine-soaked boeuf Bourguignon and garlicky snails to tasty slabs of homemade country pâté served with cornichons and a hearty red, this Art Nouveau–era bistro offers all the classics of southwestern France. Check the blackboard menu for the daily specials, delivered in generous portions. **Known for:** reasonably priced French classics; open all day and Sunday; sidewalk seating in season. **◻** *Average main: €17* ✉ *29 rue Cler, 7e, Eiffel Tower* ☎ *01–45–50–17–50* 🌐 *instagram.com/lepetitcler/?hl=en* Ⓜ *La Tour-Maubourg, École Militaire.*

Les Cocottes de Christian Constant

$$ | MODERN FRENCH | FAMILY | Chef Christian Constant has an unfailing sense of how Parisians want to eat these days, as proved by this third addition to his mini restaurant empire near the Eiffel Tower. At Les Cocottes, he's shifted the normally leisurely bistro experience into high gear, which allows him to keep prices moderate. **Known for:** cozy, no-reservation spot for elevated French comfort food; casual, child-friendly atmosphere; dishes served in cast-iron pots. **◻** *Average main: €22* ✉ *135 rue St-Dominique, 7e, Eiffel Tower* ☎ *01–45–50–10–28* 🌐 *lescocottes.paris* Ⓜ *École Militaire; Métro or RER: Pont de l'Alma.*

Le Troquet

$$ | MODERN FRENCH | FAMILY | A quiet residential street shelters one of Paris's great neighborhood bistros and among the last of the city's authentic ones, which retains its moleskin banquettes, blackboard menus, and small wooden tables where you'll touch elbows with your neighbors. Expect fresh market ingredients in a gastronomic menu that's liberal with deluxe details. **Known for:** proximity to the Eiffel Tower; sampling of the French classics; dessert soufflé du jour. **§** *Average main: €23* ✉ *21 rue François-Bonvin, 15e, Eiffel Tower* ☎ *01–45–66–89–00* 🌐 *www.restaurantletroquet.fr* ⊘ *Closed Sun., Mon., 3 wks in Aug., and 1 wk at Christmas* Ⓜ *Ségur.*

★ Le Violon d'Ingres

$$$$ | MODERN FRENCH | With chef Alain Solivérès (formerly of Taillevent) at the helm, this much-beloved outpost has taken on a new shine—and a Michelin star. The food is sophisticated and the atmosphere is lively and chic; reservations are essential. **Known for:** few minutes' walk to the Eiffel Tower; famous chef that actually cooks here; open seven days a week, a rarity in this quartier. **§** *Average main: €70* ✉ *135 rue St-Dominique, 7e, Eiffel Tower* ☎ *01–45–55–15–05* 🌐 *leviolondingres.paris* Ⓜ *École Militaire.*

L'Os à Moelle

$$ | BISTRO | FAMILY | Come for the early sitting at this buzzing bistro (reservations are essential) specializing in solid French "bistronomic" fare and you'll often discover the dining room filled with more than a few tourists—the waiters speak English perfectly. The dining room excels in such French comfort foods as leg of lamb, warm Puy lentil salad, roasted quail, and a scintillating rum-soaked baba au rhum, not to mention the namesake dish of velvety bone marrow. **Known for:** large portions at good prices; classic Parisian "blackboard" menu; well-priced wines and Champagne by the glass. **§** *Average main: €24* ✉ *3 rue Vasco de*

Gama, 15e, Eiffel Tower ☎ *01–45–57–27–27* 🌐 *www.facebook.com/losamoelleetlacave* ⊘ *Closed Sun. and Mon.* Ⓜ *Balard.*

Madame Brasserie

$$$$ | FRENCH | There's not a brasserie in Paris with a view to match the one at this eatery set on the first floor of the Eiffel Tower (the Jules Verne, helmed by chef Frédéric Anton, is on the second floor). Multiple Michelin-star chef Thierry Marx presides over this chic dining room, done up in creamy leather and blond wood, where everything is "stylish, sustainable, and cozy" (and, we might add, very expensive) with special attention to local products whenever possible. **Known for:** attentive service and good food; unbeatable views of Paris; book online and select your view. **§** *Average main: €95* ✉ *Eiffel Tower, 7e, Eiffel Tower* ☎ *01–83–77–77–78* 🌐 *www.restaurants-toureiffel.com* Ⓜ *Bir-Hakeim, Trocadéro.*

★ Shang Palace

$$$$ | CHINESE | The premiere restaurant at the beautiful Shangri-La Paris Hotel is the city's only Michelin-starred Chinese restaurant. As you sit in a jewel box of a dining room that features giant Chinese porcelains and inlaid jade paneling, you'll dine on lacquered Peking duck, sliced at your table and delivered with a flourish, and all manner of delicacies from one of the world's great cuisines. **Known for:** focus on food of southeastern China; superb wine list; best Peking duck in Paris. **§** *Average main: €58* ✉ *Shangri-La Paris Hotel, 10 av. d'Iéna, 16e, Eiffel Tower* ☎ *01–53–67–19–92* 🌐 *www.shangri-la.com/paris/shangrila/dining* ⊘ *Closed Tues. and Wed.* Ⓜ *Iéna, Trocadéro, Pont de l'Alma.*

★ Tomy & Co.

$$$$ | BISTRO | Chef Tomy Gousset, who learned his skills in some of the city's most prestigious kitchens, flies solo at this wildly popular bistro, which won its first Michelin star in 2019. The appealingly spare dining room is an excellent backdrop for some truly dazzling dishes that taste every bit as sublime as they look. **Known for:** gourmet bistro fare; inventive dishes; great wine pairings. [§] *Average main: €40* ✉ *22 rue Surcouf, 7e, Eiffel Tower* ☎ *01-45-51-46-93* ⊕ *www.tomygousset.com/tomy-and-co* ♡ *Closed weekends* Ⓜ *La Tour-Maubourg.*

 Coffee and Quick Bites

Café Coutume

$ | **CAFÉ** | **FAMILY** | A lofty space between the Musée Rodin and the Bon Marché makes this the perfect pit stop. Look for healthy salads, sandwiches, snacks, desserts, and a delicious cup of any kind of coffee drink that takes your fancy. **Known for:** some of the finest coffee in town; healthy salads for lunch; prime location near major museums. [§] *Average main: €8* ✉ *47 rue de Babylone, 7e, Eiffel Tower* ☎ *09-88-40-47-99* ⊕ *www.coutumecafe.com* ♡ *No dinner* Ⓜ *St-François-Xavier, Sèvres-Babylone.*

★ Terres de Café

$ | **CAFÉ** | A five-minute walk from the Eiffel Tower, Terre de Café is a boon to coffee lovers. It also serves gluten-free pastries, healthy fruit smoothies, and gourmet brunch options. **Known for:** fresh and healthy salads and sandwiches; delicious homemade pastries; great coffee here and in locations around Paris. [§] *Average main: €6* ✉ *67 av. de la Bourdonnais, 7e, Eiffel Tower* ☎ *01-45-50-37-39* ⊕ *www.terresdecafe.com* ♡ *No dinner* Ⓜ *École Militaire, Pont de l'Alma.*

 Hotels

Eiffel Seine Hôtel

$$ | **HOTEL** | **FAMILY** | This tiny budget boutique hotel minutes from the Eiffel Tower mixes contemporary amenities and furnishings with Art Nouveau flourishes. **Pros:** very close to the Eiffel Tower and Champ de Mars; easy métro access; reasonable rates for the area. **Cons:** breakfast not included; minimal space

in standard rooms; street noise in some rooms facing river. [§] *Rooms from: €300* ✉ *3 bd. de Grenelle, 15e, Eiffel Tower* ☎ *01-45-78-14-81* ⊕ *www.eiffelseinehotel.paris* ↝ *45 rooms* 🍴 *No Meals* Ⓜ *Bir-Hakeim.*

★ Hôtel de Londres Eiffel

$$ | **HOTEL** | Prices at this small boutique hotel in an upscale neighborhood are fairly reasonable considering all you get—top-notch service, stylish and homey decor, a lively neighborhood, a variety of amenities, and some spectacular views. **Pros:** just steps from the Eiffel Tower; quaint setting; attractive public areas. **Cons:** rooms on the small side; food not permitted in rooms; not super close to métro. [§] *Rooms from: €280* ✉ *1 rue Augereau, 7e, Eiffel Tower* ☎ *01-45-51-63-02* ⊕ *www.hotel-paris-londres-eiffel.com* ↝ *30 rooms* 🍴 *No Meals* Ⓜ *La Tour-Maubourg, École Militaire.*

Hôtel du Cadran

$$ | **HOTEL** | Well located and near sights and the métro, Hôtel du Cadran—actually two buildings run by the same management—features contemporary design that appeals as much to business travelers as to urban creative types on a budget. **Pros:** bright, whimsical rooms; large closets and windows; convenient to Rue Cler, Eiffel Tower, and Les Invalides. **Cons:** two separate buildings means you have to cross the street; lacks traditional Parisian charm; petite bathrooms. [§] *Rooms from: €310* ✉ *10 rue du Champ de Mars, 7e, Eiffel Tower* ☎ *01-40-62-67-00* ⊕ *www.cadranhotel.com* ↝ *53 rooms* 🍴 *No Meals* Ⓜ *École Militaire.*

Hôtel du Champ de Mars

$ | **HOTEL** | Around the corner from picturesque Rue Cler, this affordable hotel welcomes guests with a Provence-inspired lobby and huge picture windows overlooking a quiet street. **Pros:** good value for the location; walking distance to Eiffel Tower, Les Invalides, and Musée Rodin; quaint decor. **Cons:** minuscule rooms; no air-conditioning; inconsistent service. **§** *Rooms from: €180* ✉ *7 rue du Champ de Mars, 7e, Eiffel Tower* ☎ *01–45–51–52–30* ⊕ *www.hoteldu-champdemars.com* ↝ *25 rooms* 🍴 *No Meals* Ⓜ *École Militaire.*

★ Hotel Eiffel Blomet

$$ | HOTEL | FAMILY | Named for the cabaret a few doors down where Josephine Baker once sang, this handsome Art Deco hotel comes with a luxurious pool, hammam (steam room), and sauna. **Pros:** excellent amenities; chic rooms; good value. **Cons:** off-the-radar neighborhood; not that close to the Eiffel Tower; average breakfast. **§** *Rooms from: €230* ✉ *78 rue Blomet, 15e, Eiffel Tower* ☎ *01–53–68–70–00* ⊕ *www.hoteleiffelblomet.com* ↝ *87 rooms* 🍴 *No Meals* Ⓜ *Vaugirard, Volontaires.*

Hôtel Eiffel Trocadéro

$$ | HOTEL | A curious blend of Second Empire and rococo styling awaits guests in this hotel on a quiet corner just off Place Trocadéro. **Pros:** views of Eiffel Tower from upper floors; upscale residential district convenient to métro; organic breakfast buffet. **Cons:** no full-service restaurant; long walk to city center; basic rooms feel cramped. **§** *Rooms from: €285* ✉ *35 rue Benjamin-Franklin, 16e, Eiffel Tower* ☎ *01–53–70–17–70* ⊕ *www. hoteleiffeltrocadero.com* ↝ *17 rooms* 🍴 *No Meals* Ⓜ *Trocadéro.*

Hôtel Le Tourville

$$ | HOTEL | This cozy, contemporary haven near the Eiffel Tower, Champ de Mars, and Les Invalides is a comfortable base for exploring Paris, with quiet rooms that have crisp, damask upholstery. **Pros:** convenient location near métro; friendly service; rooms very clean. **Cons:** small standard rooms; could do with an update; no restaurant. **§** *Rooms from: €280* ✉ *16 av. de Tourville, 7e, Eiffel Tower* ☎ *01–47–05–62–62* ⊕ *www.hotel-tourville.com* ↝ *30 rooms* 🍴 *No Meals* Ⓜ *École Militaire.*

★ Hôtel Wallace

$$ | HOTEL | You'd be hard-pressed to find a more welcoming, stylish, and reasonably priced hotel in an upscale neighborhood that rarely combines all three characteristics. **Pros:** chic bar on-site; super-friendly staff; great location near the Eiffel Tower. **Cons:** hard to get a room in high season; no dinner offered; rooms are small. **§** *Rooms from: €300* ✉ *89 rue Fondary, 15e, Eiffel Tower* ☎ *01–87–53–53–30* ⊕ *www.orsohotels.com/hotel-wallace* ↝ *45 rooms* 🍴 *No Meals* Ⓜ *Cambronne.*

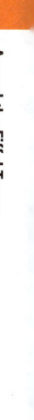

★ Le Cinq Codet

$$$ | HOTEL | Set in a 1930s former France Telecom exchange, the Art Deco–era building's streamlined contours create the ideal setting for spaces that mix modern elegance with high-tech advances, while making the most of some very Parisian views of nearby Les Invalides and the Eiffel Tower a few blocks away. **Pros:** fabulous courtyard cocktail bar; exceptional terraces with views; some of the chicest rooms in Paris. **Cons:** in a quiet part of the 7e; not a lot of nearby nightlife; not all rooms have terraces. **§** *Rooms from: €398* ✉ *5 rue Louis Codet, 7e, Eiffel Tower* ☎ *01–53–85–15–60* ⊕ *lecinqcodet.com* ↝ *67 rooms* 🍴 *No Meals* Ⓜ *École Militaire, Varenne.*

★ Le Narcisse Blanc

$$$$ | HOTEL | Set in a 19th-century Haussmannian mansion, Le Narcisse Blanc covers all the bases in luxury accommodations with a top-notch gastronomic restaurant (Cléo), stylish common areas including a pretty garden terrace, and a full-service spa with a swimming pool and fitness, sauna, and steam rooms. **Pros:** Art Deco–inspired pool, sauna, and steam room; Eiffel Tower views; lots of luxury for the price. **Cons:** hard to book during Fashion Weeks; neighborhood quiet at night; 15-minute walk to the Eiffel Tower. **§** *Rooms from: €576* ✉ *19 bd. de la Tour-Maubourg, 7e, Eiffel Tower* ☎ *01–40–60–44–32* ⊕ *www.*

lenarcisseblanc.com ↔ *37 rooms* 🍽 *No Meals* Ⓜ *La Tour-Maubourg, Assemblée Nationale.*

Le Walt

$$ | **HOTEL** | The convenient location stands out at this warm and welcoming boutique hotel in the chic district between the Eiffel Tower and Les Invalides. **Pros:** great location for sightseeing; friendly staff; some Eiffel Tower views. **Cons:** on a busy street; no hotel restaurant; rooms on the small side. 🔲 *Rooms from: €330* ✉ *37 av. de la Motte Picquet, 7e, Eiffel Tower* ☎ *01–45–51–55–83* 🌐 *www.lewaltparis.com* ↔ *25 rooms* 🍽 *No Meals* Ⓜ *École Militaire.*

 **Shangri-La Paris Hotel**

$$$$ | **HOTEL** | Displaying French elegance at its best, this impressively restored 19th-century mansion gazing across the Seine at the Eiffel Tower was once the stately home of Prince Roland Bonaparte, grandnephew of the emperor himself, and his gilded private apartments have been transformed into La Suite Impériale. **Pros:** some of the best views in Paris; excellent dining; fabulous pool. **Cons:** astronomical rates; pool open only until 9 pm; expensive breakfast. 🔲 *Rooms from: €1,200* ✉ *10 av. Iéna, 16e, Eiffel Tower* ☎ *01–53–67–19–98* 🌐 *www.shangri-la.com* ↔ *101 rooms* 🍽 *No Meals* Ⓜ *Iéna.*

 **Nightlife**

 **Bar Botaniste**

COCKTAIL BARS | This most opulent of bars offers 15 scintillating cocktails crafted with herbal elixirs, fresh fruits, flower essences, and exotic nectars in honor of Prince Roland Bonaparte, a passionate botanist and the first owner of the mansion that became the Shangri-La Paris Hotel. The cocktail menu changes every two months—all the better to keep ingredients fresh and seasonal. ✉ *Shangri-La Paris Hotel, 10 av. d'Iéna, 16e, Eiffel Tower* ☎ *01–53–67–19–98* 🌐 *www.shangri-la.com/en/paris/shangrila* Ⓜ *Iéna.*

Fitzgerald

COCKTAIL BARS | The popularity of this intimate restaurant-cocktail bar could be due to the upscale neighborhood's distinct lack of nightlife, but there's no denying its dusky allure. At cocktail hour, the bar attracts a mix of businesspeople and chic locals; at night, good music, tasty food, and plentiful drinks animate the crowd. ✉ *54 bd. de la Tour-Maubourg, 7e, Eiffel Tower* ☎ *01–45–50–38–63* 🌐 *www.fitz-group.fr/fitzgerald-paris* Ⓜ *La Tour-Maubourg, Varenne.*

Gatsby

COCKTAIL BARS | A chic cocktail bar steps from the Champ de Mars is a rare find indeed, but this one is steeped in a cosmopolitan speakeasy mystique, with wood paneling and 1920s touches (leather chairs, gramophone, old Underwood typewriter) evoking the New York of its namesake. A covered sidewalk terrace and a dance floor in the cellar add to the clubby fun, along with a small menu of tasty morsels and some very good cocktails. ✉ *64 av. Bosquet, 7e, Eiffel Tower* ☎ *01–45–51–56–24* 🌐 *le-gatsby.fr/en/home/* Ⓜ *École Militaire, La Tour-Maubourg.*

L'Eclair

COCKTAIL BARS | Tucked among the cafés on the Rue Cler, this all-purpose bistro-cum-cocktail bar's all-day and night hours (it's open until 2 am), welcoming atmosphere, and tasty cocktail concoctions make it an ideal option in a neighborhood decidedly short on late-night watering spots. ✉ *32 rue Cler, 7e, Eiffel Tower* ☎ *01–44–18–09–04* 🌐 *l-eclair.paris* Ⓜ *École Militaire.*

 **Performing Arts**

Théâtre National de Chaillot

PERFORMANCE VENUES | Housed in an imposing neoclassical building overlooking the Eiffel Tower, Théâtre National de Chaillot has a trio of venues and a total of 1,600 seats. It's dedicated to experimental, world, and avant-garde drama, dance, and music, or a mix of all three. Major names in dance—like the Ballet Royal de Suède (Royal Swedish Ballet) and William Forsythe's company—visit regularly. There are plays in English and programs for children, too. ✉ *1 pl. du Trocadéro, 16e, Eiffel Tower* ☎ *01–53–65–30–00* ⊕ *theatre-chaillot.fr* Ⓜ *Trocadéro.*

Shopping

Though this is not the neighborhood that springs to mind for a Paris shopping spree, there is plenty to engage both inveterate shoppers and those who love to just stroll and discover along the way.

One of Paris's great market streets, **Rue Cler** is a feast for the eyes and the senses, overflowing with every imaginable gourmet delight interspersed with florists, chocolatiers, organic cosmetics, wine shops, and scores of lively cafés and bistros. If you have time for only one street in this neighborhood, make it this one.

Rue St-Dominique is, hands down, the neighborhood's best street for shopping and browsing. Stretching from Invalides to the Champ de Mars, this lively thoroughfare is jam-packed with enticing one-off boutiques and high-end French clothing chains like Berenice, The Kooples, Des Petits Hauts, and ba&sh, not to mention fabulous cafés and restaurants. Here you'll find everything from decor, housewares, and jewelry to clothing for women, men, and kids.

Rue de Grenelle, parallel to Rue St-Dominique, is also a vibrant shopping street, especially as it crosses St-Germain. **Rue du Commerce**, just steps from the Eiffel Tower, is one of those fabulous stretches that no one knows about, lined with an eye-popping range of popular, attractively priced fashion chains and fun shops for everyone. **Rue de Passy**, a well-known shopping street, is elbow to elbow with French fashion chains and

high-end boutiques, plus the popular Passy Plaza mall.

Aux Merveilleux de Fred

FOOD | Lille-based pâtissier Frédéric Vaucamps riffed on an 18th-century cake recipe called the "merveilleux" and found himself at the helm of a Europe-wide empire. His version of the meringue-based confection replaced the traditional butter cream for an ethereal dome of whipped ganache in modern flavors like praline, speculoos, rose, and coffee feathered with white or dark chocolate shavings. The merveilleux come in four sizes—the smallest can be boxed for gifts. There are also brioches and breakfast pastries and the traditional Lille *gauffres*, delectable cream-filled waffles. You'll know his boutique by the giant, glittering chandelier and lines snaking down the sidewalk. ✉ *94 rue St-Dominique, 7e, Eiffel Tower* ☎ *01–47–53–91–34* ⊕ *auxmerveilleux.com/en/* Ⓜ *La Tour-Maubourg.*

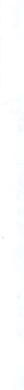

Berenice

CLOTHING | One of the more creative French chains for women's clothing, Berenice has made an international splash for its of-the-moment styles, quality fabrics, and the kind of classic tailoring Parisians adore. Separates run the gamut from bold and bright to streamlined and understated, but they're always versatile and suitable for a wide range of ages. Accessories include shoes, belts, and bags in fun materials, like python-print or studded leather. ✉ *91 rue St-Dominique, 7e, Eiffel Tower* ☎ *01–77–36–03–47* ⊕ *www.berenice.net* Ⓜ *La Tour-Maubourg.*

Blanc des Vosges

LINENS | This is your one-stop shopping destination for all of those dreamy French household textiles beloved by design magazines. Sheets of softest cotton, damask, or linen in gorgeous solid colors or romantic prints feel totally luxurious, and elegant table linens turn any table into a conversation piece. They are worth the investment, as they'll last generations (at the June and January sales, you can nab great bargains at 30%–50% off). ✉ *60 rue St-Dominique, 7e, Eiffel Tower* ☎ *01–45–55–12–19* 🌐 *www.blancdesvosges.fr* Ⓜ *La Tour-Maubourg.*

★ Comptoirs Bourdonnais

CLOTHING | A stone's throw from the Eiffel Tower, this women's boutique does all the work for you, with a handpicked collection of standout clothing and accessories from the best smaller French and European labels like Diega, Pomandere, Absolut Cashmere, Chloé Stora, Apuntob, C.T. Plage, and much more. It's an excellent one-stop shop for immediate Parisian chic. ✉ *41 av. de la Bourdonnais, 7e, Eiffel Tower* ☎ *01–45–56–01–94* 🌐 *instagram.com/comptoirs_bourdonnais* Ⓜ *École Militaire.*

Cornerluxe

CLOTHING | If new Parisian designer duds are a bit out of your price range, you might consider this classy *depot-vente* (consignment shop), where chic neighborhood ladies and men deposit last year's barely worn loot. Its clean, artfully displayed stash of A-list designer clothing, accessories, jewelry, scarves, watches, and shoes can be had for half or less than retail, plus some stellar vintage wear is also for sale. Standouts have included a crocodile Hermès Birkin bag, Cartier watches, and a Chanel leather coat. ✉ *45 av. Bosquet, 7e, Eiffel Tower* ☎ *01–44–18–31–50* 🌐 *www.cornerluxe.com* Ⓜ *Les Invalides, École Militaire.*

Des Petits Hauts

CLOTHING | This popular chain for women champions casual French fashions with a romantic feminine touch, from angora sweaters in sorbet colors to lightweight linen T-shirts. Everything from snazzy sneakers to scarves, bags, and belts is chic and top-quality. The boutique's soft, comfy jeans are especially sought after. ✉ *66 rue St-Dominique, 7e, Eiffel Tower* ☎ *01–75–44–05–92* 🌐 *despetitshauts.com* Ⓜ *La Tour-Maubourg.*

Gérard Darel

CLOTHING | This is a go-to address for top-quality Parisian fashion staples that always look of-the-moment but have the lasting power to remain stylish season after season. Ready-to-wear separates in silk, cotton, wool, cashmere, and leather come in pleasing prints and chic solids that look great on women of all ages. Look for standout leather jackets and well-priced accessories. ✉ *78 rue St-Dominique, 7e, Eiffel Tower* ☎ *01–45–54–43–07* 🌐 *gerarddarel.com* Ⓜ *La Tour-Maubourg.*

Hircus

CLOTHING | A sleek boutique, Hircus is stylish Parisians' go-to shop for chic, classic, and sustainable cashmere for men and women. Fashionably classic styles in luxuriously soft cashmere range from zip-front to cabled to striped and include featherweight models for summer—all for less than what you'd pay in high-end department stores. ✉ *101 rue St-Dominique, 7e, Eiffel Tower* ☎ *09–54–95–12–97* 🌐 *www.hircus.fr* Ⓜ *La Tour-Maubourg.*

★ Maison Chaudun

CHOCOLATE | Specializing in chocolate sculptures, pastries, and other sinful delights, this enchanting boutique is any chocolate lover's dream. Maverick chocolatier Michel Chaudun was a legend around Paris. Trained at the Maison du Chocolat, the master confectioner was the very first to strike out on his own, long before Paris became a chocolate mecca. He was also the first to introduce granules of cocoa bean into his chocolates to achieve a rich intensity. In 2015, Chaudun passed the baton to Gilles Marchal, who has more than upheld the standard. ✉ *149 rue de l'Université, 7e, Eiffel Tower* ☎ *01–47–53–74–40* 🌐 *chaudun.com* Ⓜ *La Tour-Maubourg.*

Chapter 5

THE CHAMPS-ÉLYSÉES

Updated by Jennifer Ladonne

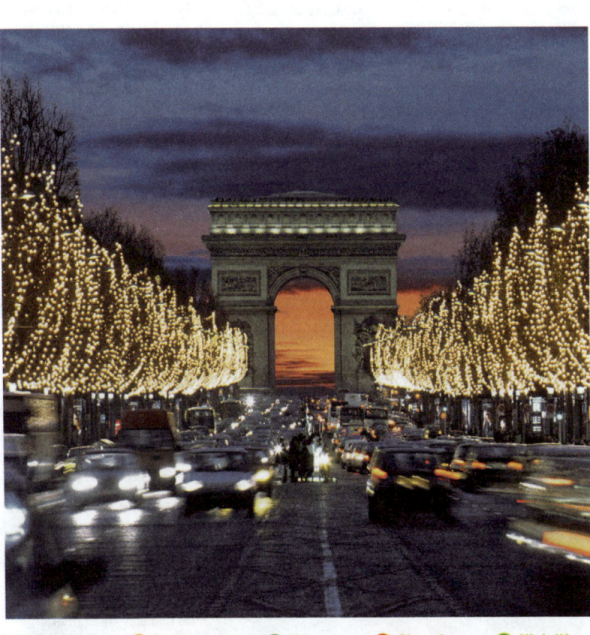

⊙ Sights	ⓘ Restaurants	🏨 Hotels	⊖ Shopping	ⓥ Nightlife
★★★★★	★★★★★	★★★★★	★★★★★	★★★★★

NEIGHBORHOOD SNAPSHOT

GETTING HERE

This neighborhood includes the 8e and 16e arrondissements. For the top of the Champs-Élysées/Arc de Triomphe, take *métro* Line 1, 2, or 6, or the RER A, to Charles-de-Gaulle–Étoile and look for the exit marked "Champs-Élysées." For the bottom of the avenue, near the Grand Palais, go to the Champs-Élysées–Clémenceau or Concorde métro station on Line 1.

MAKING THE MOST OF YOUR TIME

This neighborhood is an essential stop for every first-time visitor to Paris, and returning travelers will find plenty to do, too. The Champs-Élysées is worth a walk from end to end: start at the Arc de Triomphe if you prefer walking downhill. You can stop for (a pricey) lunch or dessert at one of the cafés or tea salons en route (Ladurée is a favorite); then detour down Avenue Montaigne, Paris's answer to Rodeo Drive or Fifth Avenue.

If your time is limited, you can come for just a stroll at night, when the Champs is alight: there are bars and nightclubs for all tastes, plus movie houses showing French films and English-language blockbusters (look for V.O., meaning *version originale*, if you prefer to see an undubbed one). At Christmastime the avenue is decked out top-to-toe in glittering lights, creating a magical atmosphere.

VIEWFINDER

The vistas up and down the Champs-Élysées are legendary. From the top of the Arc de Triomphe, you'll truly understand why this is historically called Place de l'Étoile, or "square of the star," as no fewer than 12 broad Haussmannian avenues radiate from the arc at its center. The monument's eye-popping panoramas of Paris are hands down some of the city's best. But the views of the Arc from the bottom of the avenue heading up aren't so shabby either, especially at Christmastime when the avenue is lit up like, well, a star.

TOP REASONS TO GO

■ **Avenue des Champs-Élysées.** Take a walk from the Arc de Triomphe down this splendid avenue and splurge in the upscale boutiques on and around the fabled thoroughfare. Or simply practice that oh-so-Parisian pastime of window-shopping.

■ **Grand Palais and Petit Palais.** This pair of magnificent Beaux-Arts structures, centerpieces of the 1900 World's Fair, host blockbuster art exhibitions. After 121 years of spot fixes, the glass-and-cast-iron Grand Palais closed for a top-to-toe restoration, and while the nave and main events space opened for the 2024 Olympic Games, the full reopening will happen in spring 2025.

■ **Palais de Tokyo.** A major arts center, this imposing Art Deco building is home to the city's largest exhibition space, also called the Palais de Tokyo, dedicated to experimental and contemporary art (hint: kids love it) as well as the superb Musée d'Art Moderne de Paris.

■ **Macarons from Ladurée.** Is it worth lining up for 30 minutes to get a little taste of heaven? You decide. But rest assured: the macarons, round meringue cookies made by this famous pâtissier since 1862, are as scrumptious as ever.

Make no mistake: the Champs-Élysées, while ceding some of its elegance in recent times, remains the most famous avenue in Paris—and, perhaps, the world. Like New York's Times Square or London's Piccadilly Circus, it is a mecca for travelers and locals alike.

Some Parisians complain that fast-food joints and chain stores have cheapened Avenue des Champs-Élysées, but others are more philosophical, noting that there is something here for everyone. If lunch at Ladurée is out of your budget, there's always McDonald's (and the view from its second floor is terrific).

Anchoring the Champs is the **Arc de Triomphe**, Napoléon's monument to himself. Though the soaring **Grand Palais** is partially under renovation until 2025, you can still hop across the street to enjoy the **Petit Palais's** permanent art collection (free admission), superb temporary exhibitions, and charming garden café. Between here and **Place du Trocadéro**, a busy traffic circle, you can find several museums housed in some of Paris's most impressive buildings. The **Musée Guimet** has a superlative Asian art collection, while the **Musée Yves Saint Laurent** contains 13 rooms dedicated to the master couturier's groundbreaking designs. The **Musée d'Art Moderne de la Ville de Paris**, on Avenue du Président Wilson, contains a free permanent collection of 20th-century pieces. Contemporary-art lovers should also check out what's showing next door at the trendy **Palais de Tokyo**. These twin Art Nouveau buildings, constructed for the 1937 World's Fair, are notable for their monumental facades. Across the street is the elegant **Palais**

Galliera, Paris's fashion museum, with exhibition spaces and a lovely garden with Eiffel Tower views.

Paris has ambitious plans to "green" and pedestrianize Place Charles de Gaulle—the area encircling the Arc de Triomphe—the Champs-Élysées, and Place du Trocadéro, all the way across the Seine to the Eiffel Tower. The project, first slated for completion by the 2024 Paris Olympics, will unfold in stages until 2026.

 Sights

 Arc de Triomphe

MONUMENT | Inspired by Rome's Arch of Titus, this colossal, 164-foot triumphal arch was ordered by Napoléon—who liked to consider himself the heir to Roman emperors—to celebrate his military successes. Unfortunately, Napoléon's strategic and architectural visions were not entirely on the same plane, and the Arc de Triomphe proved something of an embarrassment. Although the emperor wanted the monument completed in time for an 1810 parade in honor of his new bride, Marie-Louise, it was still only a few feet high, and a dummy arch of painted canvas was strung up to save face. Empires come and go, but Napoléon's had been gone for more than 20 years before the

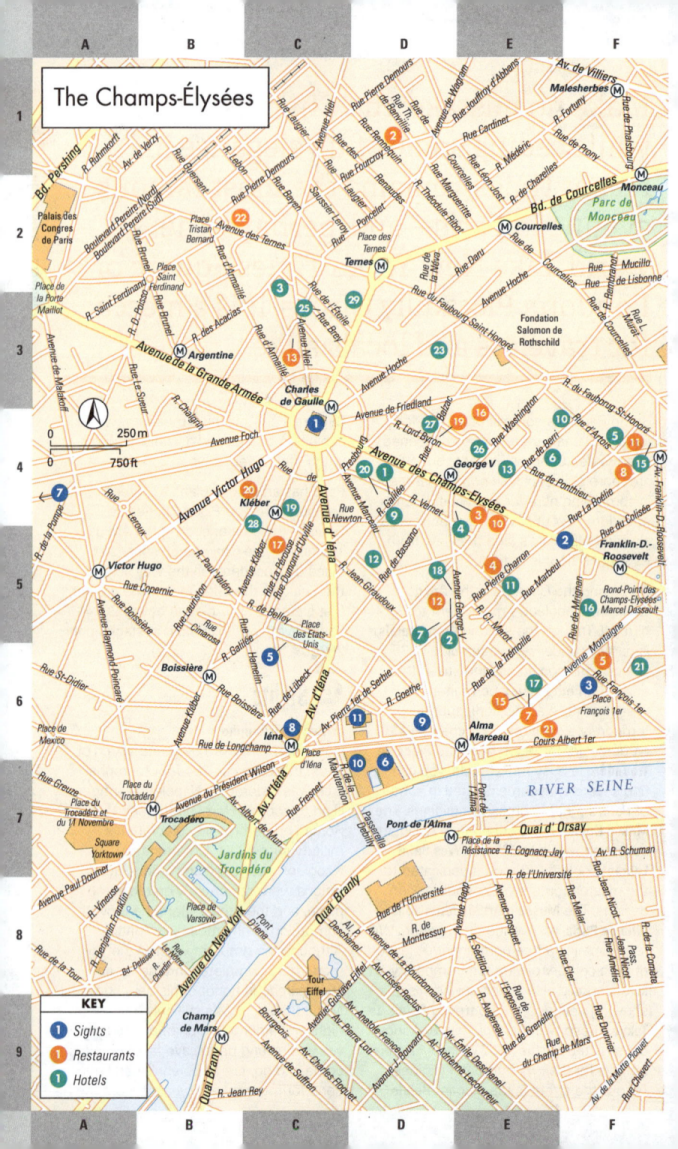

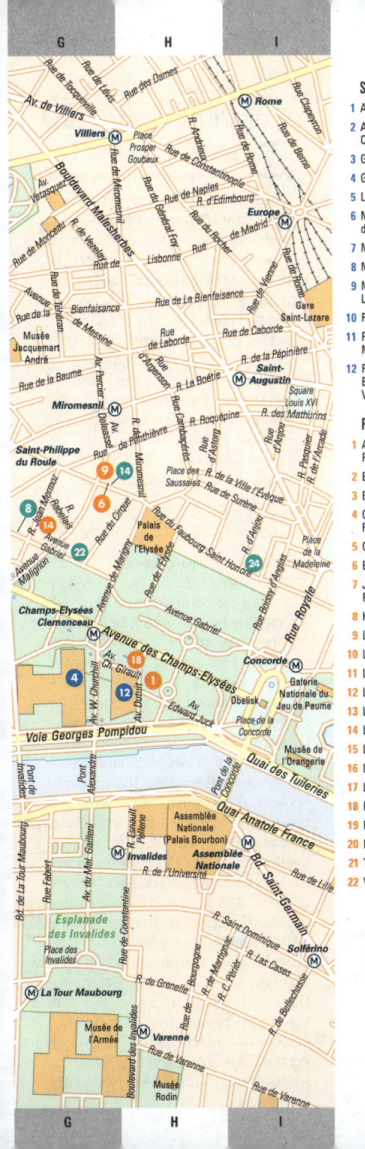

Sights ▼

#	Name	Grid
1	Arc de Triomphe	C4
2	Avenue des Champs-Élysées	E5
3	Galerie Dior	F6
4	Grand Palais	G6
5	La Maison Baccarat	C6
6	Musée d'Art Moderne de Paris	D7
7	Musée d'Ennery	A4
8	Musée Guimet	C6
9	Musée Yves Saint Laurent Paris	D6
10	Palais de Tokyo	D7
11	Palais Galliera, Musée de la Mode	D6
12	Petit Palais, Musée des Beaux-Arts de la Ville de Paris	H6

Restaurants ▼

#	Name	Grid
1	Alléno Paris au Pavillon Ledoyen	H6
2	Bistrot Flaubert	D1
3	Brasserie Fouquet's	E4
4	Café La Belle Férronnière	E5
5	Chez Savy	F6
6	Épicure	G4
7	Jean Imbert au Plaza Athénée	E6
8	Komatsubaki	F4
9	La Scène	G4
10	Ladurée	E4
11	L'Arôme	F4
12	Le Cinq	D5
13	Le Hide	C3
14	Le Mermoz	G4
15	Le Relais Plaza	E6
16	Le Taillevent	E4
17	LiLi	C5
18	Pavyllon	H6
19	Pierre Gagnaire	D4
20	Prunier	C4
21	Trente-Trois	E6
22	Vive	B2

Hotels ▼

#	Name	Grid
1	Château des Fleurs	D4
2	Four Seasons Hôtel George V Paris	D5
3	Hidden Hotel	C2
4	Hôtel Barrière Fouquet's	E4
5	Hôtel Bradford Élysées	F4
6	Hôtel de Berri Champs-Élysées	E4
7	Hôtel de Sers	D5
8	Hôtel du Rond Point des Champs-Élysées	G5
9	Hôtel Ekta	D4
10	Hôtel Elysia	F4
11	Hôtel Grand Powers	E5
12	Hôtel Keppler	D5
13	Hôtel Lancaster Paris	E4
14	Hôtel Le Bristol	G4
15	Hôtel Le 123 Élysées	F4
16	Hôtel Marignan Champs-Élysées	F5
17	Hôtel Plaza Athénée	E6
18	Hôtel Prince des Galles	D5
19	Hôtel Raphael	C4
20	Hôtel Vernet	D4
21	La Maison Champs Élysées	F6
22	La Réserve	G5
23	Le Royal Monceau Raffles Paris	D3
24	Maison Delano	I5
25	Maison Elle Paris	C3
26	Monsieur George Hôtel & Spa	E4
27	Norman Hôtel & Spa	D4
28	The Peninsula Paris	C5
29	Renaissance Paris Arc de Triomphe	D3

Arc was finally finished in 1836. A small museum halfway up recounts its history.

The Arc de Triomphe is notable for magnificent sculptures by François Rude, including the *Departure of the Volunteers in 1792,* better known as *La Marseillaise,* to the right of the arch when viewed from the Champs-Élysées. Names of Napoléon's generals are inscribed on the stone facades—the underlined names identify the hallowed figures who fell in battle.

The traffic circle around the Arc is named for Charles de Gaulle, but it's known to Parisians as L'Étoile, or "the Star"—a reference to the streets that fan out from it. Climb the stairs to the top of the arch and you can see the star effect of the 12 radiating avenues and the vista down the Champs-Élysées toward Place de la Concorde and the distant Musée du Louvre.

Ambitious plans to make visiting the Arc de Triomphe a safer and more pedestrian-friendly experience include limiting car traffic in favor of enlarged walkways and creating a wide expanse of trees extending all the way down the Champs-Élysées. It's still unclear exactly when this will happen. France's Unknown Soldier is buried beneath the arch, and a commemorative flame is rekindled every evening at 6:30. That's the most atmospheric time to visit, but, to beat the crowds, come early in the morning or buy your ticket online. ⚠ **Be wary of the traffic circle that surrounds the arch. It's infamous for accidents—including one some years ago that involved the French transport minister. Always use the underground passage from the northeast corner of Avenue des Champs-Élysées.** ✉ *Pl. Charles-de-Gaulle, 8e, Champs-Élysées* ☎ *01–55–37–73–77* 🌐 *www.paris-arc-de-triomphe.fr* 💰 *€16* ☞ *Last admission 45 mins before closing* Ⓜ *Métro or RER: Charles de Gaulle–Étoile.*

Remembering Princess Diana

The monument at Place de l'Alma, at the bottom of Avenues Montaigne and George V, has become Princess Diana's unofficial shrine, located as it is near the opening of the fateful underpass. Bouquets and messages are still placed here by her admirers—city workers regularly clean up flowers, graffiti, and photographs. The replica of the Statue of Liberty's flame predates Diana's 1997 car accident, though: it was donated by Paris-based American companies in 1989 in honor of the bicentennial of the French Revolution.

Avenue des Champs-Élysées

STREET | FAMILY | Marcel Proust lovingly described the genteel elegance of the storied Champs-Élysées (pronounced "chahnz- *eleezay,*" with an "n" sound instead of "m," and no "p") during its Belle Époque heyday, when its cobblestones resounded with the clatter of horses and carriages. Today, despite unrelenting traffic and the intrusion of chain stores and fast-food franchises, the avenue still sparkles. There's always something happening here: stores are open late (and many are open on Sunday, a rarity in Paris); nightclubs remain top destinations; and cafés offer prime people-watching, though you'll pay for the privilege. Ater all, this is Europe's most expensive piece of real estate. Along the 2-km (1¼-mile) stretch, you can find marquee names in French luxury, like Cartier, Guerlain, and Louis Vuitton. Car manufacturers lure international visitors with space-age showrooms. Old stalwarts, meanwhile, are still going strong—including the Lido cabaret and Fouquet's, whose celebrity clientele extends back to James Joyce. The avenue is also the setting for the last leg of the Tour de France bicycle race (the third or fourth Sunday in July), as well as Bastille Day (July 14) and Armistice Day (November 11) ceremonies. The Champs-Élysées, which translates to "Elysian Fields" (the resting place of the blessed in Greek mythology), began life as a cow pasture and in 1666 was transformed into a park by the royal landscape architect André Le Nôtre. Traces of its green origins are visible toward the Concorde, where elegant 19th-century park pavilions house the historic restaurants Ledoyen and Laurent. In the near future, the celebrated avenue will once again live up to its name. Plans are being considered to transform the avenue, reducing automobile traffic in favor of expanded pedestrian walkways and hundreds of new trees. ✉ *8e, Champs-Élysées* Ⓜ *Champs-Élysées–Clemenceau, Franklin D. Roosevelt, George V, Charles de Gaulle–Étoile.*

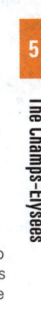

★ Grand Palais

NOTABLE BUILDING | With its curved-glass roof and sinuous Belle Époque ornamentation, you can't miss the Grand Palais, whether you're approaching from the Seine or the Champs-Élysées. This larger structure forms an elegant duo with the Petit Palais across Avenue Winston Churchill. Both buildings, adorned with mosaics and elegant sculpted friezes, were built for the 1900 World's Fair and, like the Eiffel Tower, were not intended to be permanent. That's why, after 120 years of wear and tear, the graceful yet delicate stone, glass, and cast-iron structure, home to world-class cultural, fashion, and sporting events, closed for renovation. At this writing, the Palais's galleries and central nave were set to open for the 2024 Paris Olympics, with a full reopening scheduled for 2025. The Grand Palais Éphémère, a temporary structure set on the Champ de Mars and used during the closure, is, at this writing, scheduled to be dismantled after the Olympics. ✉ *Av. Winston Churchill, 8e, Champs-Élysées* ☎ *01–40–13–48–00* 🌐 *www.grandpalais.fr* Ⓜ *Champs-Élysées–Clemenceau.*

★ Galerie Dior

SPECIALTY MUSEUM | Following on the heels of the Musée Yves Saint Laurent Paris (and helmed by its former director), this drop-dead gorgeous exhibition space, housed in the same building as the Dior flagship boutique store and restaurant, inaugurated a new direction for Dior, fusing fashion and culture, in 2022. The permanent exhibition showcases groundbreaking designs from all of the house's great designers—from Yves Saint Laurent and Gianfranco Ferré to John Galliano and Maria Grazia Chiuri—and of course iconic pieces from the master himself. This primer on the history of Paris fashion is an absolute must-see for fashion buffs, and afterward, you may be inspired to pop into the Avenue Montaigne boutique for some shopping or a quick pick-me-up at the superchic café. ✉ *11 rue François 1er, 8e, Champs-Élysées* ☎ *01–82–20–22–00* 🌐 *www.galeriedior.com* 💰 *€12* ⏰ *Closed Tues.* Ⓜ *Franklin D. Roosevelt.*

La Maison Baccarat

ART MUSEUM | Playing on the building's Surrealist legacy, designer Philippe Starck brought an irreverent Alice in Wonderland approach to the HQ and museum of the venerable Baccarat crystal firm: Cocteau, Dalí, Buñuel, and Man Ray were all frequent guests of the mansion's onetime owner, Countess Marie-Laure de Noailles. At the entrance, talking heads are projected onto giant crystal urns, and a lighted chandelier is submerged in an aquarium. Upstairs, the museum features masterworks created by Baccarat since 1764, including soaring candlesticks made for Czar Nicholas II and the perfume flacon Dalí designed for Schiaparelli. Don't miss the rotunda's "Alchemy" section by Gérard Garouste, showcasing the technical history of cutting, wheel engraving, enameling, and gilding. Contemporary crystal by top-name designers

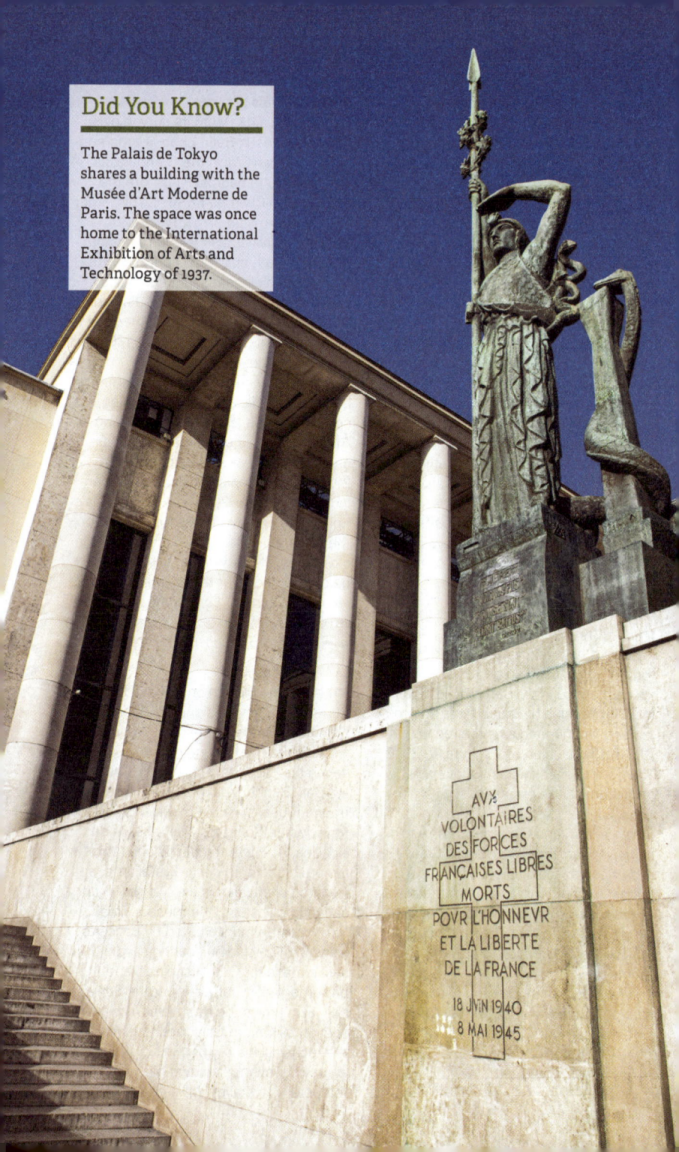

as well as stemware, vases, tableware, jewelry, chandeliers, and even furniture are sold in the on-site shop. Set aside a few moments to enjoy the little park just outside in the Place des États-Unis, with its impressive statues of Washington and Lafayette. ✉ *11 pl. des États-Unis, 16e, Champs-Élysées* ☎ *01–40–22–11–00* ⊕ *www.baccarat.fr* ✈ *€10* ♡ *Closed Sun. and Mon.* Ⓜ *Iéna.*

Musée d'Art Moderne de Paris (*Paris Museum of Modern Art*)

ART MUSEUM | Although the city's modern art museum hasn't generated a buzz comparable to that of the Centre Georges Pompidou, visiting can be a more pleasant experience because it draws fewer crowds. The Art Deco building's vast, white-walled galleries make an ideal backdrop for temporary exhibitions of 20th-century art and postmodern installation projects. The permanent collection on the lower floor takes over where the Musée d'Orsay leaves off, chronologically speaking: among the earliest works are Fauve paintings by Maurice de Vlaminck and André Derain, followed by Pablo Picasso's early experiments in Cubism. Other highlights include works by Robert and Sonia Delaunay, Chagall, Matisse, Rothko, and Modigliani. The museum also organizes excellent temporary exhibitions that rarely come with crowds. Forest, the museum's restaurant, is a lovely choice for lunch or dinner, and in warm weather, it's a prime spot for Eiffel Tower views on the Palais de Tokyo's sprawling terrace. ✉ *11 av. du Président Wilson, 16e, Champs-Élysées* ☎ *01–53–67–40–00* ⊕ *www.mam.paris.fr* ✈ *Free; temporary exhibitions from €7* ♡ *Closed Mon.* Ⓜ *Alma-Marceau, Iéna.*

★ Musée d'Ennery

ART MUSEUM | Reopened in 2023 after a years-long restoration, this jewel box of a museum—a branch of the Musée Guimet since 1943—is one of Paris's best-kept secrets, a thrilling collection of Japanese and Chinese objects d'art.

The stately rooms remain largely as they were when Clémence d'Ennery, a former actress and wife of an eminent Parisian playwright, amassed these treasures in her elegant Belle Époque mansion in the late 19th and 20th centuries. Though open to the public since 1908, it remains largely off the radar, since, until now, the museum has accepted extremely limited visitors by appointment only. Whether you're a fan of Asian art or not, it's well worth a trip to tony Avenue Foch to view the more than 7,000 objects on display, including hundreds of delightful figurines, sculptures, lacquerware, ceramics, inlaid furniture, and porcelains. Items are arranged in carved wooden cases among marble columns and gilded neoclassical woodwork. Purchase your ticket in advance on the Musée Guimet website. ✉ *59 av. Foch, 16e, Champs-Élysées* ☎ *01–56–52–53–45* ⊕ *www.guimet.fr/fr/musee-d-ennery* ✈ *€9* ♡ *Closed Tues.* Ⓜ *Porte Dauphine.*

★ Musée Guimet

ART MUSEUM | The outstanding Musée Guimet boasts the Western world's biggest collection of Asian art, thanks to the 19th-century wanderings of Lyonnaise industrialist Émile Guimet. Exhibits, enriched by the state's vast holdings, are laid out geographically in airy, light-filled rooms. Just past the entry is the largest assemblage of Khmer sculpture outside Cambodia. The second floor has statuary and masks from Nepal, ritual funerary art from Tibet, and jewelry and fabrics from India. Peek into the library rotunda, where Monsieur Guimet once entertained the city's notables; Mata Hari danced here in 1905, and the museum still hosts an impressive series of musical events. The much-heralded Chinese collection, made up of 20,000-odd objects, covers seven millennia. Recently restored and reopened, the Panthéon Bouddhique, in the Hôtel d'Heidelbach a few steps from the museum, houses Émile Guimet's collection of Japanese and Chinese works of art collected during his travels and arranged as they would appear in Buddhist temples. In the mansion's Japanese garden, authentic tea ceremonies are held in a pavilion built in the traditional Japanese style. Grab a free English-language audioguide and brochure at the museum entrance, and stop at the Salon des Porcelaines café on the lower level for a ginger milk shake or an Asian-influenced meal. The museum also has a charming bookstore. The Guimet's offshoot, the Musée d'Ennery, is housed in a Belle Époque mansion on Avenue Foch and is noted for its collection of Japanese *netsuke*, as well as 7,000 works of Chinese and Japanese art. ✉ *6 pl. d'Iéna, 16e, Champs-Élysées* ☎ *01–56–52–54–33* ⊕ *www.guimet.fr* 💰 *€13* ♡ *Closed Tues.* Ⓜ *Iéna, Boissière.*

Musée Yves Saint Laurent Paris

SPECIALTY MUSEUM | As elegant and stylish as the master couturier's groundbreaking designs, this museum is housed in the very mansion where Yves Saint Laurent did his work and entertained celebrity clients. More than 50 prototypes—including such landmarks as the Mondrian dress, the original pantsuit, and the woman's tuxedo—are on display at any one time, as are dozens of design drawings and a glittering array of jewelry. Thanks to its huge windows, the light-bathed upstairs atelier, stuffed with books and fabrics, offers an intimate glimpse into YSL's world. Be sure not to miss the touching short film detailing the relationship between Saint Laurent and his longtime partner Pierre Bergé. All of the exhibits have detailed English labeling, and a free English guide is available at reception. ✉ *5 av. Marceau, 16e, Champs-Élysées* ☎ *01–44–31–64–00* ⊕ *www.museeyslparis.com* 💰 *€10* ♡ *Closed Mon.* ☞ *Last entry 45 mins before closing* Ⓜ *Alma-Marceau.*

Palais de Tokyo

ARTS CENTER | The go-to address for some of the city's liveliest exhibitions, the Palais de Tokyo is a stripped-down venue that spotlights provocative, ambitious contemporary art. There is no permanent collection: instead, cutting-edge temporary shows are staged in a cavernous space reminiscent of a light-filled industrial loft. The programming extends to performance art, concerts, readings, and fashion shows. Night owls will appreciate the 10 pm (midnight on Thursday) closing. The museum's chic Bambini trattoria and cocktail bar—serving delicious authentic Italian cuisine and Neapolitan-style pizzas—is a regular haunt for locals, especially for cocktails, dinner, and late-night cravings, thanks to its wraparound terrace and Eiffel Tower views. But there's also a small café area at the restaurant entrance for a quick bite and glass of wine or cup of coffee. Visit the offbeat bookshop for colorful souvenirs that are as edgy and subversive as the exhibits. ✉ *13 av. du Président Wilson, 16e, Champs-Élysées* ☎ *01–81–97–35–88* ⊕ *www.palaisdetokyo.com* 💰 *€12* ♡ *Closed Tues.* Ⓜ *Iéna.*

★ Palais Galliera, Musée de la Mode

SPECIALTY MUSEUM | The city's Museum of Fashion occupies a suitably fashionable mansion—the 19th-century residence of Maria Brignole-Sale, Duchess of Galliera. Inside, exhibition spaces on two floors focus on costume and clothing design. Covering key moments in fashion history and showcasing legendary French designers, the museum's collection includes 200,000 articles of clothing and accessories that run the gamut from basic streetwear to haute couture. Galleries at the garden level focus on fashion history from the 18th century to the present via pieces from the permanent collection. Information about changing exhibitions is on the website. Don't miss the lovely 19th-century garden that encircles the palace, a favorite spot for neighborhood Parisians to take a coffee and a book. ✉ *10 av. Pierre-1er-de-Serbie, 16e, Champs-Élysées* ☎ *01–56–52–86–00* ⊕ *www.palaisgalliera.paris.fr* 💰 *€15* ♡ *Closed Mon.* Ⓜ *Iéna.*

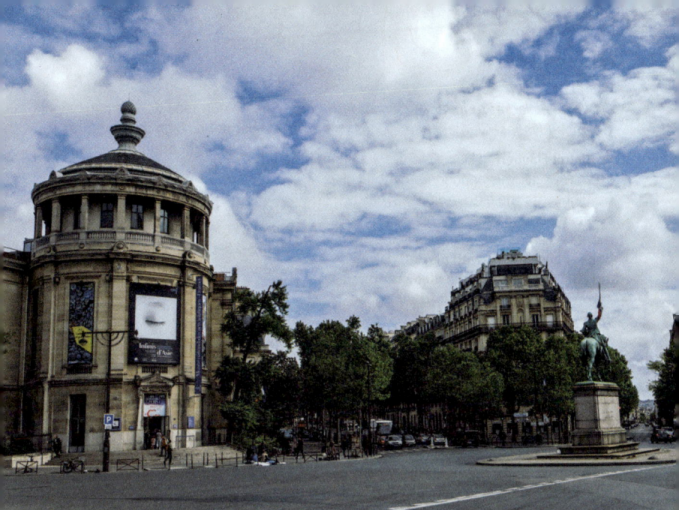

Not far from the Champs-Élysées, the Musée Guimet has one of the world's best collections of Asian art outside of Asia.

Petit Palais, Musée des Beaux-Arts de la Ville de Paris

ART MUSEUM | The "little" palace has a small, sometimes overlooked collection of excellent paintings, sculpture, and objets d'art, with works by Monet, Gauguin, and Courbet, among others. Temporary exhibitions are particularly good (and sometimes free). The building, like the Grand Palais across the street, is an architectural marvel of marble, glass, and gilt built for the 1900 World's Fair, with impressive entry doors and huge windows overlooking the river. Search directly above the main galleries for 16 plaster busts set into the wall, representing famous artists. Outside, note two eye-catching sculptures: French World War I hero Georges Clemenceau faces the Champs-Élysées, while a resolute Winston Churchill faces the Seine. In warmer weather, head to the garden café with terrace seating. ✉ *Av. Winston Churchill, 8e, Champs-Élysées* ☎ 01–53–43–40–00 🌐 *www.petitpalais.paris.fr* ✈ *Free; from €12 for temporary exhibitions* ☺ *Closed Mon.* Ⓜ *Champs-Élysées–Clemenceau.*

🍴 Restaurants

★ Alléno Paris au Pavillon Ledoyen

$$$$ | **MODERN FRENCH** | Tucked away in a quiet garden across from the Petit Palais, Ledoyen—open since 1779—is a study in Empire-style elegance (this is where Napoléon first met his eventual wife Joséphine). Star chef Yannick Alléno injects the three-star dining room with a frisson of modernity by putting fresh farmhouse ingredients front and center in his €415, nine-course tasting extravaganza (a seven-course menu is a slightly more reasonable €295, and there are à la carte options). **Known for:** reservations are essential at one of the most romantic settings in Paris; lots of cool history; langoustine tart with caviar. **$** *Average main: €120* ✉ *1 av. Dutuit, on Carré des Champs-Élysées, 8e, Champs-Élysées* ☎ 01–53–05–10–01, 🌐 *www.yannick-alleno.com/fr/* ☺ *Closed weekends and Aug.*

No lunch 🍽 Jacket required **M** *Concorde, Champs-Élysées–Clemenceau.*

★ Bistrot Flaubert

$$$$ | **FRENCH** | This handsome historic bistro highlights the extraordinary synergy that can happen when French technique meets Asian flavors. Classics like pigeon or beef come alive with pickled daikon radish, tamarind, or saké. **Known for:** sublime flavor pairings; unusually good wine list; charming decor. **$** *Average main: €34* ✉ *10 rue Gustave Flaubert, 17e, Champs-Élysées* ☎ *01–42–67–05–81* ⊕ *www.bistrotflaubert.com* ♡ *Closed Sun. and Mon. No lunch Sat.* **M** *Ternes, Courcelles.*

Brasserie Fouquet's

$$$ | **BRASSERIE** | A Champs-Élysées institution, Le Fouquet's brasserie has served steak tartare and lobster ravioli to the French royalty of stage and screen since 1899; Edith Piaf and Charles Aznavour were regulars, and the César Awards dinner is still served here every year. The brasserie's two glassed-in terraces overlook Avenue George V and the Champs-Élysées and provide an excellent spot for watching the Parisian world go by. **Known for:** hot spot for Parisian politicians and stars; classic French brasserie fare with a luxurious touch; historic dining room that's a prime people-watching spot. **$** *Average main: €29* ✉ *99 av. des Champs-Élysées, 8e, Champs-Élysées* ☎ *01–40–69–60–50* ⊕ *www.hotelsbarriere.com/en/collection-fouquets.html* **M** *George V.*

Café La Belle Ferronnière

$$ | **BRASSERIE** | A favorite of Parisians for business lunches and after-work *apéros*, this traditional brasserie prides itself on using quality ingredients from top French producers (and the family farm) for its homemade fare, along with all the joys of an authentic Parisian brasserie: a daily blackboard menu, brisk service, a generous sidewalk terrace, and convenient all-day hours (open 6:30 am until midnight). Its location a short walk from

the Champs-Élysées does mean higher prices, but not as high as the more touristy cafés right on the avenue. **Known for:** copious steak tartare; good selection of reasonable wines by the glass; great location. **$** *Average main: €23* ✉ *53 rue Pierre Charron, 8e, Champs-Élysées* ☎ *01–42–25–03–82* ⊕ *instagram.com/labelleferronniereparis/?hl=en* **M** *George V.*

Chez Savy

$$$ | **BISTRO** | Just off glitzy Avenue Montaigne, Chez Savy's Art Deco cream-and-burgundy interior is blissfully intact, occupying its own circa-1930s microcosm. Fill up on rib-sticking specialties from the Aveyron region of central France—lentil salad with bacon, foie gras (prepared on the premises), perfectly charred lamb with featherlight shoestring *frites*, and pedigreed Charolais beef. **Known for:** good prices in a pricey neighborhood; authentic brasserie experience; competent, unpretentious service. **$** *Average main: €25* ✉ *23 rue Bayard, 8e, Champs-Élysées* ☎ *01–47–23–46–98* ⊕ *www.chezsavy.com* ♡ *Closed weekends and Aug.* **M** *Franklin D. Roosevelt.*

Epicure

$$$$ | **MODERN FRENCH** | One of the most admired chefs in Paris, Éric Fréchon has been at the helm of Le Bristol Hotel's revered restaurant since 2000, with Michelin's top three-star award since 2009. Fréchon creates masterworks—say, farmer's pork cooked "from head to foot" with truffle-enhanced crushed potatoes and his famous truffle lasagna—that are both deeply satisfying yet unpretentious. **Known for:** alfresco dining in a beautiful garden in warm weather; reservations essential for this superb French provincial dining room; relatively affordable lunch menu. **$** *Average main: €185* ✉ *Hôtel Le Bristol, 112 rue du Faubourg St-Honoré, 8e, Champs-Élysées* ☎ *01–53–43–43–00* ⊕ *www.lebristolparis.*

com ◎ Closed Sun. and Mon. 👔 Jacket and tie Ⓜ Miromesnil.

★ **Jean Imbert au Plaza Athénée**

$$$$ | FRENCH | In one of the most anticipated announcements in the Parisian food world of 2021, the Plaza Athénée named talented young chef Jean Imbert, a protégé of his predecessor Alain Ducasse, as head of their new temple to gastronomy. A long marble table is the centerpiece of this opulently refurbished dining room (which seems to take Versailles as its model), and the menu is no less splendid, with options like Casparian imperial caviar, Bellevue lobster in a foie gras broth flecked with black truffle, and whole turbot masterfully boned table-side. **Known for:** gorgeous, uberopulent dining room; rising star chef and exemplary service; reservations required. **§** *Average main: €80* ✉ *Hôtel Plaza Athénée, 25 av. Montaigne, 8e, Champs-Élysées* ☎ *01–53–67–65–00* ⊕ *www.dorchestercollection.com/en/paris/hotel-plaza-athenee* ◎ *Closed Sun. and Mon. No lunch Tues.–Fri.* Ⓜ *Alma-Marceau.*

Komatsubaki

$$$$ | JAPANESE | Run by Yoichi Kino, a 30-year master sushi chef whose family has specialized in smoked eel for generations, and Ryuma Takubo, who earned a Michelin star in Japan, Komatsubaki specializes in the exquisite vegetarian cuisine favored by Japanese monks. Diners choose from three sophisticated prix-fixe menus, including a stunning vegetarian version, all served on delicate dishes and accompanied by a distinctive selection of white Burgundies, sakes, and teas. **Known for:** high-end take-out sushi; authentic dining experience on tatami mats; wine list includes white Burgundies and sake selections. **§** *Average main: €130* ✉ *3 rue d'Artois, 8e, Champs-Élysées* ☎ *01–42–25–26–78* ⊕ *www.komatsubaki-paris.com* ◎ *Closed Mon. No lunch* Ⓜ *St-Philippe du Roule.*

★ **Ladurée**

$$$ | CAFÉ | One of 100-plus locations worldwide, the largest branch of the Ladurée tea salon empire is worth the splurge, thanks to the sumptuous pastries, which steal the show. In addition to more than a dozen flavors of macarons, it has assorted cakes, sundaes, pastries, savory dishes, and beautifully boxed treats ideal for gift-giving. **Known for:** world-famous macarons; beautiful and elegant decor; pricey lunch menu. **§** *Average main: €27* ✉ *75 av. des Champs-Élysées, 8e, Champs-Élysées* ☎ *01–40–75–08–75* ⊕ *www.laduree.com* ◎ *No dinner* Ⓜ *George V.*

L'Arôme

$$$$ | MODERN FRENCH | Chef Thomas Boullault made a seamless transition when he took the helm of this storied dining room, a favorite among Parisian gourmets. Expect seasonal dishes with a touch of finesse from the open kitchen. **Known for:** masterful wine pairings; Breton crab with avocado, Japanese rice, and tomato gelée with smoked pepper; pricey prix-fixe menus (no à la carte). **§** *Average main: €140* ✉ *3 rue St-Philippe du Roule, 8e, Champs-Élysées* ☎ *01–42–25–55–98* ⊕ *www.larome-paris.com/en* ◎ *Closed weekends and Aug.* Ⓜ *St-Philippe du Roule.*

★ **La Scène**

$$$$ | FRENCH | Shortly after earning a second Michelin star from the chic open kitchen at the Hôtel Prince des Galles, Stéphanie le Quellec left to strike out on her own. Now she's regained her two stars at this gleaming dining room on the elegant Avenue Matignon, the perfect setting for the refined, scintillating cuisine that earned the former *Top Chef* winner a loyal following among Paris gastronomes. **Known for:** beautiful atmosphere; famous foie gras tart; carefully selected small-producer wines. **§** *Average main: €100* ✉ *32 av. Matignon, 8e, Champs-Élysées* ☎ *01–42–65–05–61* ⊕ *www.la-scene.paris* ◎ *Closed weekends* Ⓜ *Miromesnil, St-Philippe du Roule.*

★ **Le Cinq**

$$$$ | **MODERN FRENCH** | Christian Le Squer is among the most famous and most respected chefs in Paris, as proved by his turn here at one of the city's most deluxe dining rooms. You'll find all the luxury products you might expect—caviar, truffles, game in season—along with a masterful touch that often transforms homey Breton ingredients such as oysters or lamb into imaginative tours de force. **Known for:** reservations are essential for this Michelin-starred French fine dining; famous flowery outdoor terrace; consistently accommodating service. [5] *Average main: €120* ✉ *Four Seasons Hôtel George V, 31 av. George V, 8e, Champs-Élysées* ☎ *01–49–52–70–00* ⊕ *www.fourseasons.com/paris/dining/restaurants/le_cinq* ♡ *Closed Sun. and Mon. No lunch* 🏠 *Jacket and tie* Ⓜ *George V.*

★ **Le Hide**

$$$ | **BISTRO** | Hide Kobayashi, known as "Koba," is one of several Japanese chefs in Paris who trained with some of the biggest names in French cuisine before opening their own restaurants. Not surprisingly, this great-value bistro near the Arc de Triomphe became instantly popular (reservations are a must) with locals as well as visiting Japanese and Americans who follow the food scene. **Known for:** chic, unpretentious dining room; stellar prices for this pricey neighborhood; one of Paris's best prix-fixe menus. [5] *Average main: €27* ✉ *10 rue du Général Lanzerac, 8e, Champs-Élysées* ☎ *01–45–74–15–81* ⊕ *www.lehide.fr* ♡ *Closed Sun., 2 wks in May, and 2 wks in Aug. No lunch* Ⓜ *Charles de Gaulle–Étoile.*

Le Mermoz

$ | **BISTRO** | When the opulence of the neighborhood begins to overwhelm, this refreshing island of unpretentious pleasures is a good place to restore both body and budget. In addition to the charm of its bright, cheerful interiors—complete with mirrors, fresh flowers, globe chandeliers, and a zinc bar—you'll find a sophisticated daily menu of market-fresh dishes and small plates. **Known for:** foodie hideaway; well-priced small plates; affordable wines by the glass. [5] *Average main: €17* ✉ *16 rue Jean Mermoz, 8e, Champs-Élysées* ☎ *01–45–63–65–26* ⊕ *www.lemermozparis.fr* ♡ *Closed weekends* Ⓜ *St-Philippe du Roule, Champs-Élysées–Clémenceau.*

★ **Le Relais Plaza**

$$$$ | **FRENCH** | Parisian to its core, the Hôtel Plaza Athénée's Art Deco dining room—including a beautiful mural that's a registered historic landmark—is a cherished neighborhood treasure. Masterful updates of French classics include dishes like terrine of wild boar, langoustines and mayo, coquilles St-Jacques à la Grenobloise, and a stunning steak tartare prepared table-side. **Known for:** throwback jazz nights every last Wednesday of the month; reservations essential at this exceptional dining room; a favorite with the locals. [5] *Average main: €55* ✉ *Plaza Athénée, 21 av. Montaigne, 8e, Champs-Élysées* ☎ *01–53–67–64–00* ⊕ *www.dorchestercollection.com/fr/paris/hotel-plaza-athenee/restaurants-bars/le-relais-plaza* Ⓜ *Alma-Marceau, Franklin D. Roosevelt.*

★ **Le Taillevent**

$$$$ | **MODERN FRENCH** | Perhaps the most traditional of all Paris luxury restaurants, this two-star grande dame basks in renewed freshness under chef Giuliano Sperandio, who brings a welcome contemporary spirit that translates to daring on the plate. Dishes such as scallops meunière (with butter and lemon) are matched with contemporary choices like a splendid spelt risotto with truffles and frogs' legs or panfried duck liver with caramelized fruits and vegetables. **Known for:** reservations essential at one of the oldest names in Paris for fine French dining; discreet hangout for Paris politicians; 19th-century salon turned winter garden. **$** *Average main: €120* ✉ *15 rue Lamennais, 8e, Champs-Élysées* ☎ *01–44–95–15–01* 🌐 *www.letaillevent.com/en* ♡ *Closed weekends and Aug. No lunch Mon.* 👔 *Jacket and tie* Ⓜ *Charles de Gaulle–Étoile.*

LiLi

$$$$ | **CANTONESE** | The operatically beautiful LiLi, in the Peninsula Paris hotel, puts sophisticated Cantonese cuisine in its rightful place—the gastronomic center of the world. The menu features all the classics, raised to the status of haute cuisine: small plates of dim sum (seafood, vegetable, or pork dumplings) alongside more substantial fare like fried rice studded with market-fresh vegetables, succulent Sichuan shrimp, and barbecued suckling pig. **Known for:** authentic Peking duck and gourmet dim sum; cocktails at the Bar Kléber; reservations essential. **$** *Average main: €40* ✉ *The Peninsula Paris, 19 rue Kléber, 16e, Champs-Élysées* ☎ *01–58–12–67–50* 🌐 *www.liliparis.fr* ♡ *Closed Sun. and Mon.* Ⓜ *Kléber, Charles de Gaulle–Étoile.*

Pavyllon

$$$$ | **FRENCH** | This is a great opportunity to sample chef Yannick Alléno's cooking for a (slightly) less lofty price tag than at his three-star Pavillon Ledoyen on the same premises. Make no mistake—though guests are seated around a bar, this is as sophisticated an eatery as they come. **Known for:** outdoor dining; 15 staff to serve 20 diners; open seven days. **$** *Average main: €60* ✉ *8 av. Dutuit, 8e, Champs-Élysées* ☎ *01–53–05–10–00* 🌐 *www.yannick-alleno.com/en/restaurants-reservation/pavyllon.html* Ⓜ *Concorde, Madeleine.*

★ Pierre Gagnaire

$$$$ | **MODERN FRENCH** | If you want to venture to the frontier of contemporary cooking—and if money is no object—dinner here is a must (reservations essential). Chef Pierre Gagnaire's work is at once intellectual and poetic, often blending three or four unexpected tastes and textures in a single dish. Just taking in the menu requires concentration (ask the waiters for help), so complex are the multiline descriptions about each dish's six or seven ingredients. **Known for:** consistently ranked among the world's best (and most expensive) restaurants; combines French technical mastery with cutting-edge techniques; complicated menu descriptions. **$** *Average main: €160* ✉ *6 rue de Balzac, 8e, Champs-Élysées* ☎ *01–58–36–12–50* 🌐 *pierregagnaire.com* ♡ *Closed weekends and Aug.* Ⓜ *Charles de Gaulle–Étoile.*

★ Prunier

$$$$ | **SEAFOOD** | A Paris institution since 1925, this absolute stunner of a seafood brasserie was also one of the first restaurants to champion French-raised caviar, after the Bolshevik revolution cut the Russian supply. Fast forward to 2023, when star chef Yannick Alléno took the helm of the Art Deco dining room (one of the most spectacular historic interiors in Paris), infusing the menu with a new elegance in dishes like a caviar-flecked salmon-and-seaweed hand roll, langoustine carpaccio with caviar cream, or a perfectly prepared filet of sole, all washed down with sparkly Champagne or a crisp Bourgogne blanc. **Known for:** decor that is a historic monument; best caviar in Paris; three-starred Michelin chef. **$** *Average main: €60* ✉ *16 av. Victor Hugo, 16e, Champs-Élysées* ☎ *01–44–17–35–85* 🌐 *www.prunier.com/fr/restaurant* ♡ *Closed Mon. No dinner Sun.* Ⓜ *Étoile.*

Trente-Trois

$$$$ | **FRENCH** | Despite opening in the midst of a pandemic, in September 2021, this sumptuous contemporary dining room—tucked away in a stunner of a Belle Époque town house—achieved a Michelin star within five months. Chef Sébastien Sanjou's ingredients all have pedigrees (listed on the menu) for exceptional seasonal fare that's both refined and robust. **Known for:** beautiful atmosphere; up-and-coming chef who accommodates all palates and preferences; no à la carte options, just prix-fixe options. ⑤ *Average main: €110* ✉ *33 rue Jean Goujon, 8e, Champs-Élysées* ☎ *01–45–05–68–00* ⊕ *www.restaurant-trente-trois.com* ✡ *Closed Sun. and Mon.* Ⓜ *Alma-Marceau.*

Vive

$$$ | SEAFOOD | Culinary power couple Stéphanie Le Quellec and her husband David teamed up on this classy duplex restaurant set in a residential neighborhood close to the Arc de Triomphe that highlights the bounty of the sea. Le Quellec wisely lets the delicate flavors of the seafood speak for themselves, paired with refined complementary accents. **Known for:** maturing tuna like Angus beef; beautiful decor; two-Michelin-starred chef. ⑤ *Average main: €27* ✉ *62 av. des Ternes, 17e, Champs-Élysées* ☎ *01–42–94–07–90* ⊕ *www.vive-restaurant.com* ✡ *No dinner Sun.* Ⓜ *Ternes.*

Hotels

Château des Fleurs

$$$$ | HOTEL | Set in a flower-bedecked building on a quiet street a block from the Champs-Élysées, this Belle Époque– style hotel brings a welcome touch of whimsy to an often imposing neighborhood. **Pros:** adorable spa with ample whirlpool; close to métro and major monuments; romantic bar and restaurant. **Cons:** no security key for elevator; not all rooms have separate showers; radio audible from room next door. ⑤ *Rooms from: €620* ✉ *19 rue Vernet, 8e, Champs-Élysées* ☎ *01–47–20–41–73* ⊕ *www.chateaudesfleurs.paris/en/* ↝ *37 rooms* 🍴 *No Meals* Ⓜ *George V.*

 **Four Seasons Hôtel George V Paris**

$$$$ | HOTEL | FAMILY | As poised and polished as the day it opened in 1928, this superb hotel's original plaster detailing and 17th-century tapestries have been restored, the bas-reliefs regilded, and the marble-floor mosaics rebuilt tile by tile,

adding up to an opulence rarely equaled in the city. **Pros:** some of the best dining in the city; courtyard dining in summer; indoor swimming pool. **Cons:** several blocks from the nearest métro; definitely for the 1%; lacks the intimacy of smaller boutique hotels. ⑤ *Rooms from: €1,100* ✉ *31 av. George V, 8e, Champs-Élysées* ☎ *01–49–52–70–00* ⊕ *www.fourseasons.com/paris* ↝ *244 rooms* 🍴 *No Meals* Ⓜ *George V.*

Hidden Hotel

$$ | HOTEL | The rough-hewn wood facade heralds the eco-friendly theme of this under-the-radar boutique hotel a block from the Arc de Triomphe, and the interior follows through with handcrafted glass, wood, stone, and ceramic decor. **Pros:** a block from main métro line and Champs-Élysées; organic toiletries in recycled packaging; healthy breakfasts. **Cons:** rooms on the small side; open-plan bathrooms offer little privacy; separate entrance and breakfast area for some rooms isn't intimate. ⑤ *Rooms from: €285* ✉ *28 rue de l'Arc de Triomphe, 17e, Champs-Élysées* ☎ *01–40–55–03–57* ⊕ *www.hidden-hotel.com* ↝ *35 rooms* 🍴 *No Meals* Ⓜ *Ternes.*

Hôtel Barrière Fouquet's

$$$$ | HOTEL | Adjacent to the legendary Fouquet's Brasserie at the corner of the Champs-Élysées and Avenue George V, this luxury hotel is recognizable by its uniformed valets, parked sports cars, and elegant Haussmannian entryway. **Pros:** many rooms overlook the Champs-Élysées; very close to the métro; beautiful spa and pool. **Cons:** one of the more expensive options; bars can get overcrowded; corporate events give the place a business-hotel feel. ⑤ *Rooms from: €1,100* ✉ *46 av. George V, 8e, Champs-Élysées* ☎ *01–40–69–60–00* ⊕ *www.hotelsbarriere.com/en/collection-fouquets/paris.html* ↝ *101 rooms* 🍴 *No Meals* Ⓜ *George V.*

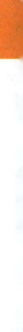

★ Hôtel Bradford Élysées

$$ | **HOTEL** | **FAMILY** | One of the Astotel group's popular Paris lodgings, this welcoming hotel follows a winning formula: annex a historic building, create attractive spaces in cheerful colors, and offer plenty of perks (free drinks, snacks, and newspapers) and service that go the whole nine yards, all for a reasonable price. **Pros:** lots of freebies, including a complimentary minibar; some rooms have period details; bargain prices. **Cons:** not in a central neighborhood; decor not to all tastes; a métro ride to many sights. **§** *Rooms from: €284* ✉ *10 rue St-Philippe du Roule, 8e, Champs-Élysées* ☎ *01–45–63–20–20* 🌐 *en.astotel.com/hotel/bradford-elysees-en/overview* ↔ *50 rooms* 🍴 *No Meals* Ⓜ *St-Philippe du Roule, Franklin D. Roosevelt.*

Hôtel de Berri Champs-Élysées

$$$$ | **HOTEL** | Set back on a quiet side street off the bustling Champs-Élysées, this opulent hotel's glass facade reveals a private garden and extravagant jewel-toned rooms filled with stylish furnishings favoring splashes of leopard. **Pros:** some rooms with garden views; iPad-controlled rooms; chic decor. **Cons:** pricey option with style that may not appeal to all; no spa; breakfasts could be better. **§** *Rooms from: €700* ✉ *18–22 rue de Berri, 8e, Champs-Élysées* ☎ *01–76–53–77–70* 🌐 *www.marriott.fr/hotels/parbe-hotel-de-berri-champs-elysees-a-luxury-collection-hotel-paris/overview* ↔ *75 rooms* 🍴 *No Meals* Ⓜ *George V, St-Philippe du Roule.*

Hôtel de Sers

$$$ | **HOTEL** | Built for the Marquis de Sers with a horse-drawn-carriage entrance, inner courtyard, expansive salons, and monumental staircase, this beautiful structure was transformed into a hotel in 1935 and later renovated with a bold modern style and hints of traditional aesthetics. **Pros:** convenient central location in the Golden Triangle; many dining options nearby; soothing Turkish bath and fitness room. **Cons:** basic rooms a bit small; no formal spa; on the expensive side. **§** *Rooms from: €500* ✉ *41 av. Pierre 1er de Serbie, 8e, Champs-Élysées* ☎ *01–53–23–75–75* 🌐 *www.hoteldesers-paris.com* ↔ *52 rooms* 🍴 *No Meals* Ⓜ *Alma-Marceau, George V.*

★ Hôtel du Rond Point des Champs-Élysées

$$ | **HOTEL** | **FAMILY** | A stylish Art Deco upgrade gave this 19th-century mansion two blocks from the Champs-Élysées a sleek period look enhanced by refined contemporary touches. **Pros:** staff couldn't be friendlier or more helpful; reasonable prices for this neighborhood; excellent location, near the Grand Palais, Concorde, and walking distance to Louvre. **Cons:** some rooms quite small; small pool; spa has only two treatment rooms. **§** *Rooms from: €290* ✉ *10 rue de Ponthieu, 8e, Champs-Élysées* ☎ *01–53–89–14–14* 🌐 *www.esprit-de-france.com/fr/hotels/hotel-rond-point-champselysees* ↔ *36 rooms* 🍴 *No Meals* Ⓜ *Champs-Élysées–Clémenceau.*

Hôtel Ekta

$$ | **HOTEL** | Two top-tier Paris designers transformed a humdrum 1960s office building into one of the city's liveliest fashion-centric boutique hotels. **Pros:** great location; in-room tea and coffee; charming garden. **Cons:** some rooms very tiny; small bathrooms; air-conditioned only after May 1. **§** *Rooms from: €290* ✉ *52 rue Galilée, 8e, Champs-Élysées* ☎ *01–53–76–09–05* 🌐 *www.hotelekta.com* ↔ *25 rooms* 🍴 *No Meals* Ⓜ *George V.*

Hôtel Elysia

$$$ | **HOTEL** | Discreet and contemporary sums up this seven-story town house steps from the hustle and bustle of the Champs-Élysées. **Pros:** extremely elegant rooms; friendly, attentive service; central location. **Cons:** small spa and gym; rooms impeccably clean but some need sprucing up; pricey breakfast. **§** *Rooms from: €460* ✉ *35 rue de Berri, 8e, Champs-Élysées* ☎ *01–53–53–20–20* 🌐 *www.*

hotelelysia.fr ↔ 35 rooms 🍴 No Meals Ⓜ St-Philippe du Roule, George V.

★ Hôtel Grand Powers

$$$$ | HOTEL | No detail was left to chance at this ravishing hotel in a restored 1920s building on a posh corner of the Golden Triangle. **Pros:** small spa and 24-hour fitness room; excellent location close to public transportation; quality in-hotel dining. **Cons:** rooms are pricey; not all rooms have views; limited fitness room. ⓘ *Rooms from: €550* ✉ *52 rue François 1er, 8e, Champs-Élysées* ☎ *01–47–23–91–05* ⊕ *www.hotelgrandpowersparis.com* ↔ *50 rooms* 🍴 *No Meals* Ⓜ *George V.*

★ Hôtel Keppler

$$ | HOTEL | FAMILY | Like your own classy pied-à-terre, the Keppler—set on a quiet street not far from the Champs-Élysées—combines traditional French and contemporary style for a comfy, lived-in elegance that invites total relaxation. **Pros:** luxurious common spaces; great in-hotel bar; elegant neighborhood. **Cons:** some rooms quite small; a walk to the nearest métro; no spa. ⓘ *Rooms from: €333* ✉ *10 rue Kepler, 16e, Champs-Élysées* ☎ *01–47–20–65–05* ⊕ *www.keppler.fr* ↔ *44 rooms* 🍴 *No Meals* Ⓜ *George V.*

Hôtel Lancaster Paris

$$$$ | HOTEL | Once a Spanish nobleman's town house, this luxurious retreat dating from 1889 and opened as a hotel in 1930 dazzles with its elegant decor, lush courtyard, and acclaimed Monsieur restaurant and sleek Copper Bay cocktail lounge. **Pros:** steps from the Champs-Élysées and five minutes from the métro; excellent seasonal menus at Monsieur Restaurant; peaceful street. **Cons:** size of rooms varies greatly; decor looks tired; no spa. ⓘ *Rooms from: €608* ✉ *7 rue de Berri, 8e, Champs-Élysées* ☎ *01–40–76–40–76* ⊕ *www.hotel-lancaster.com* ↔ *56 rooms* 🍴 *No Meals* Ⓜ *George V.*

★ Hôtel Le Bristol

$$$$ | HOTEL | FAMILY | The historic Bristol ranks among Paris's most exclusive hotels and has numerous accolades to prove it, as does its Michelin-starred restaurant. **Pros:** rooftop pool with views of Sacré-Coeur; location on luxury shopping street; one of the best restaurants in Paris. **Cons:** a few blocks from the nearest métro; old-fashioned atmosphere may not be for everyone; very expensive rates. ⓘ *Rooms from: €1,100* ✉ *112 rue du Faubourg St-Honoré, 8e, Champs-Élysées* ☎ *01–53–43–43–00* ⊕ *www.oetkercollection.com/hotels/le-bristol-paris* ↔ *188 rooms* 🍴 *No Meals* Ⓜ *Miromesnil.*

★ Hôtel Le 123 Elysées

$$ | HOTEL | Italian marble, exposed brick, rough concrete, and sleek wood mix with leather, feathers, Swarovski crystals, and fiber-optic fairy lights to give this boutique hotel a genuinely eclectic atmosphere. **Pros:** chic decor; near luxury shopping; hotel bar open daily. **Cons:** service can be impolite; no on-site restaurant; some rooms quite small for the price. ⓘ *Rooms from: €280* ✉ *123 rue du Faubourg St-Honoré, 8e, Champs-Élysées* ☎ *01–53–89–01–23* ⊕ *www.astotel.com/hotel/123-elysees/overview* ↔ *41 rooms* 🍴 *No Meals* Ⓜ *St-Philippe du Roule, Franklin D. Roosevelt.*

Hôtel Marignan Champs-Élysées

$$$$ | HOTEL | Set smack-dab in the middle of Paris's Golden Triangle, just off the Champs-Élysées, this sleek five-star hotel is a paragon of contemporary style that includes fine in-hotel dining and some breathtaking terrace views. **Pros:** stellar views from upper terraces; prices good for this standard of luxury; great location. **Cons:** a few rooms on the smaller side; not all rooms have great views; lack of outlets in bathrooms. ⓘ *Rooms from: €550* ✉ *12 rue de Marignan, 8e, Champs-Élysées* ☎ *01–40–76–34–56* ⊕ *www.hotelmarignanelyseesparis.com*

➤ 50 rooms ¶O| No Meals M Franklin D. Roosevelt.

⊕ www.raphael-hotel.com ➤ 83 rooms ¶O| No Meals M Kléber.

★ Hôtel Plaza Athénée

$$$$ | HOTEL | FAMILY | Distinguished by the scarlet flowers cascading over its elegant facade, this glamorous landmark hotel sits on one of the most expensive avenues in Paris. **Pros:** panoramic views of the Eiffel Tower and Paris; great restaurants and bar; exquisite Dior spa. **Cons:** attracts oligarchs; eye-popping prices; compact fitness room. § *Rooms from: €1,400* ✉ *25 av. Montaigne, 8e, Champs-Élysées* ☎ *01–53–67–66–65* ⊕ *www.dorchestercollection.com/paris/hotel-plaza-athenee* ➤ *208 rooms* ¶O| *No Meals* M *Alma-Marceau.*

Hôtel Prince de Galles

$$$$ | HOTEL | This glamorous Art Deco gem—opened in 1929 as the Paris hotel of choice for Edward, Prince of Wales (later King Edward VIII)—is a sleek and refined alternative to the area's more imposing palaces. **Pros:** great neighborhood; some rooms have spacious balconies with views; fabulous bar and lounge. **Cons:** some rooms on the small side; no pool; breakfast is expensive. § *Rooms from: €950* ✉ *33 av. George V, 8e, Champs-Élysées* ☎ *01–53–23–77–77* ⊕ *www.marriott.com/en-us/hotels/par/c-prince-de-galles-a-luxury-collection-hotel-paris* ➤ *159 rooms* ¶O| *No Meals* M *George V.*

Hôtel Raphael

$$$$ | HOTEL | FAMILY | This discreet, palacelike hotel was built in 1925 to cater to travelers spending a season in Paris, so every space is generously sized for long, lavish stays. **Pros:** a block from the Champs-Élysées and Arc de Triomphe; rooftop garden terrace, plus an intimate hotel bar frequented by locals; concierge helpful to families. **Cons:** decor can feel worn and dowdy; some soundproofing issues; neighborhood far from the action. § *Rooms from: €530* ✉ *17 av. Kléber, 16e, Champs-Élysées* ☎ *01–53–64–32–00*

Hotel Vernet

$$$ | HOTEL | A glamorous centenary update added 21st-century luxuries while remaining true to the beautiful bones of this boutique hotel, which first opened in the waning years of the Belle Époque. **Pros:** larger than average rooms; beautiful stained-glass ceilings designed by Gustave Eiffel; quiet street close to sights and shopping. **Cons:** coffee machines only in deluxe rooms; extras can be pricey; in-hotel dining quite expensive. § *Rooms from: €408* ✉ *25 rue Vernet, 8e, Champs-Élysées* ☎ *01–44–31–98–00* ⊕ *www.hotelvernet-paris.com* ➤ *50 rooms* ¶O| *No Meals* M *George V, Étoile.*

La Maison Champs Élysées

$$$ | HOTEL | This chic boutique hotel, in the heart of the Golden Triangle and a 10-minute walk from the city's most famous avenue, lures an art-minded fashion crowd with an eclectic modern twist on a historical Haussmannian *belle demeure* (beautiful house). **Pros:** quiet street close to métro; excellent location near both the Grand and Petit Palais; unique decor. **Cons:** some rooms seem tired; no fitness center; expensive bar. § *Rooms from: €408* ✉ *8 rue Jean Goujon, 8e, Champs-Élysées* ☎ *01–40–74–64–65* ⊕ *www.la-maison-champs-elysees.com* ➤ *57 rooms* ¶O| *No Meals* M *Franklin D. Roosevelt.*

★ La Réserve

$$$$ | HOTEL | Set in a splendid 19th-century mansion just steps from the presidential palace and the American embassy, this aristocratic lodging is one of the city's most elegant small hotels. **Pros:** top-notch spa with pool; splendid views over the Champs-Élysées and Eiffel Tower; excellent dining. **Cons:** very expensive even among its peers; can be snobby; out-of-the-way neighborhood. § *Rooms from: €1,800* ✉ *42 av. Gabriel, 8e, Champs-Élysées* ☎ *01–58–36–60–60*

⊕ www.lareserve-paris.com ↝ 40 rooms 🍴 No Meals Ⓜ Franklin D. Roosevelt.

Le Royal Monceau Raffles Paris

$$$$ | HOTEL | FAMILY | The glamorous Royal Monceau Raffles offers tons of luxury, great dining, and an artsy atmosphere along with a hefty dose of cool. **Pros:** ethereal spa and fitness center; chic private apartments; nice terrace garden. **Cons:** hefty prices; away from the heart of Paris; fitness room is small. ⓘ *Rooms from: €1,000 ✉ 37 av. Hoche, 8e, Champs-Élysées ☎ 01–42–99–88–00 ⊕ www.leroyalmonceau.com ↝ 149 rooms 🍴 No Meals Ⓜ Charles de Gaulle–Étoile.*

Maison Delano

$$$$ | HOTEL | Step inside this 18th-century mansion and you're enveloped in a welcoming vibe that extends from the beautiful courtyard terrace to its 56 splendid rooms and suites. **Pros:** opulent bathrooms; excellent French-Andalusian restaurant; central location on quiet street. **Cons:** high rates; loud music from restaurant can be distracting; no spa. ⓘ *Rooms from: €950 ✉ 4 rue d'Anjou, 8e, Champs-Élysées ☎ 01–83–96–88–88 ⊕ www.maisondelanoparis.com ↝ 56 rooms 🍴 No Meals Ⓜ Madeleine.*

Maison Elle Paris

$$$ | HOTEL | A stone's throw from the Arc de Triomphe, Maison Elle revolves around the three principles that guide the international magazine that is its namesake: "the French art of living" (seen in the crisp black, white, and chrome decor littered with Parisian fashion shots); "smiling beauty" (its wellness area, yoga classes, and organic Dr. Hauschka toiletries and beauty products); and a feminine-centric spirit, inspired by the nearby Parisian fashion addresses beloved by stylish women. **Pros:** superchic decor; great spa and free sauna and yoga room; attractive bar and breakfast area. **Cons:** small rooms; pretty lighting is for effect not efficiency; must request a softer pillow. ⓘ *Rooms from: €400 ✉ 14 rue Brey,*

17e, Champs-Élysées ☎ 01–77–35–90–00 ⊕ www.maisonelle.fr ↝ 25 rooms 🍴 No Meals Ⓜ Étoile, Ternes.

★ Monsieur George Hôtel & Spa

$$$ | HOTEL | This cosmopolitan, five-star boutique hotel, two minutes from the Champs-Élysées, brings a welcome frisson of romance to the neighborhood, with opulent, jewellike decor featuring glittering mirrors, luxe fabrics, and design-conscious furnishings. **Pros:** designed by superstar Anouska Hempel; spacious rooms and bathrooms; lovely bar and dining room. **Cons:** set on a slightly drab but quiet side street; spa quite small; not ideal for families. ⓘ *Rooms from: €500 ✉ 17 rue Washington, 8e, Champs-Élysées ☎ 01–87–89–48–48 ⊕ www.monsieurgeorge.com ↝ 46 rooms 🍴 No Meals Ⓜ George V.*

Norman Hôtel & Spa

$$$$ | HOTEL | On a quiet side street a quick jaunt from the Champs-Élysées, this handsome newcomer channels a stylish midcentury aesthetic right out of Mad Men. Cozy into a plush sofa for a cocktail in the art-filled lobby-library before dinner at Thiou restaurant, where you'll dine on upscale Thai cuisine in a dining room right out of a shelter magazine. **Pros:** cozy Omnisens spa; close to monuments and major métro hub; outdoor dining in warm weather. **Cons:** small fitness area; quite expensive in high season; lower rooms are darker. ⓘ *Rooms from: €580 ✉ 9 rue Balzac, 8e, Champs-Élysées ☎ 01–42–99–80–80 ⊕ www.hotelnorman.com ↝ 37 rooms 🍴 No Meals Ⓜ George V.*

★ The Peninsula Paris

$$$$ | HOTEL | FAMILY | A €900-million renovation restored the luster of this lavishly appointed 1908 gem and raised the bar for luxury hotels in Paris. **Pros:** world-class dining; fabulous spa and pool; amazing views from higher floors. **Cons:** price out of reach for most; not centrally located; stuffy neighborhood. ⓘ *Rooms from: €1,700 ✉ 19 av. Kléber,*

16e, Champs-Élysées ☎ 01–58–12–28–88 ⊕ www.peninsula.com/en/paris/5-star-luxury-hotel-16th-arrondissement ↝ 200 rooms ¶ No Meals Ⓜ Kléber, Charles de Gaulle–Étoile.

Renaissance Paris Arc de Triomphe

$$$ | **HOTEL** | This American-style hotel catering to corporate executives is in a predominantly business district between the Arc de Triomphe and Place des Ternes. **Pros:** walking distance to métro; spacious rooms; good discounts with Marriott points. **Cons:** neighborhood lacks character; filled with business conferences; rather unfriendly service. ⌂ *Rooms from: €493* ✉ *39 av. de Wagram, 17e, Champs-Élysées* ☎ *01–55–37–55–37* ⊕ *www.marriott.fr/hotels/parwg-renaissance-paris-arc-de-triomphe-hotel* ↝ *138 rooms* ¶ *No Meals* Ⓜ *Ternes.*

Nightlife

BARS

Apicius

BARS | Mere steps from the Champs-Élysées, Apicius offers sublime elegance. Wander through the luxe front garden and château restaurant to the sleekly modern black bar where couture cocktails are concocted to suit any cultured taste. ✉ *20 rue d'Artois, 8e, Champs-Élysées* ☎ *01–43–80–19–66* ⊕ *www.restaurant-apicius.com* Ⓜ *George V.*

Blind Bar, Maison Champs Élysées

BARS | This romantic spot in the ultra-chic Maison Champs Élysées offers a wood fire in winter and a quiet terrace in warmer months. Its impressive range of Champagnes and impeccable cocktails is well worth the stellar prices. The separate all-black cigar bar is one of the few remaining in Paris. ✉ *Hôtel La Maison Champs Élysées, 8 rue Jean Goujon, 8e, Champs-Élysées* ☎ *01–40–74–64–65* ⊕ *www.lamaisonchampselysees.com* Ⓜ *Franklin D. Roosevelt, Champs-Élysées–Clemenceau.*

Le Bar Anglais

BARS | You might find diplomats and other dignitaries discussing state affairs at this rich red den of masculinity in Hôtel Raphael, a stone's throw from the Arc de Triomphe. The hotel's Rooftop Bar, a well-guarded Parisian secret, was voted the best bar in Europe in recent years. ✉ *Hôtel Raphael, 17 av. Kléber, 16e, Champs-Élysées* ☎ *01–53–64–32–00* ⊕ *www.raphael-hotel.com* Ⓜ *Kléber, Charles de Gaulle–Étoile.*

Le Bar at George V

BARS | An ultraluxe, clubby hideaway in the Four Seasons Hotel, Le Bar at George V is perfect for stargazing from the plush wine-red armchairs, cognac in hand. Its charm still lures the glitterati, especially during Fashion Weeks. Be sure to notice the hotel's signature—and stunning—flower arrangements. ✉ *Four Seasons Hôtel George V Paris, 31 av. George V, 8e, Champs-Élysées* ☎ *01–49–52–70–00* ⊕ *www.fourseasons.com/paris/dining/lounges/le_bar* Ⓜ *George V.*

Le Bar at the Hôtel Plaza Athénée

BARS | This hotel bar par excellence has a clubby feel that lures a younger fashion crowd. Lounge in leather chairs under an Yves Klein–blue ceiling installation while sipping stylish cocktails, like the signature Rose Royal (Champagne, raspberry, and a splash of cognac). Mood lighting and music spun by a live DJ Thursday through Saturday set the tone for a glam late-night rendezvous. ✉ *Hôtel Plaza Athénée, 25 av. Montaigne, 8e, Champs-Élysées* ☎ *01–53–67–66–00* ⊕ *www.dorchestercollection.com/fr/paris/hotel-plaza-athenee/restaurants-bars/le-bar* Ⓜ *Alma-Marceau.*

 **Le Bar du Bristol**

BARS | Apparently not satisfied with its usual rich and powerful clientele, this tony spot is now vying for the impossibly hip, too. Along with enticing cocktails and rarefied spirits, Le Bar promises exceptional wines and tapas. Weekdays from 7 pm to 9:30 pm, it also showcases curated art videos on its behind-the-bar mirror screen. Chic Paris DJs heat up the scene between 9:30 pm and 2 am on Friday and Saturday. ✉ *Hôtel Le Bristol, 112 rue du Faubourg St-Honoré, 8e, Champs-Élysées* ☎ *01–53–43–43–00* ⊕ *www.oetkercollection.com/hotels/le-bristol-paris/restaurants-bar/le-bar-du-bristol/* Ⓜ *Miromesnil.*

of. The lavish bar is a great place to sip Champagne and people-watch. ✉ *116 av. des Champs-Élysées, 8e, Champs-Élysées* ☎ *01–53–33–45–50* ⊕ *lido2paris.com/en/* Ⓜ *George V.*

JAZZ CLUBS

Jazz Club Étoile

LIVE MUSIC | This moody club at Le Méridien Hotel hosts a roster of top-billed international musicians in a classy set of rooms. Check out the Sunday afternoon jazz brunch buffet and the interior garden. ✉ *Le Méridien Hotel, 81 bd. Gouvion-St-Cyr, 17e, Champs-Élysées* ☎ *01–40–68–30–42* ⊕ *www.jazzclub-paris.com* Ⓜ *Porte Maillot.*

Le Marta Paris

BARS | Swanky decor and luscious drinks are drawing the cocktail cognoscenti to this intimate lounge hidden away in the legendary Le Fouquet's Hotel. If you prefer daylight, the hotel offers two other superchic bars: Le Joy and L'Escadrille. ✉ *Le Fouquet's Paris, 46 av. George V, 8e, Champs-Élysées* ☎ *01–40–69–60–00* ⊕ *www.hotelsbarriere.com/fr/collection-fouquets/paris/restaurants-et-bars/le-marta-paris.html* Ⓜ *Georges V.*

Le Melville

LIVE MUSIC | An answer to Paris's lack of jazz supper clubs, this chic and intimate venue offers a top-notch program of live jazz and world music, along with suave cocktails and a short menu of gourmet tapas. Attentive service, a welcoming atmosphere, and an appreciative, cosmopolitan clientele make this club a good choice for a Parisian night on the town. ✉ *28 rue Jean Mermoz, 8e, Champs-Élysées* ☎ *01–40–75–00–57* ⊕ *lemelville.fr* Ⓜ *Franklin D. Roosevelt.*

CABARET

★ Crazy Horse

CABARET | This world-renowned cabaret has elevated the striptease to an art form. Founded in 1951, it's famous for gorgeous dancers and naughty routines characterized by lots of humor and very little clothing. What garments there are have been dazzlingly designed by the likes of Louboutin and Alaïa and shed by top divas (including Dita Von Teese). Reserved seats for the show start at €115. ✉ *12 av. George V, 8e, Champs-Élysées* ☎ *01–47–23–32–32* ⊕ *www.lecrazyhorseparis.com* Ⓜ *Alma-Marceau.*

Lido 2

CABARET | The storied Parisian cabaret, which hosted the likes of Josephine Baker, Edith Piaf, and Noel Coward, closed its doors in 2022 to emerge in late 2023 as the city's most glamorous music venue. Resplendent in burnished gold and red velvet, Art Deco crystal, and Venetian marble, Lido 2 is equal parts music hall, nightclub, and cabaret, featuring immersive productions that run the gamut from Stephen Sondheim musicals to a lavish 50th-anniversary staging

Performing Arts

Comédie des Champs-Élysées

THEATER | Next door to the Théâtre des Champs-Élysées, the Comédie des Champs-Élysées offers intriguing productions in its small theater. ✉ *15 av. Montaigne, 8e, Champs-Élysées* ☎ *01–53–23–99–19* ⊕ *www.comediedes-champselysees.com* Ⓜ *Alma-Marceau.*

Salle Gaveau

MUSIC | The 1,020-seat Salle Gaveau is a perfectly appointed gold-and-white hall with remarkable acoustics and a distinctly Parisian allure. It hosts chamber music, orchestral, piano, and vocal recitals. ✉ *45–47 rue la Boétie, 8e, Champs-Élysées* ☎ *01–49–53–05–07* ⊕ *www.sallegaveau.com* Ⓜ *Miromesnil.*

Salle Pleyel

CONCERTS | Once one of Paris's major classical music venues, these days Salle Pleyel's packed calendar focuses mostly on contemporary music, entertainment, and other events. The venue also hosts the annual César Awards, France's answer to the Oscars. ✉ *252 rue du Faubourg St-Honoré, 8e, Champs-Élysées* ☎ *01–42–56–13–13* ⊕ *www.sallepleyel.com* Ⓜ *Ternes.*

Théâtre des Champs-Élysées

PERFORMANCE VENUES | This was the scene of 1913's infamous Battle of the Rite of Spring, when police had to be called in after the audience ripped up seats in outrage at Stravinsky's *Le Sacre du Printemps* score and Nijinsky's choreography. Today Théâtre des Champs-Élysées is elegantly restored and worthy of a visit if only for the architecture. (It's one of Paris's most striking examples of Art Deco.) The theater also hosts first-rate opera and dance performances, along with orchestral, chamber, and Sunday morning concerts. ✉ *15 av. Montaigne, 8e, Champs-Élysées* ☎ *01–49–52–50–50* ⊕ *www.theatrechampselysees.fr* Ⓜ *Alma-Marceau.*

 Shopping

ACCESSORIES

Publicis Drugstore

ACCESSORIES | A stone's throw from the Arc de Triomphe, this trendy spot—equal parts concept store, pharmacy, cinema, and brasserie-café—is stocked with an ever-changing array of upscale wares from designer handbags and diamond bracelets to fine wine and cigars. When you're done browsing, enjoy a bite at the on-site eatery (a prix-fixe menu is available) or stop by the bakery for food to take away. What Parisians like most is its late hours: it's open until 2 am (restaurant and bar stay open till midnight). ✉ *133 av. des Champs-Élysées, 8e, Champs-Élysées* ☎ *01–44–43–79–00* ⊕ *www.*

publicisdrugstore.com Ⓜ *Charles de Gaulle–Étoile.*

BEAUTY

Guerlain

FRAGRANCES | This opulent address is a fitting home for Paris's first—and most famous—perfumer. Still the only Paris outlet for legendary perfumes like Shalimar and L'Heure Bleue, it has added several new signature scents (including Myrrhe et Délires and Cuir Beluga). Personalized bottles in several sizes can be filled on demand, or, for a mere €30,000, a customized scent can be blended just for you. Sybarites will also appreciate Guerlain's makeup, scented candles, and spa featuring its much-adored skin-care line. There's an elegant gourmet restaurant for lunch or tea, too. ✉ *68 av. des Champs-Élysées, 8e, Champs-Élysées* ☎ *01–45–62–52–57* ⊕ *www.guerlain.com* Ⓜ *Franklin D. Roosevelt.*

Parfums de Nicolaï

FRAGRANCES | Run by Guerlain family member Patricia de Nicolaï, this perfumerie sells children's, women's, and men's scents (including some unisex) as well as sprays for the home and fragrant candles. ✉ *69 av. Raymond Poincaré, 16e, Champs-Élysées* ☎ *01–44–55–02–00* ⊕ *www.pnicolai.com* Ⓜ *Victor Hugo.*

CHILDREN'S CLOTHING

★ Bonpoint

CHILDREN'S CLOTHING | Outfit the prince or princess in your life at Bonpoint (yes, royalty *does* shop here). The prices are high, but the quality is exceptional, and the adorable miniduds couldn't be more stylish: picture a perfect hand-smocked Liberty-print dress, a velvety lambskin vest, or a double-breasted cashmere sweater for Little Lord Fauntleroy. The Avenue Raymond Poincaré boutique is one of more than a dozen citywide. ✉ *64 av. Raymond Poincaré, 16e, Champs-Élysées* ☎ *01–47–27–60–81* ⊕ *www.bonpoint.com* Ⓜ *Trocadéro.*

CLOTHING

Balmain

CLOTHING | Slinky silhouettes, bare midriffs, sequins, crystals, frills, and furbelows, not to mention plenty of silver, patent leather, and cutouts: in other words, Balmain is not for shrinking violets. This may sound like a break from the couture house's ultrafeminine backstory (a favorite of '50s Hollywood idols), but in the hands of Olivier Rousteing, being feminine translates to being at home in your skin first, then dressing it up—his glamorous, highly Instagrammable flights of fancy are catnip for models, singers, and reality stars. The elegantly minimal boutique in the heart of the Golden Triangle carries the full collection and is a lovely backdrop for these opulent street wear–meets–boudoir fashions. ✉ *44 rue François 1er, 8e, Champs-Élysées* ☎ *01–47–20–57–58* 🌐 *www.balmain.com* Ⓜ *Franklin D. Roosevelt, George V.*

★ Céline

CLOTHING | Phoebe Philo, who defined this bohemian-chic label for a decade, single-handedly redefined the codes of fashion for professional women, garnering a huge and fiercely loyal following for her streamlined, minimal designs, featuring flowing pants, long, unstructured jackets, and the Cabas bag. All heads turned when bad boy Hedi Slimane, who left Saint Laurent in 2016 after rocking the label to its core, was tapped to fill Philo's comfy shoes. After his first season's glittery minis tanked, Slimane did an about-face, channeling a bourgeois art-house look that felt distinctly Parisian. Now, he's relegated the sultry looks to evening and sells tailored blouses and contoured jackets that are singularly sexy. ✉ *53 av. Montaigne, 8e, Champs-Élysées* ☎ *01–40–70–07–03* 🌐 *www.celine.com* Ⓜ *Franklin D. Roosevelt.*

★ Chanel

CLOTHING | Elegant, modern looks with sex appeal and lasting value are Chanel's stock-in-trade. Although the spectacularly beautiful Avenue Montaigne flagship takes shoppers' breath away, the heart of this revered fashion house is still the boutique at 31 rue Cambon, where Chanel once perched high up on the mirrored staircase watching audience reactions to her collection debuts. Great investments include all of Coco's favorites: the perfectly tailored suit, a lean soigné dress, or a quilted bag with a gold chain. Handbags, jewelry, shoes, and accessories are all found at the fabulous 42 avenue Montaigne boutique, opposite the flagship store. ✉ *51 av. Montaigne, 8e, Champs-Élysées* ☎ *01–44–50–73–00* 🌐 *www.chanel.com* Ⓜ *Franklin D. Roosevelt.*

★ Dior

CLOTHING | Maria Grazia Chiuri, Dior's first female designer for a label that's traditionally defined the feminine, has quickly made the House of Dior thoroughly her own. Her feminist perspective—which brings together the glamour, high style, and comfort women of all ages really want, instead of a fantastical notion best-suited for models—has transformed the house of Dior, raising it to one of the most exciting Parisian designer brands in the city, not to mention the most profitable. Furthermore, the 2022 reopening of Dior's Avenue Montaigne flagship store ushered in a new benchmark for Paris boutiques. Covering more than 105,000 square feet, this pearl of a flagship brings together haute couture and ready-to-wear items, beauty, and menswear, along with a restaurant (Monsieur Dior) and pastry shop (by chef Jean Imbert of the Plaza Athénée), three gardens, guest suites, and a gallery space bound to rival the Musée Yves Saint Laurent. ✉ *30 av. Montaigne, 8e, Champs-Élysées* ☎ *01–40–73–73–73* 🌐 *www.dior.com* Ⓜ *Franklin D. Roosevelt.*

Dolce & Gabbana

CLOTHING | Dolce & Gabbana offers a sexy, young-Italian-widow vibe with a side of moody boyfriend. Svelte silk dresses, sharply tailored suits, and plunging necklines are made for drama. Women's clothes are at the Avenue Montaigne location; men's are at 3 rue Faubourg St-Honoré. ✉ *54 av. Montaigne, 8e, Champs-Élysées* ☎ *01–42–25–68–78* 🌐 *www.dolcegabbana.com* Ⓜ *Alma-Marceau.*

Hermès

ACCESSORIES | The elegant-equestrian theme is writ large in the heritage brand's stunning Champs-Élysées flagship, where trappings in wood, leather, and gold are the backdrops for a haute couture selection of fashions, jewelry, leather goods, and, their signature silk scarves and sarongs. Everything is sumptuously displayed over three spacious floors, making the store well worth a stop, if only to dream. ✉ *24 rue du Faubourg St-Honoré, 8e, Champs-Élysées* ☎ *01–40–17–46–00* 🌐 *www.hermes.com/fr/fr/* Ⓜ *Madeleine.*

Maison Ullens

CLOTHING | A glam Golden Triangle location, a Rem Koolhaas-designed boutique, sumptuous clothes—the Belgian label's first Paris outpost hits all the marks and then some. Founded in 2013, Maison Ullens puts the focus on luxe fabrics and skins in classic-chic designs with plenty of staying power. It has everything you need for après-ski or weekends on Capri. ✉ *4 rue de Marignan, 8e, Champs-Élysées* ☎ *01–47–20–23–56* 🌐 *www.maisonullens.com* Ⓜ *Franklin D. Roosevelt.*

Marni

CLOTHING | Marni started out as a little Italian label that put a quirky spin on classic styles, employing retro-ish prints and colors (think citron yellow or seaweed green) and funky fabrics (such as rubberized cotton and filmy silks). Now it has evolved into a major player on the edgy fashion scene. Each season has something new to say—whether it's an inventive take on bold ethnic prints, ingenious knits, or eloquent color schemes. Sought-after shoes and jewelry never make it to sale time. ✉ *57 av. Montaigne, 8e, Champs-Élysées* ☎ *01–56–88–08–08* 🌐 *www.marni.com* Ⓜ *Franklin D. Roosevelt.*

★ Petit Bateau

CLOTHING | FAMILY | This beloved clothing store, originally for kids, provides a fundamental part of the classic French wardrobe from cradle to teen and beyond. The signature T-shirt—cut close to the body, with smallish shoulders—works equally well with school uniforms or vintage Chanel. Thanks to timeless designs, the high-grade cotton clothes remain wardrobe staples year after year; however, lines in cotton-silk or cotton-cashmere and popular collaborations with chic designers like Christian Lacroix or Inès de la Fressange mean there's now even more in store. There are boutiques in all the major shopping neighborhoods. Stock up: if you can find this brand back home, the prices are sure to be higher. ✉ *116 av. des Champs-Élysées, 8e, Champs-Élysées* ☎ *01–40–74–02–03* 🌐 *www.petit-bateau.fr* Ⓜ *George V.*

Prada

CLOTHING | Prada spins gold out of fashion straw. Knee-length skirts, peacock colors, cardigan sweaters, geometric prints: the waiting lists cross continents. Shoes, bags, and other accessories for men and women perennially become cult items. ✉ *10 av. Montaigne, 8e, Champs-Élysées* ☎ *01–53–23–99–40* 🌐 *www.prada.com* Ⓜ *Alma-Marceau.*

Saint Laurent Paris

CLOTHING | Anthony Vaccarello has calmed the waters at Saint Laurent with an assuredness and sleight of hand that fashion editors appreciate more every year. His recent collections have inspired the kind of praise that marks a sea change in fashion, dispensing with the rock 'n' roll glitz and overt sexiness for something less rebel-with-a-cause and more timelessly elegant. Silver evening gowns shimmer like water, and oversized suits are cut to revive movie-star glamour worthy of Katharine Hepburn. At this austere flagship store, done all in chrome and marble, you'll find ready-to-wear items (think leggings, cropped leather jackets, exquisite trenches in satin, cashmere, or leather, and bias-cut evening dresses and gowns) and all the brand's coveted accessories and jewelry too. ✉ *53 av. Montaigne, 8e, Champs-Élysées* ☎ *01–53–83–84–68* ⊕ *www.ysl.com/en-fr* Ⓜ *Franklin D. Roosevelt.*

SHOES, HANDBAGS, AND LEATHER GOODS

Berluti

SHOES | The company has been making exquisite and expensive men's shoes for more than a century. "Nothing is too beautiful for feet" is Olga Berluti's motto; she even exposes her creations to moonlight to give them an extra-special patina. One model is named after Andy Warhol; other famous clients of the past include the Duke of Windsor, Fred Astaire, and James Joyce. ✉ *26 rue Marbeuf, 8e, Champs-Élysées* ☎ *01–53–93–97–97* ⊕ *www.berluti.com* Ⓜ *Franklin D. Roosevelt.*

★ **Christian Louboutin**

SHOES | It seems the world's romance with heels so high they're potentially lethal will never end, thanks in no small part to the king of the iconic red-soled stiletto. Louboutin artfully weaves fantasy, glamour, and good, cheeky fun into his towering heels, which have graced red carpets and the gangways of private jets. But you can also find more prudent models, including kitten-heeled mules and spiky sneakers, as well as chic and functional bags and a selection of lipsticks and nail polish that blend right in with your soles. His 3,000-square-foot boutique—done up in Louboutin red, of course—offers three floors of pure fetishistic pleasure. ✉ *400 rue St-Honoré, 8e, Champs-Élysées* ⊕ *eu.christianlouboutin.com* Ⓜ *Concorde.*

Jimmy Choo

SHOES | This is the place for vampy stilettos, strappy flats, and biker boots. Recent *Belle de Jour*–inspired kitten heels are a nice respite from the famous mile-high styles that put Choo on the map. Beautiful bags, clutches, and small leather items in animal print, reptile, and metallics are deservedly popular. ✉ *41 av. Montaigne, 8e, Champs-Élysées* ☎ *01–47–23–03–39* ⊕ *www.jimmychoo.com* Ⓜ *Franklin D. Roosevelt.*

★ **Louis Vuitton**

HANDBAGS | Louis Vuitton has spawned a voracious fan base from Texas to Tokyo with its mix of classic leather goods and saucy revamped versions orchestrated by Marc Jacobs. His 2013 exit left tall boots to fill, but Nicholas Ghesquière—a daring designer who single-handedly resurrected the Balenciaga label—has done an admirable job. Melding his signature edgy modernism with vintage touches and colors, Ghesquière is taking the legendary luxe label to a glorious new level. ✉ *101 av. des Champs-Élysées, 8e, Champs-Élysées* ☎ *01–53–57–52–00* ⊕ *www.louisvuitton.com* Ⓜ *George V.*

Chapter 6

AROUND THE LOUVRE AND LES HALLES

Updated by Emily Monaco

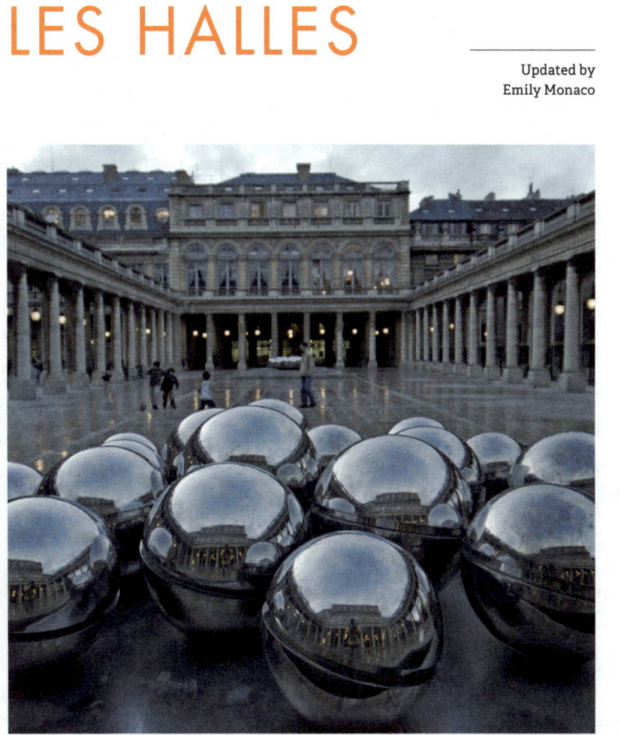

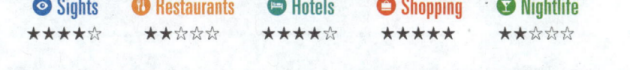

NEIGHBORHOOD SNAPSHOT

GETTING HERE

The neighborhoods here include the 1er and 2e arrondissements, from the Faubourg St-Honoré to Les Halles. If you're heading to the Louvre, take the *métro* Line 1 to the Palais-Royal–Musée du Louvre stop. For the Tuileries, use the Tuileries stop on the same line. For Place de la Concorde, use the Concorde stop on Line 1, 8, or 12. This is a good starting point for a walk on Rue St-Honoré. If you're going to Les Halles, take Line 4 to Les Halles or Line 1 to Châtelet.

MAKING THE MOST OF YOUR TIME

Try to devote two days or more—one for the Louvre alone—to this varied part of Paris. Along the narrow sidewalks of the Faubourg St-Honoré, you'll find some of the finest Parisian boutiques. Place de la Concorde is the gateway to the Tuileries gardens, which lead to the looming Louvre itself. At the eastern end of the area, Les Halles (the old market district) is booming with shops and eateries, especially around cobbled Rue Montorgueil, where traffic is mercifully restricted.

If you're headed to the Musée du Louvre, it's best to have a game plan. First step: buy your ticket online at 🌐 *www.louvre.fr.* If there is a crowd waiting to enter I. M. Pei's imposing glass pyramid, use the entrance in the underground mall, the Carrousel du Louvre (✉ *99 rue de Rivoli*).

VIEWFINDER

Standing under the ornate Arc de Triomphe du Carrousel, you can witness Paris's history unfolding: to one side, the Louvre itself, a former palace with roots in the 12th century but ultimately bearing the characteristics of its Renaissance renovation. Look to the other side, and you'll glimpse the manicured Tuileries gardens, designed by André Le Nôtre, the 17th-century royal landscape architect who would later design Versailles. Past the gardens looms the Luxor obelisk, one of a pair taken from Egypt by Napoléon, followed by the Arc de Triomphe in the distance.

TOP REASONS TO GO

■ **Musée du Louvre.** The world's first great art museum—which displays such renowned works as the serenely smirking *Mona Lisa* (*La Joconde*, in French) and the statuesque *Venus de Milo*—deserves a long visit. Plan on three hours or more, and consider going with a guide.

■ **Tuileries to Place de la Concorde.** For centuries, Parisians and visitors alike have strolled the length of this magnificent garden from the Louvre's Arc du Carrousel to the gold-tipped obelisk at Place de la Concorde.

■ **Galerie Vivienne.** The prettiest of the city's glass-roofed 19th-century shopping arcades, this passage is worth a stop to shop and photo op.

■ **Palais-Royal.** Visit these arcades and the romantic garden to understand why French writer Colette called the view from her window "a little corner of the country."

■ **Rue Montorgueil.** This historic market street is lined with food shops and cafés and is a stone's throw from some of the city's trendiest restaurants and bars.

The neighborhoods from the très chic Faubourg St-Honoré to trendy Les Halles are a study in contrasts, with the Louvre in the midst of the bustle.

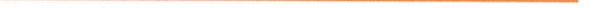

The posh **Rue du Faubourg St-Honoré**, once the stomping ground of kings and queens, is now home to the French president and assorted foreign ambassadors. Beloved by fashionistas for three centuries, it's as popular today as when royal mistresses shopped here—which explains the plethora of high-end stores (almost every luxury brand is represented). Not surprisingly, ritzy restaurants and haute hotels are here as well.

To the east, **Les Halles** (pronounced leh- *ahl*) has risen from its roots as a down-and-out market district, once described by Emile Zola as the "belly of Paris," to become a culinary destination of a wholly different kind. Vermin-infested cobbled streets have given way to trendy shops, cafés, and bars centered on Rue Montorgueil. A sweeping multiyear renovation of the former wholesale food market (which closed in 1969) gave a much-needed facelift to the plaza aboveground and the vast shopping mall below, and just steps away, the former grain exchange known as the **Bourse de Commerce** has been transformed into a contemporary art hub.

Between Faubourg St-Honoré and Les Halles, you can find some of Paris's main draws—namely the mighty **Musée du Louvre** and, just next door, the majestic **Jardin des Tuileries.** The garden is home to the **Musée de l'Orangerie**, with its curved galleries built for the express purpose of showcasing Monet's *Water Lilies*, as well as the **Jeu de Paume**, an arts center specializing in temporary contemporary

photo exhibits. Nearby, **Les Arts Décoratifs** is a must for design buffs.

In Place Colette, the stately **Comédie Française** theater is still going strong after 400 years. At the edge of the square is the psychedelic sculpture—doubling as a métro entrance—of the *kiosque des noctambules* (kiosk of the nightcrawlers), designed by artist Jean-Michel Othoniel.

Hidden just off Place Colette is the **Palais-Royal**, a romantic garden ringed by arcades with boutiques selling everything from old-fashioned music boxes to fashion-forward frocks and bedecked with the oh-so-Instagrammable *colonnes de Buren* (Buren's columns). A stone's throw away is **Galerie Vivienne**, an exquisitely restored 19th-century shopping arcade with a beautiful glass ceiling.

 Sights

 **Bourse de Commerce–Collection Pinault Paris**

ART MUSEUM | Capping one of the art world's great rivalries, the Collection Pinault Paris opened in 2021, adding another gem to the city's cultural roster. After years of false starts, tycoon François Pinault is now showcasing his billion-dollar trove of contemporary works by bold-faced names such as Mark Rothko and Damien Hirst under the historic iron-and-glass dome of the 19th-century Commerce Exchange, one of the city's most stunning, if underused, buildings. After losing a previous bid to open a museum outside Paris and taking his works to Venice instead, Gucci owner Pinault could

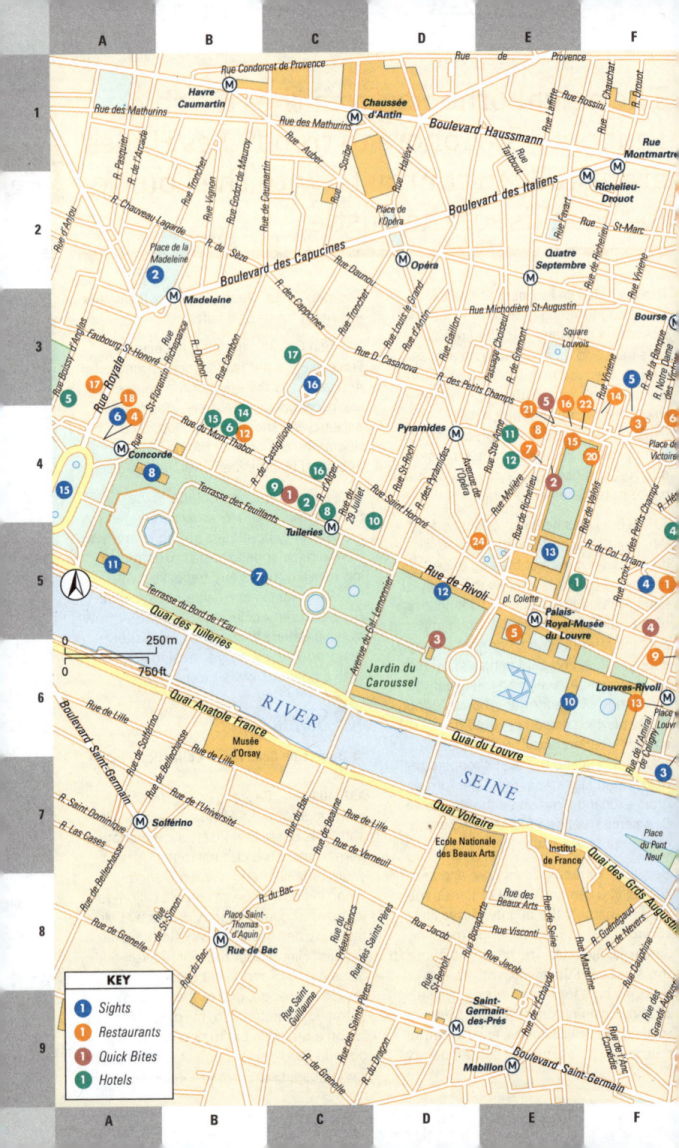

Around the Louvre

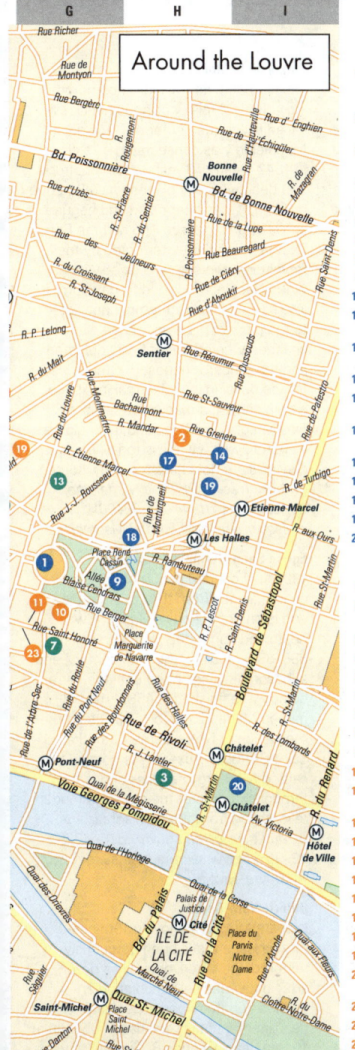

Sights ▼

1. Bourse de Commerce–Collection Pinault Paris.............. **G5**
2. Église de la Madeleine............... **B2**
3. Église Saint-Germain l'Auxerrois................. **F6**
4. Galerie Véro-Dodat...... **F5**
5. Galerie Vivienne.......... **F4**
6. Hôtel de la Marine...... **A4**
7. Jardin des Tuileries..... **B5**
8. Jeu de Paume.............. **A4**
9. Les Halles................... **G5**
10. The Louvre.................. **E6**
11. Musée de l'Orangerie..................... **A5**
12. Musée des Arts Décoratifs (MAD)....... **D5**
13. Palais-Royal................ **E5**
14. Passage du Grand-Cerf.................... **H4**
15. Place de la Concorde...................... **A4**
16. Place Vendôme........... **C3**
17. Rue Montorgueil......... **H4**
18. Saint-Eustache............ **H5**
19. Tour Jean Sans Peur... **H4**
20. Tour Saint-Jacques....... **I7**

Restaurants ▼

1. A l'Epi d'Or................ **F5**
2. Au Rocher de Cancale.................... **H4**
3. Bistrot Vivienne.......... **F4**
4. Café Lapérouse **A4**
5. Café Marly.................. **E6**
6. Chez Georges.............. **F4**
7. Ellsworth..................... **E4**
8. Juvéniles.................... **E4**
9. La Dame de Pic.......... **F6**
10. La Poule au Pot.......... **G6**
11. La Régalade Saint-Honoré............. **G6**
12. L'Ardoise................... **B4**
13. Le Fumoir................... **F6**
14. Le Grand Colbert......... **F4**
15. Le Grand Véfour.......... **E4**
16. Macéo....................... **E4**
17. Maxim's de Paris........ **A3**
18. Mimosa..................... **A4**
19. Omar Dhiab................ **G4**
20. Restaurant du Palais-Royal................ **F4**
21. Verjus....................... **E4**
22. Willi's Wine Bar........... **E4**
23. Yam'Tcha.................. **G6**
24. Zen.......................... **D5**

Quick Bites ▼

1. Angelina.................... **C4**
2. Café Kitsuné............... **E4**
3. Maison Kayser............ **D6**
4. Terres de Café............. **F5**
5. Verjus Bar à Vins........ **E4**

Hotels ▼

1. Grand Hotel du Palais Royal................. **E5**
2. Hôtel Brighton................. **C4**
3. Hôtel Britannique........ **H7**
4. Hôtel Crayon.............. **F5**
5. Hôtel de Crillon........... **A3**
6. Hôtel du Continent...... **B4**
7. Hôtel Konfidentiel....... **G6**
8. Hôtel La Tamise.......... **C4**
9. Hôtel Le Meurice........ **C4**
10. Hôtel Le Pradey.......... **D5**
11. Hôtel Louvre Sainte-Anne.................. **E4**
12. Hôtel Thérèse............. **E4**
13. Madame Rêve............. **G4**
14. Mandarin Oriental Paris............................ **B4**
15. Meliá Vendôme........... **B4**
16. Renaissance Paris Vendôme...................... **C4**
17. The Ritz..................... **C3**

only watch as archrival Bernard Arnault opened his Frank Gehry–designed Fondation Louis Vuitton in 2014. Not one to be outdone, Pinault tapped star Japanese architect Tadao Ando to carry out a nearly $140 million redesign of Paris' former grain exchange in 2017. Inside, four levels of exhibition space spiral skyward along a giant concrete cylinder ringed at the top by a walkway offering a bird's-eye view of the galleries below. The sparsity of the collections only contributes to the spaceship-like appeal of the contemporary renovation, with a handful of 19th-century details remaining: double-helix stone staircases, wooden display cases dating to 1889, the engine room on the lower level, and the realist mural adorning the underside of the dome, displaying seasonal panoramas of French traders engaged in commerce with the rest of the world. Paris Mayor Anne Hidalgo, who supplied a 50-year lease, called Pinault's creation an "immense gift" to the city. Free 20-minute tours depart daily from the ground-floor level; on the hour, tours explore the collection, while on the half-hour, they delve into the history and architecture of the building. A children's area allows kids to engage with a tour guide, discovering the collection by way of games and books, while the Halle aux Grains restaurant from Michelin-starred father-and-son team Michel and Sébastien Bras allows you to discover a tasting menu in three, five, or seven courses or an à la carte selection of upscale, contemporary French specialties. Don't miss the 100-foot-tall Medici Column on the back side of the building. It was once the stargazing perch of Marie de' Medici's powerful astrologer, Cosimo Ruggieri. Legend has it that on stormy nights, a silhouetted figure can be seen in the metal cage at the top. ✉ *2 rue de Viarmes, 1er, Louvre* ☎ *01/55–04–60–60* ⊕ *www.pinaultcollection.com/en/boursedecommerce* ✋ *€14* ♡ *Closed Tues.* Ⓜ *Les Halles; RER: Châtelet–Les Halles.*

Église de la Madeleine

CHURCH | With its rows of uncompromising columns, this enormous neoclassical edifice in the center of Place de la Madeleine was consecrated as a church in 1842, nearly 78 years after construction began. Initially planned as a Baroque building, it was later razed and begun anew by an architect who had the Roman Pantheon in mind. Interrupted by the Revolution, the site was razed yet again when Napoléon decided to transform it into a Greek-inspired temple dedicated to the glory of his army. Those plans changed when the army was defeated and the emperor deposed. Other ideas for the building included making it into a train station, a market, and a library. Finally, Louis XVIII decided it should be a church, which it still is today. Classical concerts are held here regularly, some of them free. ✉ *Pl. de la Madeleine, 8e, Louvre* ☎ *01–44–51–69–00* ⊕ *www.eglise-lamadeleine.com* Ⓜ *Madeleine.*

Église Saint-Germain l'Auxerrois

CHURCH | Founded in 500 AD, this grand church across from the Louvre's eastern end is one of the city's oldest. It was destroyed during the Norman siege in 885–886, rebuilt in the 11th century, and subsequently expanded until the current edifice was finished in 1580. The bell, named Marie, dates to 1527. During the renovation of Notre-Dame Cathedral, Saint-Germain l'Auxerrois is hosting the cathedral's liturgy services and is the temporary home of the crown of thorns relic, saved from the conflagration. ✉ *2 pl. du Louvre, 1er, Louvre* ☎ *01–42–60–13–96* ⊕ *www.saintgermainauxerrois.fr* Ⓜ *Louvre–Rivoli.*

Galerie Véro-Dodat

PEDESTRIAN MALL | A lovely 19th-century passage that's been gorgeously restored, the Véro-Dodat has a dozen artsy boutiques selling objets d'art, textiles, furniture, and accessories. The headliner tenant is Christian Louboutin at 19 Rue Jean-Jacques Rousseau, whose red-soled stilettos are favored by Angelina Jolie, Madonna, and other members of the red-carpet set. On the opposite end, at the Rue du Bouloi entrance, star cosmetics maker Terry De Gunzburg has a boutique, By Terry. ✉ *Main entrance at 19 rue Jean-Jacques Rousseau, 1er, Louvre* ⊘ *Closed Sun.* Ⓜ *Palais-Royal–Louvre.*

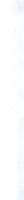

★ Galerie Vivienne

PEDESTRIAN MALL | Considered the grande dame of Paris's 19th-century *passages couverts*—the world's first shopping malls—this graceful arcade evokes an age of gaslights and horse-drawn carriages. Parisians once came to passages like this one to tread tiled floors instead of muddy streets; to see and be seen browsing boutiques under the glass-and-iron roofs. Today, the Galerie Vivienne still attracts unique retailers selling clothing, accessories, and housewares. La Marelle (No. 25) stocks secondhand designer labels, and wine merchant Legrand Filles et Fils (✉ *1 rue de la Banque*) is the place for an upscale tasting. The Place des Victoires, a few steps away, is one of Paris's most picturesque squares. In the center is a statue of an outsized Louis XIV (1643–1715), the Sun King, who appears almost as large as his horse. ✉ *Main entrance at 4 rue des Petits-Champs, 2e, Louvre* ⊘ *Closed Sun.* Ⓜ *Palais-Royal–Louvre, Bourse.*

★ Hôtel de la Marine

SPECIALTY MUSEUM | FAMILY | This splendid museum is the closest you'll get to Versailles in Paris. It took more than 200 skilled artisans and nearly $160 million to achieve what is hands down Paris's most ravishing museum to date, allowing the public a glimpse behind the elegant facade of a masterpiece of French 18th-century interior design for the first time in 250 years. No detail was overlooked in the restoration: wallpaper and curtains were painted or sewed by hand using the original 18th-century techniques; the woodwork was painstakingly stripped, restored, and gilded by master craftspeople; and decorative features were created in Paris's most rarified workshops.

The mansion is one of two twin structures built in 1758 for Louis XV to mark a new square created in his honor (now Place de la Concorde). Both buildings sat unused before the eastern facade—now the Hôtel de Crillon—was auctioned off to the Duc d'Aumont. The western edifice became the Garde-Meuble de la Couronne, the institution in charge of selecting, maintaining, and storing the king's furniture. In 1789, it became the headquarters for the navy ministry, which remained in the building for 226 years. The decrees ending slavery and the slave trade in France were signed here in 1794. Visitors can learn about the building's history through state-of-the-art interactive displays in the grand ballroom and loggia, a sprawling balcony facing Place de la Concorde with impressive views of the Assemblée Nationale and the Eiffel Tower. You can take a guided visit (in English) or grab a state-of-the-art headset; well worth it to discover the museum's fascinating history.

The museum also houses the exquisite Al Thani collection, featuring objects and artwork spanning 6,000 years and myriad civilizations, as well as an outpost of the Cordon Bleu cooking school (⊕ *www. cordonbleu.edu/paris-hoteldelamarine*). The waiting room retains lovely details of the historic mansion while state-of-the-art classrooms are equipped with top-of-the-line culinary equipment. At stations designed for two students, participants in these hands-on ateliers glean the secrets of French cuisine from professional chefs; while classes are taught in French, expert interpreters are always present to ensure English-speakers reap the full benefits. Classes start at €33 for a one-hour demonstration, but spring for the €110 two-hour Capitaine or €165 three-hour Amiral for the fullest experience.

Another great pleasure of your visit is lunch, teatime, or a cocktail at the romantic Café Lapérouse (the first offshoot of the historic Paris restaurant) or Mimosa, across the courtyard, helmed by chef Jean-François Piège, one of the city's star chefs. Both restaurants offer sumptuous interiors and outdoor dining in the interior courtyard or under the pillars overlooking Place de la Concorde. ✉ 2 pl. de la Concorde, 8e, Louvre ⊕ www.hotel-de-la-marine.paris/en ☎ From €13 Ⓜ Concord, Madeleine.

★ Jardin des Tuileries

CITY PARK | FAMILY | This quintessential French garden, with its verdant lawns, rows of manicured trees, and gravel paths, was designed by André Le Nôtre for Louis XIV. After the king moved his court to Versailles in 1682, the Tuileries became *the* place for stylish Parisians to stroll. (Ironically, the name derives from the decidedly unstylish factories that once occupied this area: they produced *tuiles*, or roof tiles, fired in kilns called *tuileries.*) Monet and Renoir captured the garden with paint and brush. It's no wonder the Impressionists loved it—the gray, austere light of Paris's famously overcast days make the green trees appear even greener.

The garden still serves as a setting for one of the city's loveliest walks. Laid out before you is a vista of must-see monuments, with the Louvre at one end and the Place de la Concorde at the other. The Eiffel Tower looms in the distance on the other side of the Seine, along with the Musée d'Orsay, accessible by a footbridge in the center of the garden.

Begin exploring the garden at the Louvre end, with the Arc du Carrousel, a stone-and-marble arch commissioned by Napoléon to showcase the bronze horses he stole from St. Mark's Cathedral in Venice. The horses were eventually returned and replaced here with a statue of a quadriga, a four-horse chariot. On the Place de la Concorde end, twin buildings bookend the garden. On the Seine side, the former royal greenhouse is now the exceptional Musée de l'Orangerie, home to the largest display of Monet's lovely *Water Lilies* series, as well as a sizable collection of early 20th-century paintings, including many Impressionist works. On the opposite end is the Jeu de Paume, which hosts some of the city's best photography exhibitions.

Note that the Tuileries is one of the best places in Paris to take kids if they're itching to run around. There's a carousel, trampolines, and, in summer, a funfair. If you're hungry, look for carts serving gelato from Amorino or sandwiches from the chain bakery Paul at the eastern end near the Louvre. Within the gated part of the gardens are four cafés with terraces. Pavillon des Tuileries near Place de la Concorde is a good place to stop for late-afternoon tea or an apéritif. ✉ *Bordered by Quai des Tuileries, Pl. de la Concorde, Rue de Rivoli, and the Louvre, 1er, Louvre* ☎ *01–40–20–90–43* ☎ *Free* Ⓜ *Tuileries, Concorde.*

Jeu de Paume

ART MUSEUM | This Napoléon III–era building at the north entrance of the Jardin des Tuileries began life in 1861 as a place to play *jeu de paume* (or "palm game"), a forerunner of tennis. It later served as a transfer point for art looted by the Germans during World War II. Rather than a permanent collection, today the ultramodern, white-walled building provides a space for temporary exhibits from up-and-comers as well as icons such as Diane Arbus, Richard Avedon, Cindy Sherman, and Robert Frank. In 2022, the museum launched the first annual Jeu de Paume festival, a celebration of multiple media that marries exhibits, screenings, concerts, and more. ✉ *1 pl. de la Concorde, 8e, Louvre* ☎ *01–47–03–12–50* ⊕ *www.jeudepaume.org* ☎ *€12* ♡ *Closed Mon.* Ⓜ *Concorde.*

Les Halles

BUSINESS DISTRICT | For 800 years, Paris was fed by the acres of food halls overflowing with meats, fish, and vegetables that made up this district. Sensuously described in Émile Zola's novel *The Belly of Paris*, Les Halles was teeming with life—though not all of it good. Hucksters and the homeless shared these streets with prostitutes, and the plague of cat-size rats didn't cease until the market moved to the suburbs in 1969. Today, you can still see stuffed pests hanging by their tails in the windows of the circa-1872 shop Julien Aurouze (✉ *8 rue des Halles*) whose sign, *Destruction des Animaux Nuisibles* (Vermin Extermination), says it all. All that remains of the 19th-century iron-and-glass market buildings designed by architect Victor Baltard is a portion of the superstructure on the southern edge of the Jardins des Halles. The Fontaine des Innocents, from 1550, at Rues Berger and Pierre Lescot, marks the site of what was once a vast cemetery before the bones were moved to the Catacombs.

After years of delays, Les Halles finally underwent one of the city's most ambitious public works projects: a sweeping €500-million renovation, completed in 2018, that has transformed the plaza and the much-maligned underground concrete mall called the Forum des Halles into a must-go destination. While the project was not without opponents, even famously grumpy Parisians were satisfied by the prospect of a prettier Les Halles—and a spruced-up train station underground. (The métro and RER station at Les Halles is one of the city's busiest transport hubs.) In an echo of the past, a 48-foot iron-and-glass canopy floats over the entrance, flooding light into the caverns below. Aboveground, a 10-acre park called the Jardin Nelson Mandela is dotted with trees, decorative pools, and play areas for kids. On the northern end, a redesigned Place René-Cassin has tiered steps centered around *L'Ecoute*, Henri

de Miller's giant head and hand sculpture. Looming behind is the magnificent church of Saint-Eustache, a Gothic gem. Movie buffs should check out the Forum des Images, which stages screenings of quirky or older films, often with notables on hand such as director Oliver Stone. Or sample some of the 7,000 films available for viewing on individual screens. To find it, enter the mall on the side of the church at the Porte Saint-Eustache.

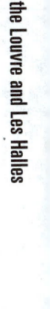

The streets surrounding Les Halles have boomed in recent years with boutiques, bars, and restaurants that have sent rents skyrocketing. Historic Rue Montorgueil is home to food shops and cafés. Running parallel, Rue Montmartre, near the church, still has a few specialty shops selling foie gras and other delicacies, though these merchants, like the butchers and bakers before them, are slowly being pushed out by trendy clothing boutiques. Steps away, Rue du Nil has become a foodie haven thanks to the Frenchie family of restaurants as well as shops from locavore trendsetters Terroirs d'Avenir. The area is also well-known for kitchen supply stores frequented by cooking amateurs and professionals alike; E. Dehillerin (✉ *18 rue Coquillière*) is rife with old-fashioned charm, while Mora (✉ *13 rue Montmartre*) is a bit more sterile but easier to navigate. ✉ *Garden entrances on Rues Coquillière, Berger, and Rambuteau. Mall entrances on Rues Pierre Lescot, Berger, and Rambuteau, 1er, Louvre* Ⓜ *Les Halles; RER: Châtelet–Les Halles.*

★ The Louvre

ART MUSEUM | Simply put, the Louvre is the world's greatest art museum—and the largest, with 675,000 square feet of works from almost every civilization on Earth. The *Mona Lisa* is, of course, a top draw, along with the *Venus de Milo* and *Winged Victory*. These and many more of the globe's most coveted treasures are

Continued on page 148

MUSÉE DU LOUVRE

Try to wrap your mind around this: The Louvre has more than 37,000 pieces of art in its collection, representing nearly every civilization on earth, and more than 675,000 square feet of exhibition space. It's gone through countless cycles of construction and demolition, expansion and renovation, starting as a medieval fortress, then becoming a royal residence before opening its doors as the Museum Central des Arts at the end of the 18th century.

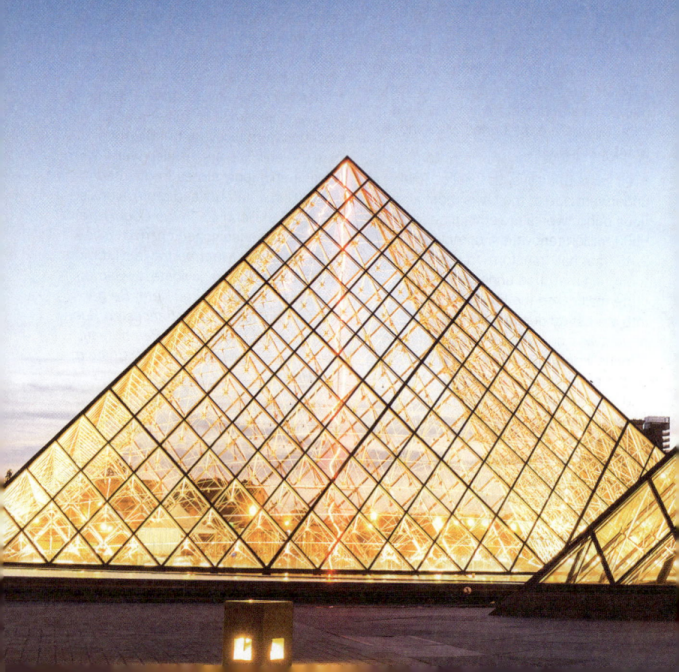

Don't make the mistake of thinking that you'll be able to see the Louvre's entire collection in one visit and still enjoy—or remember—what you've seen. The three most popular artworks here are, of course, the *Mona Lisa*, the *Venus de Milo*, and *Winged Victory*. Beyond these must-sees, your best bet is to focus on highlights that interest you the most—and don't worry about getting lost because you're bound to stumble upon something interesting. Stop by the information desk for a free color-coded map. For help navigating the collection, rent an excellent Nintendo 3DS multimedia guide, or take a daily guided tour in English. The Louvre has three wings—the Richelieu, the Sully, and the Denon—arranged like a horseshoe, with I. M. Pei's striking *Pyramide* nestled outside in the middle.

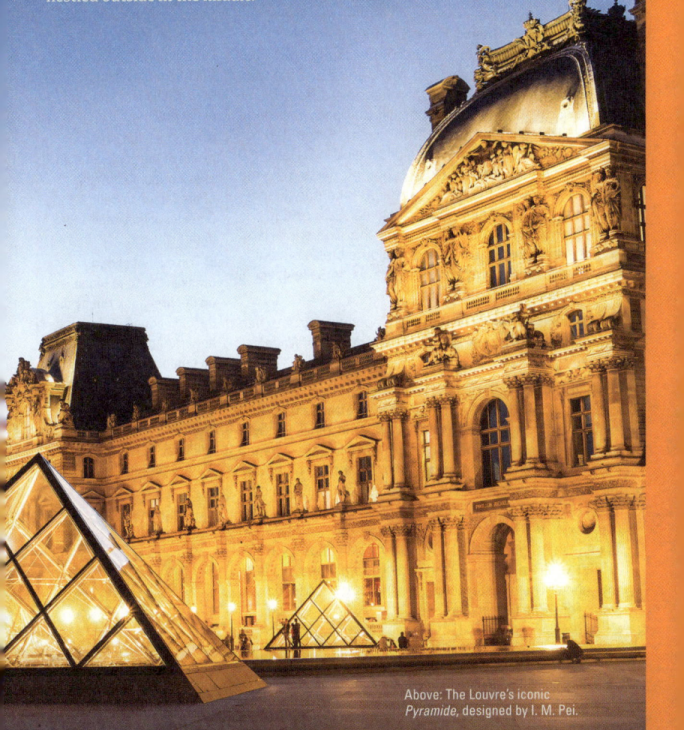

Above: The Louvre's iconic *Pyramide*, designed by I. M. Pei.

RICHELIEU WING

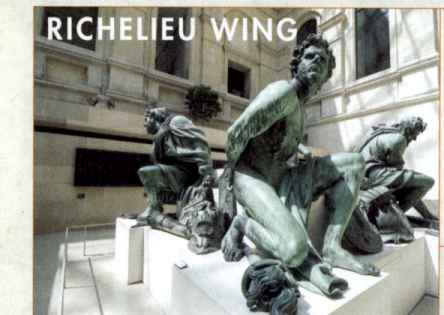

COLLECTIONS

Near East Antiquities
French Painting
French Sculpture
Northern Schools
Decorative Arts

TIPS

■ The 25 paintings by Rubens commisioned by Marie de' Medici for the Luxembourg Palace in Salle 18 on the second floor each mark an event in the queen's life.

■ To see what's on the minds of the museum staff, check out the Painting of the Month in Salle 17, French section, on the 2nd floor.

■ Take a hot chocolate break in the Café Richelieu on the first floor, run by the upscale confiseur (confectioner) Angelina. There is an outdoor terrace in summer and a tempting lunch menu.

■ Save your ticket and duck out for lunch at one of the nearby cafés.

Below Ground & Ground Floor. Entering from the *Pyramide*, head upstairs to the sculpture courtyards, Cour Marly and Cour Puget. In Cour Marly you'll find the ***Marley Horses*** (see right). Salle 2 has fragments from Cluny, the powerful Romanesque abbey in Burgundy that dominated 11th-century French Catholicism. Salles 4–6 follow the evolution of French sculpture, and in Salles 7–10 you'll find funerary art. In Cour Puget, products from the Académie Royale, the art school of 18th-century France, fill Salles 25–33. Behind this is the Near East Antiquities Collection. Salle 3's centerpiece is the Codex of Hammurabi, an 18th-century BC black-diorite stela containing the world's oldest written code of laws. In Salle 4, you'll find ***Lamassu*** (*see right*).

First Floor. Head straight through Decorative Arts to see the magnificently restored ***Royal Apartments of Napoléon III*** (*see right*).

Second Floor. Much of this floor is dedicated to French and Northern School paintings. At the entrance is a 14th-century painting of John the Good—the oldest-known individual portrait from the north of Italy. In Salle 4 hangs *The Madonna of Chancellor Rolin*, by the 15th-century Early Netherlandish master Jan van Eyck (late 14th century–1441). Peter Paul Rubens's (1577–1640) the *Disembarkation of Marie de' Medici at the Port of Marseille* is in Salle 18. In Salle 31 are several paintings by Rembrandt van Rijn (1606–69), including *Bathsheba*, his largest nude. The masterpiece of the Dutch collection is Vermeer's ***The Lacemaker*** (*see right*).

DON'T MISS

LAMASSU, 8TH CENTURY — SALLE 4

With their fierce beards and gentle eyes, these massive winged beasts are benevolent guardians straight from the dreamworld. Magical for children and adults, the strangely lifelike sculptures are located in the Near Eastern antiquities collection. The winged bull demigods are part of the Cour Khorsabad, a re-creation of the temple erected by Assyrian king Sargon II. ✦ *Richelieu, ground floor*

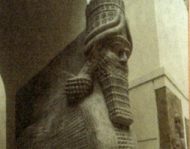

Lamassu

THE LACEMAKER, 1669–1671 — SALLE 38

This is a small but justifiably famous gem of Dutch optical accuracy (and a must-see for fans of the movie and book, *Girl with a Pearl Earring*, to see how his style evolved over a 5-year period.) Here, Jan Vermeer (1632–75) painted the red thread in the foreground as a slightly blurred jumble, just as one would actually see it if focusing on the girl. The lacemaker's industriousness represents domestic virtue, but the personal focus of the painting is far more engaging than a simple morality tale. ✦ *Richelieu, second floor*

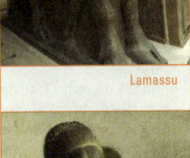

The Lacemaker

MARLY HORSES, 1699–1740 — COUR MARLY

During the dramatic 1989 reorganization of the Louvre, two courtyards were elegantly glassed over to match the entrance pyramid. The dramatic glass-roofed Marly sculpture court houses several works from Louis XIV's garden at Marly, including two magnificent winged horses by Antoine Coysevox. Later, the artist's nephew, Guillaume Coustou, created two accompanying earthbound horse sculptures for Louis XV; their fame was such that, during the Revolution, these sculptures were moved to the Tuileries gardens for public viewing. Now the four original horses greet visitors to the Richelieu Wing, ready to gallop off into the museum; replicas stand guard in the Tuileries. ✦ *Richelieu, lower ground floor*

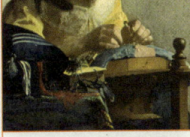

The Marly Horses

ROYAL APARTMENTS OF NAPOLÉON III, 1860s — SALLE 87

These dozen reception rooms, hung with crystal chandeliers, elaborate mirrors, and imperial velour, are a gilt-covered reminder that the Louvre was a palace for centuries, regally designed to impress. En route, you'll pass decorative items like the solid-crystal Restoration dressing table (Salle 77) that prepare you for the eye-popping luxury of the Second Empire. ✦ *Richelieu, first floor*

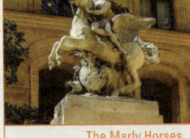

Royal Apartments of Napoléon

SULLY WING

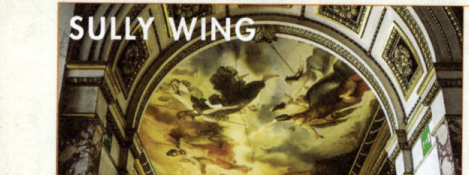

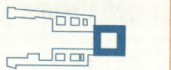

COLLECTIONS

History of the Louvre
Ancient Egypt
Near East Antiquities
Greek, Roman, & Etruscan Antiquities
French Painting
Graphic Arts
Northern Schools
Decorative Arts

TIPS

■ There is a little-known collection of pieces by Monet, Renoir, and Cezanne in Salle C on the second floor, the only Impressionist works in the Louvre.

■ There's a surprise in Salle 17 on the ground floor—the *Sleeping Hermaphrodite* by the entrance.

■ Be sure to look up as you make your way up Escalier Henri II. It took four years to complete this 16th-century vaulted ceiling.

■ Need a bathroom? There are some tucked between Salles 22 and 23 on the first floor. (And admire the colorful, 4,000-year-old Seated Scribe in Salle 22.)

■ For a breather, head to the bench in Salle 33 on the first floor and enjoy the sedate three-part ceiling by Georges Braque (1955) called *Les Oiseux (The Birds).*

Below Ground & Ground Floor. Start your visit with a journey to the roots of the Louvre—literally. From the *Pyramide* entrance, tour the 13th-century foundations of the original fortress and the **Medieval Moat** (*see right*). In Salle 12, you'll find towering **Ramses II** (*see right*). Check out the mummies and rare examples of Egyptian funerary art in Salles 14 and 15.

Upstairs, the north galleries of the Sully continue the ancient Iranian collection begun in the Richelieu Wing. Salle 16 has the 2nd-century BC ***Venus de Milo*** (*see right*), anchoring the Greek collection of Salles 7–17.

First Floor. The northern galleries of the first floor continue with the Decorative Arts collection, including works from all over Europe, and connect with the Napoléon III apartments.

Second Floor. Sully picks up French painting in the 17th century where the Richelieu leaves off. The Académiciens are best exemplified by Nicolas Poussin (1594–1665, Salle 19), the first international painting star from France. The antithesis of this style was the candlelit modest work by outsider Georges de La Tour (Salle 28), as in his *Magdalene of Night Light.*

The Académie Royale defined the standards of painting through revolution, republic, and empire. Exoticism wafted in during the Napoleonic empire, as in ***The Turkish Bath*** (*see right*) painting of Jean-Auguste-Dominique Ingres (1780–1867). Fresh energy crackled into French painting in the 18th century. Antoine Watteau (1684–1721), was known for his theatrical scenes and *fêtes galantes,* portrayals of well-dressed figures in bucolic settings. In *Pilgrimage to the Island of Cythera* (Salle 36), he used delicate brushstrokes and soft tones to convey the court set, here depicted arriving on (or departing from) Cythera, the mythical isle of love.

DON'T MISS

RAMSES II, APPROX. 1200 BC — SALLE 12

The sphinx-guarded Egyptian Wing contains the biggest display of Egyptian antiquities in the world after the Cairo museum—not surprising, considering that Egyptology as a Western concept was invented by a Frenchman, Champollion, founder of the Louvre's Egypt collection and translator of the hieroglyphics on the Rosetta Stone. This statue from the site of Tanis, presumed to be Ramses II, never fails to stop visitors' breath with its gleaming stone, beatific expression, and perfect proportions. ✚ *Sully, ground floor*

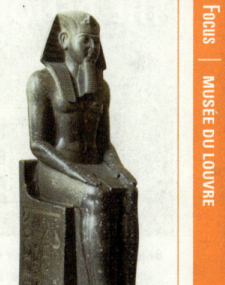

Ramses II

VENUS DE MILO, APPROX. 120 BC — SALLE 16

After countless photographs and bad reproductions, the original Aphrodite continues to dazzle. The armless statue, one of the most recognizable works of art in the world, is actually as beautiful as they say. She was unearthed on the Greek island of Milos in the 19th century and sold for 6,000 francs to the French ambassador in Constantinople, who presented her to King Louis XVIII. ✚ *Sully, ground floor*

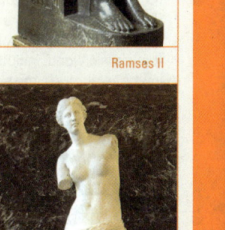

Venus de Milo

MEDIEVAL MOAT, 13TH CENTURY — MEDIEVAL LOUVRE

Wander around the perimeter of the solidly built original moat to reach the remarkable Salle Saint-Louis with its elegant columns and medieval artifacts. Keep an eye out for the parade helmet of Charles VI, which was dug up in 169 fragments and astonishingly reassembled. ✚ *Sully, lower ground floor*

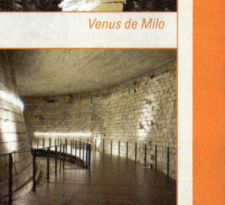

Medieval Moat

THE TURKISH BATH, 1862 — SALLE 60

Though Jean-August-Dominique Ingres' (1780–1867) long-limbed women hardly look Turkish, they are singularly elegant, and his polished immaculate style was imitated by an entire generation of French painters. This painting is a prime example of Orientalism, where Western artists played out fantasies of the Orient in their work. Popular as a society portrait painter, Ingres returned repeatedly to langorous nudes—compare the women of *The Turkish Bath* with the slinky figure in his *La Grande Odalisque*, in the Denon Wing. ✚ *Sully, second floor*

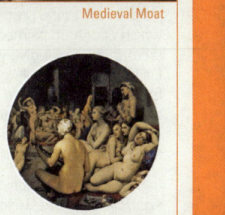

The Turkish Bath

THE DENON WING

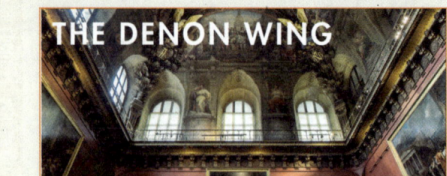

COLLECTIONS

Ancient Egypt
Greek, Roman, & Etruscan Antiquities
French Painting
Italian & Spanish Painting
Graphic Arts
Italian, Spanish, &
Northern Sculpture
African, Asian, Oceanic, &
American Arts
Arts of Islam

TIPS

■ Don't skip the coat check on the ground floor. Much of the museum is hot and stuffy.

■ Don't miss the glass case near *Winged Victory of Samothrace* on the first floor. It contains her two-fingered hand.

■ Need a bathroom? There are some tucked away at the end of the wing on the first floor near Salle 13.

Below Ground & Ground Floor. The stunning Arts of Islam wing with 30,000 square feet of gallery space is built into the Cour Visconti and topped with an undulating glass roof meant to evoke a floating head scarf. Here you'll find Europe's largest collection of treasures from across the Islamic world, including the Ottoman Empire. On the lower level, don't miss the Baptistery of Saint Louis, a 14th-century sculpted golden basin. The galleries to the south and east of the *Pyramide* entrance display early Renaissance Italian sculpture, including a 15th-century *Madonna and Child* by Florentine Dontallo (1386–1466). Drift upstairs to the Italian sculptures on the ground level, where you'll find Michelangelo's exquisite *Slaves* (1513–15) in Salle 4.

First Floor. Walk up the marble Escalier Daru to discover the sublime ***Winged Victory of Samothrace*** (*see right*), cleaned in 2014. Then head to the stunning Galerie d'Apollon (Apollo Gallery). Built in 1661 but not finished until 1851, the hall was a model for Versailles's Hall of Mirrors.

Back out and into Paintings, you'll find four by Leonardo da Vinci (1452–1519). His enigmatic, androgynous *St. John the Baptist* hangs here, along with more overtly religious works such as the 1483 *Virgin of the Rocks*. Take a close look at the pretty portrait of *La Belle Ferronnière*, which Leonardo painted a decade before the ***Mona Lisa*** (*see right*); it will give you something to compare with Lisa when you finally get to meet her in the Salle des Etats, near Salles 5 and 6. Head across to Salle 75 for an artistic 180°: the gleaming pomp and circumstance of a new empire with the ***Coronation of Napoléon*** (*see right*) by French classicist Jacques-Louis David (1748–1825).

In Salle 77 is the graphic 1819 ***The Raft of the Medusa***, (*see right*) by Théodore Géricault (1791–1824).

DON'T MISS

MONA LISA, 1503 SALLE DES ETATS

The most famous painting in the world, *La Gioconda* (*La Joconde* in French) is tougher than she looks: the canvas was stolen from the Louvre by an Italian nationalist in 1911, recovered from a Florentine hotel, and survived an acid attack in 1956. She is believed to be the wife of Francesco del Giocondo, a Florentine millionaire, and was probably 24 when she sat for this painting; some historians believe the portrait was actually painted after her death. Either way, she has become immortal through Da Vinci's ingenious "sfumato" technique, which combines glowing detail with soft, depth-filled brushwork.
✦ *Denon, first floor*

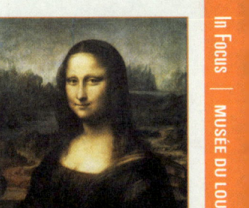

Mona Lisa

THE RAFT OF THE MEDUSA, 1819 SALLE 77

Théodore Géricault was inspired by the grim news report that survivors of a wrecked French merchant ship were left adrift on a raft without supplies. Géricault interviewed survivors, visited the morgue to draw corpses, and turned his painting of the disaster into a strong indictment of authority, the first time an epic historical painting had taken on current events in this way. Note the desperate energy from the pyramid construction of bodies on the raft and the manipulation of greenish light.
✦ *Denon, first floor*

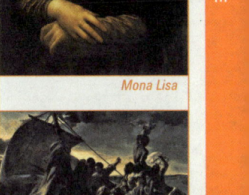

The Raft of the Medusa

WINGED VICTORY OF SAMOTHRACE, 305 BC STAIRS

Poised for flight at the top of the Escalier Daru, this exhilarating statue was found on a tiny Greek island in the northern Aegean. Depicted in the act of descending from Olympus, *Winged Victory*, or Nike to the Ancient Greeks, was carved to commemorate the naval victory of Demetrius Poliorcetes over the Persians. ✦ *Denon, first floor*

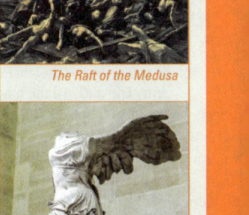

Winged Victory of Samothrace

CORONATION OF NAPOLÉON, 1805 SALLE 75

Classicist Jacques-Louis David (1748–1825) was the ultimate painter-survivor: he began his career under the protection of the king, became official designer of the Revolutionary government, endured two rounds of exile, and became one of the greatest of Napoléon's painters. Here, David avoided the politically fraught moment of December 2, 1804—when Napoléon snatched the crown from the hands of Pope Pius VII to place it upon his own head—choosing instead the romantic moment when the new emperor turned to crown Joséphine.
✦ *Denon, first floor*

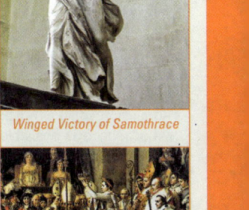

Detail from the Coronation of Napoléon

PLANNING YOUR VISIT

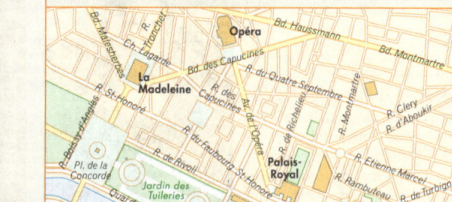

TOURS

There are 90-minute guided tours in English daily. The meeting point is at "Accueil des Groups" under the pyramid. There are also free leaflets that map out various themed, self-guided tours—some designed especially for kids. The Louvre has a phenomenal program of courses and workshops (mostly in French); see website for details.

ACCESSIBILITY

Those using wheelchairs or strollers can skip the long entry line and use the marvelous cylindrical elevator inside the entrance pyramid.

WITH KIDS

Begin your tour in the Sully Wing at the Medieval Moat, which leads enticingly to the sphinx-guarded entrance of the Egyptian Wing, a must for mummy enthusiasts. For a more in-depth visit, you can reserve private kid-centric family tours such as the Paris Muse Clues. Don't forget the Tuileries is right next door (with carnival rides in summer).

ENTRY TIPS

Booking admission tickets online in advance is the best way to avoid disappointment: the €17 timed entry guarantees admission while €15 tickets bought on-site are only sold when space is available—and given a recent decision to limit daily visitors to 30,000 (a third of the previous norm), it's unlikely that spontaneous appearances at the museum will result in a successful visit.Shorten your wait by avoiding the main entrance at the *Pyramide* and head for the entrance in the underground mall, Carrousel du Louvre. Automatic ticket machines are available. Note that crowds are thinner on Wednesday and Friday nights, when the museum is open late. Be sure to check the website for room closings; renovations are always taking place. Remember the Louvre is closed on Tuesday.

A WHIRLWIND TOUR

If you've come to Paris and feel you must go to the Louvre to see the Big Three—***Venus de Milo***, ***Winged Victory***, and ***Mona Lisa***—even though you'd rather be strolling along the Champs-Elysees, it can be done in an hour or less if you plan well. Start in Denon and head upstairs through Estruscan and Greek antiquities, walking down the long hall of sculptures until you see the *Winged Victory* in front of you. Take a right and head up the staircase through French painting to the *Mona Lisa*. Then go back down under the *Pyramide* to Sully to see the *Venus de Milo*.

- ✉ Palais du Louvre, Louvre/Tuileries
- ☎ 01–40–20–53–17 (information)
- 🌐 www.louvre.fr
- ☺ Closed Tues.
- Ⓜ Palais-Royal-Louvre, Louvre-Rivoli

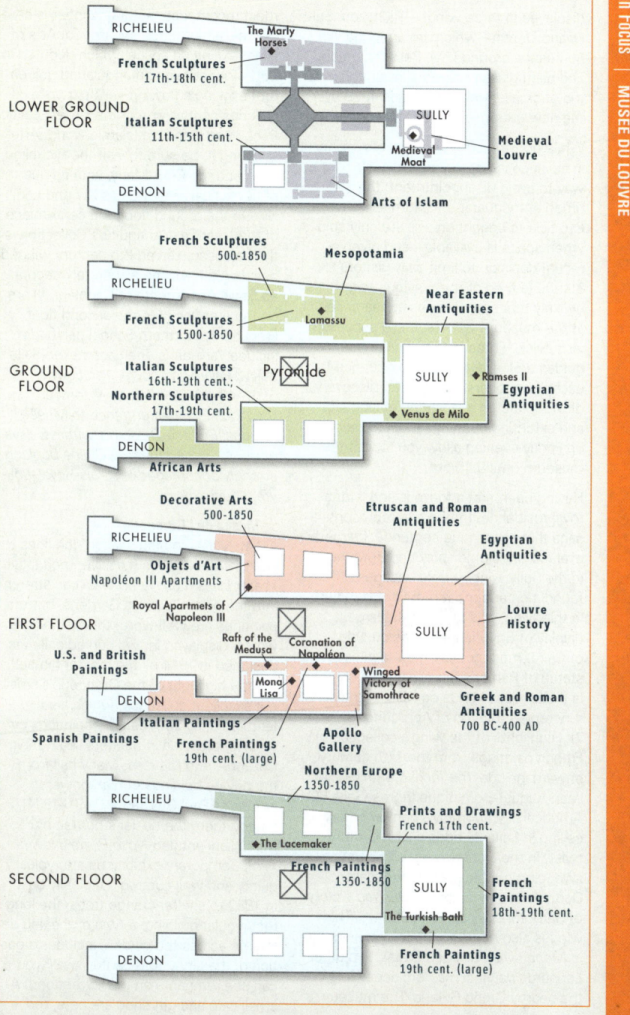

displayed in three wings—Richelieu, Sully, and Denon—which are arranged like a horseshoe around I. M. Pei's Pyramide. The giant glass pyramid surrounded by a trio of smaller ones opened in 1989 over the new entrance in the Cour Napoléon.

While booking admission tickets online in advance is not required, it's the best way to avoid disappointment: the €22 timed entry guarantees admission while €15 tickets bought on-site are only sold when space is available—and given a recent decision to limit daily visitors to 30,000 (a third of the previous norm), it's unlikely that spontaneous appearances at the museum will result in a successful visit. Slick Nintendo 3DS multimedia guides (€5), available at the entrance to each wing, offer a self-guided discovery of the museum in a variety of languages, and extended openings (*noctournes*) on Friday evening allow you to visit the museum until 9:45 pm.

Having been first a fortress and later a royal residence, the Louvre represents a saga that spans nine centuries. Its medieval roots are on display underground in the Sully wing, where vestiges of the foundation and moat remain. Elsewhere in this wing, you can ogle the largest display of Egyptian antiques outside of Cairo, most notably the magnificent statue of Ramses II (Salle 12). Upstairs is the armless Venus de Milo, a 2nd-century representation of Aphrodite (Salle 7). Highlights of the wing's collection of French paintings from the 17th century onward include *The Turkish Bath* by Jean-August-Dominique Ingres (Salle 60). American Cy Twombly's contemporary ceiling in Salle 32 adds a 21st-century twist. In the Denon wing, climb the sweeping marble staircase (Escalier Daru) to see the sublime *Winged Victory of Samothrace*, carved in 305 BC. This wing is also home to the iconic, enigmatic *Mona Lisa* (Salle des Etats); two other Leonardo da Vinci masterpieces hang in the nearby Grand Galerie. The museum's

most recent architectural wonder is here as well—the 30,000-square-foot Arts of Islam exhibition space, which debuted in 2012. Topped with an undulating golden roof evoking a flowing veil, its two-level galleries contain one of the largest collections of art from the Islamic world. After admiring it, be sure to visit the Richelieu wing and the Cour Marly, with its quartet of horses carved for Louis XIV and Louis XV. On the ground floor, the centerpiece of the Near East Antiquities Collection is the Lamassu, carved 8th-century winged beasts (Salle 4). The elaborately decorated Royal Apartments of Napoléon III are on the first floor. On the second floor, French and Northern School paintings include Vermeer's *The Lacemaker* (Salle 38). ✉ *Palais du Louvre, 1er, Louvre* ☎ *01–40–20–53–17* 🌐 *www.louvre.fr* 💰 *€22, includes entrance to Musée National Eugène-Delacroix within 2 days of use* ⏰ *Closed Tues.* 🏠 *Online booking strongly encouraged* 🚇 *Palais-Royal–Louvre, Louvre–Rivoli.*

★ Musée de l'Orangerie

ART MUSEUM | In high season, the lines to see Claude Monet's massive, meditative *Water Lilies* (*Les Nymphéas*) can stretch into the pretty Tuileries Gardens, but the paintings are well worth the wait. These works, displayed in two curved galleries designed in 1914 by the master himself, are the highlight of the Orangerie's small but excellent collection, which also features early-20th-century paintings by other Impressionist masters like Renoir, Cézanne, and Matisse. Many hail from the private holdings of high-powered art dealer Paul Guillaume (1891–1934), among them the dealer's portrait by Modigliani entitled *Novo Pilota* (*New Pilot*). Temporary exhibitions are typically quirky and well-curated. Originally built in 1852 to shelter orange trees, the long rectangular building, a twin of the Jeu de Paume across the garden, includes a portion of the city's 16th-century wall (you can see remnants on the lower floor). A small café and gift shop are here, too.

Timed entrances, easily bookable online, are strongly recommended. ☆ *Jardin des Tuileries at Pl. de la Concorde, 1er, Louvre* ☎ 01–44–77–80–07 ⊕ *www. musee-orangerie.fr* ⚡ €13 ◷ *Closed Tues.* Ⓜ *Concorde.*

Musée des Arts Décoratifs (MAD)

ART MUSEUM | The city's leading showcase of French design, Les Arts Décoratifs was rechristened the Musée des Arts Décoratifs—or MAD—in 2018 in an effort to better carve out a niche for itself. Sharing a wing of the Musée du Louvre, but with a separate entrance and admission charge, MAD is actually three museums in one spread over nine floors. The stellar collection of decorative arts, fashion, and graphics includes altarpieces from the Middle Ages and furnishings from the Italian Renaissance to the present day. There are period rooms reflecting different eras, such as the early 1820s salon of the Duchesse de Berry (who actually lived in the building), plus several rooms reproduced from designer Jeanne Lanvin's 1920s apartment. Don't miss the gilt-and-green-velvet bed of the Parisian courtesan who inspired the boudoir in Émile Zola's novel *Nana;* you can hear Zola's description of it on the free English audioguide, which is highly recommended. The second-floor jewelry gallery is another must-see.

MAD is also home to an exceptional collection of textiles, advertising posters, films, and related objects that are shown in rotating exhibitions. Before leaving, take a break at the restaurant Le Loulou, where an outdoor terrace is an ideal spot for lunch or afternoon tea (be sure to reserve—spots fill up quickly!) Shoppers should browse through the on-site boutique as well. Stocked with an interesting selection of books, paper products, toys, tableware, accessories, and jewelry, it's one of the city's best museum shops. If you're combining a visit here with the Musée du Louvre, note that the two close on different days,

so don't come on Monday or Tuesday. If you're pairing it with the exquisite Nissim de Camondo, joint tickets are available at a reduced cost. ☆ *107 rue de Rivoli, 1er, Louvre* ☎ 01–44–55–57–50 ⊕ *www. madparis.fr* ⚡ €15 ◷ *Closed Mon.* Ⓜ *Palais-Royal–Louvre.*

★ Palais-Royal

CASTLE/PALACE | This truly Parisian garden is enclosed within the former home of Cardinal Richelieu (1585–1642). The 400-year-old arcades now house boutiques and one of the city's oldest restaurants, the haute-cuisine Le Grand Véfour, where brass plaques recall former regulars like Napoléon and Victor Hugo. Built in 1629, the *palais* became royal when Richelieu bequeathed it to Louis XIII. Other famous residents include Jean Cocteau and Colette, who wrote of her pleasurable "country" view of the *province à Paris.* It was also here, two days before the Bastille was stormed in 1789, that Camille Desmoulins gave an impassioned speech sowing the seeds of Revolution. Today, the garden often hosts giant temporary art installations sponsored by another tenant, the Ministry of Culture. The courtyard off Place Colette is outfitted with an eye-catching collection of squat black-and-white columns created in 1986 by artist Daniel Buren. ☆ *Pl. du Palais-Royal, 1er, Louvre* Ⓜ *Palais-Royal–Louvre.*

Passage du Grand-Cerf

PEDESTRIAN MALL | This stately, glass-roofed arcade was built in 1825 and expertly renovated in 1988. Today, it's home to about 20 shops, many of them small designers selling original jewelry, accessories, and housewares. ☆ *Entrances at 145 rue St-Denis and 8 rue Dussoubs, 2e, Louvre* ◷ *Closed Sun.* Ⓜ *Étienne Marcel.*

Place de la Concorde

PLAZA/SQUARE | This square at the foot of the Champs-Élysées was originally named after Louis XV. It later became Place de la Révolution, where crowds

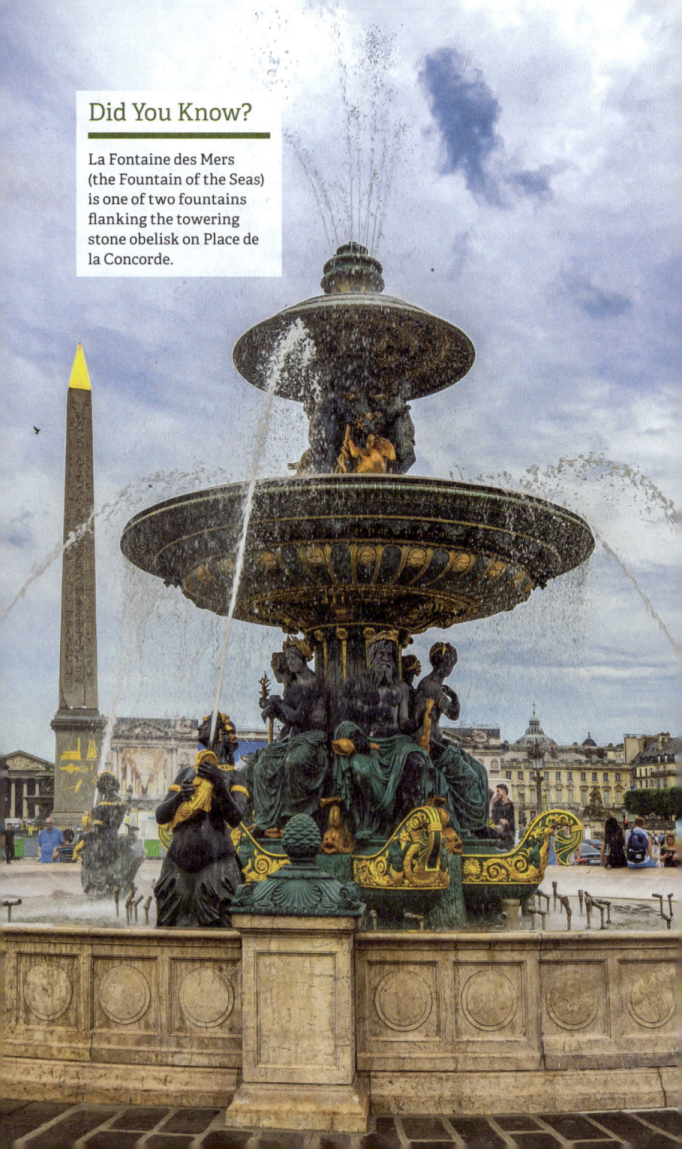

Did You Know?

La Fontaine des Mers (the Fountain of the Seas) is one of two fountains flanking the towering stone obelisk on Place de la Concorde.

cheered as Louis XVI, Marie-Antoinette, and some 2,500 others lost their heads to the guillotine. Renamed in 1836, it also got a new centerpiece: the 75-foot granite Obelisk of Luxor, a gift from Egypt quarried in the 8th century BC. Among the handsome 18th-century buildings facing the square is the Hôtel Crillon, which was originally built as a private home by Gabriel, the architect of Versailles's Petit Trianon. ✉ *Rue Royale, 8e, Louvre* Ⓜ *Concorde.*

Place Vendôme

PLAZA/SQUARE | Jules-Hardouin Mansart, an architect of Versailles, designed this perfectly proportioned octagonal plaza near the Tuileries in 1702. To maintain a uniform appearance, he gave the surrounding *hôtels particuliers* (private mansions) identical facades. It was originally called Place des Conquêtes to extoll the military conquests of Louis XIV, whose statue on horseback graced the center until Revolutionaries destroyed it in 1792. Later, Napoléon ordered his likeness erected atop a 144-foot column modestly modeled after Trajan's Column in Rome. But that, too, was toppled in 1871 by painter Gustave Courbet and his band of radicals. The Third Republic raised a new column and sent Courbet the bill, though he died in exile before paying it. Chopin lived and died at No. 12, which is also where Napoléon III enjoyed trysts with his mistress; since 1902 it has been home to the high-end jeweler Chaumet. ✉ *Pl. Vendôme, 1er, Louvre* Ⓜ *Tuileries.*

★ Rue Montorgueil

STREET | Rue Montorgueil was once the gritty oyster hub of Les Halles; now lined with food shops and cafés, the cobbled street—whose name translates to Mount Pride—is the heart of one of the city's most culinary neighborhoods. History runs deep here. Monet captured the scene in 1878, when Montorgueil was ablaze with tricolor flags during the World's Fair (see the painting in the Musée d'Orsay). Honoré de Balzac

and his 19th-century band of scribes frequented Au Rocher de Cancale at No. 78, whose famously crumbling facade has been painstakingly restored with gilt panache. Other addresses have been around for centuries: L'Escargot Montorgueil at No. 38, a favorite of Charlie Chaplin, is still graced by a giant golden snail evoking its most popular menu item, while Stohrer at No. 51 has been baking elaborate pastries since 1730. Indeed, it's pastries that reign over this small street these days, thanks to the arrivals of Fou de Pâtisseries at No. 45 and the Jeffrey Cagnes at No. 73. The street extends onto Rue des Petits-Carreaux just before Sentier métro, home to an outpost of excellent Breton crêperie Breizh Café at No. 14. Browse the boutiques on Rue Montmartre, which runs parallel, or shop for cookware at Julia Child's old haunt, E. Dehillerin, still in business at 18–20 rue Coquillière. Rue Tiquetonne is rife with bistros, and once sleepy Rue St-Sauveur became a destination when the Experimental Cocktail Club moved in at No. 37, joined by other trendy eating and drinking spots. The diminutive Rue du Nil is a foodie haven, home to Frenchie restaurant (No. 5) and wine bar (No. 6) as well as Terroirs d'Avenir's locavore shops and Plaq (No. 4), known for bean-to-bar chocolate. Even the area around Rue d'Aboukir, once far scruffier, is now a hipster fave thanks to the arrival of American-style baked goods like Boneshaker's doughnuts (No. 86) and Cookie Love's cookies (No. 84), as well as brunch spots Echo (No. 95) and Maafim (5 rue de Forges). ✉ *Rue Montorgueil, off Rue de Turbigo, 2e, Louvre* ☺ *Many shops closed Mon.* Ⓜ *Sentier, Les Halles.*

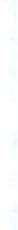

Saint-Eustache

CHURCH | Built as the market neighborhood's answer to Notre-Dame, this massive church is decidedly squeezed into its surroundings. Constructed between 1532 and 1640 with foundations dating from 1200, the church mixes a Gothic exterior (complete with impressive flying buttresses) and a Renaissance interior. On the east end (Rue Montmartre), Dutch master Rubens's *Pilgrims of Emmaus* (1611) hangs in a small chapel. Two chapels to the left is Keith Haring's *The Life of Christ,* a triptych in bronze and white-gold patina. It was given to the church after the artist's death in 1990, in recognition of the parish's efforts to help people with AIDS. On the Rue Montmartre side of the church, look for the small door to Saint Agnes's crypt, topped with a stone plaque noting the date, 1213, below a curled fish, an indication the patron made his fortune in fish. There's free entry to the weekly organ concerts. ☒ *2 impasse St-Eustache, 1er, Louvre* ⊕ *www.saint-eustache.org* Ⓜ *Les Halles; RER: Châtelet–Les Halles.*

Tour Jean Sans Peur

NOTABLE BUILDING | FAMILY | This fascinating little tower is the only remnant of a sprawling complex built on the edge of the original city walls in 1369. It is named for Jean Sans Peur (John the Fearless), the Duke of Burgundy, who gained power in 1407 after ordering the assassination of his rival, the king's brother. In 1409, as civil war raged, he had the tower erected and put his bedroom on a high floor with a bird's-eye view of approaching enemies. Carved into the vaulted second-floor ceiling—a masterwork of medieval architecture—is an ornate sculpture of an oak tree entwined with plants representing the duke's family. Children (and curious adults) will enjoy the climb up to see the restored red-velvet-lined latrine, a state-of-the-art comfort in its time. Kitschy costumed mannequins and medieval-themed exhibits covering subjects from food to furniture to hygiene lend the tower added kid appeal. Be sure to ask for English information at the entry. Note that it's open in the afternoon only. ☒ *20 rue Étienne Marcel, 2e, Louvre* ☎ *01-40-26-20-28* ⊕ *www.tourjeansanspeur.com*

✉ *€6* ♡ *Closed mornings and Mon. and Tues.* Ⓜ *Étienne Marcel.*

★ **Tour Saint-Jacques** (*Saint-Jacques Tower*)

VIEWPOINT | For centuries, this 170-foot bell tower guided pilgrims to a starting point of the Chemin de St-Jacques (Way of Saint James). Built in 1508 in the Flamboyant Gothic style, it's all that remains of the Église St-Jacques-de-la-Boucherie, which was destroyed in the French Revolution. Purchased by the city in 1836, the tower languished until a three-year renovation, completed in 2009, restored 660 tons of stone and statues, including the gargoyles hanging from the upper reaches and the figure of Saint James gracing the top. Blaise Pascal was among the medieval scientists who conducted experiments here (his involved gravity), which is why his statue sits at the base. If you wish to enter the tower, guided tours are occasionally offered in spring, summer, and early fall by reservation only. ☒ *39 rue de Rivoli, 2e, Louvre* ⊕ *boutique.toursaintjacques.fr* ✉ *Tours €12* ♡ *Closed Mon.–Thurs. and mid-Nov.–Apr.* Ⓜ *Châtelet.*

🍽 Restaurants

A l'Epi d'Or

$$$ | FRENCH | Jean-François Piège has breathed new life into A l'Epi d'Or, harking back to the 1920s, when Paris was filled with delightful classic bistros. The allure of the old-fashioned zinc bar, tiled floor, and dark wood tables invites you in; the mastery of authentic French cuisine begs you to stay. **Known for:** simple and straightforward prix-fixe menu; daily comfort-food specials; homey, traditional dining room. ◻ *Average main: €30* ☒ *25 rue Jean-Jacques Rousseau, 1er, Louvre* ☎ *01-42-36-38-12* ⊕ *www.alepidorparis.com* ♡ *Closed weekends* Ⓜ *Louvre–Rivoli.*

Au Rocher de Cancale

$$ | **FRENCH** | As its impressive facade attests, this café has a special history. It opened in 1846, when Balzac was a regular, and Rue Montorgueil was *the* place to buy oysters, though these days, the menu is more modern with salads, burgers, and brunch options, as well as a handful of classics like escargots and French onion soup. **Known for:** all-day service from 8 am to 2 am; sidewalk café with views over the bustling Rue Montorgueil; lovely dining room with panels showing scenes of 18th-century life. ⑤ *Average main: €22* ✉ *78 rue Montorgueil, 2e, Louvre* ☎ *01–42–33–50–29* Ⓜ *Les Halles.*

Bistrot Vivienne

$$$ | **FRENCH** | Set in the Galerie Vivienne, Paris's loveliest covered passage, this charmingly authentic 19th-century bistro feels both cozy and welcoming, and the food and drink are well above average. With all-day hours as well as a double terrace either inside Galerie Vivienne or on a picturesque street a few steps from the Palais Royal gardens, this is a satisfying spot for a quick coffee or glass of wine, a snack, or a full meal. **Known for:** all-day service until 11 pm; great location in the Galerie Vivienne; a handful of good vegetarian options. ⑤ *Average main: €25* ✉ *4 rue des Petits Champs, 2e, Louvre* ☎ *01–49–27–00–50* ⊕ *www.bistrotvivienne.com* Ⓜ *Bourse, Palais-Royal–Musée du Louvre.*

Café Lapérouse

$$$$ | **FRENCH** | A charming and much less infamous version of its sumptuous mothership—the legendary 250-year-old Parisian restaurant Lapérouse—this light-drenched café, housed within the beautiful Hôtel de la Marine, has all the romance of a 19th-century luxury cruseliner bound for exotic shores: plush banquettes in sorbet colors, glittering chandeliers, and touches from faraway places. It's equally wonderful for breakfast, lunch, dinner, teatime, or even a quick cocktail, indoors or on the colonnaded terrace facing Place de la Concorde or the mansion's elegant courtyard. **Known for:** bistro classics like escargots and French onion soup; menu studded with luxe ingredients like truffle and caviar; great location on Place de la Concorde. ⑤ *Average main: €40* ✉ *Hôtel de la Marine, 2 pl. de la Concorde, 8e, Louvre* ☎ *01–53–93–65–53* ⊕ *www.cafelaperouse.com* Ⓜ *Concorde.*

Café Marly

$$$ | **CAFÉ** | Run by the Costes family, this café overlooking the main courtyard of the Louvre and its famous glass pyramid is a stylish place to meet for a drink or a coffee, whether in the chic, jewel-toned dining rooms or on the Louvre's long, sheltered terrace. Regular café service shuts down during meal times, when fashion-conscious folks dig into a blend of classic bistro fare like steak tartare or duck foie gras and lighter, more international options like tom yum Chilean sea bass or kale salad with quinoa and avocado. **Known for:** a see-and-be-seen atmosphere; great views of the Louvre; all-day hours. ⑤ *Average main: €30* ✉ *Cour Napoléon du Louvre, enter from Louvre courtyard, 93 rue de Rivoli, 1er, Louvre* ☎ *01–49–26–06–60* ⊕ *cafe-marly.com* Ⓜ *Palais-Royal.*

Chez Georges

$$$$ | **BISTRO** | If you were to ask Parisian bankers, aristocrats, or antiques dealers to name their favorite bistro for a three-hour weekday lunch, many would choose Chez Georges. The traditional fare is very good, particularly the massive céleri remoulade or salade lyonnaise meant for sharing, as well as the offal ranging from liver to sweetbreads. **Known for:** excellent wine list including options by the glass; handwritten menu of French bistro classics; friendly, affable service. ⑤ *Average main: €40* ✉ *1 rue du Mail, 2e, Louvre* ☎ *01–42–60–07–11* ⊕ *www.facebook.com/chezgeorges1965* ♡ *Closed weekends, Aug., and 1 wk at Christmas* Ⓜ *Sentier.*

Ellsworth

$$$ | **FRENCH FUSION** | This spot is on Ina Garten's must-visit list in Paris, and it's not hard to see why. The succinct menu of seasonal cuisine is fresh and light, served in a simple dining room with lovely decor including wooden windowpanes and white marble tables. **Known for:** slight American accents on a contemporary French menu; delicious plant-based options; Paris's best fried chicken. **§** *Average main: €26* ✉ *34 rue de Richelieu, 1er, Louvre* ☎ *01–42–60–59–66* ⊕ *www.ellsworthparis.com* ♡ *Closed Sun.–Tues. No lunch* Ⓜ *Pyramides.*

★ Juvéniles

$$$ | **WINE BAR** | A favorite with the French and expats alike, this neighborhood bistro blends great dining with an inspired wine list and a handy location a stone's throw from the Louvre. Exquisite French ingredients are given an inspired, often slightly lighter, makeover by Chef Romain Roudeau, although hearty house-made terrines and foie gras as well as slow-cooked meat and game are frequently featured on the eclectic menu. **Known for:** great cheese selection from Neal's Yard and neighboring Madame Hisada; phenomenal wine selection on-site and takeaway; small space, so best to reserve in advance. **§** *Average main: €30* ✉ *47 rue de Richelieu, 1er, Louvre* ☎ *01–42–97–46–49* ⊕ *www.juvenile-swinebar.com* ♡ *Closed Sun. and Mon.* Ⓜ *Bourse, Pyramides.*

La Dame de Pic

$$$$ | **FRENCH** | This Michelin-starred establishment from Anne-Sophie Pic features a Provençal-accented tasting menu of specialties from the chef's native Valence, with produce-driven dishes and Southern cheeses. The dining room leans into the chef's feminine side, with pale pink accenting the cozy space otherwise decked out in leather and wood. **Known for:** open Sunday and Monday, when many other top establishments are closed; four-, five-, and seven-course prix-fixe menus with wine pairings; steps from the Louvre. **§** *Average main: €95* ✉ *20 rue du Louvre, 1er, Louvre* ☎ *01–42–60–40–40* ⊕ *www.anne-sophie-pic.com.*

La Poule au Pot

$$$$ | **FRENCH** | When Jean-François Piège took over this restaurant overlooking the former Les Halles market, he gave it a much-needed makeover while also retaining its vintage appeal. Slide into one of the red leather banquettes and peruse the menu of exquisite upscale bistro classics hailing from the height of bourgeois bistro fare (the 19th century through the 1950s) with prices to match. **Known for:** superb French classics, like frogs' legs and French onion soup; namesake "poule au pot"—stewed hen made from a recipe dating to 1935—to share; house-made tarts for dessert. **§** *Average main: €44* ✉ *9 rue Vauvilliers, 1er, Louvre* ☎ *01–42–36–32–96* ⊕ *jeanfrançoispiege.com/la-poule-au-pot* ♡ *Closed Sun. and Mon.* Ⓜ *Louvre–Rivoli.*

L'Ardoise

$$$ | **BISTRO** | Don't let the chic, updated decor fool you: this tiny, reliable bistro hasn't sacrificed substance for style. The servers are friendly, the wine list is small but well-curated, and the dining is first-rate, with a three-course dinner menu (you can order à la carte, but it's less of a bargain) of original dishes marrying terroir-driven ingredients like Charolais beef or farm-raised chicken from the Landes with contemporary touches and pretty plating. **Known for:** good-value prix-fixe menus; ever-changing traditional fare with contemporary twists; can be noisy and crowded due to its popularity. **§** *Average main: €32* ✉ *28 rue du Mont Thabor, 1er, Louvre* ☎ *01–42–96–28–18* ⊕ *www.lardoise-paris.com* ♡ *Closed Sun. and Mon.* Ⓜ *Concorde.*

★ La Régalade Saint-Honoré

$$$$ | **MODERN FRENCH** | After taking over the original La Régalade, chef Bruno Doucet kept some of what made the old

restaurant so popular (country terrines, reasonably priced wines, convivial atmosphere), but he also had a few tricks under his toque, notably creating a successful haute-cuisine-meets-comfort-food destination. With its reasonable €55 prix-fixe menu, this chic bistro has evolved into a staple of the neighborhood. **Known for:** contemporary dishes with international flair like tuna tartare, vitello tonnato, or slow-cooked veal; comfort food desserts like rice pudding or soufflé; interesting vegetarian options. **§** *Average main: €55* ✉ *123 rue St-Honoré, 1er, Louvre* ☎ *01–42–21–92–40* 🌐 *www.laregalade.paris* ⊘ *Closed Sun. and Mon.* Ⓜ *Louvre–Rivoli.*

Le Fumoir

$$$$ | **FRENCH** | Equal parts café, bar, and restaurant, Le Fumoir is a timelessly popular place to sip coffee and read the paper or enjoy an after-dinner drink. Reservations are recommended for the prix-fixe dinner as well as for the copious Sunday brunch from chef Henrik Andersson. **Known for:** good vegetarian options; reasonable prix-fixe menus at lunch, dinner, and brunch; French fare with slightly Scandinavian influences. **§** *Average main: €40* ✉ *Pl. du Louvre, 6 rue de l'Amiral-Coligny, 1er, Louvre* ☎ *01–42–92–00–24* 🌐 *www.lefumoir.com* Ⓜ *Louvre–Rivoli.*

Le Grand Colbert

$$$ | **BRASSERIE** | **FAMILY** | With its globe lamps and molded ceilings, this neighborhood institution feels elegant yet not overpolished, attracting a wonderfully Parisian mix of elderly lone diners, business lunchers, tourists, couples, and the posttheater crowd, all of whom come for the enormous seafood platters, duck foie gras with Sauternes jelly, steak tartare, and roasted chicken rendered famous by Diane Keaton in *Something's Gotta Give*. Open every day, Le Grand Colbert is also a pleasant destination for a quick bite between 3 pm and 6 pm, when most everything else is closed and the restaurant offers a French-style tea time complete with a pastry. **Known for:** towering seafood platters; standout historic decor and ambience; delightful roast chicken. **§** *Average main: €30* ✉ *2 rue Vivienne, 2e, Louvre* ☎ *01–42–86–87–88* 🌐 *www.legrandcolbert.fr* Ⓜ *Bourse.*

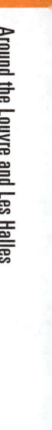

★ Le Grand Véfour

$$$$ | **MODERN FRENCH** | One of the area's most historic (and romantic) spots has welcomed everyone from Napoléon to Colette to Jean Cocteau beneath its mirrored ceiling and is still a contender for the most beautiful restaurant in Paris. This once-Michelin-starred spot has made a few changes of late, transitioning to a menu of far more reasonable (but still delicious) fare. **Known for:** gorgeous outdoor terrace overlooking the Palais Royal gardens; sumptuous historic decor dating from the 18th century; prix-fixe menu including an ever-changing plat du jour. **§** *Average main: €40* ✉ *17 rue de Beaujolais, 1er, Louvre* ☎ *01–42–96–56–27* 🌐 *www.grand-vefour.com* ⊘ *Closed Sun. and Mon.* Ⓜ *Palais-Royal.*

Macéo

$$$ | **MODERN FRENCH** | With a reasonably priced set menu, this restaurant from the owners of Willi's Wine Bar is an ideal spot for a relaxed meal after visiting the Louvre. Natural light streams through the interior, and a broad, curved staircase leads to a spacious upstairs salon: the perfect place to enjoy the seasonally motivated menu. **Known for:** modern, market-driven French fare; phenomenal wine list; convenient to the Louvre and Palais Royal gardens. **§** *Average main: €28* ✉ *15 rue des Petits-Champs, 1er, Louvre* ☎ *01–85–15–22–56* 🌐 *www.maceorestaurant.com* ⊘ *Closed Sun. and 3 wks in Aug. No lunch Sat.* Ⓜ *Palais-Royal.*

Maxim's de Paris

$$$$ | **FRENCH** | In Belle Époque Paris, Maxim's de Paris was known for being the spot where well-heeled gentlemen brought their favorite mistresses, and it long attracted a veritable who's who of

Parisians and foreign Francophiles. After falling into relative obsolescence during Pierre Cardin's three decades of ownership, hospitality group the Paris Society gave it a much-needed facelift in 2023; now the Art Nouveau institution retains its velvet banquettes, stained glass statement walls, and gorgeous light fixtures and boasts a menu of revitalized French classics. **Known for:** cocktail list calling out famous former regulars like Streisand, Hepburn, and Onassis; tableside service of French classics like excellent sole Albert or flambéed crêpes Suzette; regular music acts crooning love ballads on the central stage. ⑤ *Average main: €50* ✉ *3 rue Royale, 8e, Louvre* ☎ *01–42–65–27–94* 🌐 *www.restaurant-maxims.com* Ⓜ *Concorde.*

★ Mimosa

$$$$ | **FRENCH** | Two-Michelin-star chef Jean-François Piège is inspired by the Mediterranean Sea in this romantic dining room, the former stables of the mansion-turned-museum that is the Hôtel de la Marine. Floor-to-ceiling mirrors add grandeur to the soaring space, where a wood-fired oven turns out delicacies from land and sea. **Known for:** delightful grilled seafood designed to share; solid vegetarian options; whole menu of egg "mimosa" (deviled eggs) in a nod to the restaurant's name. ⑤ *Average main: €45* ✉ *2 rue Royale, 8e, Louvre* ☎ *01–53–93–65–52* 🌐 *www.mimosa-rueroyale.com* Ⓜ *Concorde, Madeleine.*

★ Omar Dhiab

$$$$ | **FRENCH FUSION** | Omar Dhiab's eponymous restaurant breaks with fine dining codes from the get-go: open the door to the restaurant, and you'll immediately come upon the open kitchen, where the young chef presides in jeans under his pressed chef's jacket. The laid-back ambience pervades the plain, bright dining room, where Dhaib's mastery of balancing bitter and sour is centerstage. **Known for:** more laid-back atmosphere than in most Michelin-starred spots; engaging

cuisine with a surprising approach to luxury French ingredients; wide selection of natural wines. ⑤ *Average main: €118* ✉ *23 rue Herold, 1er, Louvre* ☎ *01–42–33–52–47* 🌐 *www.omardhiab.com* ◎ *Closed weekends* Ⓜ *Bourse.*

★ Restaurant du Palais-Royal

$$$$ | **FRENCH** | This stylish restaurant serves stunning gourmet cuisine to match its gorgeous location under the arcades of the Palais-Royal. Philip Chronopoulos's Michelin-starred prix-fixe menus often revolve around exquisite seafood, but there are also lovely meat-based options. **Known for:** mainly Mediterranean-accented choices; nostalgic amuse bouches from a young Greek chef; baba au rhum that evolves with the seasons. ⑤ *Average main: €75* ✉ *Jardins du Palais-Royal, 110 Galerie Valois, 1er, Louvre* ☎ *01–40–20–00–27* 🌐 *palaisroyal-restaurant.com* ◎ *Closed weekends. No lunch Mon. and Tues.* Ⓜ *Palais-Royal.*

★ Verjus

$$$$ | **FRENCH** | One of the most creative yet affordable tasting menus awaits at this restaurant founded by American husband-and-wife team Braden Perkins and Laura Adrian. The €98 prix-fixe menu sees plant-forward, seasonally driven food paired with a modern selection of wines. **Known for:** product-driven contemporary French cuisine; very accommodating kitchen for dietary issues; wine list heavy on organic and biodynamic producers. ⑤ *Average main: €98* ✉ *52 rue de Richelieu, Louvre* ☎ *01–42–97–54–40* 🌐 *www.verjusparis.com* ◎ *Closed weekends* Ⓜ *Pyramides.*

Willi's Wine Bar

$$ | **MODERN FRENCH** | More restaurant than wine bar, this British-owned spot is a stylish haunt for Parisians and visiting gourmands who might stop in for a glass of wine at the oak bar or settle into the wood-beamed dining room. The selection of reinvented classic dishes changes daily and in accordance with the seasons. **Known for:** upscale expat hangout; fine choice of wines by the glass; good-value, three-course, prix-fixe menu. **$** *Average main: €22* ✉ *13 rue des Petits-Champs, 1er, Louvre* ☎ *01–42–61–05–09* 🌐 *www.willisweinebar.com* ⊘ *Closed Sun.* Ⓜ *Bourse.*

★ Yam'Tcha

$$$$ | **FRENCH FUSION** | Dishes at this Michelin-starred spot rely on Chinese flavors and very precise techniques. They're paired with teas by the tea sommelier, who introduces diners to earthy or grassy flavors that complement the €170 prix-fixe menu.✉✉ **Known for:** rare and unique tea pairings; one of Paris's star chefs, Adeline Grattard; close to the Louvre and Centre Pompidou. **$** *Average main: €170* ✉ *121 rue St. Honoré, 1er, Louvre* ☎ *01–40–26–08–07* 🌐 *www.yamtcha.com* ⊘ *Closed Sun. and Mon.* Ⓜ *Louvre–Rivoli, Les Halles.*

Zen

$$ | **JAPANESE** | There's no shortage of Japanese restaurants around the Louvre, but this one is a cut above much of the competition. The menu has something for every palate, from warming *donburi* to sushi and sashimi. **Known for:** good value, especially at lunchtime; plentiful seating; bright, modern space. **$** *Average main: €20* ✉ *8 rue de l'Echelle, 1er, Louvre* ☎ *01–42–61–93–99* 🌐 *www.zenrestaurantparis.fr* ⊘ *Closed Sun.* Ⓜ *Pyramides, Palais-Royal.*

 Coffee and Quick Bites

★ Angelina

$$ | **CAFÉ** | Founded in 1903 and patronized by literary luminaries like Marcel Proust and Gertrude Stein, Angelina is famous for its *chocolat "l'Africain"*—an ultrarich hot chocolate topped with whipped cream. The beautiful chestnut "Mont Blanc" pastry is the ideal accompaniment. **Known for:** the most famous hot chocolate in Paris; opulent, Belle Époque setting; long but quick moving line to get in. **$** *Average main: €22* ✉ *226 rue*

de Rivoli, 1er, Louvre ☎ *01–42–60–82–00* 🌐 *www.angelina-paris.fr* Ⓜ *Tuileries.*

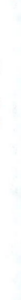

Café Kitsuné

$ | **CAFÉ** | This Japanese-inspired minichain of coffeehouses is the place to be seen during Paris Fashion Week. There are four locations in Paris: one at 208 rue de Rivoli, one at 2 place André Malraux with a full restaurant menu, one at 30 rue du Vertbois that also serves as a roastery, and this one—the original and persistent favorite, thanks in large part to the views over the Palais Royal gardens. **Known for:** branded apparel and coffee mugs; iced matcha lattes perfect for cooling down in summer; tasty cakes like shortbread, brownies, and babka including gluten-free options. **$** *Average main: €5* ✉ *51 galerie Montpensier, 1er, Louvre* ☎ *01–40–15–62–31* 🌐 *www.maisonkitsune.com* Ⓜ *Palais-Royal–Louvre.*

Maison Kayser

$ | **SANDWICHES** | **FAMILY** | Once you're done with the Louvre, this little sandwich stand adjacent to the Arc de Triomphe du Carrousel is probably the closest spot to snag something to restore you. Classic French sandwiches like ham-and-butter or tuna salad are served on fluffy baguettes reminiscent of ciabatta. **Known for:** good lunch deal that includes a sandwich, drink, and dessert; outdoor seating overlooking the Arc de Triomphe du Carrousel and the Tuileries; inexpensive prices, especially for the area. **$** *Average main: €7* ✉ *Pl. du Carrousel, 1er, Louvre* ☎ *01–40–15–01–31* 🌐 *www.maison-kayser.com* Ⓜ *Palais-Royal–Louvre.*

Terres de Café

$ | **COFFEE** | This small coffee chain was founded in 2009 by Christophe Servell, an award-winning French roaster, and today boasts Europe's largest specialty coffee range. Known for its sustainable approach to sourcing and roasting, it has a handful of pocket-size shops in the French capital tailored less to lingering than to tasting the wares before buying a bag or two to brew at home. **Known**

for: high-quality coffee beans; coffee workshops; excellent espresso drinks. ⓘ *Average main: €5* ✉ *150 rue St-Honoré, 1er, Louvre* ☎ *09–86–51–02–00* ⓦ *www.terresdecafe.com* Ⓜ *Louvre-Rivoli.*

Verjus Bar à Vins

$ | **WINE BAR** | On a nearly hidden street behind the Palais Royal gardens, this tiny wine bar invites customers to perch on metal stools at a narrow bar and enjoy a small but choice selection of wines by the glass and some very good bar snacks like top-notch olives or local Paris ham. Although not a substitute for dinner, it's great for a drink and a nosh on your way to or from somewhere else, including the excellent restaurant upstairs. **Known for:** good selection of wines by the glass; English-speaking expat hangout; atmospheric cellar setting. ⓘ *Average main: €7* ✉ *47 rue Montpensier, 1e, Louvre* ☎ *01–42–97–54–40* ⓦ *verjusparis.com* ⓒ *Closed weekends. No lunch* Ⓜ *Palais Royal–Musée du Louvre.*

Hotels

★ Grand Hotel du Palais Royal

$$$ | **HOTEL** | Despite its splashy name, this gracious five-star hotel keeps a surprisingly relaxed profile. **Pros:** wonderful seasonal cuisine (including vegetarian options) indoors and out at Café 52; an island of quiet and calm in a bustling neighborhood; great location steps from the Louvre and Palais Royal. **Cons:** not all rooms come with balconies; no pool; small fitness room. ⓘ *Rooms from: €425* ✉ *4 rue de Valois, 1er, Louvre* ☎ *01–42–96–15–35* ⓦ *www.grandhoteldupalais-royal.com* ↝ *59 rooms* 🍴 *No Meals* Ⓜ *Palais Royal–Musée du Louvre.*

Hôtel Brighton

$$ | **HOTEL** | **FAMILY** | A few of the city's most prestigious hotels face the Tuileries or Place de la Concorde, but the 19th-century Brighton occupies the same prime real estate and offers a privileged stay for a less daunting price. **Pros:**

on-site bar with cheese and charcuterie platters; tea salon serving pastries from Kevin Lacote weekends from September through April; great room service in collaboration with top chefs. **Cons:** some areas in need of repair; only half of rooms have a view; no restaurant on-site. ⓘ *Rooms from: €280* ✉ *218 rue de Rivoli, 1er, Louvre* ☎ *01–47–03–61–61* ⓦ *www.paris-hotel-brighton.com* ↝ *63 rooms* 🍴 *No Meals* Ⓜ *Tuileries.*

Hôtel Britannique

$ | **HOTEL** | Open since 1861, just a stone's throw from the Louvre and near the banks of the Seine, the romantic Britannique blends courteous English service with old-fashioned French elegance. **Pros:** on calm side street; air-conditioning in all rooms; copious breakfast buffet for a reasonable fee. **Cons:** small rooms; soundproofing could be better; decor a bit stodgy. ⓘ *Rooms from: €160* ✉ *20 av. Victoria, 1er, Louvre* ☎ *01–42–33–74–59* ⓦ *www.hotel-britannique.fr* ↝ *39 rooms* 🍴 *No Meals* Ⓜ *Châtelet.*

Hôtel Crayon

$ | **HOTEL** | Managed by artists, this hotel near the Louvre stands out thanks to its eclectic pop-art decor—expect an unusual canvas of local and international guests that's just as colorful. **Pros:** hand-painted graffiti walls; very friendly staff; curated and curious mix of modern objets d'art. **Cons:** small bathrooms; bold design might not be to all tastes; lobby lounge lacks coziness and warmth. ⓘ *Rooms from: €137* ✉ *25 rue du Bouloi, 1er, Louvre* ☎ *01–42–36–54–19* ⓦ *www.hotelcrayon.com* ↝ *26 rooms* 🍴 *No Meals* Ⓜ *Louvre.*

★ Hôtel de Crillon

$$$$ | **HOTEL** | One of the city's most historic properties reopened in 2017 after a four-year renovation and is now more sumptuous and majestic than ever. **Pros:** "Grands Appartements" designed by Karl Lagerfeld; well-equipped gym with personal trainers available on request; beautiful bar with a mile-long Champagne list. **Cons:** small pool with tough-to-find changing rooms; extra beds not available in smaller rooms; very expensive. ▌ *Rooms from: €1,810* ✉ *10 pl. de la Concorde, 8e, Louvre* ☎ *01–44–71–15–00* ⊕ *www.rosewoodhotels.com* ↝ *124 rooms* 🍴 *No Meals* Ⓜ *Concorde.*

★ Hôtel du Continent

$ | HOTEL | You'd be hard-pressed to find a budget hotel this stylish anywhere in Paris, let alone in an upscale neighborhood close to many of the city's top attractions. **Pros:** very friendly staff; all modern amenities; prime Parisian location just steps from Rue St-Honoré, arguably the city's best shopping street. **Cons:** no lobby; tiny bathrooms; bold decor not for everyone. ▌ *Rooms from: €159* ✉ *30 rue du Mont-Thabor, 1er, Louvre* ☎ *01–42–60–75–32* ⊕ *www.hotelcontinent.com* ↝ *25 rooms* 🍴 *No Meals* Ⓜ *Concorde, Tuileries.*

Hôtel Konfidentiel

$$ | HOTEL | FAMILY | Sleep beneath the preguillotined head of Marie-Antoinette or amid the turmoil of the French Revolution in one of six individually themed rooms, including the Eiffel duplex suite with a stately spiral staircase. **Pros:** terrific location near the Louvre; comfortable, unique rooms; friendly staff. **Cons:** can feel a bit enclosed; no bathtubs in bathrooms; kitschy decor doesn't suit every taste. ▌ *Rooms from: €270* ✉ *64 rue de l'Arbre Sec, 1er, Louvre* ☎ *01–55–34–40–40* ⊕ *www.konfidentiel-paris.com* ↝ *6 rooms* 🍴 *No Meals* Ⓜ *Louvre–Rivoli.*

★ Hôtel La Tamise

$$ | HOTEL | In 1878, what was a stately home owned by a noble French family was converted to an intimate hotel favored by aristocrats and, later, fashion icons. **Pros:** location on a quiet street in the heart of Paris; just steps from superlative shopping; free Mariage Frères teas on arrival. **Cons:** small lobby; no balconies; limited views of the Tuileries. ▌ *Rooms from: €219* ✉ *4 rue d'Alger, 1er, Louvre* ☎ *01–40–41–14–14* ⊕ *www.paris-hotel-la-tamise.com* ↝ *19 rooms* 🍴 *No Meals* Ⓜ *Tuileries, Concorde.*

★ Hôtel Le Meurice

$$$$ | HOTEL | FAMILY | Since 1835, Paris's first palace hotel has welcomed royalty and celebrities from the Duchess of Windsor to Salvador Dalí and continues to enchant with service, style, and views. **Pros:** stunning art and architecture; views over the Tuileries gardens; Michelin-starred dining. **Cons:** some amenities lacking like in-room coffee machine; front-desk service at times inattentive; very expensive. ▌ *Rooms from: €1,775* ✉ *228 rue de Rivoli, 1er, Louvre* ☎ *01–44–58–10–09* ⊕ *www.dorchestercollection.com* ↝ *208 rooms* 🍴 *No Meals* Ⓜ *Tuileries, Concorde.*

Hôtel Le Pradey

$$ | HOTEL | This compact boutique hotel near the Tuileries has a luxe feel, paying homage to Parisian style with rooms split between traditional *chambres* and Paris-theme suites like the Louvre and Grand Palais. **Pros:** choice of copious breakfast buffet or quick coffee and croissant; in-room massage services available; simple room service available 24 hours a day. **Cons:** smaller rooms lack closet space; rooms vary greatly in style; breakfast is relatively basic for the price. ▌ *Rooms from: €297* ✉ *5 rue St-Roch, 1er, Louvre* ☎ *01–42–60–31–70* ⊕ *www.lepradey.com* ↝ *28 rooms* 🍴 *No Meals* Ⓜ *Tuileries.*

Hôtel Louvre Sainte-Anne

$ | HOTEL | You can walk to many major sites from this small, low-key, budget property located between the Opéra and the Louvre. **Pros:** convenient location; hot-and-cold breakfast buffet (for a fee) served in a stone-vaulted cellar; reduced-mobility room available. **Cons:** very small rooms; district can feel un-Parisian; breakfast area slightly claustrophobic. ▌ *Rooms from: €167* ✉ *32 rue Ste-Anne, 1er, Louvre* ☎ *01–40–20–02–35* ⊕ *www.paris-hotel-louvre.com* ↝ *20 rooms* 🍴 *No Meals* Ⓜ *Pyramides.*

Apartment Rentals

If you favor extra space plus that special feeling of living like a local, try renting a Paris apartment. Rentals can also offer savings, especially for groups.

Check out the **Paris Tourism Office** website (@ *parisjetaime.com/eng*) for reputable agency listings. Policies differ, but you can expect a minimum required stay ranging from three to seven days, a refundable deposit payable on arrival, a possible agency fee, and maid and linen service. The following is a list of property hunters, good-value and luxury apartments, and apartment services.

Paris Perfect (@ *parisperfect.com*) manages more than 100 apartments in varying sizes around Paris, mostly on the Left Bank in the upscale 7e arrondissement. Many apartments, which are designed to feel like your very own chic pied-à-terre, have Eiffel Tower views. Luxury services,

like concierge and gourmet food tours, are often available. **Cattalan Johnson** (@ *cattalanjohnson.com*) is an established, fee-based agency specializing in rental properties. The multilingual staff has a citywide inventory of thousands of furnished apartments available for durations ranging from one week to a few years. **Citadines Apart Hotel** (☎ 01-41-05-79-05 @ *www.discoverasr.com/en/citadines*) is a chain of apartment-style hotel accommodations. They're somewhat generic but offer many services and are a good value for short stays. **Paris Attitude** (☎ 01-42-96-31-46 @ *parisattitude.com*) offers a large selection of furnished rentals, from studios to five-bedroom units, for stays from a week to a year. **Paris Vacation Apartments** (☎ 06-63-60-67-14 @ *parisvacationapartments.com*) specializes in luxury rentals, with all-inclusive prices by the week.

Hôtel Thérèse

$ | **HOTEL** | Tucked away from the traffic and crowds of Avenue de l'Opéra, this five-floor hotel named after the wife of Louis XIV is a stone's throw from regal sites like the Louvre, Palais Royal, and the historic Comédie Française theater. **Pros:** on a quiet street; cozy, charming rooms; breakfast (for a fee) can be served in room. **Cons:** rooms are relatively small for price; breakfast area located in basement; no restaurant or gym. ⓘ *Rooms from: €180* ✉ *5/7 rue Thérèse, 1er, Louvre* ☎ *01-42-96-10-01* @ *www.hoteltherese.com* ➜ *40 rooms* 🍴 *No Meals* Ⓜ *Pyramides.*

 Madame Rêve

$$$$ | **HOTEL** | You'll have the Eiffel Tower, Sacré Coeur, or the beautiful Église Saint-Eustache as your view for the night

from the arching atelier-style windows of your swanky room at this elegant hotel set in the city's beautifully restored 19th-century Louvre post office. **Pros:** refined decor in rooms and restaurants; rooftop restaurant from two-Michelin-starred chef Stéphanie Le Quellec; excellent location and views. **Cons:** hallways are long (but lovely); music a tad loud in the restaurant; indifferent service in the café. ⓘ *Rooms from: €530* ✉ *48 rue du Louvre, 1er, Louvre* ☎ *01-80-40-77-70* @ *www.madamereve.com* ➜ *82 rooms* 🍴 *No Meals* Ⓜ *Louvre-Rivoli, Châtelet-Les-Halles, Étienne Marcel.*

 Mandarin Oriental Paris

$$$$ | **HOTEL** | Of Paris's palace hotels, the Mandarin Oriental is among the most contemporary, with a soaring marble entryway and a sleek, luxe style that is a

welcome contrast to the historic grande dames. **Pros:** superlative hotel spa (contender for Paris's very best); many rooms with terraces; two gourmet restaurants helmed by Michelin-starred chef Thierry Marx. **Cons:** not much variation in standard rooms; noise from courtyard during special events; very pricey. ⑤ *Rooms from: €1,700* ✉ *251 rue St-Honore, 1er, Louvre* ☎ *01–70–98–78–88* ⊕ *www.mandarinoriental.com/paris* ↝ *135 rooms* 🍴 *No Meals* Ⓜ *Tuileries, Concorde.*

Meliá Vendôme

$$ | **HOTEL** | In a prestigious neighborhood a few minutes from the Jardin des Tuileries, Place de la Concorde, Opéra Garnier, and the Louvre, the Meliá Vendôme has handsome and spacious rooms that exude understated elegance. **Pros:** outstanding location in the city center; near world-class shopping; elegant, immaculate rooms. **Cons:** expensive breakfast; no spa or pool; in-room cooling system unreliable. ⑤ *Rooms from: €330* ✉ *8 rue Cambon, 1er, Louvre* ☎ *01–44–77–54–00* ⊕ *www.melia.com* ↝ *83 rooms* 🍴 *No Meals* Ⓜ *Concorde, Madeleine.*

★ Renaissance Paris Vendôme

$$$$ | **HOTEL** | **FAMILY** | Hiding behind a classic, 19th-century facade is this fresh, 1930s-influenced hotel, which was fully remodeled in 2018 by designer Didier Gomez. **Pros:** light-drenched suite and patio rooms with private terraces; trendy restaurant with Mediterranean-accented cuisine and 24-hour room service; full-service spa and fitness room. **Cons:** lacks authentic French character; public lounges noisy at times; packed with business groups. ⑤ *Rooms from: €506* ✉ *4 rue du Mont Thabor, 1er, Louvre* ☎ *01–40–20–20–00* ⊕ *www.marriott.com* ↝ *97 rooms* 🍴 *No Meals* Ⓜ *Tuileries.*

★ The Ritz

$$$$ | **HOTEL** | In novels, songs, and common parlance, there's not a word that evokes the romance and luxury of Paris better than the Ritz. **Pros:** spacious swimming pool; superlative selection of

bars and restaurants including a fantastic pastry counter; top-notch service. **Cons:** easy to get lost in the vast hotel; paparazzi magnet; astronomical prices. ⑤ *Rooms from: €2,100* ✉ *15 pl. Vendôme, 1er, Louvre* ☎ *01–43–16–30–30* ⊕ *www.ritzparis.com* ↝ *143 rooms* 🍴 *No Meals* Ⓜ *Opéra.*

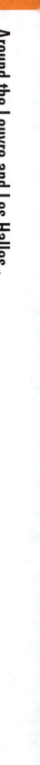

 Nightlife

BARS

Bar 8

BARS | The monolithic marble bar at the Mandarin Oriental Hotel offers an extensive Champagne list and a menu of international street food-inspired bar snacks. The outdoor terrace is especially busy during Fashion Weeks. ✉ *Mandarin Oriental Hotel Paris, 251 rue St-Honoré, 1er, Louvre* ☎ *01–70–98–78–88* ⊕ *www.mandarinoriental.com* Ⓜ *Concorde, Tuileries.*

Bar 228

BARS | Hôtel Le Meurice converted its ground-floor Fontainebleau library into the intimate Bar 228, with wood paneling and huge murals depicting the royal hunting forests of Fontainebleau. Its loyal fashion crowd is continually wooed by Philippe Starck's decor updates and lubricated with the bar's famous Bellinis. Try the Meurice Millennium cocktail, made with Champagne, rose liqueur, and Cointreau. ✉ *Hôtel Le Meurice, 228 rue de Rivoli, 1er, Louvre* ☎ *01–44–58–10–66* ⊕ *www.dorchestercollection.com* Ⓜ *Tuileries.*

★ Bar Hemingway & the Ritz Bar

BARS | Literature lovers, cocktail connoisseurs, and other drink-swilling devotees flock to these two iconic bars within the Ritz Hotel. A $400-million renovation happily didn't alter the chill vibe or the wood-paneled, club-chair decor of tiny Bar Hemingway. While mixologist mainstay and twice-named "Best Head Barman in the World" Colin Field departed the storied hotel in 2023, after 30 years behind the bar, he and his cocktails remain legendary. Try the Serendipity, the bar's most popular drink, combining Champagne with Calvados and mint. Across the elegant corridor, the more spacious Ritz Bar's 2021 renovation paved the way for an astrologically themed experience. In a style evoking Belle Époque Paris, the space's circular bar is topped by a monumental lantern whose projection of stars and constellations begins each evening at 5:30 exactly. Signature cocktails from new head bartender Romain de Courcy are built around one ingredient, like Corn made with Mexican corn whisky, ancestral corn liqueur, freeze-dried corn, and popcorn, or Grape made with white grape eau de vie, Pisco, grappa, clarified red grape juice, rosé reduction, and Syrah vinegar. ✉ *The Ritz Paris, 15 pl. Vendôme, 1er, Louvre* ☎ *01-43-16-33-74* 🌐 *www.ritzparis.com* Ⓜ *Opéra.*

★ Experimental Cocktail Club

BARS | Fashioned as a speakeasy on a tiny brick-paved street, this was one of the first bars to bring the cocktail revolution to Paris. Colorful, innovative, and ever-changing drinks are mixed with aplomb by friendly (and attractive) bartenders. By 11 pm, the bar is always packed with a mix of locals, professionals, and fashionistas. ✉ *37 rue St-Sauveur, 2e, Louvre* ☎ *01-45-08-88-09* 🌐 *www.experimentalgroup.com* Ⓜ *Réamur-Sébastopol.*

Hôtel Costes

BARS | Despite years on the scene, the bar at Hôtel Costes still draws big names—and not just during fashion weeks. Expect to cross paths with anyone from Rihanna to Leonardo DiCaprio (as long as you make it past the chilly greeting of the statuesque hostess) to enjoy classic cocktails and downtempo music from an ever-changing roster of DJs. Dressing to kill is strongly advised, especially for newcomers; otherwise,

expect all the tables to be suddenly reserved. ✉ *Hôtel Costes, 239 rue St-Honoré, Louvre* ☎ *01-42-44-50-50* 🌐 *hotelcostes.com* Ⓜ *Tuileries.*

Jefrey's

BARS | A custom-DJ'd soundtrack, enticing love seats, and truly inventive cocktails make this an easy choice for an intimate evening in sophisticated surroundings. Need further incentive to return? Jefrey's lets you keep your bottle stored on the shelf, with your name on it, for next time. ✉ *14 rue St-Sauveur, 2e, Louvre* ☎ *01-42-33-60-77* Ⓜ *Étienne Marcel.*

L'Assaggio Bar

BARS | At this gracious bar and tea salon in the Hôtel Castille (Coco Chanel's old stomping grounds), enjoy a selection of French and Italian wines or a glass of Champagne alongside an all-day menu of Italian-accented nibbles. ✉ *Hôtel Castille, 37 rue Cambon, 1er, Louvre* ☎ *01-44-58-44-58* 🌐 *www.castille.com* Ⓜ *Concorde, Madeleine.*

Le Café Noir

BARS | Parisians from *bobos* (bourgeois-bohemians) to *pompiers* (firefighters) are lured to Le Café Noir's elegantly worn digs for organic coffee during the day or a glass of natural wine come evening. In addition to cool drinks and friendly staff, the place features a pipe-smoking papier-mâché fish and a vintage leopard-print-covered motorbike. (The restaurant with the same name is unrelated.) ✉ *65 rue Montmartre, 2e, Louvre* ☎ *01-40-39-07-36* Ⓜ *Étienne Marcel.*

Le Garde-Robe

WINE BAR | One of the first bars to bring natural wine to the capital, Le Garde-Robe unites a casual atmosphere and truly knowledgeable staff for a fun, funky experience steps from the Louvre. Order a platter of cheese or charcuterie to accompany your sulfite-free bottles, and take advantage of this bar with a neighborhood feel in the heart of the city. ✉ 41 rue de l'Arbre-Sec, 1er, Louvre ☎ 01–49–26–90–60 🌐 legarderobe.net Ⓜ Louvre–Rivoli.

★ **Les Ambassadeurs**

PIANO BAR | Located within the magnificent Hôtel de Crillon, Les Ambassadeurs is perhaps the closest you'll come to experiencing the royal treatment in a real palace—it was built by order of Louis XV in 1758. Sink into one of the cozy armchairs and enjoy a *coupe* of Champagne from a list as long as the marble walls are high, or select one of a curated list of signature cocktails. All the right touches are preserved, including a frescoed ceiling adorned with twinkling chandeliers and gilt—lots of it. Live music accompanies your evening Tuesday through Saturday starting at 8. ✉ *Hôtel de Crillon, 10 pl. de la Concorde, 8e, Louvre* ☎ 01–44–71–15–00 🌐 *www.rosewoodhotels.com* Ⓜ *Concorde.*

CLUBS

Kong

DANCE CLUB | This bar is glorious not only for its panoramic skyline views but also for its manga-inspired decor and kooky, disco-ball-and-kid-sumo-adorned bathrooms. A menu of Japanese-inspired fare is offered at the rooftop restaurant, and top-shelf DJs keep patrons dancing on weekends. Valet parking is available starting at 7:30 pm. Be sure to reserve a spot head of time to avoid disappointment. ✉ *1 rue du Pont Neuf, 1er, Louvre* ☎ 01–40–39–09–00 🌐 *www.kong.fr* Ⓜ *Pont Neuf.*

JAZZ CLUBS

Duc des Lombards

LIVE MUSIC | The Duc's cozy interior and top-class jazz acts make this iconic club one of the city's most popular small venues. It's best to purchase advance tickets online or arrive early to guarantee a spot at the twice-nightly concerts at 7:30 and 10. Jam sessions Friday and Saturday

begin at midnight and last until 4 am. ✉ *42 rue des Lombards, 1er, Louvre* ☎ 01–42–33–22–88 🌐 *www.ducdeslombards.com* Ⓜ *Châtelet–Les Halles.*

Sunset-Sunside

LIVE MUSIC | This two-part club hosts French and American jazz musicians: the Sunside upstairs is devoted mostly to acoustic jazz, while the Sunset downstairs features everything from electronic jazz, fusion, and groove to classic and swing. Jam sessions have been known to last well into the wee hours. ✉ *60 rue des Lombards, 1er, Louvre* ☎ 01–40–26–46–60 🌐 *www.sunset-sunside.com* Ⓜ *Châtelet–Les Halles.*

WINE BARS

Les Caves du Louvre

WINE BAR | This 18th-century wine cellar was built by Trudon, the sommelier to King Louis XV, and tastings here are truly an experience fit for royalty. Book in advance for a tasting, cheese pairing, or even a make-your-own-wine workshop. ✉ *52 rue de l'Arbre Sec, 1er, Louvre* ☎ 01–40–28–13–11 🌐 *www.cavesdulouvre.com* Ⓜ *Louvre–Rivoli.*

Ô Château

WINE BAR | This wine bar and tasting space is the go-to for Anglophones wanting to deepen their wine knowledge and refine their palates. With more than 1,000 options, 80% of which are organic, biodynamic, or vegan, it's ideal for sampling the best French vintages. Classes in wine tasting are offered, starting at €75 for an hour-long "Tour de France" in English, with more in-depth options available including cheese pairings and Champagne cruises. Although the restaurant is closed Sunday, tastings are available daily. ✉ *68 rue Jean-Jacques Rousseau, 1er, Louvre* ☎ 01–44–73–97–80 🌐 *www.o-chateau.com* Ⓜ *Étienne Marcel.*

 **Performing Arts**

★ Comédie Française

THEATER | Founded in 1680, the Comédie Française is the most hallowed institution in French theater. It specializes in splendid classical French plays by the likes of Racine, Molière, and Marivaux. Buy tickets at the box office, by telephone, or online. If the theater is sold out, the Salle Richelieu offers steeply discounted last-minute tickets an hour before each performance. ✉ *Salle Richelieu, Pl. Colette, 1er, Louvre* ☎ *01–44–58–15–15* ⊕ *www.comedie-francaise.fr* Ⓜ *Palais-Royal–Musée du Louvre.*

Le Forum des Images

FILM | The Forum organizes thematic viewings in five state-of-the-art screening rooms, often presenting discussions with directors or film experts beforehand. Archival films and videos, workshops, and lectures are also on the schedule here. Movie tickets cost €7.20, but roundtables, discussions, and access to the film library are free; you can also download the Forum app for smartphones. ✉ *Forum des Halles, 2 rue du Cinéma, 1er, Louvre* ☎ *01–44–76–63–00* ⊕ *www.forumdesimages.fr* ♡ *Closed Mon.* Ⓜ *Châtelet–Les Halles (St-Eustache exit).*

Théâtre du Palais-Royal

THEATER | **FAMILY** | Located in the former residence of Cardinal Richelieu, this plush, 716-seat, Italian-style theater is bedecked in gold and purple. It specializes in lighter fare, like comedies and theatrical productions aimed at the under-12 set. ✉ *38 rue de Montpensier, 1er, Louvre* ☎ *01–42–97–59–76* ⊕ *theatrepalaisroyal.com* Ⓜ *Palais-Royal.*

 **Shopping**

The flagship stores of big luxury brands rub elbows here with independent boutiques and concept stores notable for their fashion cachet. The fabulous Rue St-Honoré—a bastion of Parisian chic—is the area's retail spine, but the Marché St-Honoré and the Faubourg provide tempting detours. Whatever you do, don't miss the gorgeous Palais-Royal gardens, where flashy fashion stars mix with the discreet purveyors of handmade gloves.

BEAUTY

Anne Sémonin

SKINCARE | This boutique with its own spa sells tailor-made skincare products popular with top models. Products feature seaweed and trace elements as well as essential oils. ✉ *2 rue des Petits-Champs, 2e, Louvre* ☎ *01–42–60–94–66* ⊕ *www.annesemonin.com* Ⓜ *Palais-Royal–Louvre.*

By Terry

COSMETICS | This small, refined store is the brainchild of Terry de Gunzburg, Yves Saint Laurent's former director of makeup, whose brand of ready-to-wear cosmetics is a favorite among French actresses and socialites. Upstairs, specialists create what de Gunzburg calls *haute couleur,* exclusive makeup tailored to each client (it's very expensive, and takes three weeks to create). ✉ *36 Galerie Véro-Dodat, 1er, Louvre* ☎ *01–44–76–00–76* ⊕ *www.byterry.com* Ⓜ *Palais-Royal–Louvre.*

★ Guerlain

FRAGRANCES | The world's oldest perfumer has a gorgeous Parisian flagship store, just blocks from its very first shop founded by Pierre-François Guerlain in 1828. This outpost is a sumptuous affair, offering more personalized services and customization than ever before. A tablet helps you define your olfactory profile, and experts are on-hand to guide you through a private consultation in a special room decked out in blushing velvets. You can also have a private consultation with a house "nose" to design your own fragrance. If those options are out of your price range (as they are for most mortals), you can still personalize any of the perfumer's 110 fragrances from the "perfume bar," choosing from several crystal bottles and selecting the color of your label and ribbons. ✉ *356 rue St-Honoré, 1er, Louvre* ☎ *01–42–60–68–61* ⊕ *www.guerlain.com* Ⓜ *Tuileries, Pyramides.*

Jovoy

FRAGRANCES | Representing 100 artisanal perfumers, Jovoy is the largest independent purveyor of fragrances in the world—indeed, the brand calls itself the "embassy of rare perfumes." Owner François Hénin is often on hand expounding on the unique qualities and fascinating histories of different fragrances, some of which date back hundreds of years, and many of which are exclusive to the boutique. The shop also carries fragrances for the home and a range of beautifully packaged scented candles. ✉ *4 rue de Castiglione, 1er, Louvre* ☎ *01–40–20–06–19* ⊕ *www.jovoyparis.com* Ⓜ *Tuileries, Concorde.*

★ **Les Salons du Palais-Royal Serge Lutens**

FRAGRANCES | Every year, Serge Lutens dreams up two new fragrances, which are then sold exclusively in this boutique. Each is compellingly original, from the strong *somptueux* scents often with musk and amber notes to the intense florals like Rose de Nuit. Bottles can be etched and personalized for gifts. The shop itself boasts a beautiful spiral staircase. ✉ *Jardins du Palais-Royal, 142 Galerie de Valois, 1er, Louvre* ☎ *01–49–27–09–09* ⊕ *www.sergelutens.com* Ⓜ *Palais-Royal–Louvre.*

BOOKS AND STATIONERY

Librairie Galignani

BOOKS | Dating to 1520s Venice, this venerable bookstore opened in Paris in 1801 and was the first to specialize in English-language books. Its present location, across from the Tuileries Garden on Rue de Rivoli, opened in 1856, and the wooden bookshelves, creaking floors, and hushed interior provide the perfect atmosphere for perusing Paris's best

collection of contemporary and classic greats in English and French, plus a huge selection of gorgeous art books. ✉ *224 rue de Rivoli, 1er, Louvre* ☎ *01–42–60–76–07* ⊕ *www.galignani.com* Ⓜ *Tuileries.*

Smith&Son

BOOKS | This bookseller formerly associated with chain WHSmith has stepped out on its own with this newer, independent shop that remains a must-visit for Anglophone bibliophiles. You won't just find a multitude of travel and language guides, cookbooks, and fiction for adults and children—it also has the best selection of foreign magazines and newspapers in Paris. Upstairs, enjoy a delightful afternoon tea in George Washington's former Paris apartment. ✉ *248 rue de Rivoli, 1er, Louvre* ☎ *01–53–45–84–40* ⊕ *www.smithandson.com* Ⓜ *Concorde.*

CLOTHING

★ **Acne Studios**

CLOTHING | Justly famous for its sexy, derriere-shaping jeans, this Swedish label daringly mixes genders and genres in body-hugging or oversize, asymmetrical styles that rival some of the best catwalk looks. Standout shoes, boots, and accessories—all exhibiting the brand's underplayed cool—are sold here, too. ✉ *124 Galerie de Valois, 1er, Louvre* ☎ *01–42–60–16–62* ⊕ *www.acnestudios.com* Ⓜ *Palais-Royal–Louvre.*

agnès b.

CLOTHING | This brand embodies the quintessential French approach to easy but stylish dressing. There are many branches, and the clothes are also sold in department stores, but for the fullest range go to Rue du Jour, where agnès takes up much of the street (women's and children's wear are at No. 6, menswear at No. 3). For women, classics include sleek black leather jackets, flattering black jersey separates, and trademark wide-stripe T-shirts. Children love the two-tone T-shirts proclaiming their age. And the stormy-gray velour or corduroy suits you see on those slouchy, scarf-clad men? agnès b. ✉ *3 and 6 rue du Jour, 1er, Louvre* ☎ *01-45-08-56-56* ⊕ *www.agnesb.eu* Ⓜ *Châtelet–Les Halles.*

★ Alexander McQueen

CLOTHING | The Paris flagship of this lauded label, whose global fame only skyrocketed with the design of the duchess of Cambridge's wedding gown, is glorious to behold. The late McQueen's hallmarks—tons of lace, gossamer fabrics, tartans, death's heads, and voluminous silhouettes—are all lavishly on display. Sarah Burton's dramatic gowns were the brand's signature for her 13 years as creative director; now, it's Seán McGirr, former head of ready-to-wear at JW Anderson, who has taken the lead. Shoes, accessories, and surprisingly affordable jewelry to go with the garments are available as well. ✉ *275 rue St-Honoré, 8e, Louvre* ☎ *01-70-80-78-00* ⊕ *www.alexandermcqueen.com* Ⓜ *Tuileries.*

★ Chloé

CLOTHING | Much like the clothes it sells, Chloé's flagship boutique is softly feminine and modern without being stark. Housed in an 18th-century mansion, its creamy marble floors, gold sconces, and walls in the brand's signature rosy beige are the perfect backdrop for Chemena Kamali's designs, which effortlessly continue in the vein of founder Gaby Aghion's sensibilities—unsurprising, seeing as Kamali has been connected to the brand on and off for over 20 years. Shoppers are met with the kind of sincere attention that is all but extinct in most high-end Paris shops, and sustainability is the mot d'ordre. Whether it's for a handbag or a whole new wardrobe, VIP rooms and professional stylists are available to assist anyone who calls for an appointment. ✉ *253 rue St-Honoré, 1er, Louvre* ☎ *01-55-04-03-30* ⊕ *www.chloe.com* Ⓜ *Franklin D. Roosevelt.*

Gabrielle Geppert

CLOTHING | Gabrielle Geppert's unique boutique shop takes its inspiration from 20th-century fashion's greatest hits. One part luxury vintage and one part Geppert's eponymous brand, her Palais Royal shop has it all. ✉ *31 Galerie Montpensier, 1er, Louvre* ☎ *01-42-61-53-52* Ⓜ *Palais-Royal–Musée du Louvre.*

★ Louis Vuitton

CLOTHING | The Paris-based luxury leather goods and fashion house par excellence is resplendent in an 18th-century mansion on the elegant Place Vendôme. Part fashion boutique and part art gallery, this impeccably restored locale retains the original woodwork, gilding, and stone, adding contemporary chrome, glass, and colorful works from more than 30 contemporary artists and sculptors. Covering three floors, the grand Place Vendôme store offers the entire Vuitton collection, including high-end jewelry and watches, bags and accessories, fashion, luggage, and some fabulous home furnishings on the top floor. The store even offers on-site monogramming for an even more personal touch. ✉ *2 pl. Vendôme, 1er, Louvre* ☎ *09-77-40-40-77* ⊕ *www.louisvuitton.com* Ⓜ *Concorde.*

Maison Margiela

CLOTHING | This famously elusive Belgian designer has earned a devoted following for his avant-garde styling and his innovative technique, from spiraling seams to deconstructed shirts. Women's fashion is sold at No. 28, menswear at No. 26. ✉ *26 and 28 rue de Richelieu, 1er, Louvre* ☎ *01-40-15-07-55* ⊕ *www.maisonmargiela.com* Ⓜ *Palais-Royal–Musée du Louvre.*

Miu Miu

CLOTHING | This Faubourg St-Honoré boutique dispenses with Miu Miu's Modernist ethos in favor of a Neo-Baroque sensibility—and it influences everything from the velvet wallpaper to, perhaps, a lavish pair of ruby slippers. Although the shoes and accessories scream glitz, the clothes still have a sleek refinement, with the designer's notorious tension between minimalism and opulence. ✉ *1 rue du Faubourg St-Honoré, 8e, Louvre* ☎ *01–58–62–53–20* ⊕ *www.miumiu.com* Ⓜ *Concorde.*

Rick Owens

CLOTHING | Rick Owens expertly finessed the jump from L.A. rock-star chic to Paris offbeat elegance. Lately defined more by glamour than grunge, his lush fabrics and asymmetrical designs have evolved to a new level of artistry—and wearability. Owens still loves a paradox (shrouding while revealing) and mixes high luxury with a bit of tooth and claw. You'll also find shoes, furs, jewelry, and accessories. ✉ *130–133 Galerie de Valois, 1er, Louvre* ☎ *01–40–20–42–52* ⊕ *www.rickowens.eu* Ⓜ *Palais-Royal-Musée du Louvre.*

Saint Laurent

CLOTHING | Yves Saint Laurent revolutionized women's wear in the 1970s, putting pants in couture shows for the first time. His safari jackets, "le smoking" suits, Russian-boho collections, and tailored *Belle de Jour* suits are considered fashion landmarks. Taking the helm in 2012, Hedi Slimane caused a major stir, renaming the brand, moving its headquarters, and bringing his own street-smart L.A. chic while nose-tweaking fashion journalists. In the ever-evolving game of musical chairs shaking up the major fashion houses, Anthony Vaccarello took the reins in 2017, keeping the sexy, street-smart look and adding his signature razor-sharp styling with plenty of metallics, feathers, and beading. ✉ *38 rue du Faubourg St-Honoré, 8e, Louvre* ☎ *01–42–65–74–59* ⊕ *www.ysl.com* Ⓜ *Concorde.*

DEPARTMENT STORES

★ Samaritaine

DEPARTMENT STORE | After standing empty for 16 years, the Samaritaine department store finally reopened in 2021 following

an ambitious renovation by new owners LVMH. The space dating to 1870 retains many of its Art Deco details, including its beautiful facade overlooking the Seine, and is also now home to the city's Cheval Blanc hotel. You can enter the store via Rue de la Monnaie, encountering labels from more than 600 fashion brands, including Alexander McQueen, Balenciaga, Stella McCartney, and Moschino. The new Samaritaine is also home to a spa and several eateries, including a gorgeous fifth-floor restaurant, Voyage, where you can dine on seasonal, international dishes beneath the department store's beautiful glass roof. ✉ *19 Rue de la Monnaie, 1er, Louvre* ☎ *01–88–88–60–00* ⊕ *www.dfs.com* Ⓜ *Pont Neuf.*

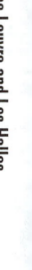

FOOD AND TREATS

Jean-Paul Hévin

CHOCOLATE | Forty masterful varieties of chocolate and some of the best pastries in Paris earned Jean-Paul Hévin his world-class chocolatier status. Devotees will be pleased to know that there are several other outposts in the capital, including one nearby at 108 rue St-Honoré. ✉ *231 rue St-Honoré, 1er, Louvre* ☎ *01–55–35–35–96* ⊕ *www.jeanpaulhevin.com* Ⓜ *Tuileries.*

Ladurée

FOOD | Founded in 1862, Ladurée oozes period atmosphere—even at the big Champs-Élysées branch (No. 75)—but nothing beats the original tearoom on Rue Royale, with its pint-size tables and frescoed ceiling. Ladurée claims a familial link to the invention of the macaron, so it's no surprise that there's a huge selection on offer. Unfortunately, service has lagged at all three of the tearooms in recent years, and the crowded space feels more like an ersatz tourist destination than the historic tearoom that it is. Still, Ladurée's stylish boxes make memorable, delicious gifts. ✉ *16 rue Royale, 8e, Louvre* ☎ *01–42–60–21–79* ⊕ *www.laduree.com* Ⓜ *Madeleine.*

La Fromagerie Du Louvre

FOOD | Cheese fans will fall in love with this little shop steps from Les Cave du Louvre, a wine cellar run by the same team. The open plan of the fromagerie allows shoppers to get up close and personal with a wide range of cheeses, from time-tested favorites like Comté and Brie to house specialties like peat whiskey-aged tomme de Savoie. And unlike many other Parisian cheese shops, it's open on Monday. The shop also offers customizable picnic boxes for one to four people that feature a selection of cheeses and charcuterie. ✉ *54 rue de l'Arbre Sec, 1er, Louvre* ☎ *09-73-89-60-23* ⊕ *www.fromageriedulouvre.com* Ⓜ *Louvre–Rivoli.*

★ **Terroirs d'Avenir**

FOOD | This shop has been at the heart of the Parisian locavore movement since 2008, when it began uniting innovative chefs with small local producers. Today, Terroirs d'Avenir also caters to individuals, with no fewer than five shops on the tiny Rue du Nil: a bakery (No. 3), butcher shop (No. 6), cheesemonger (No. 8), greengrocer (No. 7), and fishmonger (No. 8). Even if you're not planning a purchase, the picturesque cobbled street is worth a stop for a photo op. ✉ *7 rue du Nil, 2e, Louvre* ☎ *01-84-79-88-07* ⊕ *www.terroirs-avenir.fr* Ⓜ *Sentier.*

HOME DECOR

A. Simon

HOUSEWARES | Parisian chefs have been coming here for their kitchen needs for more than a century, from plates and glasses to pans and wooden spoons. The shop also offers a great selection of white porcelain. ✉ *48-52 rue Montmartre, 2e, Louvre* ☎ *01-42-33-71-65* Ⓜ *Étienne Marcel.*

Astier de Villatte

HOUSEWARES | Come here for tongue-in-chic interpretations of 18th-century table settings and furniture. You can live out your Baroque or Empire fancies with lots of mahogany and milk-white china

sets made in the artisan ceramic workshop—the only one of its kind in Paris. The paper goods come from France's last typographic printer on the outskirts of the city. Moody candles, incense, and bespoke perfumes complete the atmosphere. ✉ *173 rue St-Honoré, 1er, Louvre* ☎ *01-42-60-74-13* ⊕ *www.astierdevillatte.com* Ⓜ *Tuileries.*

★ **E. Dehillerin**

HOUSEWARES | Never mind the creaky stairs: E. Dehillerin has been around for almost 200 years and clearly knows its business. The huge range of professional cookware in enamel, stainless steel, and fiery copper is gorgeous; rely on the knowledgeable staff to locate specific items in the vast expanse of this store. During her years in Paris, Julia Child was a regular. ✉ *18-20 rue Coquillière, 1er, Louvre* ☎ *01-42-36-53-13* ⊕ *www.edehillerin.fr* Ⓜ *Les Halles.*

JEWELRY AND ACCESSORIES

Cartier

JEWELRY & WATCHES | After over two years of renovations, this historic jeweler's finally reopened its doors in 2022 to welcome devotees past the 19th-century, gold-flecked black marble facade into a massive six-story boutique. Now boasting truly contemporary flair, albeit with nods to the brand's storied past, this Cartier is airy and bright, capped by a glass ceiling that takes inspiration from the city's beloved secret courtyards. Here, longtime favorites like Trinity rings and Tank watches compete for attention with the newer Panthère, Love, and Caresse d'Orchidées collections. ✉ *13 rue de la Paix, 2e, Louvre* ☎ *01-58-18-23-00* ⊕ *www.cartier.fr* Ⓜ *Opéra.*

Dary's

JEWELRY & WATCHES | This family-run cavern teeming with artists, actors, models, and jewelry lovers offers an Ali Baba–ish shopping experience. You'll need to take your time, as the walls are filled with row upon row of antique jewels from every era, as well as more modern secondhand jewelry and vintage one-of-a-kinds. ✉ 362 *rue St-Honoré, 1er, Louvre* ☎ *01–42–60–95–23* ⊕ *www.darys-bijouterie-paris.fr* Ⓜ *Tuileries.*

LINGERIE

★ Alice Cadolle

LINGERIE | Selling lingerie to Parisians since 1889, Alice Cadolle offers some of the city's most sumptuous couture undergarments. Ready-to-wear bras, corsets, and sleepwear fill this eponymous boutique. ✉ *4 rue Cambon, 1er, Louvre* ☎ *01–42–60–94–22* ⊕ *www.cadolle.com* Ⓜ *Concorde.*

MARKETS

★ Rue du Nil

MARKET | Just steps from the popular market street Rue Montorgueil, this diminutive passage has become a foodie mecca ever since Frenchie chef Grégory Marchand set up shop here in 2009. Not only is the street home to Marchand's Michelin-starred restaurant (No. 5), wine bar (No. 6), and wine cellar (No. 9), but it also features five shops from locavore trendsetters Terroirs d'Avenir peddling everything from cheese (No. 8) to produce (No. 7) to baked goods (No. 3). Chocoholics won't want to miss Plaq at No. 4 selling exquisite single-origin chocolates, cakes, and hot cocoa. ✉ *Rue du Nil, 2e, Louvre* Ⓜ *Sentier.*

SHOES, HANDBAGS, AND LEATHER GOODS

Christian Louboutin

SHOES | These shoes carry their own red carpet with them thanks to their trademark crimson soles. Whether tasseled, embroidered, or strappy, in Charvet silk or shiny patent leather, the heels are always perfectly balanced. No wonder they set off such legendary legs as Tina Turner's and Gwyneth Paltrow's. ✉ *19 rue Jean-Jacques Rousseau, 1er, Louvre* ☎ *08–00–94–58–04* ⊕ *www.christianlouboutin.com* Ⓜ *Palais-Royal–Musée du Louvre.*

Goyard

HANDBAGS | These colorful totes are the choice of royals, blue bloods, and the like (clients have included Sir Arthur Conan Doyle, Gregory Peck, and the Duke and Duchess of Windsor). Parisians swear by their durability and longevity; they're large enough to transport a baguette and durable enough for a magnum of Champagne. Dog owners won't want to miss the "Le Chic du Chien" boutique farther down at No. 352. ✉ *233 rue St-Honoré, 1er, Louvre* ☎ *09–73–87–45–60* ⊕ *www.goyard.com* Ⓜ *Tuileries.*

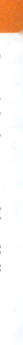

★ Hermès

ACCESSORIES | The go-to for those who prefer their logo discreet yet still crave instant recognition, Hermès was established as a saddlery in 1837, then went on to create the eternally chic Kelly (named for Grace Kelly) and Birkin (named for Jane Birkin) handbags. The silk scarves are legendary, known for their rich colors and intricate designs, which change yearly. Other accessories are also extremely covetable: enamel bracelets, dashing silk-twill ties, and small leather goods. During semiannual sales, in January and July, prices are slashed by up to 50%, and the crowds line up for blocks. ✉ *24 rue du Faubourg St-Honoré, 8e, Louvre* ☎ *01–40–17–46–00* ⊕ *www.hermes.com* Ⓜ *Concorde.*

Lancaster

HANDBAGS | A household name in France for 100 years, Lancaster has a reputation for style and craftsmanship. Its bags are chic and sporty, with an emphasis on practicality, and all the classic models are available in this spaceship-modern boutique. Look for the popular crossbody Besace bag (it's made of patent leather or soft cowhide and comes in a rainbow of colors). ✉ *422 rue St-Honoré, 8e, Louvre* ☎ *01–42–28–88–88* ⊕ *www.lancaster.com* Ⓜ *Concorde.*

Maison Fabre

HATS & GLOVES | Until you've eased on an exquisite pair of gloves handcrafted by Fabre, you probably haven't experienced the sensation of having a second skin far superior to your own. Founded in 1924, this historic *gantier* is known for styles ranging from classic to haute: picture elbow-length croc leather, coyote-fur mittens, and peccary driving gloves. ✉ *128–129 Galerie de Valois, 1er, Louvre* ☎ *01–42–60–75–88* 🌐 *www.maisonfabre.com* Ⓜ *Palais-Royal–Musée du Louvre.*

Pierre Hardy

SHOES | With Vivier and Louboutin, Pierre Hardy completes the triumvirate of anointed Paris shoe designers. Armed with a pedigree—Dior, Hermès, Balenciaga—Hardy opened his own boutique in 2003 and made serious waves. The luxe bags are ever popular, and the shoes are unmistakable: sky-scraping platforms and wedges or demure kitten heels double as sculpture with breathtaking details and luscious colors. ✉ *156 Galerie de Valois, 1er, Louvre* ☎ *01–42–60–59–75* 🌐 *www.pierrehardy.com* Ⓜ *Palais-Royal–Musée du Louvre.*

Roger Vivier

SHOES | Long known for his Pilgrim-buckle shoes and inventive heels, Roger Vivier's name is being resurrected through the creativity of uber-Parisienne Inès de la Fressange and the expertise of shoe designer Gherardo Felloni. The results are easily some of the best shoes in town: leather boots that mold to the calf perfectly, towering rhinestone-encrusted or feathered platforms for evening, and vertiginous crocodile pumps. ✉ *29 rue du Faubourg St-Honoré, 8e, Louvre* ☎ *01–53–43–00–85* 🌐 *www.rogervivier.com* Ⓜ *Concorde.*

Chapter 7

LES GRANDS BOULEVARDS

Updated by
Jennifer Ladonne

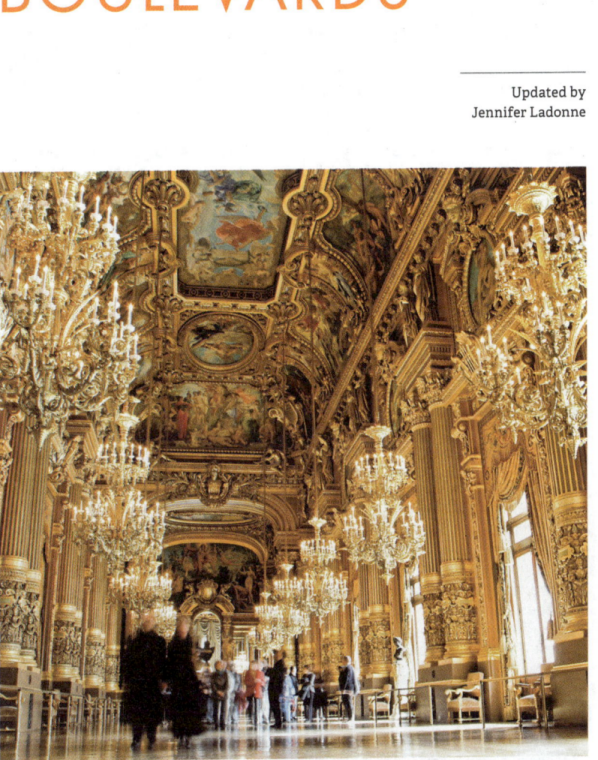

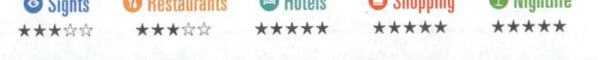

NEIGHBORHOOD SNAPSHOT

GETTING HERE

This neighborhood covers parts of the 2e, 3e, 8e, and 9e arrondissements. There are myriad ways of getting to the major sights in these areas; however, for the major landmarks we mention, take the *métro* to the Opéra station, named for the opulent opera house. Just behind it, you can find Paris's historic department stores Galeries Lafayette and Au Printemps, each with three buildings (women's, men's, home) along Baron Haussmann's wide avenues, known as the Grands Boulevards. If you're planning to visit the numerous small and wonderful museums, take the métro to Parc Monceau for the Musée Nissim de Camondo, Musée Cernuschi, and Musée Jacquemart-André (if you don't mind a little walk). For the Musée National Gustave Moreau, the métro stop St-George is the closest, but you can also head to Pigalle and walk through the still-elegant historic Nouvelle Athènes neighborhood, where such artistic luminaries as Georges Sand, Frédéric Chopin, Victor Hugo, Eugène Delacroix, and Jean Auguste Dominique Ingres lived, worked, and played.

MAKING THE MOST OF YOUR TIME

If you're a serious shopper, plan to spend a day, or at least a long morning, in this neighborhood, beginning with the department stores near the Chausée-d'Antin–La Fayette or Havre-Caumartin métro stops (best to go on weekday mornings when the crowds are thinner). Then check out the shopping and food scene on Rue d'Aboukir and the elegant shops surrounding Place des Victoires. From here, head east on Rue Étienne Marcel, lined with boutiques, as well as the old market streets Rues Montmartre, du Louvre, and du Jour. Don't miss the historic covered galleries (Paris's first shopping malls): the soaring glass Passages Jouffroy and Verdeau, and Paris's oldest, Passage des Panoramas, just across the street.

If shopping isn't your bag, plan on a long afternoon's visit: tour the Opéra Garnier and one or two museums, or bring a picnic lunch to lovely Parc Monceau on the western edge.

TOP REASONS TO GO

■ **Les Grands Magasins.** Sample a new perfume under the magnificent dome at Galeries Lafayette; update your look, snack at the food halls, or gaze at Parisian rooftops from the eighth-floor outdoor restaurant terraces at Au Printemps or Galeries Lafayette.

■ **Opéra Garnier.** It may not be haunted by the Phantom, but this 19th-century opera house still dazzles.

■ **Parc Monceau.** Join the well-dressed children of well-heeled Parisians and frolic on some of the prettiest lawns in the city.

■ **Musée Jacquemart-André.** This superb permanent collection (set to reopen in fall 2024) in the former home of husband-and-wife art collectors is well worth a view, and the temporary exhibitions are excellent.

■ **Musée National Gustave Moreau.** You'd swear the artist had just left for a moment, so well preserved is his home and atelier, where he created his Symbolist works.

■ **Les Passages Couverts.** Stroll the passages Jouffroy, Verdeau, and Panoramas to experience what the original shopping malls were like 150 years ago.

In Belle Époque Paris, the Grands Boulevards were the place to see and be seen: in the cafés, at the opera, or in the ornate *passages couverts* (glass-roofed arcades that served as the world's first malls).

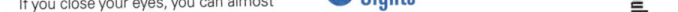

If you close your eyes, you can almost imagine the Grands Boulevards immortalized on canvas by the Impressionists, with well-attired Parisians strolling wide avenues dotted with shops, cafés, grand hotels, and horse-drawn carriages—all set against a backdrop of stately Haussmannian buildings. Today, despite the chain stores, sidewalk vendors, and fast-food joints, the Grands Boulevards remain one of the city's shopping epicenters, home to the most popular *grands magasins* (department stores), Galeries Lafayette and Au Printemps, near Place de l'Opéra.

Shopping aside, the Grands Boulevards are a cultural destination anchored by the magnificent **Opéra Garnier,** commissioned by Napoléon III. The neighborhood is also home to some of the city's best small museums, all former private collections housed in 19th-century *hôtels particuliers* (mansions) or town houses that alone are worth the trip. The exquisite **Musée Jacquemart-André** displays an impressive collection of Italian Renaissance art, while the jewel-box **Musée Nissim de Camondo** remembers one family's tragic demise. The **Musée Cernuschi** has a dazzling array of Asian art, and the **Musée National Gustave Moreau** is an offbeat tribute to the Symbolist master.

 **Sights**

★ **Au Printemps**

STORE/MALL | Encompassing a trio of upscale department stores (Printemps Mode, Printemps Beauté-Maison-Enfant, and Printemps Homme), this vast, venerable retailer has been luring shoppers since 1865 and has lately upped its glamour quotient with elegant storewide restorations—most recently, a spiffed-up, historic grand staircase connecting the main entrances of the Haussmann flagship (Printemps Femme) with the panoramic restaurant Le 7ème Ciel. Besides the clothes, shoes, jewelry, beauty, housewares, and everything else, there are appealing dining options here. The top floor of the main building (Printemps Homme) has been completely renovated and is home to Printemps du Goût, a celebration of French cuisine. Here you can eat in style while taking in spectacular views, either from inside via floor-to-ceiling windows or outside on the wraparound terrace. Noted chefs and food artisans—including master cheese-maker Laurent Dubois, chef *pâtissier* Nina Métayer, and artisanal crêperie Malo—oversee a gourmet cornucopia. One floor down, Bar Perché "literary café" serves snacks, coffee, and drinks all day in a chic-casual Parisian apartment setting with glorious city views. You can also opt for a leisurely shopping break at Bleu Coupole, on the sixth floor of Printemps Femme under

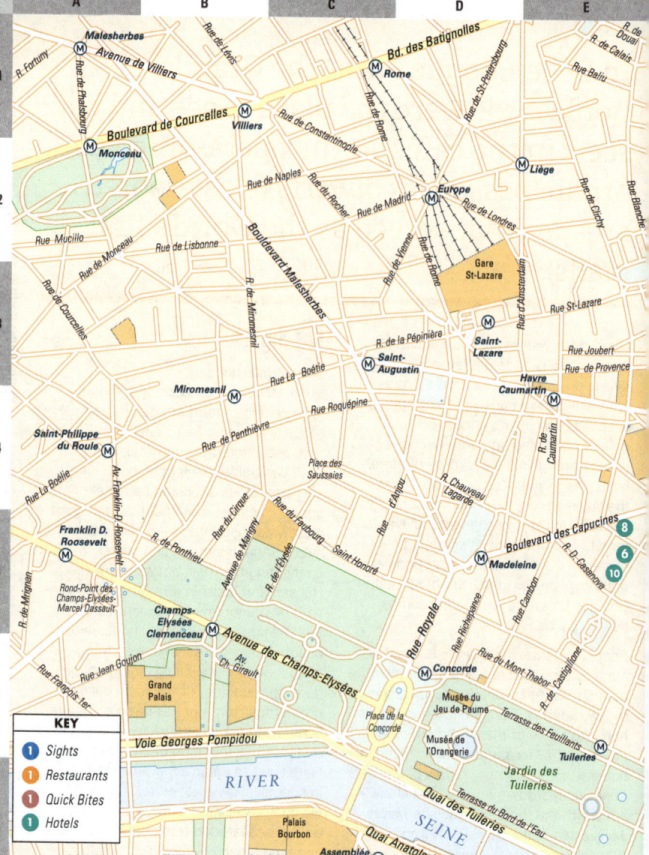

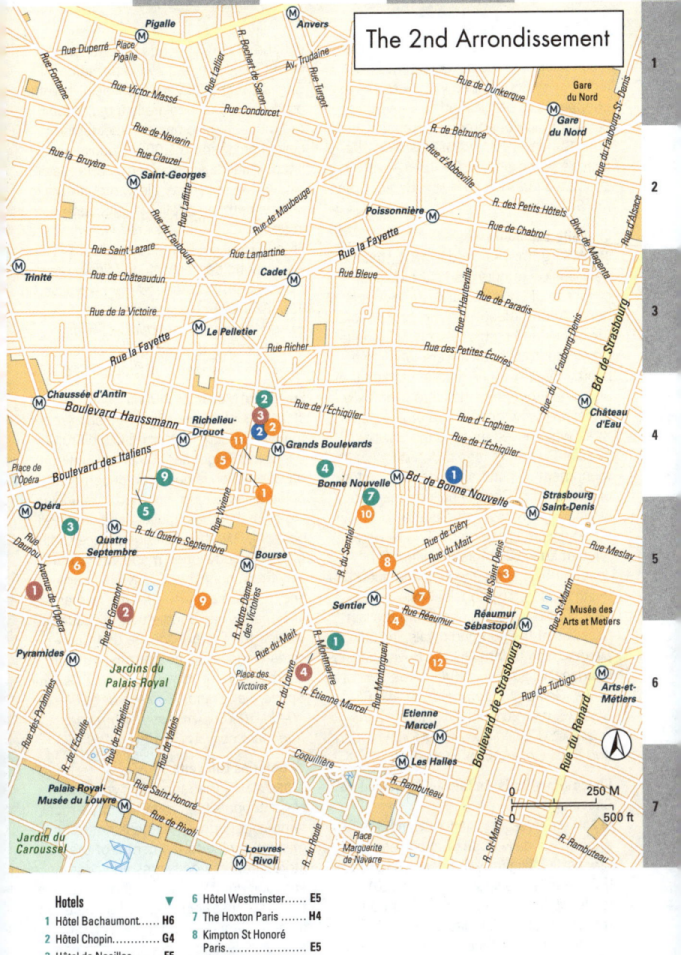

the famous stained-glass cupola, or the magnificent terrace of restaurant Perruche, with 360-degree views over Paris. Shoppers will be pleased to know that Paris's grand department stores are now open Sunday. ✉ *64 bd. Haussmann, 9e, Grands Boulevards* ☎ *01–42–82–50–00* ⊕ *www.printemps.com* Ⓜ *Havre-Caumartin, St-Lazare.*

Chapelle Expiatoire

CHURCH | Commissioned in 1815, this neoclassical temple marks the original burial site of Louis XVI and Marie-Antoinette. After the deposed monarchs took their turns at the guillotine on Place de la Concorde, their bodies were taken to a nearby mass grave. A loyalist marked their place, and their remains were eventually retrieved by the dead king's brother, Louis XVIII, who moved them to the Basilica of Saint-Denis. He then ordered the monument (which translates to Expiatory, or Atonement, Chapel) built on this spot, in what is now the leafy Square Louis XVI off Boulevard Haussmann. Two massive white-marble sculptures by François Joseph Bosio show the king and queen being succored by angels, while stone tablets below are inscribed with the last missives of the doomed royals, including pleas to God to forgive their Revolutionary enemies. ✉ *Sq. Louis-XVI, 29 rue Pasquier, 8e, Grands Boulevards* ☎ *01–42–65–35–80* ⊕ *www.chapelle-expiatoire-paris.fr* 💰 *€7* ⊘ *Closed Sun. and Mon. yr-round and Tues. Oct.–Mar.* Ⓜ *St-Augustin.*

Choco-Story Paris: Le Musée Gourmand du Chocolat

SPECIALTY MUSEUM | **FAMILY** | Considering that a daily dose of chocolate is practically obligatory in Paris, it's hard to believe that this spot (opened in 2010) is the city's first museum dedicated to the sweet stuff. Exhibits on three floors tell the story of chocolate from the earliest traces of the "divine nectar" in Mayan and Aztec cultures, through to its introduction in Europe by the Spanish, who added milk and sugar to the spicy,

dark brew and launched a Continental craze. There are detailed explanations in English, with many for the kids. While the production of chocolate is a major topic, the museum also has a respectable collection of some 1,000 chocolate-related artifacts, such as terra-cotta Mayan sipping vessels (they blew into straws to create foam) and delicate chocolate pots in fine porcelain that were favored by the French royal court. Frequent chocolate-making demonstrations finish with a free tasting. ✉ *28 bd. de Bonne Nouvelle, 10e, Grands Boulevards* ☎ *01–42–29–68–60* ⊕ *www.museeduchocolat.fr* 💰 *€15; €18 with a cup of hot chocolate* Ⓜ *Bonne-Nouvelle, Strasbourg, St-Denis.*

Fragonard Musée du Parfum

SPECIALTY MUSEUM | More of a showroom than a museum, the small exhibit run by *parfumier* Fragonard above its boutique on Rue Scribe is heavy on decorative objects associated with perfume, including crystal bottles, gloves, and assorted bibelots. The shop is a good place to find gifts, like body lotion made with royal jelly (from honeybees), myriad soaps, and, of course, perfume. True fragrance aficionados can double their pleasure by visiting the Théâtre Musée des Capucines-Fragonard, another minimuseum nearby (✉ 39 bd. des Capucines). ✉ *9 rue Scribe, 9e, Grands Boulevards* ☎ *01–40–06–10–09* ⊕ *musee-parfum-paris.fragonard.com* 💰 *Free* Ⓜ *Opéra.*

★ Galeries Lafayette

STORE/MALL | The stunning Byzantine glass *coupole* (dome) of the city's most famous department store is not to be missed. Amble to the center of the main store, amid the perfumes and cosmetics, and look up. If you're not shopping, visit the (free) first-floor Galerie des Galeries, an art gallery devoted to fashion, applied arts, and design; or have lunch at one of the many restaurants, including Créatures rooftop bar and restaurant in the main store, with its panoramic city views. Chic Café Coutume, on the third

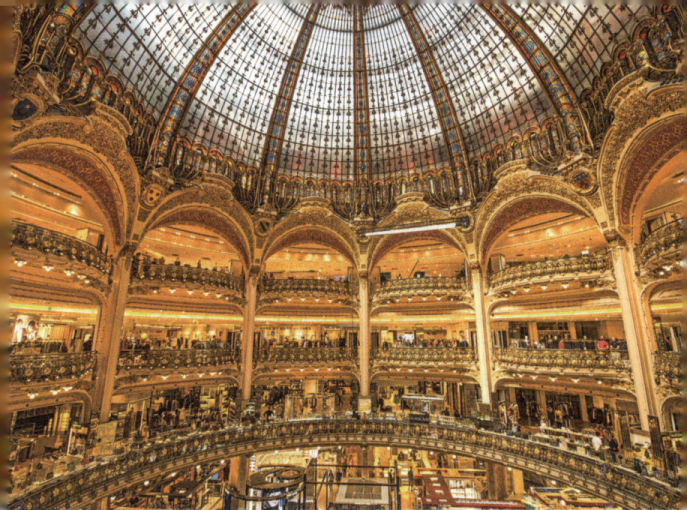

The interior of the Galeries Lafayette department store—especially the ceiling—almost outshines the fabulous merchandise.

level under the main building's famous coupole, serves craft coffee and delicious snacks. If you prefer a Champagne brunch, stop in at the Wine Gate, with 100 wines to taste with gourmet bites and up-close views of the coupole. The top floor of the main store is a good place to pick up interesting Parisian souvenirs. Across the street in Galeries Maison, the gourmet food hall has one of the city's best selections of delicacies and several restaurants, including Top Chef Pierre Sang's Korean delights and elegant La Maison de la Truffe lunch bar. Don't miss Duclot La Cave on Galeries Maison/ Gourmet's first floor, where 2,500 bottles of wine from France and around the world are on display—you can sample dozens of them at the semicircular wine bar. ✉ *35–40 bd. Haussmann, 9e, Grands Boulevards* ☎ *01–42–82–34–56* 🌐 *haussmann.galerieslafayette.com* Ⓜ *Chaussée d'Antin–La Fayette, Havre-Caumartin.*

Hôtel Drouot

OTHER ATTRACTION | Hidden away in a small antiques district, not far from the Opéra Garnier, is Paris's central auction house, said to be the oldest in the world. Drouot sells it all: vintage clothes, haute-couture gowns, tchotchkes, ornate Chinese lacquered boxes, rare books, art, and wine. Anyone can attend the sales and viewings, which draw a mix of art dealers, ladies who lunch, and art amateurs hoping to discover an unknown masterpiece. Check the website to see what's on the block. Don't miss the small galleries and antiques dealers in the Quartier Drouot, a warren of small streets around the auction house, notably on Rues Rossini and de la Grange-Batelière. ✉ *9 rue Drouot, 9e, Grands Boulevards* ☎ *01–48–00–20–20* 🌐 *www.drouot.com* ✉ *Free* ⊘ *Closed Sun.* Ⓜ *Richelieu-Drouot.*

★ Musée Cernuschi

ART MUSEUM | Wealthy Milanese banker and patriot Enrico (Henri) Cernuschi fled to Paris in 1850 after the new Italian government collapsed, only to be arrested during the 1871 Paris Commune. He subsequently decided to wait out the unrest by traveling and collecting Asian art. Upon his return 18 months later, he had a special mansion built on the edge of Parc Monceau to house his treasures, notably a two-story bronze Buddha from Japan. Reopened in 2020 after restoration, France's second-most-important collection of Asian art, after the Musée Guimet, expanded its galleries to include objects never before displayed, widening the collection to include more works from Japan, Korea, and Vietnam. Cernuschi had an eye not only for the bronze pieces he adored but also for Neolithic pottery (8000 BC), *mingqi* tomb figures (AD 300–900), and an impressive array of terra-cotta figures from various dynasties. A collection highlight is La Tigresse, a bronze wine vessel in the shape of a roaring feline (11th century BC), purchased after Cernuschi's death. Although the museum is free, there is a charge for temporary exhibitions. ✉ 7 *av. Velasquez, 8e, Grands Boulevards* ☎ *01–53–96–21–50* 🌐 *www.cernuschi.paris.fr* 💰 *Free; €10 for temporary exhibitions* ⏰ *Closed Mon.* Ⓜ *Monceau.*

Musée Grévin

SPECIALTY MUSEUM | FAMILY | If you like wax museums, this one founded in 1882 ranks among the best. Pay the steep entry price and ascend a grand Phantom of the Opera–like staircase into the Palais des Mirages, a mirrored salon from the 1900 Paris Exposition that transforms into a hokey sound-and-light show the kids will love. (It was a childhood favorite of designer Jean-Paul Gaultier, who is in the collection, of course.) From there, get set for a cavalcade of nearly 300 statues, from Elvis to Ernest Hemingway, Picasso to the late Queen Elizabeth II. Every king of France is here, along with Mick Jagger and George Clooney, plus scores of French singers and celebrities. ✉ *Passage Jouffroy, 10 bd. Montmartre, 9e, Grands Boulevards* ☎ *01–47–70–85–05* 🌐 *www.grevin-paris.com* 💰 *From €20* Ⓜ *Grands Boulevards.*

★ Musée Jacquemart-André

ART MUSEUM | Among the city's best small museums, the opulent Musée Jacquemart-André (closed at this writing; due to reopen in September 2024 after a yearlong restoration; check before visiting) is home to a huge collection of art and furnishings lovingly assembled in the late 19th century by banking heir Edouard André and his artist wife, Nélie Jacquemart, when this was their home. Their midlife marriage in 1881 raised eyebrows—he was a dashing bachelor and a Protestant, and she, no great beauty, hailed from a modest Catholic family. Still, theirs was a happy union fused by a common passion for art. For six months every year, the couple traveled, most often to Italy, where they hunted down works from the Renaissance, their preferred period. Their collection also includes masterworks by French painters Fragonard, Jacques-Louis David, and François Boucher, plus Dutch masters van Dyck and Rembrandt. The Belle Époque mansion itself is a major attraction. Its elegant ballroom, equipped with collapsible walls operated by then-state-of-the-art hydraulics, could hold 1,000 guests. The winter garden was a wonder of its day, spilling into the *fumoir,* where André would share cigars with the *grands hommes* (important men) of the time. You can tour the separate bedrooms—his in dusty pink, hers in pale yellow. The former dining room, now an elegant café, features a ceiling by Tiepolo. Don't forget to pick up the free audioguide in English, and do inquire about the current temporary exhibition, which is usually top-notch. Plan on a Sunday visit, and enjoy the popular brunch (€32) in the café from 11 am to 2:30 pm. Reservations are not accepted, so come early or late to avoid waiting in line. ✉ *158 bd. Haussmann, 8e, Grands Boulevards* ☎ *01–45–62–11–59* 🌐 *www.musee-jacquemart-andre.com* 💰 *€12* Ⓜ *St-Philippe du Roule, Miromesnil.*

Musée National Gustave Moreau

ART MUSEUM | Visiting the quirky town house and studio of painter Gustave Moreau (1826–98) is well worth your time. With an eye on his legacy, Moreau—a high priest of the Symbolist movement—created an enchanting gallery to showcase his dark paintings, drawings, and sculpture. The first-floor rooms trace Moreau's "sentimental journey"; their walls are festooned with family portraits and works offered by close friends and allies like Chassériau, Fromentin, and Degas. The two light-flooded top floors house Moreau's vast workshops, where hundreds of paintings, watercolors, and more than 4,000 drawings give a broad overview of his techniques and subjects. Some of the pieces appear unfinished, such as *Unicorns* (No. 213), inspired by the medieval tapestries in the Musée de Cluny: Moreau refused to work on it further, spurning the wishes of a wealthy would-be patron. His interpretations of Biblical scenes and Greek mythology combine flights of fantasy with a keen use of color, shadow, and tracings influenced by Persian and Indian miniatures. There are wax sculptures and cupboards with sliding vertical doors containing small-format paintings. The Symbolists loved objects, and Moreau was no different. His cramped private apartment on the second floor is jam-packed with bric-a-brac, and artworks cover every inch of the walls. ✉ *14 rue de la Rochefoucauld, 9e, Grands Boulevards* ☎ *01–48–74–38–50* ⊕ *www.musee-moreau.fr* ✉ *€8* ♡ *Closed Tues.* Ⓜ *Trinité, St-Georges.*

Musée National Jean-Jacques Henner

ART MUSEUM | French artist Jean-Jacques Henner (1829–1905) was a star in his day, and although his luminous nudes and clear-eyed portraits are largely forgotten now, the handsomely renovated 19th-century mansion-cum-museum stocked with his works is an interesting stop for art enthusiasts. Henner painted more than 400 portraits, including a

substantial number sold in America, with a Realist's eye, yet there is much beauty here as well: witness *Lady with Umbrella*, a portrait of a fur-clad aristocrat with glistening blue eyes. Many of his soft-featured nudes betray other influences. Don't miss them in the light-filled atelier on the museum's third floor, where they share space with a series of religious paintings, notably the haunting *Saint Sebastian* and a stark portrayal of a lifeless Christ, whose luminescent white skin is offset by a shock of flaming red hair. There is some information in English. ✉ *43 av. de Villiers, 17e, Grands Boulevards* ☎ *01–47–63–42–73* ⊕ *www.musee-henner.fr* ✉ *€8* ♡ *Closed Tues.* Ⓜ *Malesherbes.*

★ Musée Nissim de Camondo

HISTORIC HOME | The story of the Camondo family is steeped in tragedy, and it's all recorded within the walls of this superb museum. Patriarch Moïse de Camondo, born in Istanbul to a successful Jewish banking family, built his showpiece mansion in 1911 in the style of the Petit Trianon at Versailles and stocked it with some of the most exquisite furniture, wainscoting, artworks, and bibelots of the mid- to late 18th century. Despite his vast wealth and purported charm, his wife left him five years into their marriage. Then his son, Nissim, was killed in World War I. Upon Moïse's death in 1935, the house and its contents were left to the state as a museum named for his lost son. A few years after Moïse's death, daughter Béatrice, her husband, and two children were deported from France and murdered at Auschwitz. No heirs remained, and the Camondo name died out. Today, the house is an impeccable tribute to Moïse's life. Besides the mansion's grand spaces such as various living rooms, a visit includes some of the family's private apartments, the kitchen, scullery, and the servants' dining room. There's also a chic contemporary café with a lovely terrace in the adjoining former garage. ✉ *63 rue de Monceau, 8e,*

Grands Boulevards ☎ *01–53–89–06–50* ⊕ *www.madparis.fr/Musee-Nissim-de-Camondo-125* ✉ *€15; €22 joint ticket with Musée des Arts Décoratifs* ☺ *Closed Mon.* Ⓜ *Villiers, Monceau.*

★ Opéra Garnier

PERFORMANCE VENUE | Haunt of the Phantom of the Opera and the real-life inspiration for Edgar Degas's paintings of dancers, the gorgeous Opéra Garnier is one of two homes of the National Opera of Paris. The building, the Palais Garnier, was begun in 1860 by then-unknown architect Charles Garnier, who finished his masterwork 15 long years later, way over budget. Festooned with (real) gold leaf, colored marble, paintings, and sculpture from the top artists of the day, the opera house was about as subtle as Versailles and sparked controversy in post-Revolutionary France. The sweeping marble staircase, in particular, drew criticism from a public skeptical of its extravagance. But Garnier, determined to make a landmark that would last forever, spared no expense. The magnificent grand foyer is one of the most exquisite salons in France. In its heyday, the cream of Paris society strolled all 59 yards of the vast hall at intermission, admiring themselves in the towering mirrors. To see the opera house, buy a ticket for an unguided visit, which allows access to most parts of the building, including a peek into the auditorium. There is also a small ballet museum with a few works by Degas and the tutu worn by prima ballerina Anna Pavlova when she danced her epic *Dying Swan* in 1905. To get to it, pass through the unfinished entrance built for Napoléon III and his carriage (construction was abruptly halted when the emperor abdicated in 1870). On the upper level, you can see a sample of the auditorium's original classical ceiling, which was later replaced with a modern version painted by a septuagenarian Marc Chagall. His trademark willowy figures encircling the dazzling crystal chandelier—today the world's

third largest—shocked an unappreciative public upon its debut in 1964. Critics who fret that Chagall's masterpiece clashes with the fussy crimson-and-gilt decor can take some comfort in knowing that the original ceiling is preserved underneath, encased in a plastic dome.

The Opéra Garnier hosts the Paris Ballet as well as a few operas each season (most are performed at the Opéra Bastille). Tickets cost €10–€230 and should be reserved as soon as they go on sale—typically a month ahead at the box office, earlier by phone or online; otherwise, try your luck last-minute. To learn about the building's history and get a taste of aristocratic life during the Second Empire, take an entertaining English-language tour (daily at 11 am and 2:30 pm, €14) or rent an audioguide (€5) and proceed at your own pace. To complete the experience, dine at Coco—an over-the-top Belle Époque *folie* recalling the glamorous 1920s, and helmed by chef Julien Chicoisne—or browse through the Palais Garnier gift shop for ballet-inspired wares, fine Bernardaud porcelain depicting the famous Chagall ceiling, honey from the Opéra's own rooftop hives, and an exceptional selection of themed DVDs and books. ✉ *Pl. de l'Opéra, 9e, Grands Boulevards* ☎ *08–92–89–90–90 (€0.35 per min), 01–71–25–24–23 from outside France* ⊕ *www.operadeparis.fr* ✉ *€15 with temporary exhibition; €19 for tours* Ⓜ *Opéra.*

Parc Monceau

CITY PARK | FAMILY | This exquisitely landscaped, 20-acre park began in 1778 as the Duc de Chartres's private garden. Though some of the land was sold off under the Second Empire (creating the exclusive real estate that now borders the park), the refined atmosphere and some of the fanciful faux ruins have survived. Immaculately dressed children play under the watchful eye of their nannies, while lovers cuddle on the benches. In 1797, André Garnerin, the world's first-recorded parachutist, staged a

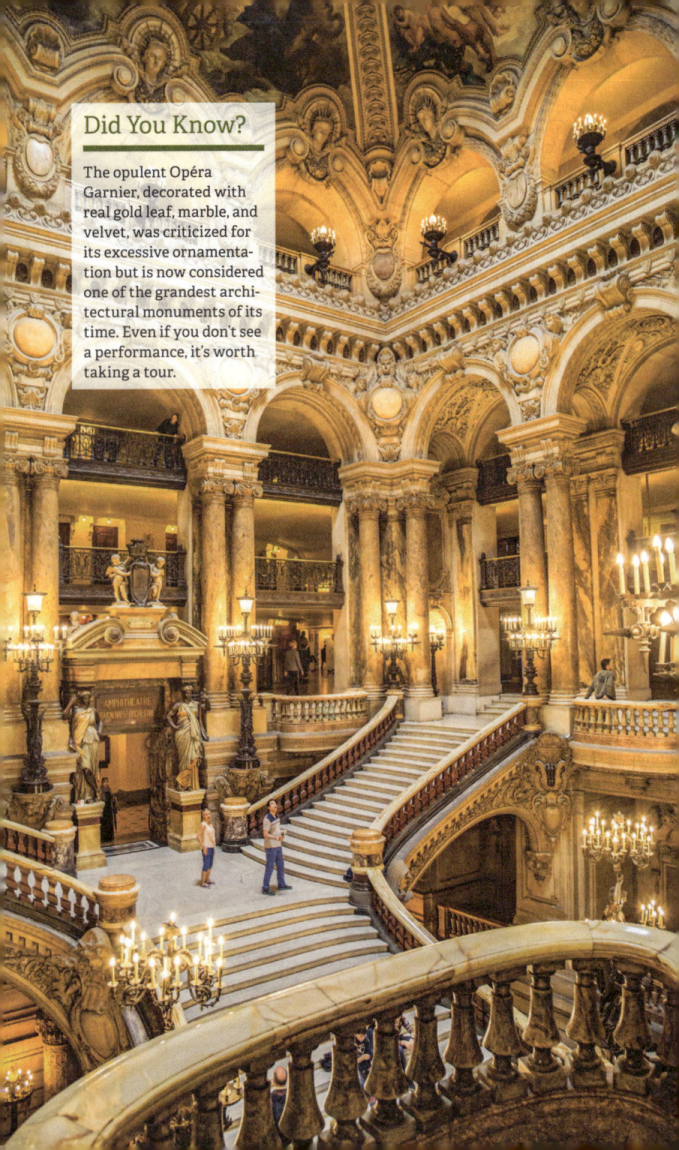

Did You Know?

The opulent Opéra Garnier, decorated with real gold leaf, marble, and velvet, was criticized for its excessive ornamentation but is now considered one of the grandest architectural monuments of its time. Even if you don't see a performance, it's worth taking a tour.

landing in the park. The rotunda—known as the Chartres Pavilion—is surely the city's grandest public restroom: it started life as a tollhouse. ✉ *Entrances on Bd. de Courcelles, Av. Velasquez, Av. Ruysdaël, and Av. van Dyck, 8e, Grands Boulevards* Ⓜ *Monceau.*

Restaurants

★ Abri Soba

$$ | JAPANESE | Those unable to score a sought-after table at chef Katsuaki Okiyama's restaurant Abri should have better luck at this small soba bar tucked away on a back street off the Faubourg-Montmartre. The chef's savory homemade buckwheat noodles are the big draw—enjoy them hot or cold, paired with duck and leeks, fried tofu and mushrooms, or more imaginative concoctions like eel, cod intestine, and the freshest sashimi. **Known for:** no reservations—try to arrive early; good selection of natural wines and Japanese whiskeys; crème brûlée with matcha-sesame seed ice cream. **§** *Average main: €22* ✉ *10 rue Saulnier, 9e, Grands Boulevards* ✡ *Closed Sun. and Mon.* Ⓜ *Cadet.*

★ Astair

$$ | BRASSERIE | This classy brasserie in the heart of the Passage des Panoramas, Paris's oldest and most picturesque covered gallery, has much more going for it than just good looks. Every item on its tempting menu of French classics—from *oeufs mayonnaise* and *soupe à l'oignon* to frogs' legs and octopus *à la Provençal*, a house specialty—is made with the freshest market ingredients and perfectly cooked, beautifully presented, and served with a smile. **Known for:** beautiful historic setting; friendly and welcoming atmosphere; exceptional dining without breaking the bank. **§** *Average main: €23* ✉ *19 passage des Panoramas, 2e, Grands Boulevards* ☎ *09-81-29-50-95* 🌐 *www.astair.paris* Ⓜ *Grands Boulevards, Bourse.*

Au Petit Riche

$$$ | BRASSERIE | You'll have no doubt what city you're in at this classic Parisian brasserie where you can sample all the French delicacies you'll never find at home, like *quenelle de brochet* with sauce Nantua (a sort of fritter made with pike—a traditional specialty of Lyon); *tête de veau* with tangy sauce ravigote (capers, shallots, tarragon, chervil, and parsley); poached haddock à l'Anglaise; and a fabulous *millefeuille de boudin noir* (blood sausage pastry). Be sure to try the excellent frites, and do not skimp on dessert: their crème brûlée is legendary. **Known for:** beautiful decor and attentive service; more elegant than your average brasserie; superb crème brûlée. **§** *Average main: €25* ✉ *25 rue Le Peletier, 9e, Grands Boulevards* ☎ *01-47-70-68-68* 🌐 *www.restaurant-aupetitricbe.com* Ⓜ *Le Peletier, Chausée d'Antin-Lafayette.*

Bouillon Chartier

$ | BISTRO | FAMILY | So-named to recall one of the Parisian soup restaurants (*bouillons*) popular among workers in the early 20th century, Bouillon Chartier is part of the Gérard Joulie group of bistros and brasseries, which discreetly updated the menu without changing the fundamentals. People come here more for the *bonhomie* and the stunning 1896 interior than the cooking, which could be politely described as unambitious—then again, where else can you find a plate of foie gras for €8? **Known for:** Paris's last truly authentic bouillon, with 19th-century ambience; extensive menu with gentle prices; no reservations. **§** *Average main: €12* ✉ *7 rue du Faubourg-Montmartre, 9e, Grands Boulevards* ☎ *01-47-70-86-29* 🌐 *www.bouillon-chartier.com* Ⓜ *Montmartre.*

Brasserie Dubillot

$ | BRASSERIE | FAMILY | There's nothing quite like a good old-fashioned Paris brasserie... except, perhaps, for a good old-fashioned Paris neobrasserie, a new genre that takes the best of the classic eatery—lively atmosphere, copious menu options, all-day hours, traditional decor—and adds a 21st-century vibe, all at reasonable prices. At Dubillot, you'll find the French classics—*oeufs mayonnaise,* house-made country pâté, steak tartare, smoked trout, leg of lamb, and crispy frites—along with well-priced wines by the bottle or glass. **Known for:** brasserie classics with locally sourced ingredients; fun and spirited ambience; no reservations. **§** *Average main: €16* ✉ *222 rue St-Denis, 2e, Grands Boulevards* ☎ *01–88–61–51–24* ⊕ *lanouvellegarde.com/fr/brasserie-dubillot* **M** *Réaumur-Sébastopol, Strasbourg St-Denis.*

Breizh Café

$ | **FRENCH** | **FAMILY** | This most stalwart of Breton addresses in the French capital is known for its savory buckwheat galettes and sweet wheat-flour crêpes, best enjoyed with a glass of local Breton cider. The city boasts several outposts of this restaurant; this one quite near the Les Halles market area is known for its cozy vaulted cider cellar, with more than 40 ciders to sample. **Known for:** organic buckwheat galettes with fillings like truffled ham, Basque chorizo, and raw-milk raclette cheese; nonstop service throughout the day; outdoor tables overlooking a lively pedestrian shopping street. **§** *Average main: €15* ✉ *14 rue des Petits Carreaux, 2e, Grands Boulevards* ☎ *01–42–33–97–78* ⊕ *www.breizhcafe.com* **M** *Sentier.*

Café de la Paix

$$$ | **FRENCH** | A pinnacle of Second Empire opulence, this Paris landmark was once an obligatory stop on the sophisticated gastronome's tour of Paris and a favorite watering hole among the likes of Victor Hugo, Gustave Flaubert, Arthur Conan Doyle, Josephine Baker, and Marlene Dietrich. While superfresh, heaping seafood platters are your best bet here, you'll do just as well with a classic French dish or an *apéro* on the terrace as the sun sets over the Opéra Garnier across the street—a magical Parisian scene indeed. **Known for:** breathtaking decor; Paris institution with a history; spectacular buffet brunch. **§** *Average main: €28* ✉ *5 pl. de l'Opéra, 9e, Grands Boulevards* ☎ *01–40–07–36–36* ⊕ *www.cafedelapaix.fr* **M** *Opéra, Havre-Caumartin.*

★ Caffè Stern

$$$ | **ITALIAN** | Lodged in one of Paris's most picturesque historic passages, the Italian Caffè Stern—a listed monument updated by designer Philippe Starck—is loaded with the sort of antique charm that makes a cup of coffee and dessert feel like a romantic moment in time. Full meals are a more elegant—and expensive—affair, though teatime (3 pm–6 pm) and the prix-fixe lunch (€30) make for a more manageable splurge. **Known for:** superb historic setting in the Passage des Panoramas; gorgeous decor; top-notch Italian food. **§** *Average main: €27* ✉ *47 Passage des Panoramas, 2e, Grands Boulevards* ☎ *01–75–43–63–10* ⊕ *www.alajmo.it* ✡ *Closed Sun. and Mon.* **M** *Grands Boulevards, Bourse.*

Drouant

$$$$ | **MODERN FRENCH** | **FAMILY** | Best known for the literary prizes awarded here since 1914, Drouant has shed its dusty image to become a forward-thinking restaurant. The playful menu revisits the French hors d'oeuvres tradition with starters that come as a series of four plates; diners can pick from themes such as French classics (like a deconstructed leek salad) or convincing minitakes on Thai and Moroccan dishes. **Known for:** France's most prestigious literary prize, the Prix Goncourt, awarded here; good for same-day reservations; elegant atmosphere, but prices can add up. **§** *Average main: €33* ✉ *16–18 pl. Gaillon, 2e, Grands Boulevards* ☎ *01–42–65–15–16* ⊕ *www.drouant.com* **M** *Pyramides.*

★ Frenchie

$$$$ | **BISTRO** | Set in a brick- and stone-walled building on a pedestrian street near Rue Montorgueil, Frenchie has quickly become one of the most hard-to-book bistros in town, with tables reserved months in advance, despite two seatings each evening. This success is due to the good-value, €140 five-course dinner menu (prix fixe only); boldly flavored dishes such as calamari gazpacho with squash blossoms or melt-in-the-mouth braised lamb with roasted eggplant and spinach are excellent options. **Known for:** casual, laid-back atmosphere that belies the ultrasophisticated dishes; extensive and original wine list; graciously accommodating to vegetarians. **§** *Average main: €40* ✉ *5 rue du Nil, 2e, Grands Boulevards* ☎ *01–40–39–96–19* 🌐 *www.frenchie-restaurant.com* ♡ *Closed weekends, 2 wks in Aug., and 10 days at Christmas. No lunch* Ⓜ *Sentier.*

★ Frenchie Bar à Vins

$$ | **WINE BAR** | If this weren't one of Paris's most outstanding wine bars, the wait and the metal tractor seats might be a deterrent. Yet wine lovers would be hard-pressed to find a better venue for sampling a great list of French wines and inspired selections from Italy and Spain—every one of them sold by the bottle or glass—with superb tapas to match. **Known for:** choice selection of natural wines from France and Europe; rare expertise in natural, organic, and biodynamic wines; no reservations, so go when it opens (7 pm) to avoid line. **§** *Average main: €22* ✉ *6 rue du Nil, 2e, Grands Boulevards* 🌐 *www.frenchie-bav.com* ♡ *Closed weekends. No lunch* Ⓜ *Sentier.*

Golden Poppy

$$$$ | **VEGETARIAN** | The luminous, California-inspired dining room (named for the state flower) is the only French outpost of French-born chef Dominique Crenn, who became the first woman to earn three Michelin stars for Atelier Crenn in San Francisco. This was a hotly anticipated opening in 2023, and Crenn's choice to exclude all meat in favor of a fish- and plant-based menu produce puts her in a rarified category in Paris. **Known for:** gourmet sustainable seafood and vegetarian fare; Asian and Latin American flavors in artfully composed dishes; charming setting and garden. **§** *Average main: €35* ✉ *24 rue Cadet, 9e, Grands Boulevards* ☎ *01–55–07–85–10* 🌐 *goldenpoppy.com* Ⓜ *Cadet.*

★ La Bourse et La Vie

$$$$ | **BISTRO** | After a takeover by the French-trained American star chef Daniel Rose back in 2015, this bistro stalwart transformed from a duckling to a swan, with elegant revamps of its bistro decor and an upgrade on its deeply satisfying French comfort-food classics. All meals begin with superb *gougères* (warm, cheesy puffs), and, if you're wise, will end with dessert. **Known for:** melt-in-your-mouth steak frites and rich veal pot-au-feu stew; one of the best tartes tatin in Paris; reservations are essential. **§** *Average main: €42* ✉ *12 rue Vivienne, 2e, Grands Boulevards* ☎ *01–42–60–08–83* 🌐 *www.labourselavie.com* ♡ *Closed weekends* Ⓜ *Bourse.*

Lazare

$$$ | **BRASSERIE** | With so many of Paris's fabled brasseries co-opted by upscale chains, the 2013 opening by three-Michelin-star chef Eric Frechon of this modern take on the traditional brasserie in the St-Lazare train station was met with curiosity and joy. Though prices are commensurate with his status, Frechon doesn't skimp on the classics: steak tartare, escargot, and charcuterie all make memorable appearances. **Known for:** quick dining before catching a train; can usually snag a seat sans reservation; classic brasserie atmosphere and cooking. **§** *Average main: €25* ✉ *108 rue St-Lazare, 8e, Grands Boulevards* ☎ *01–45–23–42–06* 🌐 *www.lazare-paris.fr* Ⓜ *St-Lazare.*

★ Louis

$$$$ | **FRENCH** | It may not be the most glamorous or the most well known of the city's Michelin-starred restaurants, but this intimate, prix-fixe dining room in an authentic part of town is one of the best. Be prepared to be both wowed and surprised with choices from chef Stéphane Pitré, who is known for his precise, original dishes that offer Asian touches without a hint of pretension. **Known for:** intimate dining room with individual attention; happily accommodating to those with food preferences and allergies; excellent options at lunchtime, outstanding options at dinner. ⑤ *Average main: €45* ✉ *23 rue de la Victoire, 9e, Grands Boulevards* ☎ *01–55–07–86–52* ⊕ *www.stephanepitre.fr* ⊘ *Closed weekends* Ⓜ *Le Peletier, Notre-Dame-de-Lorette.*

✉ *24 rue du Sentier, 2e, Grands Boulevards* ☎ *01–73–74–77–28* ⊕ *www.restaurant-pantagruel.com* ⊘ *Closed weekends* Ⓜ *Grands Boulevards, Sentier.*

Racines

$$$ | **WINE BAR** | Originally a *cave à manger* (a wine bar/bistro) serving natural wines and top-quality French fare, Racines made the foodie world rejoice in 2018 when adulated Sardinian-born chef Simone Tondo took the helm and introduced a small but stellar menu of Italian comfort dishes mixed with French stalwarts. The old tile floors, wooden tables, and location in the atmospheric Passage des Panoramas, Paris's oldest covered arcade, only add to the ambience. **Known for:** hard-to-find Italian wines; homemade tagliatelli with slow-cooked beef; reservations are essential. ⑤ *Average main: €27* ✉ *8 Passage des Panoramas, 2e, Grands Boulevards* ☎ *01–40–13–06–41* ⊕ *www.racinesparis.com* ⊘ *Closed 3 wks in Aug.* Ⓜ *Grands Boulevards, La Bourse.*

Oinari

$ | **JAPANESE** | This restaurant is small but mighty when it comes to fresh and delicious Japanese comfort food in the form of *inari age*: sushi rice wrapped in fried tofu (that used here is imported from Kyoto) and topped with vegetables, fish, or meat. The menu also features delicious udon, donburi, gyoza, and mochi for dessert. **Known for:** near Sacré-Coeur; expert sake pairings; good-value bento boxes. ⑤ *Average main: €14* ✉ *34 rue la Bruyère, 9e, Grands Boulevards* ☎ *06–60–06–08–10* ⊕ *www.oinariparis.com* ⊘ *Closed Sun. No lunch Sat. No dinner Mon. and Tues.* Ⓜ *St-Georges, Blanche.*

Shabour

$$$$ | **MEDITERRANEAN** | You could hear the buzz for miles when this beautiful dining room opened in 2019, and it's only gotten louder thanks to a shiny new Michelin star. Jerusalem-born chef Assaf Granit brings his formidable talent and imagination to Israeli and Asian-inspired dishes on the set-price tasting menu (there's no à la carte). Candlelit at night, the small but beautiful dining room is the perfect backdrop to an unforgettable meal. **Known for:** to-die-for desserts; unusual wines; perfect for a romantic dinner. ⑤ *Average main: €144* ✉ *19 rue St-Sauveur, 2e, Grands Boulevards* ☎ *06–95–16–32–87* ⊕ *www.restaurant-shabour.com* ⊘ *Closed Sun. No lunch Mon.–Thurs.* Ⓜ *Réamur–Sébastopol, Sentier, Bonne Nouvelle.*

Pantagruel

$$$$ | **FRENCH** | Chef Jason Gouzy won a Michelin star less than a year after the 2020 opening of this sought-after restaurant, where each dish resembles a gemlike work of art. The sleekly romantic dining room perfectly mirrors what's on the menu: dishes of exceptional imagination and refinement with an emphasis on seasonal market-fresh vegetables, seafood, and meticulously sourced meats. **Known for:** good prices for this quality of cuisine; lovely atmosphere; excellent wines by the glass. ⑤ *Average main: €45*

Vivant 2

$$ | **FRENCH** | There's something about this sleek little wine bar that attracts top talent before they really hit the big time. Currently, it's a whole new culinary

adventure under the helm of Mexican chef Robert Mendoza, whose sublime concoctions have Parisians coming back again and again. **Known for:** excellent, inventive food; vegetarian options; outstanding wine list, with at least 20 choices by the glass. **§** *Average main: €21* ✉ *43 rue des Petites Écuries, 10e, Grands Boulevards* ☎ *01–42–46–43–55* ⊕ *www.vivantparis.com* ✡ *Closed weekends. No lunch* Ⓜ *Château d'Eau, Bonne Nouvelle.*

 Coffee and Quick Bites

 Cédric Grolet Opéra

$ | **CAFÉ** | Pastry chef extraordinaire Cédric Grolet made his name at Le Meurice, the palace hotel just down the street, with his exquisite sculpted fruits—glorious trompe-l'oeil versions of the real thing made with various chocolates filled with creamy fruit or nut ganache. At this cafe near the Opéra, you can sample the master's sublime cookies and breakfast pastries along with other gourmet delights. **Known for:** some of the most masterfully designed sweets in Paris; gourmet tea and coffee; perfect breakfast pastries. **§** *Average main: €12* ✉ *35 av. de l'Opéra, 2e, Grands Boulevards* ☎ *01–83–95–21–02* ⊕ *cedric-grolet.com* ✡ *Closed Mon. and Tues.* Ⓜ *Quatre-Septembre.*

Juji-Ya

$ | **JAPANESE** | One of Paris's first bento-box cafés (it's also a Japanese grocer), this cozy spot on storied Rue Ste-Anne offers an array of delicious eats, from smoked eel and grilled salmon to crispy chicken, fried tofu, and yummy veggie sides like marinated seaweed—a house specialty—and sesame spinach. For a meal on the go, this is the place. **Known for:** bento boxes to go; long lines, so arrive early for lunch; Japanese gourmet groceries. **§** *Average main: €15* ✉ *46 rue Ste-Anne, 9e, Grands Boulevards* ☎ *01–42–86–02–22* ⊕ *www.jujiya-bento.com* ✡ *Closed Sun. No dinner Mon.–Wed.* Ⓜ *Pyramides, Bourse, Quatre-Septembre.*

 Le Valentin

$ | **BAKERY** | A head-turning variety of luscious pastries, classic French breakfast sweets and breads, ice cream, chocolates, and homemade jams will tempt every sweet tooth at this charming bakery and tearoom. Tucked into the historic covered Passage Jouffroy, Le Valentin is a picturesque spot for breakfast, lunch, or teatime—or buy a box of irresistible French-Alsatian sweets to enjoy on the go. **Known for:** set in an 1845 covered passage; notable croissants and chocolate bread with Valrhona chocolate; French-Alsatian specialties. **§** *Average main: €7* ✉ *30–32 Passage Jouffroy, 9e, Grands Boulevards* ☎ *01–47–70–88–50* ⊕ *www.levalentin.paris* Ⓜ *Grands Boulevards.*

 Matamata

$ | **CAFÉ** | This tiny gem of a coffee shop may not have the ambience of Paris's historic brasserie cafés, but it does have something you won't find in any brasserie in Paris—reliably excellent coffee served with care and enthusiasm. What's more, a small menu of delicious homemade sweets and sandwiches and salads at lunchtime pretty much covers all your restorative needs. **Known for:** consistently great coffee drinks of all kinds; quality beans sourced from around the world; friendly atmosphere and clean-lined modern space. **§** *Average main: €7* ✉ *58 rue d'Argout, 2e, Grands Boulevards* ☎ *01–71–39–44–58* ⊕ *www.matamat-acoffee.com* ✡ *Closed Sun. No dinner* Ⓜ *Sentier.*

Noir Coffee Shop & Torréfacteur

$ | **COFFEE** | Part of a stylish new chain proliferating around Paris, this sleek café inhabits the entrance of a formerly run-down historic on the picturesque, and newly chic, Rue Richer—home of the Folies Bergère. Coffee lovers can enjoy their cuppa (or matcha, chai, and so forth) from velvet banquettes or high up on a balcony overlooking the soaring, light-filled space with a views down

Rue Saulmier. **Known for:** ethically grown coffee roasted in Paris; long coffee menu, but also some teas and a variety of pastries and cookies; location near many unique boutiques. [S] *Average main: €6* ✉ *33 rue Richer, 9e, Grands Boulevards* ☎ ⊕ *noircoffeeshop.com* ◎ *No dinner* Ⓜ *Le Peletier.*

Hotels

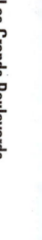

Chouchou Hotel

$$ | **HOTEL** | A distinctly bohemian vibe reigns in this oh-so-Parisian hotel, which opened in 2020 in a 19th-century Haussmannian building that's just a stone's throw from the Opéra Garnier. **Pros:** central location; excellent restaurant, oyster bar, and lounge; top-quality bath products. **Cons:** rooms are rather small, though cozy; suites are expensive; no fitness room (but there are yoga classes). [S] *Rooms from: €350* ✉ *11 rue du Helder, 9e, Grands Boulevards* ☎ *01–87–44–54–79* ⊕ *www.chouchouhotel.com* ⇝ *63 rooms* 🍴 *No Meals* Ⓜ *Chaussée d'Antin-Lafayette, Opéra.*

★ Hôtel Bachaumont

$$$ | **HOTEL** | This sleek 2015 revival of a 100-year-old neighborhood hotel that closed in the 1970s is a newfound favorite with the international set, whether staying the night or just stopping in for a stylish bite or drink at the wildly popular cocktail bar. **Pros:** central location in a vibrant up-and-coming neighborhood; chic nightlife on the premises; retro interiors. **Cons:** nearby métro can disturb sensitive sleepers in lower-floor rooms; room service can be slow; gym small and basic. [S] *Rooms from: €345* ✉ *18 rue Bachaumont, 2e, Grands Boulevards* ☎ *01–81–66–47–00* ⊕ *www.hotelbachaumont.com* ⇝ *49 rooms* 🍴 *No Meals* Ⓜ *Sentier.*

Hôtel Chopin

$ | **HOTEL** | A unique mainstay of the district, the Chopin—set within the atmospheric Passage Jouffroy—recalls its 1846 birth date with a creaky-floored lobby, aged woodwork, and its own homey charm. **Pros:** charmed location; close to major métro station; great nightlife district. **Cons:** thin walls; single rooms are very small; few amenities. [S] *Rooms from: €190* ✉ *10 bd. Montmartre, at 46 Passage Jouffroy, 9e, Grands Boulevards* ☎ *01–47–70–58–10* ⊕ *www.hotelchopin-paris-opera.com* ⇝ *36 rooms* 🍴 *No Meals* Ⓜ *Grands Boulevards.*

★ Hôtel de Nell

$$$ | **HOTEL** | Tucked in a picturesque corner of a chic, up-and-coming neighborhood ripe for exploration, this serenely beautiful hotel offers contemporary luxury with clean lines and uncluttered spaces designed by French architect Jean-Michel Wilmotte. **Pros:** good dining and bar on premises; interesting neighborhood to explore; beautiful, peaceful rooms. **Cons:** area deserted at night; far from the major Paris attractions; lacks a spa. [S] *Rooms from: €351* ✉ *9 rue du Conservatoire, 9e, Grands Boulevards* ☎ *01–44–83–83–60* ⊕ *www.hoteldenell.com* ⇝ *33 rooms* 🍴 *No Meals* Ⓜ *Bonne Nouvelle.*

Hôtel de Noailles

$$ | **HOTEL** | With a nod to the work of postmodern designers like Putman and Starck, this stylish boutique hotel is both contemporary and cozy. **Pros:** 15- to 20-minute walk to the Louvre and Opéra; a block from the airport bus; nice breakfast included. **Cons:** no interesting views; some bathrooms in need of renovation; small elevator. [S] *Rooms from: €303* ✉ *9 rue de la Michodière, 2e, Grands Boulevards* ☎ *01–47–42–92–90* ⊕ *www.hotelnoailles.com* ⇝ *56 rooms* 🍴 *Free Breakfast* Ⓜ *Opéra.*

★ Hôtel des Grands Boulevards

$$ | **HOTEL** | At this chic hotel, tucked away in plain sight on Boulevard Poissonnière, even the smallest of the minimalist jewel-toned rooms (some with balconies or garden terraces) feels elegant, with tall windows, marble touches, and

Marie-Antoinette-worthy draped headboards. **Pros:** beautifully designed rooms; chic on-site cocktail bar, restaurant, and rooftop bar; lots of outdoor spaces and some fabulous private terraces. **Cons:** rooms facing the courtyard bar can be noisy at night if windows are open; not every room has a balcony; some rooms quite tiny. ⑤ *Rooms from: €320* ✉ *17 bd. Poissonnière, 2e, Grands Boulevards* ☎ *01–85–73–33–33* ⊕ *www.grandsboulevardshotel.com* ↝ *50 rooms* 🍴 *No Meals* Ⓜ *Bonne Nouvelle, Grands Boulevards.*

Hôtel Gramont Opéra

$$ | **HOTEL** | Near the Opéra Garnier and some of the city's best department stores, this family-owned boutique hotel has lots of little extras that make it a great value. **Pros:** breakfast buffet (for a fee) with eggs made to order; personal and professional service; connecting rooms for families. **Cons:** singles have no desk; small bathrooms; elevator doesn't go to top floor. ⑤ *Rooms from: €250* ✉ *22 rue Gramont, 2e, Grands Boulevards* ☎ *01–42–96–85–90* ⊕ *www.hotelgramontparis.com* ↝ *25 rooms* 🍴 *No Meals* Ⓜ *Quatre-Septembre.*

Hôtel Langlois

$$ | **HOTEL** | This darling hotel gained a reputation as one of the more atmospheric budget sleeps in the city, although rates have since crept up. **Pros:** excellent views from the top floor; close to department stores and Opéra Garnier; historical decor. **Cons:** noisy street; a bit out of the way; some sagging furniture and worn fabrics. ⑤ *Rooms from: €210* ✉ *63 rue St-Lazare, 9e, Grands Boulevards* ☎ *01–48–74–78–24* ⊕ *www.hotel-langlois.com* ↝ *27 rooms* 🍴 *No Meals* Ⓜ *Trinité.*

Hôtel Littéraire Le Swann, BW Premier Collection

$$ | **HOTEL** | Paying homage to France's greatest literary lion, Marcel Proust, this original, modern *hôtel littéraire* is located in the novelist's old stomping grounds and immerses guests in his world, from the downstairs library filled with his works (including manuscripts and first editions) to the poetic quotes etched on glass partitions in each room—not to mention the complimentary madeleines. **Pros:** not far from the big department stores; good breakfasts; views from some rooms. **Cons:** some street noise; most rooms on the small side; bathrooms are minuscule. ⑤ *Rooms from: €240* ✉ *15 rue de Constantinople, 8e, Grands Boulevards* ☎ *01–45–22–80–80* ⊕ *www.hotel-leswann.com* ↝ *81 rooms* 🍴 *No Meals* Ⓜ *Europe, Villiers, Rome.*

★ Hôtel Parister

$$ | **HOTEL** | A glamorous addition to the fabulous (if off-the-beaten-path) 9e arrondissement, the Parister flaunts its design creds in even the tiniest of details, from its gorgeous common spaces to its sparse but elegant rooms. **Pros:** soothing modern decor in guest rooms; pool, steam room, and fitness center; elegant on-site restaurant. **Cons:** great neighborhood but off the beaten path; a little pricey for the location; some rooms on the small side. ⑤ *Rooms from: €340* ✉ *19 rue Saulnier, 9e, Grands Boulevards* ☎ *01–80–50–91–91* ⊕ *www.hotelparister.com* ↝ *45 rooms* 🍴 *No Meals* Ⓜ *Cadet.*

Hôtel Westminster

$$ | **HOTEL** | On one of the most prestigious streets in Paris, between the Opéra and Place Vendôme, this mid-19th-century inn happily retains its old-world feel. **Pros:** prestigious location near major sights; soothing steam room; popular jazz bar. **Cons:** a bit old-fashioned; some rooms overlook an air shaft; poor bathroom plumbing. ⑤ *Rooms from: €350* ✉ *13 rue de la Paix, 2e, Grands Boulevards* ☎ *01–42–61–57–46* ⊕ *www.warwickhotels.com/hotel-westminster* ↝ *102 rooms* 🍴 *No Meals* Ⓜ *Opéra.*

The Hoxton Paris

$$$ | **HOTEL** | In 2017, the urban-chic trendsetting Hoxton brand transformed an 18th-century mansion in Paris's up-and-coming Sentier district into this

hip hostelry with a chic restaurant, three cocktail bars—including the charming Jacques Bar tucked away on the second floor—and a welcoming community vibe. **Pros:** cool neighborhood with lots to explore; attractive contemporary decor in historic mansion setting; memorable bar scene. **Cons:** off-the-radar neighborhood not for everyone; restaurant is just average; the most affordable rooms have very few frills. 5 *Rooms from: €370* ✉ *30–32 rue du Sentier, 2e, Grands Boulevards* ☎ *01–85–65–75–00* 🌐 *www.thehoxton.com* ↔ *172 rooms* 🍴 *Free Breakfast* Ⓜ *Grands Boulevards, Bonne Nouvelle.*

★ InterContinental Paris Le Grand

$$$ | **HOTEL** | Sarah Bernhardt and Sir Arthur Conan Doyle adored this elegant Belle Époque hotel, an epitome of Haussmannian grandeur inaugurated in 1862 by the Empress Eugenie herself, and in 2021 it was given a dazzling renovation—the guest rooms, many with eye-popping views of the Opéra Garnier, blend old-world luxury with 21st-century glamour. **Pros:** the best breakfast buffet in Paris; lovely spa and winter garden; terraces with breathtaking Parisian views. **Cons:** the 4 miles of hallways can get confusing; not all terraces overlook the opera house; some rumbling from the métro below on lower floors. 5 *Rooms from: €500* ✉ *2 rue Scribe, 9e, Grands Boulevards* ☎ *01–40–07–32–32* 🌐 *www.parislegrand.intercontinental.com* ↔ *458 rooms* 🍴 *No Meals* Ⓜ *Opéra.*

★ Kimpton St Honoré Paris

$$$$ | **HOTEL** | The chic Kimpton line's first Parisian outpost opened in 2021 inside a stunning Art Nouveau landmark building—once part of the upscale Samaritaine department store—and each of the deco-inspired rooms is different: some offer balconies, others stellar views to the Eiffel Tower or the Opéra a stone's throw away. **Pros:** walking distance to major sights; some rooms have balconies with great views; stellar rooftop cocktail bar with astounding panoramas. **Cons:**

pricey restaurant; bar can get crowded; only two rooms in the spa. 5 *Rooms from: €540* ✉ *27–29 bd. des Capucines, 2e, Grands Boulevards* ☎ *01–80–40–76–10* 🌐 *www.kimptonsthonoreparis.com* ↔ *149 rooms* 🍴 *No Meals* Ⓜ *Opéra.*

★ La Fantaisie

$$$$ | **HOTEL** | Entering this newcomer hotel set in a vibrant, lightly-touristed quarter of Paris is like stepping into an enchanted garden. **Pros:** beautiful decor and spa; everything you need on-site, including excellent restaurant; stellar views from rooftop garden. **Cons:** spa too intimate for more than six people; prices high for this neighborhood; cocktails great but pricey. 5 *Rooms from: €600* ✉ *24 rue Cadet, 9e, Grands Boulevards* ☎ *01–55–07–85–07* 🌐 *www.lafantaisie.com* ↔ *73 rooms* 🍴 *No Meals* Ⓜ *Cadet.*

La Maison Favart

$$$ | **HOTEL** | An atmospheric indoor pool, relaxing sauna, and around-the-clock concierge are some of the reasons this jewel-box hotel is such a popular choice—add 18th-century charm, reasonable rates, good service, and beautifully decorated rooms, and it's no wonder why this hotel, named after the founders of the Comic Opera, pleases those who demand discreet elegance and creature comforts. **Pros:** lovely rooms and interior design; spacious bathrooms; easy walking distance to the sights. **Cons:** high demand for best rooms; impractical use of space in some rooms; no spa. 5 *Rooms from: €378* ✉ *5 rue de Marivaux, 2e, Grands Boulevards* ☎ *01–42–97–59–83* 🌐 *www.lamaison-favart.com* ↔ *39 rooms* 🍴 *No Meals* Ⓜ *Quatre-Septembre.*

★ Park Hyatt Paris – Vendôme

$$$$ | **HOTEL** | Understated luxury with a contemporary Zen vibe differentiates this Hyatt from its more classic neighbors between Place Vendôme and Opéra Garnier, and it's also distinguished by its designation as one of Paris's 12 "palace" hotels, meaning it reaches a certain level of luxury, service, and amenities beyond even a five-star hotel. **Pros:** stylish urban-chic design; the latest technology; only in-suite spa tubs in Paris. **Cons:** as part of a chain, it can feel anonymous; many corporate events held here; very expensive. ⑤ *Rooms from: €1,400* ✉ *3–5 rue de la Paix, 2e, Grands Boulevards* ☎ *01–58–71–12–34* 🌐 *www.hyatt.com* ↝ *148 rooms* 🍴 *No Meals* Ⓜ *Concorde, Opéra.*

Pley Hotel

$$ | HOTEL | Life's one big playground at this chic hotel that adds lightness and fun—not to mention serious style—to a neighborhood that can be a bit uppity. **Pros:** excellent rooftop bar with Eiffel Tower views; fun decor that nods to Paris's radio history; good location between Arc de Triomphe and Parc Monceau. **Cons:** cozy rooms can feel small; no proper spa; traffic noise in street-side rooms. ⑤ *Rooms from: €230* ✉ *214 rue du Faubourg St-Honoré, Grands Boulevards* ☎ *01–42–25–26–27* 🌐 *www.pley-hotel.com* ↝ *100 rooms* 🍴 *No Meals* Ⓜ *George V, Ternes.*

Nightlife

BARS

Corcoran's Irish Pub

PUB | This roomy pub, with several locations in central Paris, has an ample menu, a sleek bar, a pool table, and old-timey photos and quotations on the walls—such as "He who opens his mouth most is the one who opens his purse least." It's basically a classic Irish pub. Copious plates of pub food and frosty glasses of beer fuel conversation. Dancing at night has a regulated guy-to-girl ratio, so men shouldn't try coming alone. ✉ *23 bd. Poissonière, 2e, Grands Boulevards* ☎ *01–40–39–00–16* 🌐 *grands-boulevards.corcoransirishpub.fr* Ⓜ *Grands Boulevards.*

Duke's Bar

BARS | A favorite not only for its prestigious location between Opéra and Place Vendôme but also for its worn-leather chairs and English-private-club feel, the Westminster Hotel's bar offers drinks like the James Bond and Duke's Martini. At times, you get the feeling that Monsieur Hercule Poirot is lurking just behind that wing chair. ✉ *Westminster Hotel, 13 rue de la Paix, 2e, Grands Boulevards* ☎ *01–42–61–57–46* 🌐 *www.warwickhotels.com/hotel-westminster* Ⓜ *Opéra.*

Harry's Bar

BARS | Also known as Harry's New York Bar, this cozy, wood-paneled hangout decorated with dusty college pennants is popular with expats and American-loving French people who welcome the ghosts of Ernest Hemingway and F. Scott Fitzgerald, both of whom drank themselves unconscious here. Gershwin composed *An American in Paris* in the piano bar downstairs, and the Bloody Mary is said to have originated on-site. ✉ *5 rue Daunou, 2e, Grands Boulevards* ☎ *01–42–61–71–14* 🌐 *www.harrysbar.com* Ⓜ *Opéra.*

 **Jacques' Bar**

COCKTAIL BARS | Tucked away beyond a cobbled courtyard and up a winding back stairway, this cozy (only 24 seats) bar achieves an intimate, parloresque ambience thanks to floral chintz wallpaper, plush armchairs and poufs, and Asian rugs. For a hotel bar, it has well-priced Moroccan-inspired cocktails and small plates, making settling in for the evening a tempting option. Considering the Hoxton Hotel's other bustling spaces, this is a nice little getaway. It gets crowded, so arrive early. ✉ *30–32 rue du Sentier, 2e, Grands Boulevards* ☎ *01–85–65–75–01* 🌐 *thehoxton.com/paris/jacques-bar* Ⓜ *Bonne Nouvelle.*

Magniv

BARS | One of the newer outposts in a neighborhood with plenty to choose from, this scene-y hangout strikes a cool balance between a cocktail lounge, a Mediterranean restaurant, and a club— it's all of these. Set on three floors, Magniv has streamlined, vaguely futuristic decor, arched mirrors, and dusky lighting—perfect for dining, drinking, or dancing. Expect inventive tapas and truly delicious cocktails. ✉ 37 *rue du Sentier, 2e, Grands Boulevards* ☎ *01–40–26–14–94* ⊕ *www.magnivrestaurant.fr* Ⓜ *Bonne Nouvelle.*

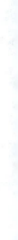

 The Shell

COCKTAIL BARS | Parisian cocktail lovers squeeze into this beautiful, intimate space—the beating heart of the Hôtel des Grands Boulevards—to imbibe some of the city's most ingenious and delicious cocktails concocted by a trailblazing mixologist. But the innovation doesn't end there. The Shell specializes in "mocktails" and lets drinkers watching their intake choose their dosage of alcohol, with commensurate prices, starting at €9. Anyone can get behind The Shell's motto: "No more hangovers."✉ *Hôtel des Grands Boulevards, 17 bd. Poissonnière, 2e, Grands Boulevards* ☎ *01–85–73–33–32* ⊕ *www.grandsbouievardshotel.com* Ⓜ *Grands Boulevards, Bonne Nouvelle.*

CLUBS

Silencio

DANCE CLUB | David Lynch named his nightclub after a reference in his Oscar-nominated hit, *Mulholland Drive.* Silencio, which hosts concerts, films, and other performances, is open only to members and their guests until 11 pm; after that everyone is allowed. Guest DJs spin until 4 am Tuesday through Thursday, and until 6 am on Friday and Saturday. ✉ *142 rue Montmartre, 2e, Grands Boulevards* ☎ *01–40–13–12–33* ⊕ *www.lesilencio.com* Ⓜ *Bourse.*

LIVE MUSIC

 New Morning

LIVE MUSIC | At New Morning—the premier spot for serious fans of avant-garde jazz, folk, and world music—the look is spartan, and the mood reverential. ✉ *7*

rue des Petites-Ecuries, 10e, Grands Boulevards ☎ *01–45–23–51–41* ⊕ *www.newmorning.com* Ⓜ *Château d'Eau.*

 Performing Arts

Casino de Paris

THEATER | Once a favorite of the immortal Serge Gainsbourg, Casino de Paris (a performance venue, not a gaming casino) has a horseshoe balcony and a cramped but cozy music-hall feel, and it presents everything from performances by touring musicals to Lorde and Belle & Sebastian concerts. This is where Josephine Baker performed in the early '30s with her leopard, Chiquita. ✉ *16 rue de Clichy, 9e, Grands Boulevards* ☎ *08–92–69–89–26* ⊕ *www.casinodeparis.fr* Ⓜ *Trinité.*

 Folies Bergère

MUSIC | Many an arts career was launched at this institution, where Josephine Baker charmed the city clad in nothing but a banana skirt and pearls, and icons such as Charlie Chaplin, Maurice Chevalier, and Mistinguett made their big Paris debuts. The 1926 Art Deco facade is a listed historic monument, but the opulent interiors hark back to its Belle Époque heyday as Paris's most daring cabaret. Nowadays, Dita Von Teese and other cabaret acts perform here regularly, but you'll also find more family-style shows, including dance, solo acts, and musicals. ✉ *32 rue Richer, 9e, Grands Boulevards* ☎ *01–44–79–98–60* ⊕ *www.foliesbergere.com/en.*

 Le Grand Rex

FILM | Since it opened in 1932, the Grand Rex—a designated historic landmark— has been Europe's largest cinema, with 2,800 seats in its main auditorium and Paris's largest screen. The cinema's history is almost as colorful as its superb Art Deco architecture, considered some of the finest in the city. Although some films are in French or are dubbed in French, many of the international films are in their original language (including

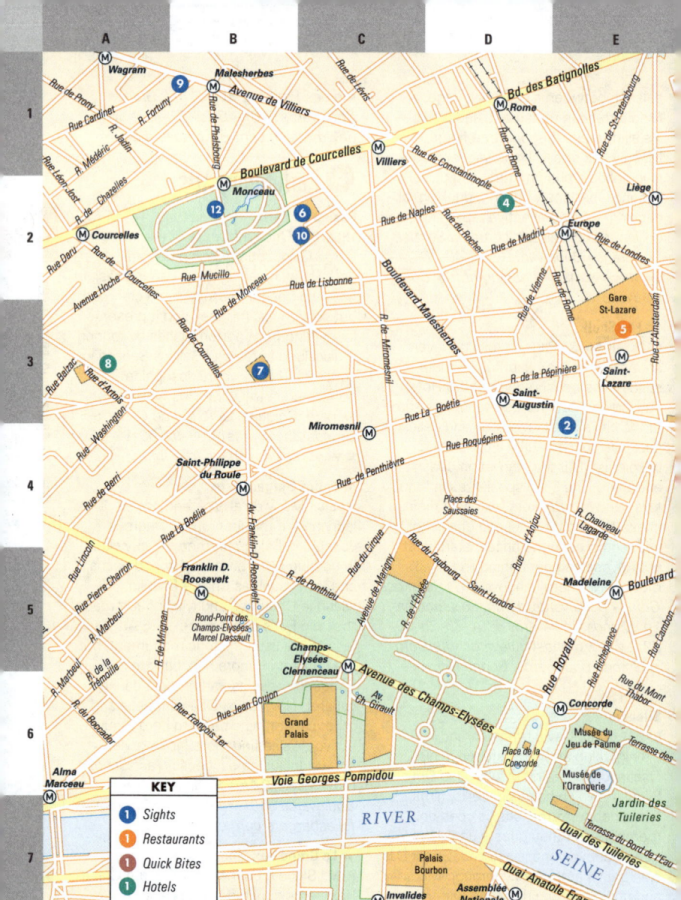

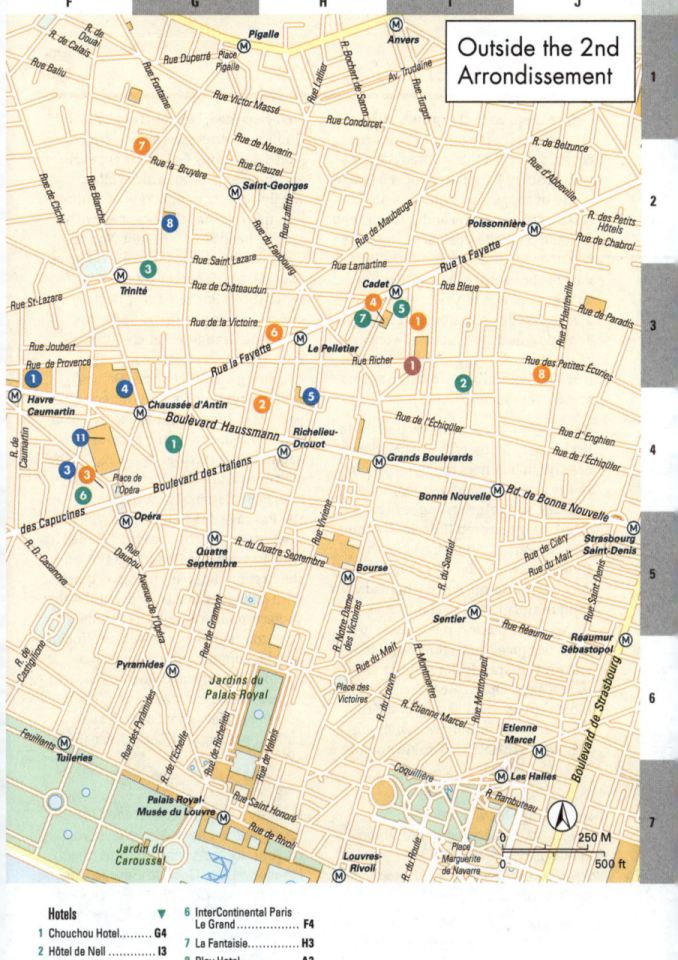

Paris's Covered Arcades

Before there were the *grands magasins*, there were the *passages couverts*, covered arcades that offered the early-19th-century Parisian shopper a hodgepodge of shops under one roof and a respite from the mud and grit of streets that did not have sidewalks. Until the rise of department stores in the latter part of the century, they would rule as the top places not just to shop but also to wander, socialize, and take tea. Technical and architectural wonders of the time, the vaulting structures of iron and frosted glass inspired artists and writers such as Émile Zola.

Of the 150 arcades built around Paris in the early 1800s, only about a dozen are still in business today, mostly in the 2e and 9e arrondissements. Two arcades still going strong are the fabulously restored **Galerie Vivienne** (✉ *4 rue Petits Champs, 2e*) and the **Galerie Véro-Dodat** (✉ *19 rue Jean-Jacques Rousseau, 1er*), both lined with unique and glamorous boutiques. Three other modest passages enjoying a renaissance can be found end to end off the Grands Boulevards, east of Place de l'Opéra. Begin with the most refined, the **Passage Jouffroy** (✉ *10–12 bd. Montmartre, 9e*), which is home to the Musée Grévin and the

well-regarded, budget-friendly Hôtel Chopin. There's an eclectic array of shops, including Galerie Fayet at No. 34, founded in 1909, which sells a wildly eccentric collection of umbrellas and walking sticks capped with animal heads and whatnot. You can outfit your dollhouse at Pain d'Épices (No. 29), which stocks thousands of miniatures. Pop out at the northern end of Passage Jouffroy and cross Rue de la Grange-Batelière into the **Passage Verdeau** (9e), where the charming Le Bonheur des Dames sells everything for embroideries like your grandma used to make (No. 8) or Thierry Ruby's art- and exotica-filled cabinet of curiosities at No. 12. On the southern end of the Passage Jouffroy, across Boulevard Montmartre, is the **Passage des Panoramas** (2e), the granddaddy of the arcades. Opened in 1799, Passage des Panoramas became the first public space in Paris equipped with gaslights in 1817. A few philatelist shops remain, though the arcade is now dominated by restaurants, including the popular wine bar-bistros Racines (No. 8) and Coinstot Vino (No. 26, *bis*), the chic Astair bistro (No. 19), and the perfect spot for an Italian coffee or teatime at Caffè Stern (No. 47).

many in English) with French subtitles. ✉ *1 bd. Poissonnière, 2e, Grands Boulevards* ☎ *01–45–08–93–89* 🌐 *www.legrandrex.com* Ⓜ *Bonne Nouvelle, Grands Boulevards.*

★ L'Olympia

CONCERTS | Paris's legendary music hall hosts an eclectic roster of performances encompassing genres that range from gospel and jazz to French chanson to rock. Edith Piaf rose to fame after a series of Olympia concerts, and Jeff

Buckley's famous *Live at the Olympia* was recorded here. Nowadays, you can see top acts ranging from Beach House to Lady Gaga to George Benson. ✉ *28 bd. des Capucines, 9e, Grands Boulevards* ☎ *08–92–68–33–68* 🌐 *www.olympiahall.com* Ⓜ *Madeleine, Opéra.*

★ Opéra Comique

OPERA | France's third-oldest theatrical institution is a gem of an opera house whose reputation was forged by its former director, *enfant terrible* Jérôme

Savary. In addition to staging operettas, the hall hosts modern dance, classical concerts, and vocal recitals. Tickets, which vary widely in price, can be purchased at the theater, online, or by phone. ✉ *1 pl. Boieldieu, 2e, Grands Boulevards* ☎ *01–70–23–01–00* ⊕ *www.opera-comique.com* Ⓜ *Richelieu-Drouot.*

★ Salle Cortot

MUSIC | This acoustic jewel was built in 1929 by Auguste Perret, who promised to construct "a concert hall that sounds like a Stradivarius." You can buy tickets for jazz and classical concerts only at the box office 30 minutes before each show; check the website for information on advance purchases. Free student recitals are offered at 12:30 pm on Tuesday and Thursday from October to April, and on some Wednesday afternoons from January to May. ✉ *78 rue Cardinet, 17e, Grands Boulevards* ☎ *01–47–63–47–48* ⊕ *www.sallecortot.com* Ⓜ *Malesherbes.*

★ Théâtre Mogador

THEATER | One of Paris's most sumptuous theaters features musicals and other productions with a pronounced popular appeal (think *The Lion King* or *Holiday on Ice*). Many of the shows here are subtitled in English, thanks to Theatre in Paris (⊕ *theatreinparis.com*). ✉ *25 rue de Mogador, 9e, Grands Boulevards* ☎ *01–53–32–32–32* ⊕ *www.theatremogador.com* Ⓜ *Trinité.*

 Shopping

BARGAIN SHOPPING

Monoprix

DEPARTMENT STORE | **FAMILY** | With branches throughout the city, this is *the* French dime store par excellence, stocking everyday items like cosmetics, groceries, toys, kitchenware, and more. Monoprix also has a line of stylish, inexpensive, basic wearables for the whole family—particularly adorable kids' clothes—and it isn't a bad place to stock up on French chocolate, jams, or *confit de canard* at

reasonable prices. ✉ *21 av. de l'Opéra, 1er, Grands Boulevards* ☎ *01–42–61–78–08* ⊕ *www.monoprix.fr* Ⓜ *Opéra.*

BEAUTY AND FRAGRANCES

Make Up For Ever

COSMETICS | Poised at the back of a courtyard, this store is a must-stop for makeup artists, models, actresses, and divas of all stripes. The riotous color selection includes hundreds of hues for foundation, eye shadow, powder, and lipstick. ✉ *5 rue de la Boétie, 8e, Grands Boulevards* ☎ *01–53–05–93–30* ⊕ *www.makeupforever.com* Ⓜ *St-Augustin.*

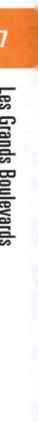

★ Nose

FRAGRANCES | Off the bustling Rue Montmartre, this unique concept store is Paris's perfume and skin-care central—a must for seekers of that elusive perfect fragrance. After you're installed at the bar (with refreshment), you'll be given a detailed questionnaire on the in-house iPad to pinpoint five or 10 scents from 500 niche perfumes that correspond to your deepest self. There's also a super range of European skin-care products, scented candles, and other delicious surprises. ✉ *20 rue Bachaumont, 2e, Grands Boulevards* ☎ *01–40–26–46–03* ⊕ *noseparis.com* Ⓜ *Sentier, Étienne Marcel.*

CLOTHING

Anouschka

VINTAGE | A former model, Anouschka has set up shop in her apartment (open by appointment only, Monday through Saturday) and has rack upon rack of vintage clothing dating from the 1930s to the '80s. It's the perfect place to find a '50s cocktail dress in mint condition or a mod jacket for him. She calls this a "designer laboratory," and teams from top fashion houses often pop by looking for inspiration. ✉ *6 av. du Coq, 9e, Grands Boulevards* ☎ *01–48–74–37–00* Ⓜ *St-Lazare, Trinité.*

★ **By Marie**

SPECIALTY STORE | At her multibrand concept store, jewelry designer and general fashionista-about-town Marie Gas does the work for you, mixing women's wear designers you already know and love (Spalwart, Ulla Johnson) with French and European *créateurs* that you definitely want to know (and will love). Browse a seasonal collection of everything from ready-to-wear to jewelry, leather goods, perfume, and design objects for the home. ✉ *44 rue Étienne Marcel, 2e, Grands Boulevards* ☎ *01–42–33–36–04* ⊕ *www.bymarie.com* Ⓜ *Sentier, Étienne Marcel.*

Charvet

CLOTHING | The Parisian equivalent of a Savile Row tailor, Charvet is a conservative, aristocratic institution. It's famed for made-to-measure shirts, exquisite ties, and accessories; for garbing John F. Kennedy, Charles de Gaulle, and the duke of Windsor; and for its regal address. Although the exquisite silk ties, in hundreds of colors and patterns, and custom-made shirts for men are the biggest draws, refined pieces for women and girls, as well as adorable miniatures for boys, round out the collection. ✉ *28 pl. Vendôme, 1er, Grands Boulevards* ☎ *01–42–60–30–70* ⊕ *instagram.com/ charvet_official* Ⓜ *Opéra.*

Eric Bompard

CLOTHING | This cashmere shop provides stylish Parisians with luxury cashmere in every color, style, and weight; yarns range from light as a feather to a hefty 50-ply for the jaunty caps. The store caters to men and women (there are some kids' models, too). Styles are updated seasonally yet tend toward the classic. ✉ *75 bd. Haussmann, 8e, Grands Boulevards* ☎ *01–42–68–00–73* ⊕ *www. eric-bompard.com* Ⓜ *Miromesnil.*

★ **Y's Yohji Yamamoto**

CLOTHING | Yamamoto's voluminous, draped, and highly coveted Y's label fully expresses itself in this sleek backdrop of white and chrome. Don't expect a varied palette; the clothing comes mostly in his signature black, with splashes of red, beige, and white. But do expect sophisticated, classic clothes for women and men that never go out of style. ✉ *25 rue du Louvre, 2e, Grands Boulevards* ☎ *01–42–21–42–93* ⊕ *www. yohjiyamamoto.co.jp* Ⓜ *Étienne Marcel, Bourse, Louvre-Rivoli.*

FOOD AND TREATS

À la Mère de Famille

CANDY | **FAMILY** | This enchanting shop dates from 1761 and is the oldest continuously open confectionary in Paris. Though it has gone the way of the chain, with multiple boutiques in Paris, À la Mère de Famille retains its authenticity and is well versed in French regional specialties as well as old-fashioned bonbons, chocolates, marzipan, ice creams, and more. ✉ *35 rue du Faubourg-Montmartre, 9e, Grands Boulevards* ☎ *01–47– 70–83–69* ⊕ *www.lameredefamille.com* Ⓜ *Cadet.*

Fauchon

FOOD | The most iconic of Parisian food stores is expanding globally, but its flagship is still behind the Madeleine church. Established in 1886, Fauchon sells renowned pâté, honey, jelly, tea, and private-label Champagne. Expats come for hard-to-find foreign foods (think U.S. pancake mix or British lemon curd), while those with a sweet tooth make a beeline to the pâtisserie for airy, ganache-filled macarons. There's also a café for a quick bite. Be prepared, though: prices can be eye-popping—marzipan fruit for €100 a pound?! ✉ *26 pl. de la Madeleine, 8e, Grands Boulevards* ☎ *01–70–39–38–00* ⊕ *www.fauchon.com* Ⓜ *Madeleine.*

★ **G. Detou**

FOOD | Join Paris's chefs and head for G. Detou (get it, *j'ai de tout*—I have everything), just off the wonderful Marché Montorgeuil, for an absolutely astounding range of baking staples, nuts, chocolate, canned rarities, and other

French and European delicacies. Basically, a bit of, well … everything. ✉ *58 rue Tiquetonne, 2e, Grands Boulevards* ☎ *01–42–36–54–67* Ⓜ *Étienne Marcel, Réaumur–Sébastopol.*

★ Rrraw

CHOCOLATE | Just when Paris thought its already phenomenal chocolate scene couldn't get any better, chocolatier Frédéric Marr opened this chic chocolate factory and boutique in 2007. Now the words "healthy" and "chocolate" appear together in the organic, nondairy, vegan (and yes, tasty) confections made here from unheated raw beans to preserve all the nutrients, subtle flavors, and (minimal) natural sugars. There's no resisting the chic metal boxes filled with bite-size truffles perfumed with flavors like sesame-rose, hazelnut-vanilla, or honey-pollen, as well as *tablettes* (bars) and baking chocolate, a boon for vegan cooks. It's known for its vegan, gluten-free, organic, and low-sugar products, but it also has delicious hot chocolate. Plus, you can watch chocolate being made on the premises. ✉ *8 rue de Mulhouse, 2e, Grands Boulevards* ☎ *01–45–08–84–04* ⊕ *www.rrraw.fr* Ⓜ *Bonne Nouvelle.*

★ Stohrer

FOOD | This institution opened in 1730, thanks to Louis XV's Polish bride, who couldn't bear to part with her pastry chef and thus brought Nicholas Stohrer along with her to Paris. Today, it has all the to-die-for pastries that made the bakery's name, including the famous *baba au rhum* that originated here, as well as a tantalizing range of other sweets, breads, and savory prepared foods to go. ✉ *51 rue Montorgueil, 2e, Grands Boulevards* ☎ *01–42–33–38–20* ⊕ *stohrer.fr* Ⓜ *Étienne Marcel, Réaumur–Sébastopol.*

HOME DECOR

★ Design et Nature

SPECIALTY STORE | Harking back to the Victorian era, when every chic household had a stuffed bird or small mammal, this outstanding cabinet of curiosities mixes jewel-like butterflies and insects with astonishing specimens of wild animals, including giraffes, lions and tigers, polar bears, antelopes, zebras, and exquisite birds. (Note that all of the animals died of natural causes in zoos.) More comical or whimsical pieces include pastel-color chickens, winged monkeys or mice, and the Poe chandelier, complete with a raven. All items come with certification for easy export and can be shipped anywhere. ✉ *4 rue d'Aboukir, 2e, Grands Boulevards* ☎ *01–43–06–86–98* ⊕ *www.designetnature.fr* Ⓜ *Étienne Marcel, Pyramides, Palais Royal–Musée du Louvre.*

★ Maison Sarah Lavoine

HOUSEWARES | Come here to learn the secrets of Paris's chicest apartments and upscale boutique hotels, brought to you by the sought-after Parisian designer herself. The boutique carries everything from textiles, throw pillows, tableware, and accessories to furnishings and lighting, all in Lavoine's signature jewel colors and luxe textures and shapes. ✉ *6 pl. des Victoires, 2e, Grands Boulevards* ☎ *01–40–13–75–75* ⊕ *www.maisonsarahlavoine.com* Ⓜ *Bourse.*

JEWELRY AND ACCESSORIES

Chanel Jewelry

JEWELRY & WATCHES | The iconic design elements of the pearl-draped designer are in evidence in Chanel Jewelry: witness the quilting (reimagined for gold rings), camellias (now brooches), and shooting stars (used for Chanel's first jewelry collection in 1932, now appearing as diamond rings). ✉ *18 pl. Vendôme, 1er, Grands Boulevards* ☎ *01–40–98–55–55* ⊕ *www.chanel.com* Ⓜ *Tuileries, Opéra.*

Dinh Van

JEWELRY & WATCHES | Just around the corner from Place Vendôme's titan jewelers, Dinh Van thumbs its nose at in-your-face opulence. The look here is refreshingly spare. Bestsellers include a hammered-gold-orb necklace and leather-cord bracelets joined with geometric shapes in white or yellow gold, some with pavé diamonds. ✉ *16 rue de la Paix, 2e, Grands Boulevards* ☎ *01–42–61–74–49* ⊕ *www.dinhvan.com* Ⓜ *Opéra.*

LINGERIE

Erès

LINGERIE | This brand revolutionized the bathing suit in the free-spirited '60s. Engineered to move freely with the body, these ingenious cuts liberated women from bones and padding. Lingerie followed in 1998, offering the same flawless craftsmanship and supreme comfort. Sexy without a hint of trashiness, Erès puts out some of the finest and most sophisticated lingerie and bathing suits in Paris season after season. ✉ *2 rue Tronchet, 8e, Grands Boulevards* ☎ *01–47–42–28–82* ⊕ *www.eresparis.com* Ⓜ *Madeleine.*

MARKETS

★ Marché Montorgeuil

MARKET | One of Paris's oldest and most colorful market streets, with its roots in the 12th century, still harbors addresses that hark back to the 18th century. To get the full effect, start at Rue Réaumur, and walk this cobbled pedestrian street all the way to the Forum des Halles, past shops displaying every French delicacy, from cheese and chocolate to oysters and pastry, interspersed with bustling cafés. Stop in at Société des Huîtres d'Étretat (1777), at Nos. 61–63, purveyors of oysters to Marie-Antoinette, or grab a divine pastry at Stohrer (1730) at No. 51. ✉ *Rue Montorgeuil, 2e, Grands Boulevards* Ⓜ *Étienne Marcel, Réaumur–Sébastopol.*

★ Rue du Nil

MARKET | Once a sordid spot where grifters convened to count the daily take, this minuscule street, tucked away in the up-and-coming Sentier neighborhood in arrondissement 2e, is now foodie central. It all began with the Frenchie empire—takeout, wine bar, and gastronomic restaurant—then their suppliers followed. Now, the cobbled street is lined with chic eateries and purveyors of everything from fresh fish and fruits to tempting breads and pastries, and boasts one of Paris's best gourmet coffee shops (L'Arbre à Café, No. 10). ✉ *Rue du Nil, Grands Boulevards.*

Rue Lévis

MARKET | Near Parc Monceau, this is one of Paris's more vibrant and oldest market streets, dating back to the 1600s. Though some cut-rate boutiques lately encroached, you'll find plenty of the authentic good stuff, from cured Iberian ham to every French specialty under the sun. ✉ *Rue Lévis, 17e, Grands Boulevards* Ⓜ *Villiers.*

TOYS

★ Pain d'Épices

TOYS | **FAMILY** | This toy shop has anything you can imagine for the French home (and garden) in miniature, such as Lilliputian croissants, wine decanters, and minuscule instruments in their cases. Build-it-yourself dollhouses include a 17th-century town house and a *boulangerie* storefront. Upstairs are do-it-yourself teddy-bear kits and classic toys. ✉ *29 Passage Jouffroy, 9e, Grands Boulevards* ☎ *01–47–70–08–68* ⊕ *www.paindepices.fr* Ⓜ *Grands Boulevards.*

WINE

Les Caves Augé

WINE/SPIRITS | One of the best wine shops in Paris, Les Caves Augé has been in operation since 1850. It's just the ticket, whether you're looking for a rare vintage, a select Bordeaux, or a seductive bubbly for a tête-à-tête. English-speaking experts are on hand to guide you through an excellent collection of small-producer, organic, and natural wines, as well as select grower-producer Champagnes. ✉ *116 bd. Haussmann, 8e, Grands Boulevards* ☎ *01–45–22–16–97* Ⓜ *St-Augustin.*

Chapter 8

MONTMARTRE

Updated by
Jack Vermee

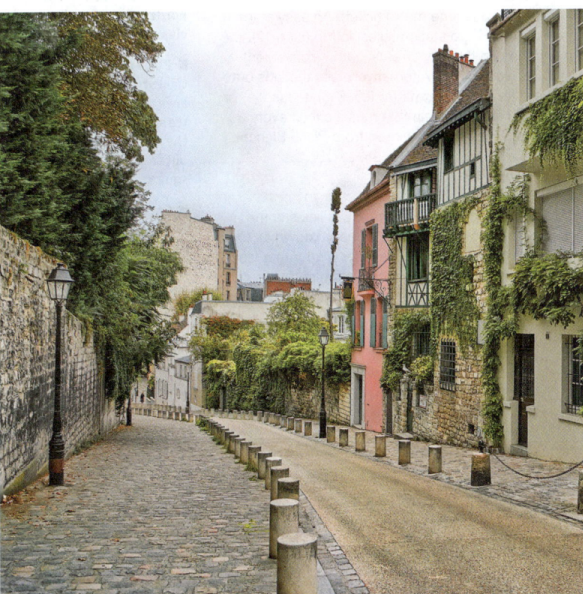

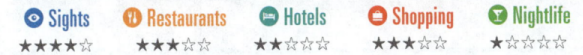

NEIGHBORHOOD SNAPSHOT

MAKING THE MOST OF YOUR TIME

Devote a day to this neighborhood if you want to see more than the obligatory Sacré-Coeur Basilica. If possible, avoid weekends, when the narrow—and extremely hilly—streets are jam-packed.

GETTING HERE

Montmartre is in the 18e arrondissement. Take Line 2 to Anvers *métro* station, and then take the funicular (one métro ticket) up to Sacré-Coeur. Or take Line 12 to Abbesses station and take your time wandering the cobbled streets and staircases that lead up to the basilica. For a scenic tour, hop the public bus, Montmartrobus (one métro ticket). An easy starting point is the métro station Jules-Joffrin (Line 12): the bus winds up the hilly streets, with a convenient stop at Sacré-Coeur. Alternatively, pile the kids onto Le Petit Train de Montmartre (€5–€10), a bus disguised as a minitrain that runs a circuit every 30 minutes (every hour in winter) from Place Blanche.

PAUSE HERE

Directly behind the Sacré-Coeur Basilica sits the lovely park and green space formally known as the Square Marcel Bleustein Blanchet. With great views of Paris's northeast quadrant, it is the perfect spot to recharge your batteries before tackling Sacré-Coeur itself.

TOP REASONS TO GO

■ **Basilique du Sacré-Coeur.** The best view of Paris is worth the climb—or the funicular ride—especially at twilight when the city lights create a magnificent panorama below the hill of Montmartre.

■ **Place du Tertre.** This bustling square beside Sacré-Coeur teems with crowds of tourists and hordes of street artists clamoring to paint them.

■ **Place des Abbesses.** Capture the village ambience that makes Montmartre special by exploring the tiny streets branching out from this picturesque square.

■ **Carré Roland Dorgelès.** Bring your camera to this little square overlooking a pair of classic Montmartre sights: the city's only vineyard and the famous Au Lapin Agile cabaret.

Montmartre has become almost too charming for its own good. Yes, it feels like a village (if you wander off the beaten path); yes, there are working artists here (though far fewer than there used to be); and yes, the best view of Paris is yours for free from the top of the hill (if there's no haze).

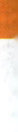

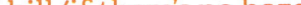

That's why on any weekend day, year-round, you can find scores of visitors crowding these cobbled alleys, scaling the staircases that pass for streets, and queuing to see Sacré-Coeur, the "sculpted cloud," at the summit.

If you're lucky enough to have a little corner of Montmartre to yourself, you'll understand why locals love it so. Come at nonpeak times, on a weekday, or in the morning or later in the evening. Stroll around **Place des Abbesses**, where the rustic houses and narrow streets escaped the heavy hand of urban planner Baron Haussmann. Until 1860 the area was, in fact, a separate village, dotted with windmills. Always a draw for bohemians and artists, many of whom had studios at what is now the **Musée de Montmartre** and the **Bateau-Lavoir**, Montmartre has been home to such painters as Suzanne Valadon and her son Maurice Utrillo, Picasso, van Gogh, Géricault, Renoir, and, of course, Henri de Toulouse-Lautrec, whose iconic paintings of the cancan dancers at the **Moulin Rouge** are now souvenir-shop fixtures.

While you can still see shows at the Moulin Rouge in Place Blanche and the pocket-size cabaret **Au Lapin Agile**, much of the entertainment here is on the rather unwholesome side—the area around Pigalle is the city's largest red-light district, though "SoPi" (as hipster residents call it) is far tamer than it used to be and is now dotted with upscale cocktail bars. Boulevard de Clichy was virtually an artists' highway at the turn of the 20th century: Degas lived and died at No. 6, and Picasso lived at No. 11. The *quartier* is a favorite of filmmakers (the blockbuster *Moulin Rouge* was inspired by it), and visitors still seek out Café des Deux Moulins at 15 rue Lepic, the real-life café (unfortunately with a remodeled look) where Audrey Tautou waited tables in 2001's *Amélie*. In 1928, **Studio 28** opened as the world's first cinema for experimental films.

 Sights

★ Basilique de St-Denis

CHURCH | Built between 1136 and 1286, St-Denis Basilica is one of the most important Gothic churches in France. It was here, under dynamic prelate Abbé Suger, that Gothic architecture (typified by pointed arches and rib vaults) was said to have made its first appearance. The kings of France soon chose St-Denis as their final resting place, and their richly sculpted tombs—along with what

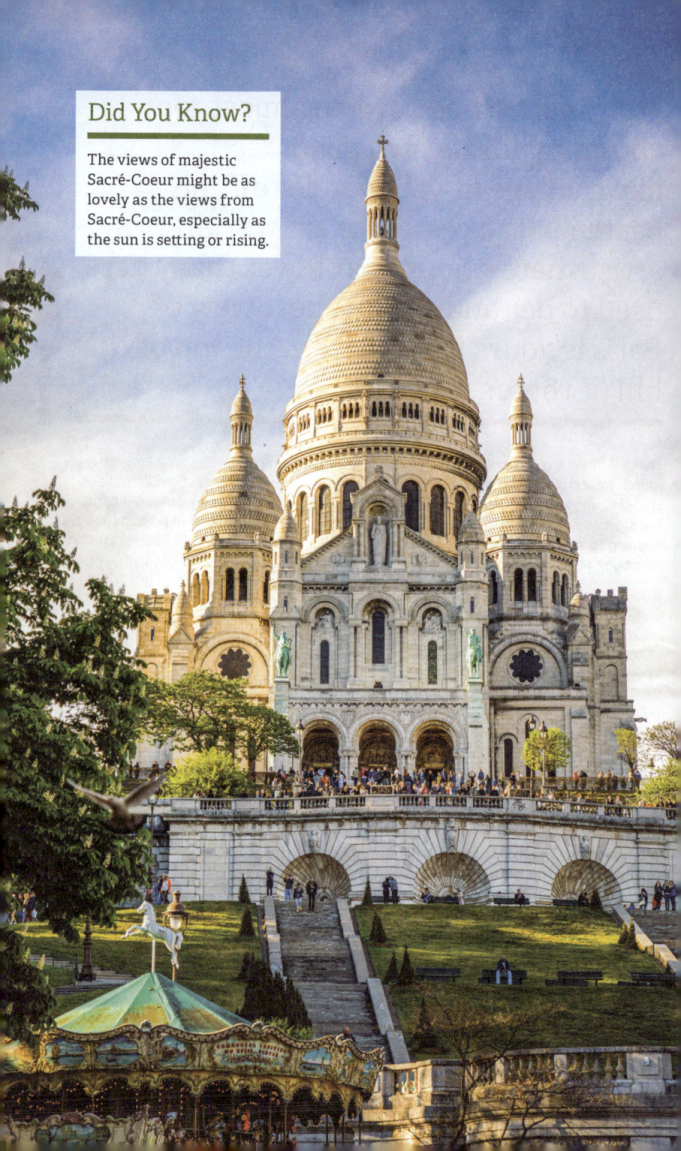

remains of Suger's church—can be seen in the choir area at the east end. The basilica was battered during the Revolution; afterward, however, Louis XVIII reestablished it as the royal burial site by moving the remains of Louis XVI and Marie-Antoinette here to join centuries' worth of monarchical bones. The vast 13th-century nave is a brilliant example of structural logic; its columns, capitals, and vault are a model of architectural harmony. The facade, retaining the rounded arches of the Romanesque that preceded the Gothic period, is set off by a small rose window, reputedly the oldest in France. Check out the extensive archaeological finds, such as a Merovingian queen's grave goods. Occasional guided tours in English are offered (see website for exact times); if you'd rather explore on your own, audioguides are available for €3, as is a free English-language information leaflet. ✉ *1 rue de la Légion d'Honneur, St-Denis* ☎ *01–48–09–83–54* ⊕ *www.saint-denis-basilique.fr* ✈ *€11* Ⓜ *Basilique de St-Denis.*

Picasso Lived Here

Montmartre is virtually littered with "Picasso Lived Here" plaques. The artist resided at three different addresses in the area: on Rue Gabrielle when he first arrived; at the Bateau-Lavoir; and at 11 boulevard de Clichy.

Inside, expect another visual treat—namely the massive golden mosaic set high above the choir. Created in 1922 by Luc-Olivier Merson, *Christ in Majesty* depicts Christ with a golden heart and outstretched arms, surrounded by various figures, including the Virgin Mary and Joan of Arc. It remains one of the largest mosaics of its kind. In the basilica's 262-foot-high campanile hangs La Savoyarde, one of the world's heaviest bells, weighing about 19 tons.

★ Basilique du Sacré-Coeur

CHURCH | It's hard not to feel as though you're ascending to heaven when you visit Sacred Heart Basilica, the white castle in the sky, perched atop Montmartre. The French government commissioned it in 1873 to symbolize the return of self-confidence after the devastating years of the Commune and Franco-Prussian War, and architect Paul Abadie employed elements from Romanesque and Byzantine styles when designing it—a mélange many critics dismissed as gaudy. Construction lasted until World War I, and the church was finally consecrated in 1919. Many people now come to Sacré-Coeur to admire the superlative view from the top of its 271-foot-high dome. But if you opt to skip the climb up the spiral staircase, the view from the front steps is still ample compensation for the trip.

The best time to visit Sacré-Coeur is early morning or early evening, and preferably not on a Sunday, when the crowds are thick. If you're coming to worship, there are daily Masses. ■ TIP→ **To avoid the steps, take the funicular, which costs one métro ticket each way.** ✉ *Pl. du Parvis-du-Sacré-Coeur, 18e, Montmartre* ☎ *01–53–41–89–00* ⊕ *www.sacre-coeur-montmartre.com* ✈ *Basilica free, dome €8* Ⓜ *Anvers, plus funicular; Jules Joffrin plus Montmartrobus.*

Bateau-Lavoir

HISTORIC HOME | The birthplace of Cubism isn't open to the public, but a display in the front window details this unimposing spot's rich history. Montmartre poet Max Jacob coined the name because the original structure here reminded him of the laundry boats that used to float in the Seine, and he joked that the warren of paint-splattered artists' studios needed

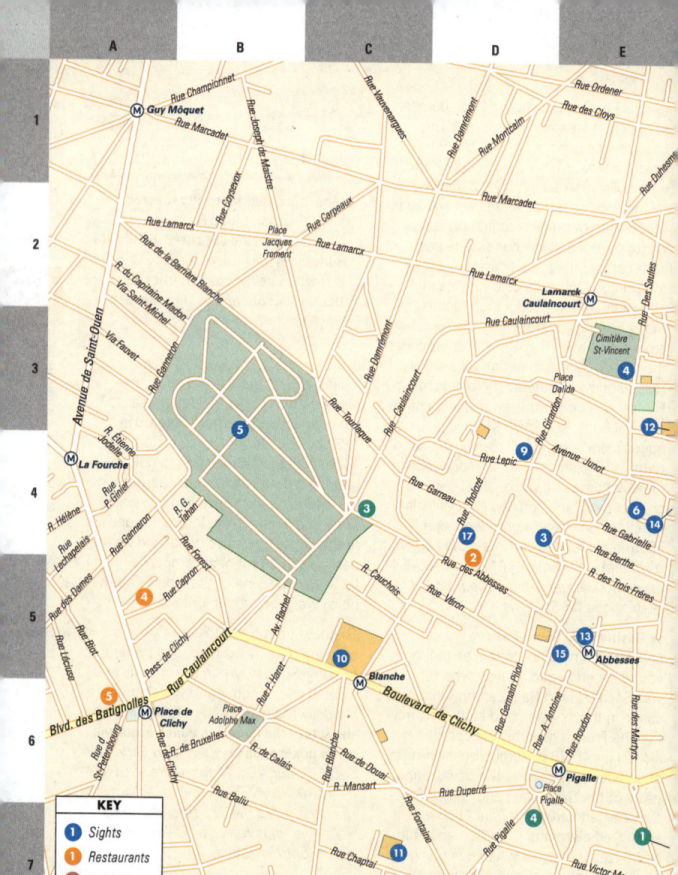

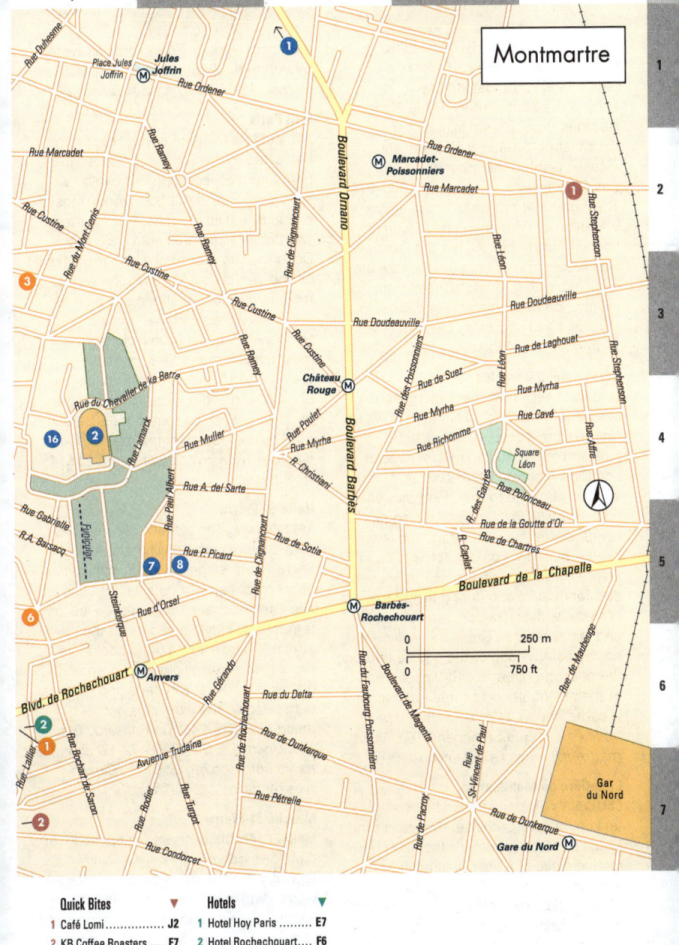

a good hosing down (wishful thinking, because the building had only one water tap). It was in the Bateau-Lavoir that, early in the 20th century, Pablo Picasso, Georges Braque, and Juan Gris made their first bold stabs at Cubism, and Picasso painted the groundbreaking *Les Demoiselles d'Avignon* in 1906–07. The experimental works of the artists weren't met with open arms, even in liberal Montmartre. All but the facade was rebuilt after a fire in 1970. Like the original building, though, the current incarnation houses artists and their studios. ✉ *13 pl. Émile-Goudeau, 18e, Montmartre* Ⓜ *Abbesses.*

Carré Roland Dorgelès

PLAZA/SQUARE | This unassuming square is a perfect place to take in two of Montmartre's most photographed sights: the pink-and-green Au Lapin Agile cabaret and Clos Montmartre, Paris's only working vineyard. The former, famously painted by Camille Pissarro, still welcomes revelers after over 160 years; the latter can be visited via guided tours (€39, in French) organized by the nearby Musée de Montmartre and during the annual Fête de Jardins (Garden Festival) weekend in September. The stone wall on the northwestern edge of the square borders the peaceful Cimetière St-Vincent, one of the neighborhood's three atmospheric cemeteries. ✉ *Corner of Rue des Saulnes and Rue St-Vincent, 18e, Montmartre* Ⓜ *Lamarck-Caulaincourt.*

Cimetière de Montmartre

CEMETERY | Overshadowed by better-known Père-Lachaise, this cemetery is just as picturesque. It's the final resting place of a host of luminaries, including painters Degas and Fragonard; Adolphe Sax, inventor of the saxophone; dancer Vaslav Nijinsky; filmmaker François Truffaut; and composers Hector Berlioz and Jacques Offenbach. The Art Nouveau tomb of novelist Émile Zola (1840–1902) lords over a lawn near the

entrance—though Zola's remains were moved to the Panthéon in 1908. ✉ *20 av. Rachel, 18e, Montmartre* Ⓜ *Blanche.*

Dalí Paris

ART MUSEUM | One of several museums dedicated to the Surrealist master, the permanent collection in this exhibition space includes about 300 works, mostly etchings and lithographs. Among the two-dozen sculptures are versions of Dalí's melting bronze clock and variations on the *Venus de Milo*. Since he was a multimedia pioneer ahead of his time, there are videos with Dalí's voice, and temporary exhibits have included the mustachioed man's foray into holograms. There's plenty of information in English, and audioguides (meant more for children) can be rented for €3. ✉ *11 rue Poulbot, 18e, Montmartre* ☎ *01–42–64–40–10* ⊕ *www.daliparis.com* 💰 *€14* Ⓜ *Abbesses.*

Halle St-Pierre

ART MUSEUM | The elegant iron-and-glass, 19th-century market hall at the foot of Sacré-Coeur stages dynamic exhibitions of *art brut,* "raw" or outsider and folk art. The international artists featured are contemporary in style and outside the mainstream. There's also a good bookstore and a café serving light, well-prepared dishes, such as savory tarts and quiches with salad on the side, plus homemade desserts. ✉ *2 rue Ronsard, 18e, Montmartre* ☎ *01–42–58–72–89* ⊕ *www. hallesaintpierre.org* 💰 *€10* ♡ *Closed weekends in Aug.* Ⓜ *Anvers.*

Marché St-Pierre

MARKET | **FAMILY** | This self-described "fabric kingdom" has been selling Parisians their curtains for more than 90 years. With five floors, it actually stocks a lot more than draperies, including bolts of fine silk, feather boas, and spangled cushions. Among the regulars here are the designers who create the famous windows at Hermès. The Marché

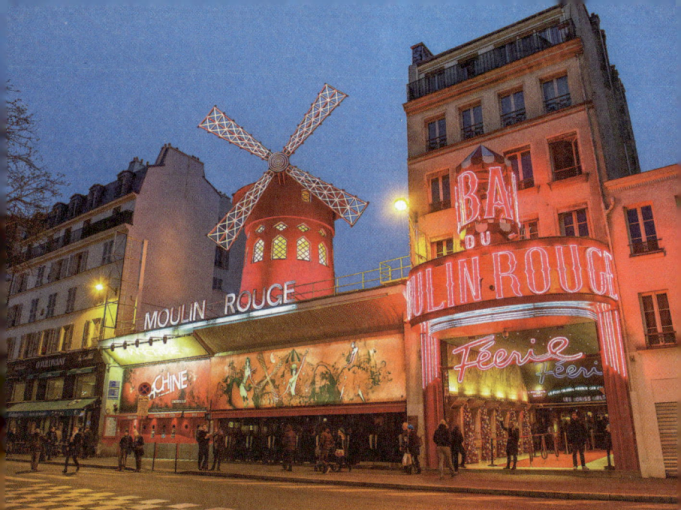

Perhaps the most famous cabaret in the world, the Moulin Rogue is where the cancan dance is said to have originated.

anchors a fabric district that extends to the neighboring streets; each shop is a bit different from the next. ✉ 2 *rue Charles Nodier, 18e, Montmartre* ☎ 01–42–06–92–25 🌐 *www.marchesaintpierre.com* ◷ *Closed Sun.* Ⓜ *Anvers.*

Moulin de la Galette

WINDMILL | Of the 14 windmills (*moulins*) that used to sit atop this hill, only two remain. They're known collectively as Moulin de la Galette, a name taken from the bread the owners once produced. The more storied of the two is Le Blute-Fin: in the late 1800s there was a dance hall on the site, famously captured by Renoir (you can see the painting in the Musée d'Orsay). A facelift restored the windmill to its 19th-century glory; however, it is on private land and can't be visited. Down the street is the other moulin, Le Radet. ✉ *Le Blute-Fin, at corner of Rue Lepic and Rue Girardon, 18e, Montmartre* Ⓜ *Abbesses.*

★ Moulin Rouge

PERFORMANCE VENUE | When this world-famous cabaret opened in 1889, aristocrats, professionals, and the working classes alike all flocked to ogle the scandalous performers (the cancan was considerably kinkier in Toulouse-Lautrec's day, when girls kicked off their knickers). There's not much to see from the outside except for tourist buses and sex shops; if you want to catch a show inside, ticket prices start at €113. Souvenir seekers should check out the Moulin Rouge gift shop (around the corner at 11 rue Lepic), which sells official merchandise, from jewelry to sculptures, by reputable French makers. ✉ *82 bd. de Clichy, 18e, Montmartre* ☎ 01–53–09–82–82 🌐 *www.moulinrouge.fr* 💰 *From €113* Ⓜ *Blanche.*

Musée de la Vie Romantique

SPECIALTY MUSEUM | A visit to the charming Museum of Romantic Life, dedicated to novelist George Sand (1804–76), will transport you to the countryside.

A Scenic Walk in Montmartre

One of Paris's most charming walks begins at the Abbesses métro station (Line 12). Explore the streets ringing **Place des Abbesses**, or begin the walk immediately by heading west along Rue des Abbesses. Turn right on Rue Tholozé and note the historic movie house, **Studio 28**, at No. 10. At the top of the street is Le Blute-Fin, a windmill portrayed in a well-known work by Renoir; a right on Rue Lepic takes you past the only other windmill still standing, Le Radet. Take a left here onto Rue Girardon, to **Place Dalida**, marked with a voluptuous bust of the beloved French singer who popularized disco. (Yolanda Gigliotti, aka Dalida, lived until her death in 1987 at 11 bis, rue d'Orchampt, one of the city's narrowest streets, opposite Le Radet.)

The stone house behind Dalida's bust is the 18th-century **Château des Brouillards**, whose name, Castle of the Mists, is taken from the light fog that used to cloak this former farmland. Detour down the romantic alley of the same name. Renoir is said to have lived in the château before moving to the small house across the way at No. 8. From Place Dalida, head down winding Rue de l'Abreuvoir, one of the most photographed streets in Paris. Pissarro kept a pied-à-terre at No. 12. The stone-and-wood-beam house at No. 4 was once home to a historian of the Napoleonic wars whose family symbol was an eagle.

Notice the wooden sundial with a rooster and the inscription: "When you chime, I'll sing." At the pink-and-green **Maison Rose** restaurant, committed to canvas by resident artist Maurice Utrillo, turn left on Rue des Saules, where you'll find Paris's only working vineyard, **Clos de Montmartre**.

Across the street is the famous cabaret **Au Lapin Agile**, still going strong. On the opposite corner, a stone wall rings the **Cimetière St-Vincent**, one of the city's smallest cemeteries, where Utrillo is buried. Backtrack up Rue des Saules and take the first left onto Rue Cortot to the **Musée de Montmartre**, once home to a bevy of artists, including Suzanne Valadon (mother of Utrillo), whose second-floor studio has been completely restored. A few doors down, at No. 6, the composer Erik Satie, piano player at Le Chat Noir nightclub, lived during a penniless period in a 6- by 4-foot flat with a 9-foot ceiling (and two pianos, stacked on top of each other). At the corner of Rue Mont-Cenis, the white water tower Château d'Eau still services the neighborhood. Turn right to reach **Place du Tertre**, a lively square packed with tourists and street artists. Easily overlooked is **St-Pierre de Montmartre**, one of the city's oldest churches, founded in 1147. End your walk at the basilica **Sacré-Coeur**, and enjoy one of the best views of Paris from the city's highest point.

Occupying a pretty 1830s mansion in a tree-lined courtyard, the small permanent collection features drawings by Delacroix and Ingres, among others, though Sand is the undisputed star. Displays include glass cases stuffed with her jewelry and even a mold of the hand of composer

Frédéric Chopin—one of her many lovers. The museum, about a five-minute walk from the Musée National Gustave Moreau, is in a picturesque neighborhood once called New Athens, a reflection of the architectural tastes of the writers and artists who lived and worked in the area. There is usually an interesting temporary exhibit here, too. The garden café (open mid-March to mid-October) is a lovely spot for lunch or afternoon tea. ✉ *16 rue Chaptal, 9e, Pigalle* ☎ *01–55–31–95–67* 🌐 *www.museevieromantique.paris.fr* 💰 *Free; temporary exhibits from €7* ⏰ *Closed Mon.* Ⓜ *Blanche, Pigalle, St-Georges.*

Musée de Montmartre

ART MUSEUM | During its turn-of-the-20th-century heyday, this building—now home to Montmartre's historical museum—was occupied by painters, writers, and cabaret artists. Foremost among them was Pierre-Auguste Renoir, who painted *Le Moulin de la Galette* (an archetypal scene of sun-drenched revelers) while living here. Recapping the area's colorful past, the museum has a charming permanent collection, which includes many Toulouse-Lautrec posters and original Eric Satie scores. An ambitious renovation, completed in 2014, doubled its space by incorporating both the studio apartment once shared by mother-and-son duo Suzanne Valadon and Maurice Utrillo (now fully restored) and the adjoining Demarne Hotel (which has been redesigned to house temporary exhibitions). The lovely surrounding gardens—named in honor of Renoir—have also been revitalized. An audioguide is included in the ticket price. ✉ *12 rue Cortot, 18e, Montmartre* ☎ *01–49–25–89–39* 🌐 *www.museedemontmartre.fr* 💰 *€15 (€5 gardens only)* Ⓜ *Lamarck–Caulaincourt.*

Place des Abbesses

PLAZA/SQUARE | This triangular square is typical of the countrified style that has made Montmartre famous. Now a hub for shopping and people-watching, the *place* is surrounded by hip boutiques, sidewalk cafés, and shabby-chic restaurants—a prime habitat for the young, neo-bohemian crowd and a sprinkling of expats. Trendy streets like Rue Houdon and Rue des Martyrs have attracted small designer shops, trendy secondhand

clothing stores, and even a *pâtisserie* specializing in meringues. Many retailers remain open on Sunday afternoon. ✉ *Rue des Abbesses at Rue la Vieuville, 18e, Montmartre* Ⓜ *Abbesses.*

Place du Tertre

PLAZA/SQUARE | Artists have peddled their wares in this square for centuries. Busloads of tourists have changed the atmosphere, but if you come off-season—when the air is chilly and the streets are bare—you can almost feel what it was like when up-and-coming Picassos lived in the houses that today are given over to souvenir shops and cafés. ✉ *East end of Rue Norvin, Pl. du Tertre, 18e, Montmartre* Ⓜ *Abbesses.*

Saint Jean l'Évangéliste de Montmartre

CHURCH | This eye-catching church with a compact Art Nouveau interior was the first modern house of worship built in Paris (1897–1904) and the first to be constructed of reinforced cement. Architect Anatole de Baudot's revolutionary technique defied the accepted rules at the time with its use of unsupported masonry; critics, who failed to stop construction, feared the building would crumble under its own weight. Today the church attracts a steady flow of visitors curious about its unusual Moorish-inspired facade of redbrick and curved arches. Note the tiny clock at the top left of the bell tower and the handsome stained-glass windows. Free concerts and art exhibitions are staged in the church from time to time. ✉ *19 rue des Abbesses, 18e, Montmartre* ☎ *01–46–06–43–96* 🌐 *www.saintjeandemontmartre.com* Ⓜ *Abbesses.*

Saint-Pierre de Montmartre

CHURCH | Tucked in the shadow of mighty Sacré-Coeur is one of the oldest churches in Paris. Built in 1147 on the site of a 5th-century temple to the god Mars, this small sanctuary with its impressive sculpted metal doors was once part of a substantial Benedictine abbey. Besides

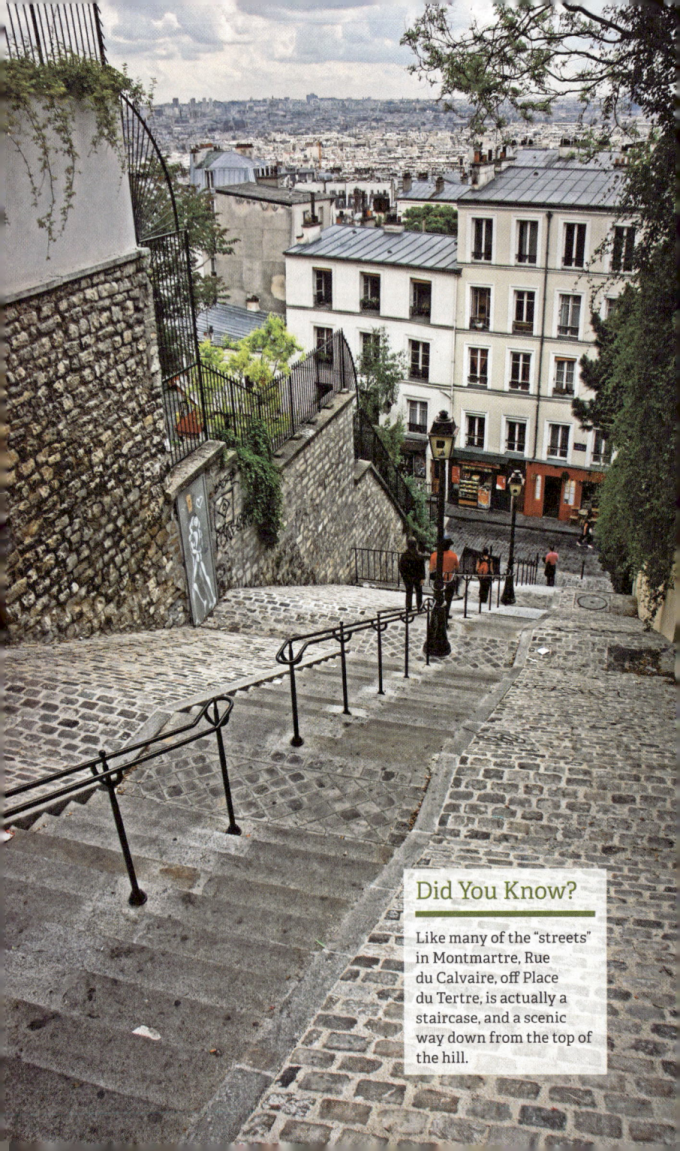

Did You Know?

Like many of the "streets" in Montmartre, Rue du Calvaire, off Place du Tertre, is actually a staircase, and a scenic way down from the top of the hill.

the church, all that remains is a small cemetery, now closed (you can see it through the ornate metal door on the left as you enter the courtyard). Renovated multiple times through the ages, Saint-Pierre combines various styles. Interior elements, such as the columns in the nave, are medieval; the facade dates to the 18th century, with renovations in the 19th century; and the stained-glass windows are 20th century. Maurice Utrillo's 1914 painting of the titular saint hangs in the Musée de l'Orangerie. Admission is free; English audioguides are €3. ✉ *2 rue du Mont Cenis, off Pl. du Tertre, 18e, Montmartre* ☎ *01–46–06–57–63* ⊕ *www.saintpierredemontmartre.net* Ⓜ *Anvers.*

Studio 28

OTHER ATTRACTION | This little movie house has a distinguished history. When it opened in 1928, it was the first theater in the world purposely built for *art et essai*, or experimental film, and Luis Buñuel and Salvador Dalí's *L'Age d'Or* caused a riot when it premiered here. Through the years artists and writers came to see "seventh art" creations by directors such as Jean Cocteau, François Truffaut, and Orson Welles. Today it's a repertory cinema, showing first-runs, just-runs, and previews—usually in their original language. Movies are screened beginning at 2 pm daily, and tickets cost €10. In the back of the movie house is a cozy bar and café that has a quiet outdoor terrace decorated with murals of film stars. Oh, and those charmingly bizarre chandeliers in the *salle*? Cocteau designed them. ✉ *10 rue Tholozé, 18e, Montmartre* ☎ *01–46–06–47–45* ⊕ *www.cinema-studio28.fr* ✈ *Movie tickets €10* Ⓜ *Abbesses.*

 Restaurants

Perched above central Paris, Montmartre is buzzing with a hip vibe. Idyllic as the portrayal of Montmartre might seem in Jean-Pierre Jeunet's film *Amélie*,

it's surprisingly close to reality. Though decidedly out of the way, Montmartre is still one of the most desirable areas in Paris, seamlessly blending the trendy and the traditional. The less picturesque neighborhood around Gare du Nord and Gare de l'Est is making its mark on the culinary milieu: besides classic brasseries, tucked-away bistros, and the city's most authentic Indian restaurants, there is a new generation of cafés and gastro-bistros exploding onto the scene.

Citrons et Huîtres

$ | **SEAFOOD** | With a name that translates to "lemons and oysters," this compact oyster bar—a notable addition to Pigalle's thriving food scene—is the perfect stop for a casual apéro of succulent oysters (imported daily from coastal France) and a glass of crisp vin blanc. But don't resist the urge to stay for dinner: the wildly creative chef (also a chef at the beautiful Hotel Rochechouart next door) presents beautiful small seafood dishes (think cured sardines, crab rolls on brioche, and house-smoked salmon) flecked with fresh flowers and herbs. **Known for:** great prices; sidewalk dining in summer; lively atmosphere. **$** *Average main: €12* ✉ *57 bd. Marguerite de Rochechouart, 9e* ☎ *07–64–29–26–66* ⊕ *www.citron-sethuitres.com* ⊘ *Closed Sun. and Mon.* Ⓜ *Pigalle, Anvers.*

La Mascotte

$$$$ | **BRASSERIE** | Though everyone talks about the "new Montmartre," exemplified by a wave of chic residents and throbbingly cool cafés and bars, the old Montmartre is alive and well at the untrendy-and-proud-of-it Mascotte. This old-fashioned café-brasserie—which dates from 1889, the same year that saw the opening of the Tour Eiffel and the Moulin Rouge—is a local favorite. **Known for:** copious oyster and seafood platters; sidewalk dining in summer; typical Belle Époque Montmartre atmosphere. **$** *Average main: €34* ✉ *52 rue des Abbesses,*

18e, Montmartre ☎ *01–46–06–28–15*
🌐 *www.la-mascotte-montmartre.com*
Ⓜ *Abbesses.*

 **L'Arcane**

$$$$ | **FRENCH** | Once a well-guarded foodie secret, a Michelin star brought this singular restaurant, tucked behind the Sacré-Coeur, richly deserved acclaim. Now the dining room is packed with diners enjoying impeccable contemporary French cuisine that's gorgeously presented and full of flavor. **Known for:** vividly imagined cuisine on multicourse tasting menus; location near the Sacré-Coeur; more affordable five-course lunch menu. **§** *Average main: €165* ✉ *52 rue Lamarck, 18e* ☎ *01–46–06–86–00* 🌐 *www.restaurantlarcane.com* ♡ *Closed Sun., Mon., Aug., 1 wk in mid-Apr., and last wk of Dec. No lunch Tues.–Thurs.* Ⓜ *Lamarck-Cauliancourt.*

 **Le BAL Café par Le RECHO**

$ | **CAFÉ** | **FAMILY** | Set in a bright, modern space on a tiny street in the lower reaches of Montmartre, the popular Le BAL Café caters to a diverse clientele who come for the great coffee, delicious homey food, lively crowd, and the art gallery/bookstore. Italian- and French-inspired cuisine (like spelt risotto with mushrooms, hazelnuts, and creamed spinach) during the week rests alongside a traditional weekend brunch menu featuring items like tender pancakes, fried eggs with ham and roasted tomatoes, and buttery scones with jam. **Known for:** great brunches and reliably good coffee; art gallery on the premises; outdoor terrace on a quiet passageway. **§** *Average main: €16* ✉ *6 impasse de la Défense, 18e, Montmartre* ☎ *01–44–70–75–51* 🌐 *www.le-bal.fr/le-bal-cafe-par-le-recho* ♡ *Closed Mon. and Tues. No dinner* Ⓜ *Pl. de Clichy.*

Le Cyrano

$ | **BISTRO** | This "bistronomic" (think "bistro" and "gastronomic") outpost set in a classic Art Nouveau–era bistro—complete with romantic mosaics and a marble bar that made it a favorite meeting place of the Surrealists—draws a lively food-centric crowd that's wild about chef Charleyne Valet's tasty sharable plates. Bistro favorites include egg parfait with smoked potato mousse and sunchoke chips, a delicious riff on grandmère's lentil soup, or haddock with raisins and almonds all served with a small but deftly curated selection of natural wines. **Known for:** affordable prices; location right off of lively Place de Clichy; supertrendy vibes. **§** *Average main: €17* ✉ *3 rue Biot, 17e* ☎ *01–40–07–55–05* 🌐 *www.lecyranoparis.com* Ⓜ *Pl. de Clichy.*

Le Progrès

$$ | **BRASSERIE** | This photo op–ready corner café draws a quirky mix of hipsters, artists, and discriminating tourists. The food is good and includes classics like steak tartare and escargots from Burgundy. **Known for:** good value for your money; excellent cheeseburger and fries; lively atmosphere. **§** *Average main: €20* ✉ *7 rue des Trois Frères, 18e, Montmartre* ☎ *01–42–64–07–37* 🌐 *www.facebook.com/leprogresmontmartre* Ⓜ *Abbesses.*

 Coffee and Quick Bites

Café Lomi

$ | **COFFEE** | A trailblazer on the Paris gastro-coffee scene, out-of-the-way Café Lomi first supplied expertly roasted single-origin coffees to the first wave of barista cafés and top restaurants. Now Lomi's industrial-chic loft is equal parts roaster, café, workshop, and pilgrimage stop for hard-core coffee lovers, serving a range of splendid brews along with cookies, cakes, and other confections. **Known for:** industrial-chic space; coffee roasted on the premises; consistently excellent brews. **§** *Average main: €10* ✉ *3 ter rue Marcadet, 18e* ☎ *09–51–27–46–31* 🌐 *www.lomi.cafe* ♡ *Closed Sun., Mon., and 3 wks in Aug.* Ⓜ *Marcadet-Poissonnière.*

KB Coffee Roasters

$ | **CAFÉ** | Set at a leafy crossroads on the lively Rue des Martyrs, this is a top pick in this vibrant neighborhood for a quick stop or to linger with a device. The coffee (roasted at their atelier-café Back in Black) is always good, as are the many other beverage options, both hot and cold, and the food—from healthy salads and sandwiches to yummy pastries—is exactly what's needed to get you revved up for your next Paris adventure. **Known for:** spacious outdoor setting; healthy snacks; open daily. ⑤ *Average main: €6* ✉ *53 av. Trudaine, 9e* ☎ *01–56–92–12–41* ⊕ *www.kbcafeshop.com* Ⓜ *Anvers, Notre-Dame-de-Lorette.*

 Hotels

Like a village unto itself, off-the-beaten-path Montmartre and its equally picturesque hotels provide a homey retreat after a day of sightseeing. There's much to explore here, and the old cobbled streets and hidden historic corners harbor lodgings as varied as old, gated mansions and quaint mom-and-pop hotels.

Hotel Hoy Paris

$$ | **HOTEL** | Ethical, sustainable, "zero waste," and entirely focused on your well-being, this distinctive property with feng shui–correct rooms and "indulge and enjoy" as its motto has made quite a splash since its 2020 debut. **Pros:** numerous healthy details; yoga and wellness classes offered on-site; superb bar and plant-based restaurant. **Cons:** wellness classes cost extra; no TVs; not ideal for hedonists. ⑤ *Rooms from: €200* ✉ *68 rue des Martyrs, 9e* ☎ *01–77–37–87–20* ⊕ *www.hoyparis.com* ↝ *19 rooms* 🍴 *No Meals* Ⓜ *Pigalle, St-Georges.*

Hotel Rochechouart

$ | **HOTEL** | This beautiful hotel located in a 1929 building at the foot of Montmartre has been returned to its roaring 1920s glory, with everything from the handsome Art Deco–inspired guest rooms (some with Sacré-Coeur-facing balconies) to the dreamy candlelit restaurant and jewel-like Mikado dance hall in the basement recalling a romantic, cosmopolitan Paris. **Pros:** excellent in-hotel drinking and dining; focus on sustainability; superb oyster bar. **Cons:** some rooms lack views; no lobby; no spa or fitness room. ⑤ *Rooms from: €186* ✉ *55 bd. Marguerite de Rochechouart, 9e, Pigalle* ☎ *01–42–81–91–00* ⊕ *www.hotelrochechouart.com* ↝ *106 rooms* 🍴 *No Meals* Ⓜ *Anvers, Pigalle.*

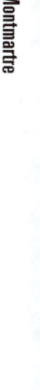

★ **Hotel Terrass"**

$$ | **HOTEL** | If you feel like being away from it all, but in a fairly self-sufficient setting with a good on-site restaurant and a chic bar with stupendous views, this is the place. **Pros:** panoramic views of all of Paris; awesome terrace bar; welcoming common areas with complimentary coffee. **Cons:** basic rooms are small; four-night-minimum stay in high season; some street noise. ⑤ *Rooms from: €320* ✉ *12–14 rue Joseph de Maistre, 18e* ☎ *01–46–06–72–85* ⊕ *www.terrass-hotel.com* ↝ *92 rooms* 🍴 *No Meals* Ⓜ *Blanche, Abbesses.*

Le Pigalle Paris

$$$ | **HOTEL** | The rooms here may not be huge, but they do give you the chance to have your very own Parisian lodging at the foot of Montmartre, packed with lovely touches like chic contemporary-vintage decor, provocative art prints and books, a record player with vinyl records, a fluffy bed, Le Labo toiletries, and quintessential Parisian views. **Pros:** good prices; close to fantastic nightlife; great neighborhood to explore. **Cons:** immediate area might not be to everyone's liking; open-plan bathrooms not for everyone; rooms very small. ⑤ *Rooms from: €410* ✉ *9 rue Frochot, 9e, Pigalle* ☎ *01–48–78–37–14* ⊕ *www.lepigalle.paris* ↝ *40 rooms* 🍴 *No Meals* Ⓜ *Pigalle.*

 Nightlife

Vestiges of this *quartier's* absinthe-tinged heyday, immortalized by Toulouse-Lautrec and Renoir, still endure in the cabarets and clubs that extend from the heights of Montmartre down to louche Pigalle's newly vibrant cocktail bar and dance scene.

BARS

Café la Fourmi

BARS | One of Montmartre's trendiest addresses, Café la Fourmi has a funky, spacious bar-café where cool locals party. It's open until 2 am every night but Friday and Saturday, when it's open until 4 am. ✉ *74 rue des Martyrs, 18e, Montmartre* ☎ *01–42–64–70–35* ⊕ *www.facebook.com/thomascubat* Ⓜ *Pigalle.*

Cave des Abbesses

WINE BAR | Locals head to this charming retro-looking *caviste* (wineshop) and wine bar for a glass of something special with a side of oysters, or perhaps La Grande Mixte, a platter of charcuterie, terrine, and cheese (€23). ✉ *43 rue des Abbesses, 18e, Montmartre* ☎ *01–42–52–81–54* ⊕ *www.cavesbourdin.fr/cave-des-abbesses-montmartre* Ⓜ *Abbesses.*

★ Dirty Dick

COCKTAIL BARS | An updated version of the classic tiki lounge, this stylish option in the hip South Pigalle (SoPi) neighborhood comes complete with lurid lighting, life-size totems, and retro rattan furniture. All the exotic drinks you'd expect at a Polynesian beach hut (or '60s motel lounge) are here—including fruity cocktails, a range of rums, and punch bowls with names like Amazombie. ✉ *10 rue Frochot, 9e, Pigalle* ☎ *01–48–78–74–58* ⊕ *www.facebook.com/dirtydickparis* Ⓜ *Pigalle.*

Le Rendez-Vous des Amis

BARS | This makes an intriguing midway breather if you climb the hill of Montmartre by foot. Le Rendez-Vous des Amis has a jovial staff, eclectic music, and a century's worth of previous patrons immortalized in painted murals. ✉ *23 rue Gabrielle, 18e, Montmartre* ☎ *01–46–06–01–60* Ⓜ *Abbesses.*

Le Sancerre

BARS | Café/restaurant by day, Le Sancerre turns into an essential watering hole for Montmartrois and artists at night (until 2 am), with Belgian beers on tap and an impressive list of cocktails. Locals love its traditional old-school vibe. ✉ *35 rue des Abbesses, 18e, Montmartre* ☎ *01–42–58–08–20* ⊕ *www.lesancerreparis.com* Ⓜ *Abbesses.*

★ Paname Brewing Company

BREWPUBS | One of Paris's first and best microbreweries on the city's exploding brewery scene, Paname offers a dozen masterful craft beers, plus limited-time specials, and a fabulous terrace on a plum spot facing the Canal de la Villette. ✉ *41 bis, quai de la Loire, 19e* ☎ *01–40–36–43–55* ⊕ *www.panamebrewingcompany.com* Ⓜ *Crimée, Laumière, Ourcq.*

CABARET

★ Au Lapin Agile

CABARET | An authentic survivor from the 19th century, Au Lapin Agile considers itself the doyen of cabarets. Founded in 1860, it inhabits the same modest house that was a favorite subject of painter Maurice Utrillo. It became the home-away-from-home for Braque, Modigliani, Apollinaire, and Picasso—who once paid for a meal with one of his paintings, then promptly exited and painted another that he named after this place. There are no topless dancers; this is a genuine French cabaret with songs, poetry, and humor (in French) in a publike setting. Entry—with one drink included—is €35, and it's cash only at the door (online prepayment by credit card is available). ✉ *22 rue des Saules, 18e, Montmartre* ☎ *01–46–06–85–87* ⊕ *au-lapin-agile.com* ♡ *Closed Sun., Mon., and Wed.* Ⓜ *Lamarck–Caulaincourt.*

Chez Michou

CABARET | Although the always-decked-out-in-blue owner, Michou, passed away in early 2020, the over-the-top show dances on. It features performers on stage in extravagant drag, with high camp for a radically different cabaret experience. Dinner shows are €130, €160, and €195, or you can watch from the bar for €55, one drink included. ✉ *80 rue des Martyrs, 18e, Montmartre* ☎ *01–46–06–16–04* ⊕ *www.michou.com* Ⓜ *Pigalle.*

Performing Arts

Cinéma des Cinéastes

FILM | **FAMILY** | Catch previews of feature films, as well as documentaries, shorts, children's movies, and rarely shown flicks at Cinéma des Cinéastes. Near the Montmartre neighborhood, it's an old cabaret transformed into a movie house and wine bar. ✉ *7 av. de Clichy, 17e, Montmartre* ☎ *01–53–42–40–20* ⊕ *www.cinema-des-cineastes.fr* ✉ *€10* Ⓜ *Pl. de Clichy.*

★ La Cigale

CONCERTS | Artists like Maurice Chevalier and Arletty were once a staple of this small concert hall in the storied Montmartre neighborhood before cabaret and vaudeville moved in. Today it's one of Paris's top pop and contemporary music venues; artists like Adele and Coldplay played here in their early days. ✉ *120 bd. de Rochechouart, 18e, Montmartre* ☎ *01–49–25–89–99* ⊕ *www.lacigale.fr* Ⓜ *Pigalle, Anvers.*

★ Le Louxor

FILM | First opened in 1921, Le Louxor has since been returned to its original Egyptian-theme splendor. Now the city's grandest cinema, this Art Deco beauty is gorgeously appointed—all in rich ocher with jewel-toned velvet seating—and shows a roster of contemporary international art films in three cinemas. Have a drink at the top-floor bar or balcony for spectacular views of the neighborhood and Sacré-Coeur. ✉ *170 bd. Magenta, 10e, Montmartre* ☎ *01–44–63–96–96* ⊕ *www.cinemalouxor.fr* ✉ *€11* Ⓜ *Barbès–Rochechouart.*

Théâtre des Abbesses

THEATER | Part of the Théâtre de la Ville, Théâtre des Abbesses is a 400-seat venue in Montmartre. It features lesser-known theater acts, musicians, and up-and-coming choreographers, who often make it onto the program in the Théâtre de la Ville the following year. ✉ *31 rue des Abbesses, 18e, Montmartre* ☎ *01–42–74–22–77* ⊕ *www.theatre-delaville-paris.com* Ⓜ *Abbesses.*

Shopping

To avoid an uphill climb, the Abbesses métro stop on Rue de la Vieuville is a good starting point for serious shoppers. From here, descend picturesque Rue des Martyrs all the way down to Notre-Dame-de-Lorette. The route promises a cornucopia of captivating boutiques that sell everything from chic antiques and offbeat fashion to gourmet food.

CLOTHING

A.P.C. Surplus

CLOTHING | A surplus store steps away from Sacré-Coeur, there's no need to wait for sales here; funky classics can always be found for up to 50% off. ✉ *20 rue André del Sarte, 18e, Montmartre* ☎ *01–42–62–10–88* ⊕ *www.apc.fr* Ⓜ *Château Rouge.*

MARKETS

★ Marché aux Puces St-Ouen

(*Clignancourt*)

MARKET | This picturesque market on the city's northern boundary still lures crowds on Friday from 8 am to noon, and weekends and Monday from 10 am to 6 pm, but its once-unbeatable prices are now a relic. Packed with antiques booths and *brocante* stalls, the century-old, miles-long labyrinth has been undergoing a mild renaissance lately: its 15 covered "marchés" now house all manner of artisans and creators as well as buzzworthy shops and galleries (some of which keep weekend-only hours). Destination cafés and eateries—including the popular La Chopes des Puces, where Django Reinhardt used to jam, and the chic MOB Hotel—also attract a hip Paris contingent. Arrive early to pick up the best loot, then linger over a meal or *apéro*. Be warned, though: if there's one place in Paris where you need to know how to bargain, this is it. If you're arriving by métro, walk under the overpass and take the first left at the Rue de Rosiers to reach the center of the market. Note that stands selling dodgy odds and ends (think designer knockoffs and questionable gadgets) set up around the overpass. These blocks are crowded and gritty; be careful with your valuables here and throughout the marché. ✉ *18e, Montmartre* ⊕ *www.marcheauxpuces-saintouen.com* Ⓜ *Porte de Clignancourt, Garibaldi, Mairie de St-Ouen.*

Chapter 9

THE MARAIS

Updated by
Jennifer Ladonne

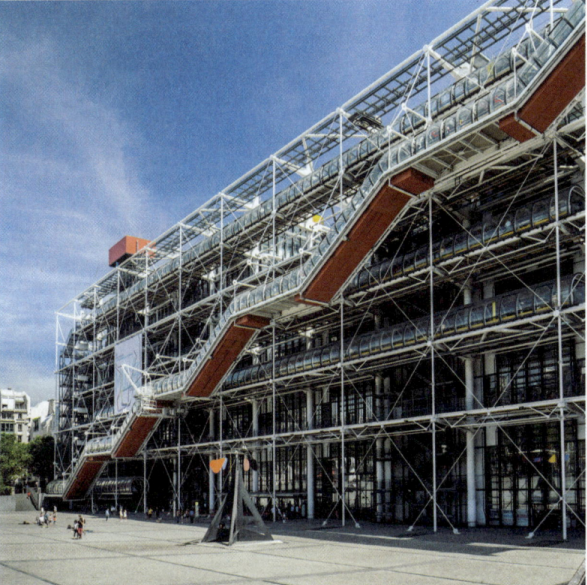

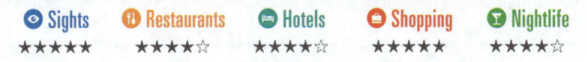

NEIGHBORHOOD SNAPSHOT

MAKING THE MOST OF YOUR TIME

One day in the Marais might seem painfully short, but it would allow you to take a do-it-yourself walking tour, peek into private courtyards, and picnic in Place des Vosges as you proceed. Leave at least two days if your itinerary includes the Centre Pompidou and the Musée Picasso. In three days you could cover some of the smaller museums, which are well worth visiting as many are housed in exquisite mansions. If time permits, wander the edges of the 3e arrondissement to see the charming streets, away from the crowds, or drop into the quirky-artsy Musée de la Chasse et de la Nature or science-centric Musée des Arts et Métiers. Sunday afternoon is a lively time because many shops are open. As Paris's most concentrated—and chicest—shopping neighborhood, you'll want to reserve at least an afternoon for discovering its many-splendored boutiques. This neighborhood thrives after dark as well: business is brisk at cafés and bars—particularly those favored by the LGBTQ+ community.

GETTING HERE

The Marais includes the 3e and 4e arrondissements. It's a pleasant walk from Beaubourg—the area around Centre Pompidou—into the heart of the Marais. Rue Rambuteau turns into Rue des Francs-Bourgeois, which runs into Place des Vosges. If you're going by *métro*, the most central stops are St-Paul or Hôtel de Ville on Line 1. If you're going to the Pompidou, take Line 1 to Hôtel de Ville or Line 11 to Rambuteau. For the Musée Picasso, the closest stop is St-Sébastien-Froissart on Line 8. For the 3e arrondissement, you can get off at any of the stops on métro Line 8: République, Filles du Calvaire, St-Sébastien-Froissart, or Chemin Vert. In fact, métro lines 3, 5, 8, 9, and 11 all converge at the République stop, which exits at Place de la République, at the top of the haut Marais (3e).

TOP REASONS TO GO

■ **Centre Pompidou.** Paris's leading modern art museum is also a vast (and architecturally ambitious) arts center that presents films, theater, performance art, and dance performances.

■ **Place des Vosges.** The prettiest square in the French capital surrounds a manicured park, where benches and inviting patches of grass are ideal if you're in need of a siesta.

■ **Musée National Picasso-Paris.** Spectacularly renovated, this museum is a must-see for fans of the Spanish master, who painted some of his best work while living in the city.

■ **Shopping.** This is Paris's largest, most diverse, and most fashionable neighborhood, with more boutiques than you could visit in a week, let alone a day.

■ **Jewish history.** The old Jewish quarter has two world-class sites: Mémorial de la Shoah (the Holocaust Memorial) and the Musée d'Art et d'Histoire du Judaïsme.

From swampy to swanky, the Marais has a fascinating history, having remade itself many times and today retaining a myriad array of identities. It's the city's epicenter of cool, with hip boutiques, designer hotels, and art galleries galore. It's also the hub of Paris's LGBTQ+ community, and, though fading, it's the nucleus of Jewish life. You could easily spend your entire visit to Paris in this neighborhood—there is that much to do.

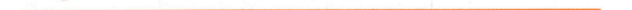

"Marais" means swamp, and that is exactly what this area was until the 12th century, when it was converted to farmland. In 1605, Henri IV began building the Place Royale (today's Place des Vosges, the oldest square in Paris), which touched off a building boom, and the wealthy and fabulous moved in. Despite the odors—the area was one of the city's smelliest—it remained the chic quarter until Louis XIV transferred his court to Versailles, trailed by dispirited aristocrats unhappy to decamp to the country. Merchants took over their exquisite *hôtels particuliers* (private mansions), which are some of the city's best surviving examples of French Baroque and Renaissance architecture. Here you can see the hodgepodge of narrow streets that so vexed Louis Napoléon and his sidekick, Baron Haussmann, who feared a redux of the famous *barricades* that Revolutionaries threw up to thwart the monarchy. Haussmann leveled scores of blocks like these, creating the wide, arrow-straight avenues that are a hallmark of modern Paris. Miraculously, the Marais escaped destruction, though much of it fell victim to neglect and ruin. Thanks to restoration efforts over the past half-century, the district is enjoying its latest era of greatness, and the apartments here—among the city's oldest—are also some of the most in demand, with *beaucoup* charm, exposed beams, and steep crooked staircases barely wide enough for a supermodel. (Should you be lucky enough to find an elevator, don't expect it to fit your suitcase.) Notice the impressive *portes cochères*, the huge doors built to accommodate aristocratic carriages that today open into many sublime courtyards and hidden gardens.

The 4e arrondissement, the Marais's glitzier half, is sandwiched between two opposite poles—the regal **Place des Vosges** in the east and the eye-teasing modern masterpiece **Centre Pompidou** in the west. Between these points you'll find most of the main sights, including the **Musée Picasso**, the **Maison Européenne de la Photographie**, and the **Musée**

Carnavalet, set in a splendid Renaissance mansion and the best place to see how the city evolved through the ages. To tour an exquisitely restored 17th-century hôtel particulier, visit the **Musée Cognacq-Jay** or wander into the manicured back garden of the magnificent **Hôtel de Sully**. The quieter 3e arrondissement of the Marais, around Rue de Bretagne, has become one of Paris's most in-demand residential areas—and one of the most interesting to explore. Here you'll find intriguing, off-the-tourist-track boutiques, bars, and galleries, plus notable attractions such as the **Musée des Arts and Métiers**, Europe's oldest science museum, and the **Musée de la Chasse et de la Nature**, one of Paris's most delightful museums.

Paris's **Jewish quarter** (the Pletzl, Yiddish for "little place") has existed in the Marais in some form since the 13th century and still thrives around Rue des Rosiers, even as hipster hangouts encroach on the traditional bakeries and delis. Not far away is the beating heart of the gay Marais, radiating out from Rue Vieille du Temple and Rue des Archives, along Rue St-Croix de la Bretonnerie to Rue du Temple. It's filled with trendy shops, cool cafés, and lively nightspots popular with LGBTQ+ folks but welcoming to all.

Sights

Agoudas Hakehilos Synagogue

SYNAGOGUE | Art Nouveau genius Hector Guimard built this unique synagogue (also called Synagogue de la Rue Pavée) in 1913 for a Polish-Russian Orthodox association. The facade resembles an open book: Guimard used the motif of the Ten Commandments to inspire the building's shape and its interior, which can only rarely be visited. Knock on the door, and see if the caretaker will let you upstairs to the balcony, where you can admire Guimard's well-preserved decor. Like other Parisian synagogues, its front door was dynamited by Nazis on Yom Kippur, 1941. The Star of David over the

door was added after the building was restored. ✉ *10 rue Pavé, 4e, Marais Quarter* ☎ *01–48–87–21–54* Ⓜ *St-Paul.*

Archives Nationales

ARCHIVE | Thousands of important historical documents are preserved inside the Hôtel de Soubise and Hôtel de Rohan—a pair of spectacular buildings constructed in 1705 as private homes. Fans of the decorative arts will appreciate a visit to the former, where the well-preserved private apartments of the Prince and Princess de Soubise are among the first examples of the rococo style, which preceded the more somber Baroque opulence of Louis XIV. The Hôtel de Soubise also has a museum that displays documents dating from 625 to the 20th century. Highlights include the Edict of Nantes (1598), the Treaty of Westphalia (1648), the wills of Louis XIV and Napoléon, and the Declaration of Human Rights (1789). Louis XVI's diary is also here, containing his sadly clueless entry for July 14, 1789—the day the Bastille was stormed and the French Revolution was launched. The Hôtel de Rohan, open to the public only during Patrimony Weekend in September, was built for Soubise's son, Cardinal Rohan. Before you leave, notice the medieval turrets in the courtyard: this is the Porte de Clisson, all that remains of a stately 14th-century mansion. ✉ *60 rue des Francs-Bourgeois, 3e, Marais Quarter* ☎ *01–40–27–60–96* ⊕ *www.archives-nationales.culture.gouv.fr/fr/web/guest/site-de-paris* ✈ *Free* ☺ *Closed Tues.* Ⓜ *Rambuteau.*

Centre Pompidou

ART MUSEUM | FAMILY | Love it or hate it, the Pompidou is certainly a unique-looking building, and it holds some of the city's best contemporary art, from the 20th century to the present day. Most Parisians have warmed to the industrial, Lego-like exterior that caused a scandal when it opened in 1977. Named after French president Georges Pompidou (1911–74), it was designed by

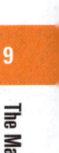

then-unknown architects Renzo Piano and Richard Rogers, who put the building's guts on the outside and color-coded them: water pipes are green, air ducts are blue, electrics are yellow, and things like elevators and escalators are red.

The Musée National d'Art Moderne (Modern Art Museum, entrance on Level 4) occupies the top two levels. Level 5 is devoted to modern art from 1905 to 1960, including major works by Matisse, Modigliani, Marcel Duchamp, and Picasso. Level 4 is dedicated to contemporary art from the '60s on, including video installations. The Galerie d'Enfants (Children's Gallery) on the mezzanine level has interactive exhibits designed to keep the kids busy. Outside, next to the museum's sloping plaza—where throngs of teenagers hang out (and where there's free Wi-Fi)—is the Atelier Brancusi. This small, airy museum contains four rooms reconstituting Brancusi's Montparnasse studios with works from all periods of his career. On the opposite side, in Place Igor-Stravinsky, is the Stravinsky fountain, which has 16 gyrating mechanical figures in primary colors, including a giant pair of ruby red lips. On the opposite side of Rue Rambuteau, on the wall at the corner of Rue Clairvaux and Passage Brantôme, is the appealingly bizarre, mechanical, brass-and-steel clock, *Le Défenseur du Temps.*

The Pompidou's permanent collection takes up very little of the massive building, which also contains temporary exhibition galleries, including a special wing for design and architecture; the free, highly regarded reference library (university students often line up on Rue Renard to get in); and the basement, with its two cinemas, theater, dance venue, and a small, free exhibition space. On your way up the escalator, you'll have spectacular views of Paris, ranging from Tour Montparnasse to the left, around to the hilltop Sacré-Coeur on the right.

Major plans to renovate and expand the museum to the tune of €260 million have

been delayed the past few years, but developments are finally starting to take shape. Artwork will begin being moved to other locations in Paris starting in October 2024, and the museum itself, along with its performance halls and library, will no longer be accessible to the public starting in March 2025, with construction beginning sometime in 2026. The current plan is for the museum to be fully closed to the public for five years, with a predicted reopening in 2030. ✉ *Pl. Georges-Pompidou, 4e, Marais Quarter* ☎ *01–44–78–12–33* 🌐 *www.centrepompidou.fr* ✉ *Center access free, Atelier Brancusi free, museum and exhibits from €15 (free access to permanent collection 1st Sun. of month)* ⌚ *Closed Tues.* Ⓜ *Rambuteau.*

Église Saint-Merry

CHURCH | This impressive Gothic church in the shadow of the Centre Pompidou was completed in 1550. Notable features include the turret (it contains the oldest bell in Paris, cast in 1331) and an 18th-century pulpit supported on carved palm trees. There are free concerts here Saturday at 8 pm and Sunday at 4 pm. ✉ *76 rue de la Verrerie, 4e, Marais Quarter* ☎ *01–42–71–93–93* 🌐 *www. paroissesaintmerry.fr* Ⓜ *Hôtel de Ville.*

★ Fondation Henri Cartier-Bresson

ART MUSEUM | Henri Cartier-Bresson, the legendary artist-photojournalist and co-creator of the Magnum photo agency, launched this foundation with his wife Martine Franck, a British-Belgian portrait and documentary photographer, and their daughter Melanie. The soaring, light-filled gallery showcases a collection of 50,000 original prints along with an exceptional series of solo exhibitions from notable photographers. The foundation's bookstore itself is a draw for photography buffs. ✉ *79 rue des Archives, 3e, Marais Quarter* ☎ *01–40–61–50–50* 🌐 *www. henricartierbresson.org* ✉ *€10* ⌚ *Closed Mon.* Ⓜ *République, Filles du Calvaire, Rambuteau.*

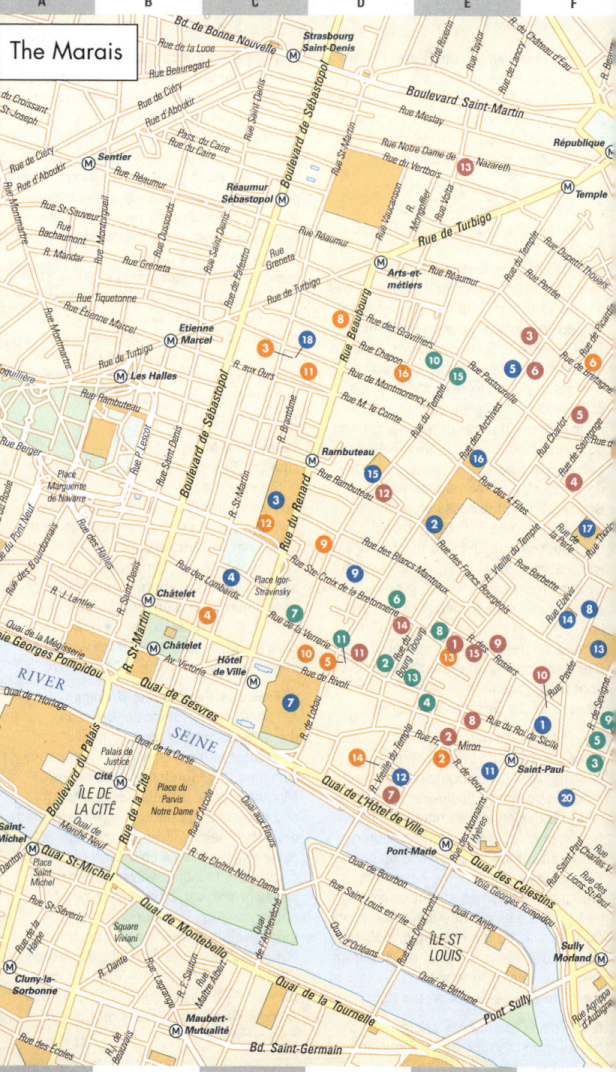

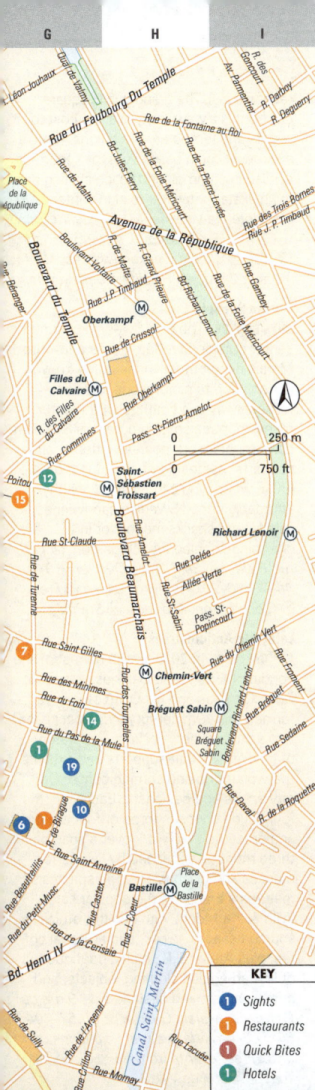

Sights ▼

1 Agoudas Hakehilos Synagogue F7
2 Archives Nationales.....E5
3 Centre Pompidou C5
4 Église Saint-Merry........C5
5 Fondation Henri Cartier-Bresson...............E4
6 Hôtel de Sully G7
7 Hôtel de Ville C6
8 Institut Suédois F6
9 Lafayette Anticipations D5
10 Maison de Victor Hugo...............G7
11 Maison Européenne de la Photographie E7
12 Mémorial de la Shoah D7
13 Musée Carnavalet....F6
14 Musée Cognacq-Jay....F6
15 Musée d'Art et d'Histoire du Judaïsme (mahJ)....D4
16 Musée de la Chasse et de la Nature..............E4
17 Musée National Picasso-Paris F5
18 Nicolas Flamel's Home.......................C3
19 Place des Vosges......G7
20 St-Paul-St-Louis..........F7

Restaurants ▼

1 Assemblages...............G7
2 Au Bourguignon du Marais...................E7
3 Auberge Nicolas Flamel C3
4 Benoît......................C6
5 Boubalé....................D6
6 Café Charlot F4
7 Café des Musées G6
8 Datsha Underground...D3
9 Grand Coeur...............D5
10 La Table Cachée D6
11 L'Ambassade d'Auvergne.................C4
12 Le Georges C5
13 Les Philosophes E6
14 Nellu.........................D7
15 Ogata.......................F4
16 Parcelles...................D4

Quick Bites ▼

1 Au Petit Fer à Cheval....E6
2 Au Petit Versailles Café E7
3 Bontemps..................F3
4 Breizh Café F5
5 Chez Alain Miam Miam F4
6 Gramme....................F4
7 La Caféothèque D7
8 La Tartine E7
9 L'As du Fallafel E6
10 Le Loir dans la Theière F6
11 Maison Aleph D6
12 Pain de Sucre.............D5
13 Philippe Conticini E2
14 Une Glace à Paris D6
15 Yann Couvreur E6

Hotels ▼

1 Cour des Vosges..........G7
2 Hôtel Bourg Tibourg....D6
3 Hôtel Caron.................F7
4 Hôtel Caron de Beaumarchais E6
5 Hôtel de JoBo..............F7
6 Hôtel de la Bretonnerie...................D6
7 Hôtel Duo C6
8 Hôtel Dupond-Smith....E6
9 Hôtel Jeanne d'Arc G7
10 Hôtel Jules & Jim........E3
11 Hôtel Le Grand Mazarin D6
12 Hôtel Sookie...............G4
13 9Confidentiel E6
14 Pavillon de la Reine.....G6
15 Sinner.......................E4

Hôtel de Sully *(Hôtel de Béthune-Sully)*
NOTABLE BUILDING | This early Baroque gem, built in 1624, is one of the city's loveliest *hôtels particuliers* (grand town houses). Like much of the area, it fell into ruin until the 1950s, when it was rescued by the institute for French historic monuments (the Centre des Monuments Nationaux), which is based here. The renovated headquarters aren't open to the public, but you're welcome to enjoy the equally lovely garden. Stroll through it, past the Orangerie, to find a small passage into nearby Place des Vosges. Sully's best buddy, King Henri IV, would have lived there had he not been assassinated in 1610. An on-site bookstore (with a 17th-century ceiling of exposed wooden beams) sells specialized English-language guides to Paris. ✉ 62 rue St-Antoine, 4e, Marais Quarter ☎ 01–44–61–20–00 🌐 www.hotel-de-sully.fr ⊘ Bookstore closed Mon. Ⓜ St-Paul.

Hôtel de Ville

GOVERNMENT BUILDING | Overlooking the Seine, City Hall contains the residence and offices of the mayor. The original Renaissance structure was built by François I in 1535–51 and added to by both Henry IV and Louis XIII in the early 17th century. In 1871 it was sacked and burned during the final days of the Paris Commune. Rebuilt in an almost exact replica of the original in 1874, it is one of Paris's most stunning buildings, made all the more dramatic by elaborate nighttime lighting. The adjoining public library stages frequent free exhibits celebrating famous photographers like Doisneau or Atget and their notable subjects, often the city itself. (The entrance is on the side across from the department store BHV.) Alas, the impressive interior of the main administrative building, with its lavish reception halls and staircases, is open only for independent visits during Patrimony Weekend in September. If your French is good, however, free guided tours are given biweekly in summer, weekly in other seasons (call two months ahead for information and

reservations). The grand public square out front is always lively, playing host to events and temporary exhibitions. There's a carousel and a beach volleyball court (or similar) in summer, and an ice-skating rink (with skate rental available) in winter. ✉ Pl. de l'Hôtel-de-Ville, 4e, Marais Quarter ☎ 01–42–76–43–43 tours 🌐 www.paris.fr 💰 Free ⊘ Closed weekends ☞ Access for visits at 29 rue de Rivoli Ⓜ Hôtel de Ville.

Institut Suédois

ARTS CENTER | The only Swedish cultural center outside Sweden, this is a favorite Marais hang-out for those in the know, not only for its picturesque location, tucked away in a beautiful 18th-century mansion, but also its program of Swedish contemporary art, open-air cinema, and concerts. Its best-kept secret is the Café FICA, where you can feast on healthy, affordably priced Swedish sandwiches, salads, and snacks indoors or in the charming cobbled French garden. ✉ 11 rue Payenne, 3e, Marais Quarter ☎ 01–44–78–80–20 🌐 www.ccs.si.se 💰 Free ⊘ Closed Mon. and Tues. Ⓜ St-Paul.

Lafayette Anticipations

ART GALLERY | In 2018, at the behest of the Fondation Entreprise Galeries Lafayette, Rem Koolhaas and his OMA studio transformed this 19th-century industrial space into a streamlined, six-floor "laboratory of innovation" that supports and exhibits the work of up-and-coming contemporary artists and designers. Each year, the foundation chooses three or four artists and presents their work over a span of three months, enhanced by live performances and discussions. The space also features a branch of the popular café Wild & the Moon, with healthy, ethically sourced snacks, juices, and artisanal coffee, plus Atelier E.B., a chic boutique full of limited-edition clothing, objects, and gifts by artists and designers. ✉ 9 rue du Plâtre, 4e, Marais Quarter ☎ 01–57–40–64–17 🌐 www.lafayetteanticipations.com/en 💰 Free; events from €5 ⊘ Closed Tues. Ⓜ Hôtel de Ville.

Maison de Victor Hugo

HISTORIC HOME | France's most famous scribe lived in this house on the southeast corner of Place des Vosges between 1832 and 1848. It's now a museum dedicated to the multitalented author. In Hugo's apartment on the second floor, you can see the tall desk, next to the short bed, where he began writing his masterwork *Les Misérables* (as always, standing up). There are manuscripts and early editions of the novel on display, as well as others such as *Notre-Dame de Paris*, known to English readers as *The Hunchback of Notre-Dame*. You can see illustrations of Hugo's writings, including Bayard's rendering of the impish Cosette holding her giant broom (which has graced countless *Les Miz* T-shirts). The collection includes many of Hugo's own, sometimes macabre, ink drawings (he was a fine artist), and furniture from several of his homes. Particularly impressive is the room of carved and painted Chinese-style wooden panels that Hugo designed for the house of his mistress, Juliette Drouet, on the island of Guernsey, when he was exiled there for agitating against Napoléon III. Try to spot the intertwined Vs and Js (hint: look for the angel's trumpet in the left corner). A recent restoration not only spiffed up the house but made the museum fully accessible to people with physical or mental disabilities and impaired sight or hearing, with improved touch screens and audioguides. It also added a lovely garden and a café by Paris's famous pastry shop Maison Mulot. ✉ 6 *pl. des Vosges, 4e, Marais Quarter* ☎ 01–42–72–10–16 🌐 www.maisonsvictorhugo.paris.fr ✈ Free; from €6 for temporary exhibitions ⊘ Closed Mon. Ⓜ St-Paul, Bastille.

★ **Maison Européenne de la Photographie** (*Center for European Photography*)

ART MUSEUM | Much of the credit for the city's ascendancy as a hub of international photography goes to Maison Européenne de la Photographie (MEP). Set in a landmark 17th-century mansion with a contemporary addition, MEP hosts up to four simultaneous exhibitions, which change about every three months, along with theme visits, workshops, and programs for kids. Shows feature an international crop of photographers and video artists. Works by superstar Annie Leibovitz or the late designer-photographer Karl Lagerfeld may overlap with a collection of self-portraits by an up-and-coming artist, and there are also regular retrospectives of photos by Doisneau, Cartier-Bresson, Man Ray, and other classics from MEP's vast private collection. The center has an excellent library, bookstore, and a café that spills out into the courtyard in warm months. Programs are available in English, and English-language tours are sometimes offered. ✉ 5/7 *rue de Fourcy, 4e, Marais Quarter* ☎ 01–44–78–75–00 🌐 www.mep-fr.org ✈ €12 ⊘ Closed Mon. and Tues., between exhibitions Ⓜ St-Paul.

★ **Mémorial de la Shoah** (*Memorial to the Holocaust*)

HISTORY MUSEUM | The first installation in this compelling memorial and museum is the deeply moving Wall of Names, tall plinths honoring the 76,000 French Jews deported from France to Nazi concentration camps, of whom only 2,500 survived. Opened in 2005, the center has an archive on the victims, a library, and a gallery hosting temporary exhibitions. The permanent collection includes riveting artifacts and photographs from the camps, along with video testimony from survivors. The children's memorial is particularly poignant and not for the faint of heart—scores of backlit photographs show the faces of many of the 11,000 murdered French children. The crypt, a giant black marble Star of David, contains ashes recovered from the camps and the Warsaw ghetto. You can see the orderly drawers containing small files on Jews kept by the French police. (France officially acknowledged the Vichy government's role only in 1995.) The history of anti-Semitic persecution in the world is revisited, as well as the rebounding state of Jewry today. There is a free guided tour in English the second Sunday of every month at 3. ✉ *17 rue Geoffroy l'Asnier, 4e, Marais Quarter* ☎ *01–42–77–44–72* ⊕ *www.memorialdelashoah.org* ⚡ *Free* ♡ *Closed Sat.* Ⓜ *Pont Marie, St-Paul.*

⊕ *www.carnavalet.paris.fr* ⚡ *Free; around €7 for temporary exhibitions* ♡ *Closed Mon.* Ⓜ *St-Paul.*

Musée Cognacq-Jay

ART MUSEUM | One of the loveliest museums in Paris, this 16th-century, rococo-style mansion contains an outstanding collection of mostly 18th-century artwork in its rooms of *boiserie* (intricately carved wood paneling). A tour through them allows a rare glimpse into the lifestyle of wealthy 19th-century Parisians. Ernest Cognacq, founder of the department store La Samaritaine, and his wife, Louise Jay, amassed furniture, porcelain, and paintings—notably by Fragonard, Watteau, François Boucher, and Tiepolo—to create one of the world's finest private collections of this period. Some of the best displays are also the smallest, like the tiny enamel medallion portraits showcased on the second floor, and on the third floor, the glass cases filled with exquisite inlaid snuff boxes, sewing cases, pocket watches, perfume bottles, and cigar cutters. Exhibits are labeled in French only, but free pamphlets and €5 audioguides are available in English. ✉ *8 rue Elzévir, 3e, Marais Quarter* ☎ *01–40–27–07–21* ⊕ *www.museecognacjay.paris.fr* ⚡ *Free; €9 for temporary exhibitions* ♡ *Closed Mon.* Ⓜ *St-Paul.*

★ Musée d'Art et d'Histoire du Judaïsme (mahJ)

HISTORY MUSEUM | This excellent museum traces the tempestuous backstory of French and European Jews through art and history. Housed in the refined 17th-century Hôtel St-Aignan, exhibits have good explanatory texts in English, but the free English audioguide adds another layer of insight; guided tours in English are also available on request (€4 extra). Highlights include 13th-century tombstones excavated in Paris; a wooden model of a destroyed Eastern European synagogue; a roomful of early paintings by Marc Chagall; and Christian Boltanski's stark two-part tribute to Shoah

★ Musée Carnavalet

HISTORY MUSEUM | If it has to do with Parisian history, it's here: this fascinating hodgepodge of artifacts and art ranges from prehistoric canoes used by the Parisii tribes to the cork-lined bedroom where Marcel Proust labored over his evocative novels. Thanks to scores of paintings, drawings, photographs, furniture, and scale models, nowhere else in Paris can you get such a precise picture of the city's evolution through the ages. The museum fills more than 100 rooms in two adjacent mansions, the Hôtel Le Peletier de St-Fargeau and the Hôtel Carnavalet. The latter is a Renaissance jewel that was the home of writer Madame de Sévigné from 1677 to 1696. Throughout her long life, she wrote hundreds of frank and funny letters to her daughter in Provence, giving an incomparable view of both public and private life during the time of Louis XIV. The museum offers a glimpse into her world, but its collection covers far more than just the 17th century. The exhibits on the Revolution are especially interesting, with scale models of guillotines and a replica of the Bastille prison carved from one of its stones. Louis XVI's prison cell is reconstructed along with mementos of his life, even medallions containing locks of his family's hair. Other impressive interiors are reconstructed from the Middle Ages through the rococo period and into Art Nouveau—showstoppers include the Fouquet jewelry shop and the Café de Paris's original furnishings. The sculpted garden at ✉ *16 rue des Francs-Bourgeois* is open from April to the end of October. ✉ *16 rue des Francs-Bourgeois, 4e, Marais Quarter* ☎ *01–44–59–58–58*

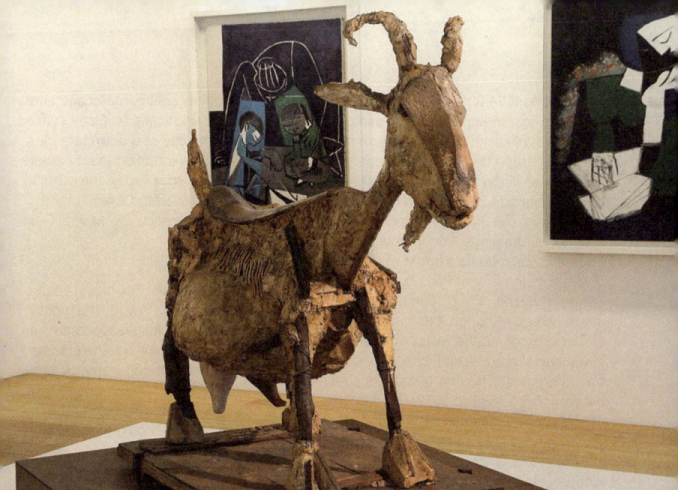

The Musée Picasso Paris highlights various works from Pablo Picasso, including his longtime devotion to sculpture.

(Holocaust) victims in the form of plaques on an outer wall naming the (mainly Jewish) inhabitants of the Hôtel St-Aignan in 1939, and canvas hangings with the personal data of the 13 residents who were deported and died in concentration camps. The museum also mounts excellent temporary exhibitions, like the recent "Chagall, Modigliani, Soutine: Paris as a School, 1940." The rear-facing windows offer a view of the Jardin Anne Frank. To visit the garden, use the entrance on Impasse Berthaud, off Rue Beaubourg, just north of Rue Rambuteau. ✉ *71 rue du Temple, 3e, Marais Quarter* ☎ *01-53-01-86-60* 🌐 *www.mahj.org* ✉ *€11 with temporary exhibitions* ⊘ *Closed Mon.* Ⓜ *Rambuteau, Hôtel de Ville.*

★ **Musée de la Chasse et de la Nature**

HISTORY MUSEUM | FAMILY | Mark this down as one of Paris's most distinctive—and fascinating—collections around the theme of "humans and nature." The museum, housed in the gorgeous 17th-century Hôtel de Guénégaud, features lavishly appointed rooms stocked with animal- and hunt-theme art and sculpture by the likes of Rubens and Gentileschi, as well as antique weaponry and taxidermy interspersed with contemporary works by artists such as Jeff Koons, Sophie Calle, and Walton Ford. In a tribute to Art Nouveau, the decor incorporates chandeliers and railings curled like antlers. Older kids will appreciate the jaw-dropping Trophy Room's impressive menagerie of beasts, not to mention the huge polar bear stationed outside. There is a lovely multimedia exhibit on the myth of the unicorn, as well as charming interactive displays on antique weaponry and bird calls. Temporary exhibits take place on the first floor, with works scattered throughout the permanent collection. There's also a spacious café. ✉ *62 rue des Archives, 3e, Marais Quarter* ☎ *01-53-01-92-40* 🌐 *www.chassenature.org* ✉ *€12* ⊘ *Closed Mon.* Ⓜ *Rambuteau.*

★ **Musée National Picasso-Paris**

ART MUSEUM | Home to the world's largest public collection of Picasso's inimitable oeuvre, this spectacular museum covers almost 54,000 square feet in two buildings: the splendid 17th-century Hôtel Salé and a sprawling structure in the back garden dedicated to temporary exhibitions. Diego Giacometti's exclusively designed furnishings in the former are a bonus. The 200,000-plus paintings, sculptures, drawings, documents, and other archival materials (most of them donated to the City of Paris by Picasso or his family members) span the artist's entire career. Although it doesn't include his most recognizable works, it does contain many of the pieces Picasso himself treasured most. The first two floors cover his work from 1895 to 1972. The top floor illustrates his relationship to his favorite artists: landscapes, nudes, portraits, and still life works taken from his private collection detail his "artistic dialogue" with Cézanne, Gauguin, Degas, Rousseau, Matisse, Braque, Renoir, Modigliani, Miró, and others. The basement centers on Picasso's workshops, with photographs, engravings, paintings, and sculptures that document or evoke key pieces created at the Bateau Lavoir, Château de Boisgeloup, Grands-Augustins, Villa La Californie, and his farmhouse, Notre-Dame-de-Vie, in Mougins. With excellent temporary exhibitions and plenty of multimedia components and activities that cater to kids, this is ideal for children and adult art lovers alike. ■ TIP→ **Buy tickets online well in advance of your planned visit. Also, try to avoid visiting on weekends, when the crowds are largest.** ✉ *5 rue de Thorigny, 3e, Marais Quarter* ☎ *01–85–56–00–36* 🌐 *www.museepicassoparis.fr* ✈ *From €11* ⊘ *Closed Mon.* Ⓜ *St-Sébastien–Froissart.*

series. A wealthy scribe, merchant, and dabbler in the mystical arts, Flamel willed his home to the city as a dormitory for the poor—on the condition that boarders pray daily for his soul. Today, the building contains apartments and a restaurant. ✉ *51 rue Montmorency, 3e, Marais Quarter* Ⓜ *Rambuteau.*

★ Place des Vosges

PLAZA/SQUARE | FAMILY | The oldest square in Paris and—dare we say it—the most beautiful, Place des Vosges represents an early stab at urban planning. The precise proportions offer a placid symmetry, but things weren't always so calm here. Four centuries ago, this was the site of the Palais des Tournelles, home to King Henry II and Queen Catherine de' Medici. The couple staged regular jousting tournaments, and Henry was fatally lanced in the eye during one of them in 1559. Catherine fled to the Louvre, abandoning her palace and ordering it destroyed. In 1612, the square became Place Royale on the occasion of Louis XIII's engagement to Anne of Austria. Napoléon renamed it Place des Vosges to honor the northeast region of Vosges, the first in the country to pony up taxes to the Revolutionary government. At the base of the 36 redbrick-and-stone houses—nine on each side of the square—is an arcaded, covered walkway lined with art galleries, shops, and cafés. There's also an elementary school, a synagogue (whose barrel roof was designed by Gustav Eiffel), and several chic hotels. The formal, gated garden's perimeter is lined with chestnut trees; inside are a children's play area and a fountain. Aside from hanging out in the park, people come here to visit the house, now a museum, of the man who once lived at No. 6—Victor Hugo, the author of *Les Misérables* and *Notre-Dame de Paris* (aka *The Hunchback of Notre-Dame*).

■ TIP→ **One of the best things about this park is that you're actually allowed to sit—or snooze or snack—on the grass during spring and summer.**

Nicolas Flamel's Home

HISTORIC HOME | Built in 1407 and reputed to be the oldest house in Paris (though other buildings also claim that title), this abode has a mystical history. Harry Potter fans should take note: this was the real-life residence of Nicolas Flamel, the alchemist whose sorcerer's stone is the source of immortality in the popular book

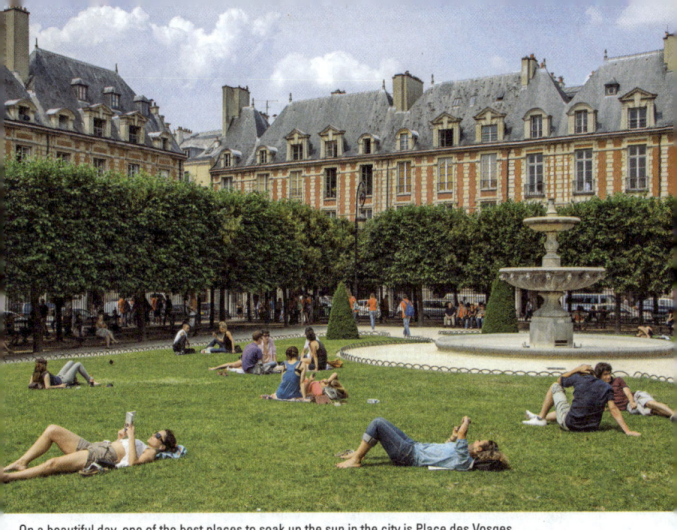

On a beautiful day, one of the best places to soak up the sun in the city is Place des Vosges.

There is no better spot in the Marais for a picnic: you can pick up fixings at the nearby street market on Thursday and Sunday morning. (It's on Boulevard Richard Lenoir between Rues Amelot and St-Sabin.) The most likely approach to Place des Vosges is from Rue de Francs-Bourgeois, the main shopping street. However, for a grander entrance, walk along Rue St-Antoine until you get to Rue de Birague, which leads directly into the square. ✉ *Off Rue des Francs-Bourgeois, near Rue de Turenne, 4e, Marais Quarter* Ⓜ *Bastille, St-Paul.*

St-Paul–St-Louis

CHURCH | The leading Baroque church in the Marais, its dome rising 180 feet above the crossing, was begun in 1627 by the Jesuits, who modeled it after their Gesù church in Rome. Recently cleaned on the outside but dark and brooding inside, it contains Delacroix's *Christ on the Mount of Olives* in the transept and a shell-shape holy-water font at the entrance. The font was donated by Victor Hugo, who lived in nearby Place des Vosges. Hugo's beloved daughter, Léopoldine, was married here in 1843, though she met a tragic end less than seven months later, when she fell into the Seine and drowned, along with her husband Charles, who tried to save her. ✉ *99 rue St-Antoine, 4e, Marais Quarter* ☎ 01–42–72–30–32 🌐 *www.spsl.fr* Ⓜ *St-Paul.*

Restaurants

★ **Assemblages**

$ | **WINE BAR** | At this restaurant set on a pretty street leading right into the Place des Vosges, it's hard to know if you've landed in someone's chic private salon or their woodworking studio. Carpenter and wine lover Eric Wilmot shares his passion for wood and wine (and Harley-Davidsons) in this stylishly intimate space, featuring Persian rugs and velvet chaises, where you can indulge in some stupendous wines handpicked by the owner and served alongside a tempting array of nibbles—homemade foie gras, smoked salmon, artisanal cheeses, and some seriously decadent desserts. **Known for:** hard-to-find wines; intimate atmosphere with a carpentry shop behind glass; gorgeous interiors. **§** *Average main: €16* ✉ *7 rue de Birague, 4e, Marais Quarter* ☎ *09–52–58–61–12* 🌐 *www.instagram. com/assemblages.paris* ✡ *Closed Mon.* Ⓜ *St-Paul, Bastille, Chemin Vert.*

Au Bourguignon du Marais

$$$ | **BISTRO** | This handsome, contemporary Marais bistro and wine bar is the perfect place to enjoy traditional fare and excellent Burgundies served by the glass and bottle. Unusual for Paris, food is served nonstop from noon to 11 pm, and you can drop by just for a glass of wine in the afternoon. **Known for:** traditional bistro atmosphere; hearty Burgundian cuisine; sidewalk dining with nice views of the Marais. **§** *Average main: €27* ✉ *52 rue François-Miron, 3e, Marais Quarter* ☎ *01–48–87–15–40* 🌐 *aubourguignondu-marais.fr* Ⓜ *St-Paul.*

Auberge Nicolas Flamel

$$$$ | **FRENCH** | There's some serious magic happening at this off-the-radar retreat set in one of Paris's oldest buildings (from 1407), once the laboratory of alchemist Nicolas Flamel. The intimate space, mixing ancient beams, stone, and wood with a streamlined contemporary design, is perfect for the chef's bewitching combinations in signature dishes like Breton langoustine with herbs crowned with caviar or roasted monkfish with tender carrots and bottarga. **Known for:** one Michelin star; top-quality seasonal ingredients; stunning wines. **§** *Average main: €60* ✉ *51 rue de Montmorency, 3e, Marais Quarter* ☎ *01–42–71–77–78* 🌐 *au-berge.nicolas-flamel.fr* ✡ *Closed weekends* Ⓜ *Étienne Marcel, Rambuteau.*

Benoît

$$$$ | **BISTRO** | Without changing the vintage 1912 setting, superchef Alain Ducasse and Thierry de la Brosse of l'Ami Louis have subtly improved the menu, with dishes such as marinated salmon, frogs' legs in a morel-mushroom cream sauce, and an outstanding *cassoulet* served in a cast-iron pot. It's a splurge to dine here, so go all the way, and top off your meal with the caramelized tarte tatin or a rum-doused baba. **Known for:** glorious Marais setting overlooking the Seine with equally romantic interior; affordable prix-fixe lunch menu; charming outdoor terrace in warm weather. **§** *Average main: €40* ✉ *20 rue St-Martin, 4e, Marais Quarter* ☎ *01–42–72–25–76* 🌐 *www. benoit-paris.com* ✡ *Closed Aug. and 1 wk in Feb.* Ⓜ *Châtelet.*

Boubalé

$$$$ | **ISRAELI** | Every night is a party at this ebullient Marais eatery in the chic Le Grand Mazarin hotel, where stylish locals enjoy Israeli chef Assaf Granit's Jewish comfort foods just like his Ashkenazi grandma used to make. Think gravlax with a sauce of arak and beet juice, creamy aioli, and crunchy capers; tender lamb ravioli; chicken livers with candied egg yolk and mustard pickles; and a scrumptious deep-dish fruit crumble with a dollop of fennel ice cream for dessert. **Known for:** fun party atmosphere; inventive and delicious Jewish cuisine; discoveries to be made on the wine list. **§** *Average main: €35* ✉ *Hôtel Le Grand Mazarin, 6 rue des Archives, 4e, Marais Quarter* ☎ *07–81–45–41–58* 🌐 *www. boubaleparis.com* Ⓜ *Hôtel de Ville.*

Café Charlot

$$ | **CAFÉ** | It may not have the healthiest food in the Marais, and the coffee may not be third wave, but that doesn't keep chic locals from packing into it on a sunny (or even not-so-sunny) day. The people-watching from this choice spot—at the intersection of the à la mode shopping street Rue Charlot and the bustling Rue de Bretagne—is top-notch, and the café's 1950s film noir charm is irresistible. **Known for:** hearty, delicious French staples and well-priced wines by the glass; chic, lively atmosphere; open daily from 7 am to 2 am. **§** *Average main: €22* ✉ *38 rue de Bretagne, 3e, Marais*

Quarter ☎ 01-44-54-03-30 ⊕ www.lecharlot-paris.com Ⓜ Filles du Calvaire.

Café des Musées

$$ | BISTRO | A true neighborhood haunt, this bustling little bistro near the Musée Picasso offers a convivial slice of Parisian life at a good value. Traditional French bistro fare is adapted to a modern audience. **Known for:** reliable bistro fare; warm and friendly service; proximity to Marais museums. ⑤ *Average main: €20* ✉ 49 rue de Turenne, 3e, Marais Quarter ☎ 01-42-72-96-17 ⊕ www.lecafedesmusees.fr Ⓜ St-Paul.

Datsha Underground

$$$ | FRENCH FUSION | If you're seeking good food among a chicest-of-chic crowd, this beautifully designed restaurant—whose sole aim is to provide you a "sensorial experience"—is just the place. Chef Baptiste Trudel, a *Top Chef* contender, concocts gastronomic dishes that you might find at a fantasy of a Russian country getaway—beef tartare with red wine-shallot "caviar" or a rich black pudding of squid and mushrooms—paired with wines from a truly impressive list. **Known for:** great people-watching; knowledgeable sommelier; innovative French-Russian fare. ⑤ *Average main: €25* ✉ 57 rue des Gravilliers, 3e, Marais Quarter ☎ 01-43-56-95-09 ⊕ www.datshaunderground.com ♡ *Closed Mon. No dinner Sun. No lunch Tues. and Wed.* Ⓜ Arts et Métiers.

Grand Coeur

$$$ | MODERN FRENCH | Soaring ceilings with exposed beams, globe lighting, velvet chairs, and marble-top tables give this superchic eatery the look of a classic brasserie gone upscale. The menu, designed by three-star chef Mauro Colagreco of the world-renowned Mirazur restaurant on the Riviera, features market-fresh French classics complemented by a wine list with plenty of by-the-glass offerings. **Known for:** spacious courtyard terrace; chic decor; menu designed by a "World's Best Chef." ⑤ *Average main: €30*

✉ 41 rue du Temple, 4e, Marais Quarter ☎ 01-58-28-18-90 ⊕ www.grandcoeur.paris Ⓜ Hôtel de Ville, Rambuteau.

L'Ambassade d'Auvergne

$$ | BISTRO | At this rare authentic Parisian bistro that refuses to change, settle into the dining room in an ancient Marais house to try rich, rib-sticking dishes from the Auvergne, a sparsely populated region in central France. Indulge in a heaping serving of the superb lentils in goose fat with bacon or Salers beef in red wine sauce with *aligot* (mashed potatoes with cheese). **Known for:** copious quantities of classic French cuisine; excellent price-to-quality ratio; chocolate mousse for dessert. ⑤ *Average main: €23* ✉ 22 rue du Grenier St-Lazare, 3e, Marais Quarter ☎ 01-42-72-31-22 ⊕ ambassade-auvergne.fr Ⓜ Rambuteau.

La Table Cachée

$$$ | FRENCH | Tucked away like a boudoir behind a green velvet curtain in the lingerie department of the famous BHV department store hides this elegant dining room. It's an excellent choice for a shopping break or a gourmet dinner after store hours, when veteran chef Michel Roth pulls out the stops in dishes like buttery chicken paté or pan-fried foie gras to start, followed by haddock in a vibrant beet reduction with caviar, and ending with a clementine-and-white chocolate mille-feuille. **Known for:** far exceeding expectations for a department store restaurant; true gourmet cuisine; to-die-for views from the outdoor terrace. ⑤ *Average main: €25* ✉ 55 rue de la Verrerie, 4e, Marais Quarter ☎ 01-42-74-91-86 ⊕ www.bhv.fr/magasins/vivez-bhv/un-petit-creux/la-table-cachee-par-michel-roth ♡ *Closed Sun. and Mon.* Ⓜ Hôtel de Ville.

Le Georges

$$$ | MODERN FRENCH | One of those showstopping rooftop venues so popular in Paris, Le Georges preens atop the Centre Georges Pompidou. Part of the Costes brothers' empire, the establishment trots out fashionable

dishes such as sesame-crusted tuna and coriander-spiced beef fillet flambéed with cognac. **Known for:** stunning views of central Paris and beyond from the terrace; indifferent service; hit-or-miss pricey food. ◼ *Average main: €32* ✉ *Centre Pompidou, 6th fl., 19 rue Beaubourg, 4e, Marais Quarter* ☎ *01–44–78–47–99* ⊕ *restaurantgeorgesparis.com* ♡ *Closed Tues.* Ⓜ *Rambuteau.*

Les Philosophes

$$ | **FRENCH** | All of Paris seems to collide at this lively corner café in the heart of the Marais, where you'll find pretty much whatever is your pleasure any time of the day or night. Slide into a red banquette, or take a seat on the wide wraparound terrace to watch the world go by while indulging in generous servings of all the French classics, a glass of wine, or coffee and dessert. **Known for:** extensive menu; lively atmosphere; decent prices. ◼ *Average main: €19* ✉ *28 rue Vieille du Temple, 4e, Marais Quarter* ☎ *01–48–87–49–64* ♡ *Closed Mon. and Tues.* Ⓜ *Hôtel de Ville.*

Nellu

$$ | **FRENCH** | This spot has quickly become a go-to for its chic atmosphere, small gourmet plates, and natural wines from around the world. Olivier Garcia, ex-sous-chef at the one-Michelin-star restaurant Tamara, presides over a small but tantalizing menu that includes a scrumptious oyster gratin with miso and caramelized shallots or melt-in-your-mouth pressed beef shoulder with seaweed and rhubarb. **Known for:** laid-back atmosphere; great wines by the glass; excellent location. ◼ *Average main: €23* ✉ *5 rue du Pont Louis Philippe, 4e, Marais Quarter* ☎ *9–73–89–43–24* ⊕ *www.restaurant-nellu.com* ♡ *No lunch* Ⓜ *Pont Marie.*

Ogata

$$$$ | **JAPANESE** | Housed in an 18th-century Marais mansion on a picturesque backstreet, this Japanese restaurant, bar, tearoom, pastry shop, and boutique redefines preciousness. It took four years for the architect and owner to construct, and every detail is a triumph of Japanese craftsmanship—from the rough *wabi-sabi* walls to the graceful sculptural touches to the ethereal porcelain tea and dinnerware used in the restaurant and for sale in the boutique. **Known for:** jaw-droppingly beautiful; top-quality products in the restaurant, tearoom—and everywhere else!; more than the usual Parisian attitude. ◼ *Average main: €42* ✉ *16 rue Debelleyme, 3e, Marais Quarter* ☎ *01–80–97–76–80* ⊕ *ogata.com/paris* ♡ *Closed Mon. and Tues.* Ⓜ *Filles du Calvaire, St-Paul.*

 **Parcelles**

$$$ | **FRENCH** | One of the city's best-kept secrets, this gem of bistro has been a fixture since 1936, and the new owners have retained the old-world vibe that's ever harder to come by in Paris, especially in the Marais. Cozy and full of charm—with beamed ceilings, stone walls, and a timeless decor—the atmosphere perfectly highlights chef Julien Chevallier's deliciously down-to-earth and seasonally inspired meats, fish, and charcuterie. **Known for:** excellent selection of natural wines; charming old-world feel; lovely terrace seating. ◼ *Average main: €28* ✉ *13 rue Chapon, 3e, Marais Quarter* ☎ *01–43–37–91–64* ⊕ *www.parcelles-paris.fr* ♡ *Closed Sun. No dinner Sat.* Ⓜ *Arts et Métiers, Rambuteau.*

 Coffee and Quick Bites

Au Petit Fer à Cheval

$ | **BISTRO** | This cozy bar is always packed, and tables often spill out onto the sidewalk. Come for a hearty meal, a cup of coffee, or a glass of wine. **Known for:** late night hours until 2 am; charming sidewalk seating; well-prepared classics like beef tartare and duck confit. ◼ *Average main: €16* ✉ *30 rue Vieille du Temple, 4e, Marais Quarter* ☎ *01–42–72–47–47* ⊕ *www.cafeine.com* ♡ *Closed Mon. and Tues.* Ⓜ *Hôtel de Ville, St-Paul.*

★ Bontemps

$ | **FRENCH** | This charming courtyard café-tearoom grew out of an adorable pastry shop (next door) specializing in the French *sablé*, those classic melt-in-your-mouth butter cookies, with an assortment of ethereal cream fillings. Marble-topped tables, velvet chairs, and other vintagelike touches make this one of the neighborhood's most charming spots for lunch, brunch, or dessert. **Known for:** vintage atmosphere; top-notch homemade food and pastries; high prices. § *Average main: €17* ✉ *57 rue de Bretagne, 3e, Marais Quarter* ☎ *01–42–74–10–68* ⊕ *bontemps.paris* ♡ *Closed Mon. and Tues.*

★ Breizh Café

$ | **FRENCH** | **FAMILY** | Eating a crêpe in Paris might seem clichéd, until you venture into this modern offshoot of a Breton crêperie. The plain, pale-wood decor is refreshing, but what really makes the difference are the ingredients—farmers' eggs, unpasteurized Gruyère, shiitake mushrooms, Valrhona chocolate, homemade caramel, and extraordinary butter from a Breton dairy farmer. **Known for:** some of the best crêpes in Paris; adventurous ingredients; Cancale oysters on the half shell. § *Average main: €13* ✉ *109 rue Vieille du Temple, 3e, Marais Quarter* ☎ *01–42–72–13–77* ⊕ *www.breizhcafe.com* ♡ *Closed Aug.* Ⓜ *St-Sébastien–Froissart.*

Chez Alain Miam Miam

$ | **SANDWICHES** | You may be tempted to call it a sandwich stand, but for Parisians it's more of a pilgrimage point at the beloved Marché des Enfants-Rouges. Alain's inspired creations burst with organic vegetables (raw or roasted), artisanal cheeses, locally cured ham, roast chicken, or pastrami, among other gourmet fillings, lodged between slices of bread, a buckwheat galette, or a *socca* (a Provençale flatbread made with chickpea flour). **Known for:** good price for the quantity and quality; top ingredients; a favorite Parisian address. § *Average main: €11*

✉ *26 rue Charlot, 3e, Marais Quarter* ☎ *09–86–17–28–00* ♡ *Closed Mon. and Tues. No dinner* Ⓜ *Filles du Calvaire.*

Gramme

$ | **CAFÉ** | "Gastro-café" may be the best description of this pint-size coffee shop with an inventive menu of seasonal fare. You can enjoy your artisanal coffee, homemade lemonade, kombucha, or glass of organic wine with dishes inspired by Paris's cultural mix: pulled pork banh mi, a "dwitch" sandwich on brioche with caramelized bacon, fried egg, and miso topped with fresh herbs. **Known for:** all-day hours; delicious pastries and inventive snacks; great coffee. § *Average main: €11* ✉ *86 rue des Archives, 3e, Marais Quarter* ☎ *09–50–92–20–23* ⊕ *www.grammeparis.fr* ♡ *Closed Mon. and Tues. No dinner* Ⓜ *Arts et Métiers, Filles du Calvaire.*

★ La Caféothèque

$ | **CAFÉ** | This was Paris's first coffee bar, founded by former Guatemalan ambassador to France turned coffee ambassador, Gloria Montenegro. With three spacious rooms, all coffee preparations under the sun, and a daily special brew chosen from among dozens of varieties of meticulously sourced beans from plantations around the globe, this is a Paris institution. **Known for:** rigorously sourced, hard-to-find beans; excellent coffee of the day; all roasting done in-house. § *Average main: €4* ✉ *52 rue de l'Hotel de Ville, 4e, Marais Quarter* ☎ *01–53–01–83–84* ⊕ *www.lacafeotheque.com* ♡ *No dinner* Ⓜ *Pont Marie, St-Paul.*

L'As du Fallafel

$ | **MIDDLE EASTERN** | **FAMILY** | For one of the cheapest, tastiest meals in Paris, look no further than the fantastic falafel stands on the pedestrian Rue de Rosiers, where L'As (the Ace) is widely considered the best of the bunch, with lunchtime lines that extend down the street. A falafel sandwich costs €7 to go or €9 in the dining room, and it's heaping with grilled eggplant, cabbage, hummus, tahini, and hot sauce. **Known for:** the best, freshest, and biggest falafel sandwich in town; fast takeout or seated service at lunch; shawarma sandwiches. ◾ *Average main: €10* ✉ *34 rue des Rosiers, 4e, Marais Quarter* ☎ *01–48–87–63–60* ⊘ *Closed Sat. No dinner Fri.* Ⓜ *St-Paul.*

La Tartine

$ | FRENCH | This calm café-brasserie on busy Rue de Rivoli is a local favorite with an extensive wine list. Though the food is nothing to write home about, its authentic brasserie atmosphere and inexpensive wines by the glass from every region of France make it a great place for a quick pick-me-up or an apéro on the go. **Known for:** total lack of snobbery; reasonably priced Champagne; authentic Art Deco interior. ◾ *Average main: €16* ✉ *24 rue de Rivoli, 4e, Marais Quarter* ☎ *01–42–72–76–85* ⊕ *www.latartineparis.fr* Ⓜ *St-Paul.*

Le Loir dans la Théière

$ | FRENCH | Sink into a comfy armchair at this popular tearoom, whose name translates to "the Dormouse in the Teapot" (from *Alice's Adventures in Wonderland*). The savory tarts are good, but the real stars are desserts like the decadent chocolate crumble tart or mile-high lemon meringue pie. **Known for:** scrumptious desserts; shabby-chic setting; popular Sunday brunch (expect lines). ◾ *Average main: €15* ✉ *3 rue des Rosiers, 4e, Marais Quarter* ☎ *01–42–72–90–61* ⊕ *www.leloirdanslatheiere.com* ⊘ *No dinner* Ⓜ *St-Paul.*

★ Pain de Sucre

$ | BAKERY | A dazzling array of gourmet pastries here includes all the classics in imaginative and delicious flavor combinations. There are also impossibly moist individual cakes, Paris's best *baba au rhum*, sublime cookies, and the specialty *guimauve*, a flavored, melt-in-your-mouth marshmallow. **Known for:** some of Paris's best pastries; gourmet sandwiches; take-out options for picnics. ◾ *Average main: €8* ✉ *14 rue Rambuteau, 3e, Marais Quarter* ☎ *01–45–74–68–92* ⊕ *www.*

patisseriepaindesucre.com ⊘ *Closed Tues. and Wed. No dinner* Ⓜ *Rambuteau.*

★ Une Glace à Paris

$ | ICE CREAM | Smoked chocolate … orange-carrot-ginger … coffee–black cardamom … these are just a few of the intriguing ice cream and gelato flavors featured at Paris's Instagram-famous *glacier*. Expect only the best seasonal ingredients plus cream and sugar in the ice creams and loads of fresh fruit in the nondairy sorbets. **Known for:** imaginative and creative flavor pairings; lots of nondairy and gluten-free choices; free samples. ◾ *Average main: €6* ✉ *15 rue St-Croix de la Bretonnerie, 4e, Marais Quarter* ☎ *01–49–96–98–33* ⊕ *uneglaceaparis.fr* ⊘ *Closed Mon. and Tues. No dinner* Ⓜ *Hôtel de Ville.*

Au Petit Versailles Café

$ | CAFÉ | It's worth a visit to this popular café just to see the listed historic ceilings and delightfully old-fashioned interiors. The sweets may not reach the ambition of some of the designer pâtisseries in the neighborhood, but it's as picturesque spot as can be for a coffee and a classic tarte tatin, eclair, raspberry tart, or a savory Croque Monsieur for lunch in the or on the sidewalk terrace in warm weather. **Known for:** historic decor; great spot for people-watching; charming sidewalk tables. ◾ *Average main: €7* ✉ *1 rue Tiron, 4e, Marais Quarter* ☎ *08–93–02–53–61* ⊕ *www.instagram.com/aupetitversaillesdumarais* ⊘ *Closed Sun.* Ⓜ *St-Paul.*

Maison Aleph

$ | BAKERY | Pastry chef Myriam Sabeta's carved out a whole new niche in French sweets with her creations influenced by her childhood in Aleppo, Syria. Her signature "nids" are based on *kadaïf*, the buttery angel hair pastries of the Levant, which Sabet fills with cream and dried or candied fruit in original flavors such as Damascus rose, chocolate-sumac, or lemon-cardamom. **Known for:** exotic flavors; imaginative takes on Levantine pastries; delicious and nutritious gourmet cereal bars. ⑤ *Average main: €6* ✉ *20 rue de la Verrerie, 4e, Marais Quarter* ☎ *09–83–03–42–02* ⊕ *www.maisonaleph.com* Ⓜ *Hôtel de Ville.*

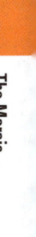

★ Philippe Conticini

$ | **BAKERY** | Conticini's riffs on beloved French classics include a divine Paris-Brest that contrasts a crunchier *pâte à chou* with an ethereal almond-hazelnut cream. Plus, his *viennoiserie* (croissants, *pain au chocolat,* brioches, and *pain au raisins*) are a revelation: the Chignon Praliné, filled with a homemade Nutella and topped with roasted hazelnuts, redefines the breakfast pastry. **Known for:** one of Paris's top pastry chefs; Cirrus, a CBD-infused pastry; best breakfast pastries in town. ⑤ *Average main: €6* ✉ *31 rue Notre Dame de Nazareth, 3e, Marais Quarter* ☎ *01–42–78–93–25* ⊕ *www.philippeconticini.fr* Ⓜ *République.*

Yann Couvreur

$ | **BAKERY** | You'll find all of this brilliant young pastry chef's latest and classic creations at this handsome pâtisserie and café, but good luck choosing between the tasty options. Known for his ambitious and subtle flavor pairings and over-the-top decadence, you'll be wowed by pastries like the Entremets Isatis, a pecan biscuit with pecan praline, creamy vanilla-bean ganache, and vanilla caramel; his exquisite lemon merengue tart topped with a tangy dollop of lemon crème; or the signature Mille Feuilles Madagascar. **Known for:** ambitious flavor pairings; beautiful café; reasonable prices for a gourmet pâtisserie. ⑤ *Average main: €6* ✉ *23 bis, rue des Rosiers, 4e, Marais Quarter* ☎ *No phone* ⊕ *www.yanncouvreur.com* Ⓜ *St-Paul.*

 Hotels

★ Cour des Vosges

$$$$ | **HOTEL** | This luxurious hotel set in a 16th-century building right on the city's most beautiful square is quite splendid, with its opulent guest rooms and suites decked out with beamed ceilings, bespoke furnishings, and a vast collection of contemporary artworks. **Pros:** art-centric decor; pretty pâtisserie-tearoom with a terrace; butler service. **Cons:** exclusive vibe may not suit everyone; restaurant serves only light dinner fare; exhorbitant prices. ⑤ *Rooms from: €790* ✉ *19 pl. des Vosges, 4e, Marais Quarter* ☎ *01–42–50–30–30* ⊕ *www.courdesvosges.com* ↝ *12 rooms* 🍴 *No Meals* Ⓜ *St-Paul, Chemin Vert, Bastille.*

Hôtel Bourg Tibourg

$$ | **HOTEL** | Subdued lighting and rich jewel tones announce the blend of romance and chic cultivated by the Hôtel Bourg Tibourg, designed by Paris superstar Jacques Garcia. **Pros:** in the heart of the trendy Marais; moderate prices; great nightlife district. **Cons:** small and poorly lit rooms; no restaurant; lounge area gets crowded. ⑤ *Rooms from: €300* ✉ *19 rue du Bourg Tibourg, 4e, Marais Quarter* ☎ *01–42–78–47–39* ⊕ *www.bourgtibourg.com* ↝ *30 rooms* 🍴 *No Meals* Ⓜ *Hôtel de Ville.*

Hôtel Caron

$$ | **HOTEL** | On a relatively quiet side street, this contemporary boutique bed-and-breakfast may be petite, but many thoughtful extras—free Wi-Fi and non-alcoholic minibar beverages, L'Occitane toiletries—make it as accommodating as bigger hotels. **Pros:** excellent location in center of Paris; friendly staff; great amenities. **Cons:** only enough storage for small suitcases; no hotel restaurant or bar; tight space in bathrooms. ⑤ *Rooms from: €275* ✉ *3 rue Caron, 4e, Marais Quarter* ☎ *01–40–29–02–94* ⊕ *www.hotelcaron.com* ↝ *18 rooms* 🍴 *No Meals* Ⓜ *St-Paul.*

★ Hôtel Caron de Beaumarchais

$$ | **HOTEL** | For that traditional French feeling, book into this intimate, affordable, romantic hotel—the theme is the work of former next-door-neighbor Pierre-Augustin Caron de Beaumarchais, a supplier of military aid to American revolutionaries and the playwright who penned *The Marriage of Figaro* and *The Barber of Seville*. **Pros:** cozy Parisian decor of yesteryear; breakfast in bed served until noon; excellent location within easy walking distance of major monuments. **Cons:** small rooms with few amenities; busy street of bars and cafés can be noisy; may feel old-fashioned for younger crowd. **§** *Rooms from: €230* ✉ *12 rue Vieille du Temple, 4e, Marais Quarter* ☎ *01–42–72–34–12* ⊕ *www.carondebeaumarchais.com* ↝ *19 rooms* 🍴 *No Meals* Ⓜ *Hôtel de Ville.*

★ Hôtel de JoBo

$$$ | **HOTEL** | On a small street, just steps from the Place des Vosges and the Musée Picasso, this hotel takes its name and stylish spirit from Joséphine Bonaparte herself. **Pros:** excellent location close to the Seine; small, intimate atmosphere; steps from the métro. **Cons:** common area can feel claustrophobic; breakfast not included in standard rates; fire station across the street can mean lots of sirens. **§** *Rooms from: €370* ✉ *10 rue d'Ormesson, 4e, Marais Quarter* ☎ *01–48–04–70–48* ⊕ *www.hoteldejobo.paris* ↝ *24 rooms* 🍴 *No Meals* Ⓜ *St-Paul, Bastille.*

Hôtel de la Bretonnerie

$$ | **HOTEL** | This small hotel with exposed wooden beams and traditional styling sits on a side street in a 17th-century hôtel particulier (a grand town house) that's just a few minutes from the Centre Pompidou and the numerous bars and cafés of Rue Vieille du Temple. **Pros:** typical Parisian character; moderate prices for the area; free Wi-Fi access. **Cons:** quality and size of the rooms vary greatly; no air-conditioning; rooms facing street can be noisy. **§** *Rooms from: €230* ✉ *22 rue Ste-Croix-de-la-Bretonnerie, 4e, Marais Quarter* ☎ *01–48–87–77–63* ⊕ *www.hotelparismaraisbretonnerie.com* ↝ *29 rooms* 🍴 *No Meals* Ⓜ *Hôtel de Ville.*

Hôtel Duo

$$ | **HOTEL** | Architect Jean-Philippe Nuel used bold colors and dramatic lighting

in his update of this hotel, and although some rooms still have the original 16th-century beams, the overall feel is functional urban-chic. **Pros:** central location near shops and cafés; walking distance to major monuments; decent prices for this neighborhood. **Cons:** neighborhood noise, especially in ground-floor rooms; service not always delivered with a smile; small standard rooms and bathrooms. **§** *Rooms from: €330* ✉ *11 rue du Temple, 4e, Marais Quarter* ☎ *01–42–72–72–22* ⊕ *www.duo-paris.com* ↝ *58 rooms* 🍴 *No Meals* Ⓜ *Hôtel de Ville.*

★ Hôtel Dupond-Smith

$$$ | **HOTEL** | If it weren't your chic destination for the night, you could easily walk right by this boutique hotel set on a tiny street. **Pros:** quality buffet breakfast; in-room massage service; ideally located. **Cons:** small common area; limited honor bar; small staff. **§** *Rooms from: €365* ✉ *2 rue des Guillemites, 4e, Marais Quarter* ☎ *01–42–76–88–99* ⊕ *www.hoteldupondsmith.com* ↝ *8 rooms* 🍴 *No Meals* Ⓜ *Hôtel de Ville.*

Hôtel Jeanne-d'Arc

$$ | **HOTEL** | This hotel is prized for its unbeatable location off tranquil Place du Marché Ste-Catherine, one of the city's lesser-known pedestrian squares, and for its gentler prices in an ever more costly neighborhood. **Pros:** charming street close to major attractions; good value for the Marais; lots of drinking and dining options nearby. **Cons:** noisy garbage trucks and late-night revelers on the square after midnight; rooms quite small; no air-conditioning. **§** *Rooms from: €260* ✉ *3 rue de Jarente, 4e, Marais Quarter* ☎ *01–48–87–62–11* ⊕ *www.hoteljeannedarc.com* ↝ *35 rooms* 🍴 *No Meals* Ⓜ *St-Paul.*

★ Hôtel Jules & Jim

$$ | **HOTEL** | In the less-traveled corner of the trendy Marais district, this contemporary boutique hotel with an easy-to-miss industrial facade and three buildings set around a historic courtyard feels almost like an art gallery. **Pros:** bright and modern; stylish bar; close to public transportation. **Cons:** the small "Jules" rooms are best for those traveling light or staying just one night; no restaurant; no in-room coffeemakers. **§** *Rooms from: €300* ✉ *11 rue des Gravilliers, 3e, Marais Quarter* ☎ *01–44–54–13–13* ⊕ *www.hoteljulesetjim.com* ↝ *23 rooms* 🍴 *No Meals* Ⓜ *Arts et Métiers.*

Hôtel Le Grand Mazarin

$$$$ | **HOTEL** | This charmingly eccentric hotel, decked out in sherbet hues and dreamy furnishings, brings a breath of fresh air to the Marais. **Pros:** chic central neighborhood; fully equipped for people with disabilities; excellent spa, pool, and restaurant on-site. **Cons:** small lobby; pricey; no dedicated elevator to spa and pool so you might be caught in your robe. **§** *Rooms from: €550* ✉ *17 rue de la Verrerie, 4e, Marais Quarter* ☎ *01–83–64–00–65* ⊕ *www.legrandmazarin.com* ↝ *61 rooms* 🍴 *No Meals* Ⓜ *Hôtel de Ville.*

Hôtel Sookie

$$ | **HOTEL** | Set at one of the Haut Marais's trendiest crossroads, this vintage-theme and jazz-inspired newcomer (its name comes from a tune by guitarist Grant Green) fits perfectly into the beating heart of the neighborhood. **Pros:** excellent location in the heart of the Marais; superfriendly staff; top-notch café. **Cons:** rooms are a bit small (but cozy); tiny bathrooms; breakfast not included in rates. **§** *Rooms from: €240* ✉ *2 bis, rue Commines, 3e, Marais Quarter* ☎ *01–40–29–01–33* ⊕ *www.hotelsookie.com* ↝ *50 rooms* 🍴 *No Meals* Ⓜ *Filles du Calvaire, St-Sébastien-Froissart.*

9Confidentiel

$$$ | **HOTEL** | This glamorous Philippe Starck–designed property takes the art and poetry of Cocteau-era Paris as its theme and couldn't be more stylish or better located. **Pros:** luxury touches, like the Codage amenities and sophisticated tearoom; nice views from some rooms

(be sure to ask); small but very helpful and friendly staff. **Cons:** on the pricey side; many rooms quite small; no fitness center. **§** *Rooms from: €360* ✉ *58 rue du Roi de Sicile, 4e, Marais Quarter* ☎ *01–86–90–23–33* ⊕ *www.hotel-9confidentiel-paris.fr* ↝ *29 rooms* 🍴 *No Meals* Ⓜ *St-Paul, Hôtel de Ville.*

Pavillon de la Reine

$$$$ | **HOTEL** | Hidden off regal Place des Vosges behind a stunning garden courtyard, this enchanting château has gigantic beams, chunky stone pillars, and a weathered fireplace that speaks to its 1612 origins. **Pros:** historic character; quiet setting; free loaner bikes. **Cons:** expensive for the area and the room size; nearest métro is a few blocks away; the interior design lacks a uniform theme. **§** *Rooms from: €650* ✉ *28 pl. des Vosges, 3e, Marais Quarter* ☎ *01–40–29–19–19* ⊕ *www.pavillon-de-la-reine.com* ↝ *54 rooms* 🍴 *No Meals* Ⓜ *Bastille, St-Paul.*

Sinner

$$$$ | **HOTEL** | The crowd of chic locals and bank of fog rolling out over the bar are the first clues that you've stepped into one of the Marais's trendiest addresses. **Pros:** super comfy beds; great location; cozy spa. **Cons:** extremely dark hallways; teensy pool; expensive across the board. **§** *Rooms from: €600* ✉ *116 rue du Temple, 3e, Marais Quarter* ☎ *01–42–72–20–00* ⊕ *www.sinnerparis.com* ↝ *43 rooms* 🍴 *No Meals* Ⓜ *Arts et Métiers, Filles du Calvaire, République.*

Nightlife

BARS

Bar at the Hotel Jules & Jim

BARS | The look here is something between a chic contemporary Paris apartment and a low-key lounge. Enjoy a cocktail over a good book from the bar library, or relax with a smooth drink in front of the outdoor fireplace. ✉ *Hotel Jules & Jim, 11 rue des Gravilliers, 3e,*

Marais Quarter ☎ *01–44–54–13–13* ⊕ *www.hoteljulesetjim.com* Ⓜ *Arts et Métiers, Rambuteau.*

Bar Nouveau

BARS | Cozy up to the marble horseshoe bar under the Art Nouveau decor of this tiny bar that recalls a Belle Époque salon de thé. In the underground cellar, the vibe is decidedly darker and cozier. But the main draw for the whole space is the cocktails, crafted by three of Paris's top mixologists, who pooled their talents after stints at notable Paris watering holes. Ingredients like Thai rice awamori, crème de banane, vodka, and salt (the Sarbacane) surprise and delight. ✉ *5 rue des Haudriettes, 3e, Marais Quarter* ⊕ *www.instagram.com/bar_nouveau* Ⓜ *Rambuteau.*

Bar Sotto

COCKTAIL BARS | Set in a vaulted cellar under a chic Italian restaurant, this speakeasy-style bar lets you imbibe all the classics (Negroni, Sidecar, Amaretto Sour, Cosmo, etc.) along with deliciously romantic concoctions (like the Lolita) accompanied by small plates and the strains of a vinyl jukebox. ✉ *45 rue de Poitou, 3e, Marais Quarter* ☎ *01–42–72–49–12* ⊕ *www.carbonisparis.com* Ⓜ *Filles du Calvaire, Rambuteau.*

★ Candelaria

BARS | Steamy Candelaria is a taquería by day and a cocktail lounge by night. The tang of tequila hangs in the air at this hip hideaway, where deftly crafted drinks are poured for a contented crowd. ✉ *52 rue de Saintonge, 3e, Marais Quarter* ☎ *01–42–74–41–28* ⊕ *www.candelaria-paris.com* Ⓜ *Filles du Calvaire.*

Grazie

BARS | Equal parts cocktail bar and gourmet pizzeria, this stylish offspring of the übercool concept store Merci promises top-quality libations and stone-oven-baked pizza. The decor is industrial-rustic, with pressed-tin ceilings and a corrugated-iron bar, all enhanced by mood lighting. It's jam-packed with neighborhood hipsters, so reservations are a must. ✉ *91 bd. Beaumarchais, 3e, Marais Quarter* ☎ *01–42–78–11–96* ⊕ *www.graziegraze.fr* Ⓜ *St-Sébastien–Froissart.*

La Belle Hortense

BARS | This spot is heaven for anyone who ever wished they had a book in a bar (or a drink in a bookstore). The *bar littéraire* is the infamous spot where gal-about-town Catherine M. launched her *vie sexuelle* that became a bawdy best seller. ✉ *31 rue Vielle-du-Temple, 4e, Marais Quarter* ☎ *01–48–04–74–60* Ⓜ *St-Paul.*

★ Le Mary Celeste

BARS | Half-price oysters at happy hour (6–7 pm) aren't the only reason this refreshingly unpretentious cocktail bar is wildly popular. One of a trilogy of superhip watering holes (including Candelaria and Glass) opened by a trio of expat restaurateurs, its craft cocktails, microbrews, natural wines, and standout tapas menu deliver the goods and then some. If you're planning to dine, reserve ahead online. ✉ *1 rue Commines, 3e, Marais Quarter* ☎ *No phone* ⊕ *www.lemarycesleste.com* Ⓜ *St-Sébastian–Froissart.*

Le Trésor

BARS | On a tiny street that's a tad separated from the sometimes-maddening crowd of the Marais, this large, lively Auvernian café has mismatched Baroque furnishings and a chill vibe, but its biggest appeals are the sprawling outdoor terrace (heated in winter) and late weekend hours. ✉ *9 rue du Trésor, 4e, Marais Quarter* ☎ *01–42–71–35–17* ⊕ *www.restaurantletresor.com* Ⓜ *St-Paul.*

Little Red Door

BARS | Behind the red door, you'll discover a dark, cozy lounge that has style, sophistication, and atmosphere without the attitude. Creative cocktails—supplemented by artisanal beers and well-chosen wines by the glass (the last of which aren't always easy to come by in a cocktail bar)—can be enjoyed from a cushy velour bar stool or cubbyhole alcove. ✉ *60 rue Charlot, 3e, Marais Quarter* ☎ 01–42–71–19–32 🌐 *www.lrdparis.com* Ⓜ *Filles du Calvert.*

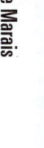

Serpent a Plume

COCKTAIL BARS | Any place whose tagline is "cocktails and pajamas" is bound to be a good time, especially when located in the vaulted 17th-century cellar of a town house smack dab on the Place des Vosges. Surprising cocktails fuel the anything-goes atmosphere that often includes late-night dancing and revelry. ✉ *24 pl. des Vosges, 3e, Marais Quarter* ☎ 01–45–31–77–83 🌐 *serpentaplume.com* Ⓜ *Chemin Vert.*

★ Sherry Butt

BARS | On a quiet street close to the Bastille, Sherry Butt's relaxed loftlike atmosphere, imaginative drinks, whiskey flights, and tasty bar menu draw a lively crowd that appreciates meticulously crafted cocktails. A DJ spins on weekends. ✉ *20 rue Beautreillis, 4e, Marais Quarter* ☎ 09–83–38–47–80 🌐 *www.sherrybuttparis.com* Ⓜ *Bastille, Sully-Morland.*

LGBTQ+ BARS

Café Cox

BARS | "Le Cox" is a prime gay pickup joint that's known for its live DJ sets. Its extended Sunday happy hour—from 6 pm to 2 am—is a rollicking good time. ✉ *15 rue des Archives, 4e, Marais Quarter* ☎ 01–42–72–08–00 🌐 *www.cox.fr* Ⓜ *Hôtel de Ville.*

Duplex Bar

BARS | Young tortured-artist types flock to this low-key club—one of the oldest gay bars in the city—to enjoy the frequent art exhibitions, alternative music, and mood-inspiring ambient lighting. It's open from 8 pm to 2 am, except on Friday and Saturday when it's open till 4 am. ✉ *25 rue Michel-Le-Comte, 3e, Marais Quarter* ☎ 01–42–72–80–86 Ⓜ *Rambuteau.*

La Mutinerie

GATHERING PLACE | Run by a female-only collective, this feminist bar is described as "a space run by and for queers, women, trans people, dykes and bis." It's a chic spot for drinks, music, and dancing, but there's plenty beyond socializing over a drink. Artist exhibitions, discussion nights, writing workshops, and stand-up shows make this more a place of community. ✉ *176 rue St-Martin, 3e, Marais Quarter* ☎ 01–42–72–70–59 🌐 *www.lamutinerie.eu* Ⓜ *Étienne Marcel.*

Le Bar'Ouf

BARS | You'll know by the billiards, board games, and friendly laid-back vibe that this lesbian bar run by two women isn't your usual drinking spot, but a convivial neighborhood meeting place where you can let your hair down and enjoy a drink among friends. ✉ *182 rue St-Martin, 3e, Marais Quarter* ☎ 06–08–13–61–12 🌐 *www.lebaroufparis.com* Ⓜ *Étienne Marcel.*

Raidd Bar

BARS | The ever-popular Raidd has a dark downstairs bar and potent drinks. The men are hot, and so is the steamy shower show presented after 11 pm—not for timid voyeurs. ✉ *23 rue du Temple, 3e, Marais Quarter* ☎ 01–42–77–04–88 🌐 *www.facebook.com/leraiddparis* Ⓜ *Hôtel de Ville, St-Paul.*

 Performing Arts

Café de la Gare

THEATER | This spot offers an opportunity to experience a particularly Parisian form of entertainment, the *café-théâtre*—part satire, part variety revue—jazzed up with slapstick humor and performed in a café salon. You'll need a good grasp of French slang and current events to keep up with the jokes. There's no reserved seating; doors open 15 minutes before showtime. ✉ *41 rue du Temple, 4e, Marais Quarter* ☎ 01–42–78–52–51 🌐 *www.cdlg.org* Ⓜ *Hôtel de Ville.*

Théâtre de la Ville Sarah-Bernhardt

MODERN DANCE | A top spot for contemporary dance, you'll find French and international troupes choreographed by the world's best—like William Forsythe and Anne-Teresa de Keersmaeker's Rosas company. Concerts and theatrical performances are also part of the season. Book early; shows sell out quickly. ✉ *2 pl. du Châtelet, 4e, Marais Quarter* ☎ *01-42-74-22-77* ⊕ *www.theatredelaville-paris.com* Ⓜ *Châtelet.*

 Shopping

ANTIQUES AND COLLECTIBLES

Village St-Paul

ANTIQUES & COLLECTIBLES | This clutch of streets, in the beautiful historic netherworld, tucked between the fringes of the Marais and the banks of the Seine, has many antiques shops. ✉ *Enter from Rue St-Paul, 4e, Marais Quarter* ⊕ *www.levillagesaintpaul.com* Ⓜ *St-Paul.*

BEAUTY

★ Amalthéa

COSMETICS | There's nothing more luxurious for your face, body, and hair than these 100% natural, organic, and chemical-free beauty products. This beautiful, understated boutique in the Haut Marais is the perfect place for the kinds of beauty products that get results. Forget the multiple cleansers, creams, and serums, this four-step no-nonsense beauty regime delivers radiant skin in a matter of weeks. All products are refillable and the boutique ships to its many fans overseas. ✉ *39 rue des Gravilliers, 3e, Marais Quarter* ☎ *01-70-23-75-35* ⊕ *www.amalthea.bio* Ⓜ *Arts et Métier, Rambuteau.*

★ Officine Universelle Buly 1803

FRAGRANCES | This elegant little "pharmacy" could have been here for a hundred years, thanks to the genteel ambience of the shop featuring a line of irresistible all-natural fragrances and luscious beauty concoctions for the face and body. Choose from a range of

lotions in delicate scents like tuberose, orange blossom, and damask rose or create your own according to skin type. The charming tea and coffee bar, where you can sit for a snack or drink, was imported straight from Italy. ✉ *45 rue de Saintonge, 3e, Marais Quarter* ☎ *01-42-72-28-92* ⊕ *www.buly1803.com* Ⓜ *Filles du Calvaire.*

BOOKS AND STATIONERY

Calligrane

STATIONERY | This sleek boutique near the Pont Marie carries a selection of 200 handmade papers from around the world, unique stationery, cards, and writing instruments as well as artwork made on and with, yep, paper. It's an oh-so-Parisian source for personalized calling cards and stationery. ✉ *6 rue du Pont Louis-Philippe, 4e, Marais Quarter* ☎ *01-48-04-09-00* ⊕ *www.calligrane.fr* Ⓜ *Pont Marie.*

Ofr

NEWSSTAND | Ofr gets magazines from the most fashionable spots in the world before anyone else. The store is messy, but you can rub shoulders with photo and press agents while checking out the latest in underground, art, and alternative monthlies. ✉ *20 rue Dupetit-Thouars, 3e, Marais Quarter* ☎ *01-42-45-72-88* Ⓜ *St-Paul.*

CHILDREN'S CLOTHING

Bonton

CHILDREN'S CLOTHING | FAMILY | Bonton takes the prize for most-coveted duds among those who like to think of children as fashion accessories. (Moms may find some useful wardrobe pointers, too.) Sassy separates in saturated colors layer beautifully, look amazing, and manage to be perfectly kid-friendly. Bonton sells toys and furniture, too. ✉ *5 bd. des Filles du Calvaire, 3e, Marais Quarter* ☎ *01-42-72-34-69* ⊕ *www.bonton.fr* Ⓜ *Filles du Calvaire.*

CLOTHING

AB33

CLOTHING | AB33 is like a sleek boudoir—complete with comfy chairs and scented candles—and the clothes here are unabashedly feminine. Separates in luxury fabrics from top designers, irresistible silk lingerie, dainty jewelry, and a selection of accessories celebrate that certain French *je ne sais quoi.* ✉ *33 rue Charlot, 3e, Marais Quarter* ☎ *01–42–71–02–82* ⊕ *www.ab33.fr* Ⓜ *Filles du Calvaire.*

The Broken Arm

CLOTHING | Like the ready-made Duchamp "artwork" for which it is named, the Broken Arm projects a minimalist cool that puts the concept back in concept store. A hypercurated selection of A-list brands for men and women includes vivid separates from the likes of Martin Margiela, Raf Simons, and the sublime Christophe Lemaire. A choice selection of objects and accessories (books, hats, shoes, jewelry, and leather goods) elevates the everyday to art. ✉ *12 rue Perrée, 3e, Marais Quarter* ☎ *01–44–61–53–60* ⊕ *www.the-broken-arm.com* Ⓜ *Temple.*

Comptoir des Cotonniers

CLOTHING | Comfortable, affordable, *au courant* clothes make this chain popular. Its reputation is built on smart, wearable styles that stress ease over fussiness. Separates in natural fibers—cotton, silk, and cashmere blends—can be light and breezy or cozy and warm, but they are always soft, flattering, and in a range of beautiful colors. ✉ *33 rue des Francs-Bourgeois, 4e, Marais Quarter* ☎ *01–42–76–95–33* ⊕ *www.comptoir-descotonniers.com* Ⓜ *St-Paul.*

COS

CLOTHING | COS—which stands for Collection of Style—is the H&M group's answer to fashion sophisticates, who flock here in droves for high-concept, minimalist designs with serious attention to quality tailoring and fabrics at a reasonable price. Classic accessories and shoes look more expensive than they are. ✉ *4*

rue des Rosiers, 4e, Marais Quarter ☎ *01–44–54–37–70* ⊕ *www.cosstores.com* Ⓜ *St-Paul.*

★ The Frankie Shop

CLOTHING | This small-but-mighty boutique has quickly become chic Parisians' go-to place for affordable, eminently wearable, and ever-stylish urban classics. From stunning leather trenches to flowing suits and elegant evening wear, you'll find all the best in urban basics for home, office, and evening. These beautiful basics will never go out of style. ✉ *14 rue St-Claude, 3e, Marais Quarter* ☎ *01–49–96–52–39* ⊕ *eu.thefrankieshop.com* Ⓜ *St-Sébastien Froissart.*

Free 'P' Star

CLOTHING | Don't let the chaos at Free 'P' Star discourage you—there's gold in them there bins. Determined seekers on a budget can reap heady rewards, at least according to the young hipsters who flock here for anything from a floor-sweeping peasant skirt to a cropped chinchilla cape. A second Marais branch at 61 rue de la Verrerie is equally stuffed to the gills. ✉ *52 rue de la Verrerie, 4e, Marais Quarter* ☎ *01–42–76–03–72* ⊕ *www.freepstar.com* Ⓜ *Hôtel de Ville.*

FrenchTrotters

CLOTHING | The flagship store features an understated collection of contemporary French-made clothes and accessories for men and women that emphasize quality fabrics, classic style, and cut over trendiness. You'll also find a handpicked collection of exclusive collaborations with cutting-edge French brands (like sleek leather-and-suede booties by Avril Gau for FrenchTrotters), as well as FrenchTrotters' namesake label and a limited selection of housewares for chic Parisian apartments. ✉ *128 rue Vieille du Temple, 3e, Marais Quarter* ☎ *01–44–61–00–14* ⊕ *www.frenchtrotters.fr* Ⓜ *St-Sébastien–Froissart.*

L'Eclaireur

CLOTHING | This Rue de Sevigné boutique is Paris's touchstone for edgy, up-to-the-second styles. L'Eclaireur's knack for uncovering new talent and championing established visionaries is legendary—no surprise after 30 years in the business. Hard-to-find geniuses, like leather wizard Isaac Sellam and British prodigy Paul Harnden, coexist with luxe labels such as Ann Demeulemeester, Jil Sander, and Maison Margiela. ✉ *40 rue de Sevigné, 3e, Marais Quarter* ☎ *01-48-87-10-22* ⊕ *leclaireur.com* Ⓜ *St-Paul.*

L'Habilleur

CLOTHING | L'Habilleur is a favorite with the fashion press and anyone looking for a deal. For women, there's a great selection from Harley of Scotland, Wax London, and Henrik Vibskov. Men can find elegant suits from Scandinavian designers. ✉ *44 rue de Poitou, 3e, Marais Quarter* ☎ *01-48-87-77-12* ⊕ *habilleur.fr* Ⓜ *St-Sébastien-Froissart.*

Majestic Filatures

CLOTHING | Wearing a Majestic cashmere-cotton blend T-shirt, dress, cardigan, or blazer is like spending the day cocooned in your favorite jammies. Fans have been known to buy five pairs of the silky-soft leggings in one go, just to be sure they never run out. The fact that you'll look totally stylish is the icing on the cake. ✉ *7 rue des Francs-Bourgeois, 4e, Marais Quarter* ☎ *01-57-40-62-34* ⊕ *www.majesticfilatures.com* Ⓜ *St-Paul.*

★ Merci

CLOTHING | Paris's favorite concept store assembles top fashions for men and women, home furnishings (including those irresistible French bed and bath linens), vintage, jewelry, and housewares all plucked straight from top-tier French, European, and American designers. Every two months the store features a new design concept in the main entrance, with themes that range from Merci en Rose (featuring all things pink) to American Surf & Skate. The store's three cafés make lingering among Paris's fashion elite a pleasure. ✉ *111 bd. Beaumarchais, 3e, Marais Quarter* ☎ *01-42-77-00-33* ⊕ *www.merci-merci.com* Ⓜ *St-Sébastien-Froissart.*

Pretty Box

VINTAGE | The owners of Pretty Box have scoured Europe for unique pieces from the '20s through the '80s. Women love the superstylish belts, shoes, and bags—many in reptile—sold here for a fraction of what they'd cost new, along with an eccentric selection of cool separates and Bettie Page–era lingerie. The men's collection includes vintage French military coats, sharkskin suits, and a gaggle of riotously patterned shirts. ✉ *46 rue de Saintonge, 3e, Marais Quarter* ☎ *01-48-04-81-71* Ⓜ *St-Sébastien-Froissart.*

★ Roseanna

CLOTHING | An absolute favorite address for the kind of beautifully designed, offbeat yet sexy wardrobe staples we've come to expect from Paris designers. First carried only in top boutiques and concept stores, this sought-after label opened its own boutique only recently. You'll find tons here to love that you won't see on anyone else, including shoes and accessories. ✉ *5 rue Froissart, 3e, Marais Quarter* ☎ *09-86-62-58-32* ⊕ *roseanna.fr* Ⓜ *St-Sébastien-Froissart, Filles du Calvaire.*

Safe Urban Concept

CLOTHING | The Marais's newest concept store is devoted to the sustainable and the selective, in a space that delivers the best in Parisian fashion (including small Parisian labels and limited editions) and beauty lines, along with a chic little café for a nice lunch or coffee and an art gallery. Look for the all-natural, made-in-France beauty lines Estampe and La Crème Libre all-natural face care products. ✉ *11 rue Commines, 3e, Marais Quarter* ☎ *01-42-72-49-12* ⊕ *www.safe-urban.com* Ⓜ *Filles du Calvaire.*

Stella Pardo

CLOTHING | This Parisian knitwear label's gorgeous sweaters, vests, coats, throws, and pillows are all handcrafted with featherweight Peruvian alpaca. Along with signature knitwear, you'll find other separates, bags, and accessories. Basically everything in this charming boutique, including the furnishings, is for sale. ✉ *51 rue de Turenne, 3e, Marais Quarter* ☎ *09–67–48–13–98* 🌐 *www.stellapardo.com/en* Ⓜ *Chemin Vert.*

Studio W

CLOTHING | If you're nostalgic for the days of Studio 54, sashay over to Studio W, where a rare Loris Azzaro gold-chain top or a plunging Guy Laroche beaded couture dress in crimson mousseline has Liza and Bianca written all over it. With plenty of jewelry, shoes, bags, and even gloves to match, this elegant boutique is a must-see for fashion divas who don't mind spending a little more for sublimity. ✉ *21 rue du Pont aux Choux, 3e, Marais Quarter* ☎ *01–44–78–05–02* Ⓜ *St-Sébastien–Froissart.*

Tom Greyhound

CLOTHING | This sleek, streamlined concept store gets you down to business. Not only will you find a handpicked selection of clothes and accessories for men and women by top-name designers, but there are also plenty of smaller, cooler labels to discover. ✉ *19 rue de Saintonge, 3e, Marais Quarter* ☎ *01–44–61–36–59* 🌐 *www.tomgreyhound.com* Ⓜ *Filles du Calvaire.*

★ Valentine Gauthier

CLOTHING | Glamour, nonchalance, and serious chic are what make these highly sophisticated separates standouts for the contemporary woman-on-the-go. Even Gauthier's more tailored, masculine styles manage to feel feminine and romantic, and she doesn't shy away from gauzy silks or colorful prints. A Paris insider favorite, her sleek boutique—on an up-and-coming Haut Marais shopping street not far from the concept store

Merci—carries clothes, accessories, and her sought-after shoes. ✉ *88 bd. Beaumarchais, 3e, Marais Quarter* ☎ *01–75–57–14–33* 🌐 *valentinegauthier.com* Ⓜ *St-Sébastien–Froissart, Chemin Vert, Richard Lenoir.*

Vintage Clothing Paris

VINTAGE | It's worth a detour to the Marais's outer limits to visit Vintage Clothing Paris, where the racks read like an A-list of designer greats—Margiela, Valentino, Comme des Garçons, and Mugler, just to name a few. Brigitte Petit's minimalist shop is the fashion insider's go-to spot for rare pieces that stand out in a crowd, like a circa-1985 Alaïa suede skirt with peekaboo grommets and a jaunty Yves Saint Laurent Epoch Russe hooded cape. ✉ *10 rue de Crussol, 11e, Marais Quarter* ☎ *01–48–07–16–40* 🌐 *www.vintageclothingparis.com* Ⓜ *Filles du Calvaire, Oberkampf.*

Zadig & Voltaire

CLOTHING | Zadig & Voltaire rocks the young fashionistas by offering street wear at its best: racy camisoles, cashmere sweaters in gorgeous colors, cropped leather jackets, and form-fitting pants to cosset those tiny French derrieres. Branches abound in every chic corner of Paris. ✉ *42 rue des Francs-Bourgeois, 3e, Marais Quarter* ☎ *01–44–54–00–60* 🌐 *www.zadig-et-voltaire.com* Ⓜ *St-Paul.*

Zadig & Voltaire Stock

CLOTHING | Here you'll find new unsold stock from last season. There's a great selection of beautiful cashmere sweaters, silk slip dresses, rocker jeans, and leather jackets, all in their signature luscious colors, for 33%–60% off. ✉ *22 rue Bourg Tibourg, 4e, Marais Quarter* ☎ *01–44–59–39–64* 🌐 *www.zadig-et-voltaire.com* Ⓜ *Hôtel de Ville.*

DEPARTMENT STORES

★ BHV

DEPARTMENT STORE | Short for Bazar de l'Hôtel de Ville, Le BHV Marais houses an enormous basement hardware store that sells everything from doorknobs to cement mixers and has to be seen to be believed. The fashion offerings for men, women, and kids feature many of the top labels, and there's a fabulous, not-too-crowded lingerie department on the fifth floor. But BHV is most noted for its high quality home-decor items, electronics, stationery, and office supplies. If you're looking for typically French housewares (like those heavy, gold-rimmed café sets, gorgeous linens, or Savon de Marseille), this is the place. The extensive men's store is across the street at 36 rue de la Verrerie. Perched on the top level is Le Perchoir, a cozy rooftop cocktail bar overlooking the city skyline. ✉ *52 rue de Rivoli, 4e, Marais Quarter* ☎ *09–77–40–14–00* ⊕ *www.bhv.fr* Ⓜ *Hôtel de Ville.*

FOOD AND TREATS

★ Artefact

SPECIALTY STORE | Tea lovers will adore this art-centric tea boutique and *salon* set in a 17th-century stone building in the upper Marais, near the Centre Pompidou. In contrast to the behemoth sellers—Mariage Frères, Palais des Thés, and Dammann Frères—who focus on quantity over quality, this shop's hand-selected varieties come from surprising places around the world (oolong from Georgia, anyone?) and small artisanal producers. The friendly owners, a husband-and-wife team, love to share their extensive knowledge, and a tasting flight of four pots in the adorable tearoom is a delight. Upstairs is reserved for artists' books and limited-edition artworks. There's also a tempting array of handmade porcelain teaware. ✉ *23 rue des Blancs Manteaux, 3e, Marais Quarter* ☎ *01–40–09–96–58* ⊕ *www.artefact-marais.com* Ⓜ *Rambuteau, Hôtel de Ville.*

Eataly

FOOD | This is Paris's one-stop-shop for all things Italian—cheeses, charcuterie, fresh and dried pasta, olive oil, sauces, pastries, wines—you name it, it's here. There's also a restaurant, café, and two wine bars on the premises. On weekends it's teeming with neighborhood foodies, so best to go in the morning or linger at apéro hour over specialty olives and a glass of wine. ✉ *37 rue Ste-Croix de la Bretonnerie, 4e, Marais Quarter* ☎ *01–83–65–81–00* ⊕ *www.eataly.fr/pages/eataly-paris-marais* Ⓜ *Hôtel de Ville.*

Izraël

FOOD | This place isn't called the "*épicerie du monde*" for nothing. Izraël is a one-stop shop for any spice under the sun, plus those hard-to-find items you'd otherwise spend days tracking down. Bins overflowing with every variety of candied fruit, nuts, beans, olives, pickles, and preserved fish give this tiny shop the air of an exotic bazaar. You'll also find all manner of canned goods, candies, rare spirits, and baking necessities. ✉ *30 rue François Miron, 4e, Marais Quarter* ☎ *01–42–72–66–23* Ⓜ *St-Paul.*

Jacques Genin

CHOCOLATE | Genin offers great chocolate: not too sweet, with handpicked seasonal ingredients for the velvety ganaches. The tea salon is a great spot to sample one of Genin's masterful takes on classic French pastries and a voluptuous *chocolat chaud.* ✉ *133 rue de Turenne, 3e, Marais Quarter* ☎ *01–45–77–29–01* ⊕ *www.jacques-genin.fr* Ⓜ *Filles du Calvaire, Oberkampf.*

Le Palais des Thés

SPECIALTY STORE | White tea, green tea, black tea, tea from China, Japan, Indonesia, South America, and more: you can expect a comprehensive tea experience here. Try one of the flavored varieties, such as Hammam, a traditional Turkish recipe with date pulp, orange flower, rose, and red berries. ✉ *64 rue Vieille du Temple, 3e, Marais Quarter* ☎ *01–48–87–80–60* ⊕ *www.palaisdesthes.com* Ⓜ *St-Paul.*

Mariage Frères

SPECIALTY STORE | Mariage Frères, with its colonial *charme* and wooden counters, has 100-plus years of tea purveying behind it. Choose from more than 450 blends from 32 countries, not to mention teapots, teacups, books, and tea-flavor biscuits and candies. High tea and light lunches are served here and at several other Paris locations. ✉ *30 rue du Bourg-Tibourg, 4e, Marais Quarter* ☎ *01–42–72–28–11* ⌂ *www.mariage-freres.com* Ⓜ *Hôtel de Ville.*

Méert

FOOD | The first Paris offshoot of the famous patisserie and tea salon in Lille (one of France's oldest) specializes in the *gauffre,* a delicate waffle handmade in the original 19th-century molds and wrapped in gilt-paper packages. Native to Belgium and northern France, Méert's version is treasured for its light cream center perfumed with Madagascar vanilla. There are also chocolates, pastries, and flavored *guimauves,* the airy French marshmallows. ✉ *16 rue Elzévir, 3e, Marais Quarter* ☎ *01–49–96–56–90* ⌂ *www.meert.fr* Ⓜ *St-Paul.*

HOME DECOR

Cire Trudon

HOUSEWARES | One of a slew of cannily resurrected ancient brands, Cire Trudon traces its origins to a Paris candle works founded in 1643, later dubbed the royal candle supplier in 1811. Now this bijoux of a boutique carries elegant tapers and sublimely scented candles in a range of sophisticated fragrances dreamed up by Parisian perfumers and poured into elegant Italian glasses. Cheeky wax busts of French personages—made in partnership with the Réunion des Musées Nationaux, makers of the official replicas from French museums—are for chic Parisian apartments. You'll also find a line of perfumes for you and your home. ✉ *11 rue Ste-Croix de la Bretonnerie, 4e, Marais Quarter* ☎ *01–42–77–90–88* ⌂ *www.trudon.com* Ⓜ *Hôtel de Ville.*

★ Empreintes

HOUSEWARES | The *raison d'être* of the organization Métiers d'Art is to reward and promote French *savoir faire*—the traditional expertise of France's many fine craftspeople and artists passed down from generation to generation. To this end—and to the delight of local bobos (short for *bourgeois-bohème* or bourgeois-bohemians) decorating their Marais lofts—Métiers d'Art opened the capital's first crafts "concept store," which assembles the work of dozens of craftspeople and artists on four floors, including impeccably crafted glassware, porcelain, jewelry, leather goods, furnishings, housewares, fine art, and much more. It's an excellent place for a souvenir of French *art de vivre.* ✉ *5 rue de Picardie, 3e, Marais Quarter* ☎ *01–40–09–53–80* ⌂ *www.empreintes-paris.com* Ⓜ *Temple, République, Filles du Calvaire.*

Le Monde Sauvage

HOUSEWARES | Le Monde Sauvage is a must-visit for home accessories. Expect reversible silk bedspreads in rich colors, velvet throws, hand-quilted bed linens, silk floor cushions, colorful rugs, and the best selection of hand-embroidered curtains in silk, cotton, linen, or velvet. ✉ *21 rue Sévigné, 4e, Marais Quarter* ☎ *01–44–61–02–61* ⌂ *www.lemondesauvage.com* Ⓜ *St-Paul.*

Muji

HOUSEWARES | *Kanketsu* (simplicity) is the guiding philosophy at Muji, and the resulting streamlined designs are all the rage in Europe. Must-haves include a collection of mini-necessities—travel essentials, wee office gizmos, purse-size accoutrements, plus the best notebooks and pens around. They're so useful and adorable you'll want them all. ✉ *47 rue des Francs–Bourgeois, 4e, Marais Quarter* ☎ *01–49–96–41–41* ⌂ *www.muji.eu* Ⓜ *St-Paul.*

Van der Straeten

HOUSEWARES | Paris designer Hervé van der Straeten started out creating jewelry for Saint Laurent and Lacroix, designed a perfume bottle for Christian Dior, and then moved on to making rather baroque-style and often wacky furniture. In his loft gallery-cum-showroom, furniture, lighting, and startling mirrors are on display. ✉ *11 rue Ferdinand Duval, 4e, Marais Quarter* ☎ *01–42–78–99–99* ⊕ *www.vanderstraeten.fr* Ⓜ *St-Paul.*

JEWELRY AND ACCESSORIES

Audrey Langlois

JEWELRY & WATCHES | Beautiful, affordable, wearable—these are just a few of the words that spring to mind to describe this Parisian designer's line of sumptuous creations that mix rich gold-plate with semiprecious stones—lapis, turquoise, azurite, and agate—with designs that can be both fragile and bold. These pieces for all occasions put just the right touch on any outfit. The beautiful, cozy boutique is a must-visit for lovers of unique, one-off pieces you won't find anywhere else. ✉ *66 rue du Temple, 3e, Marais Quarter* ⊕ *www.audreylanglois-paris.fr* Ⓜ *Rambuteau.*

★ Titlee

JEWELRY & WATCHES | This whimsical jewelry line finally open a dedicated boutique, home to its entire cast of lovable creatures—from ghosts and jack-o-lanterns to owls and dolphins to rocket ships and PAC-MAN—all so colorful and captivating you can't stop at just one. There's also a superchic line of bracelets, necklaces, and rings, but the real showstoppers are the pins, perfect accents on anything from an evening gown to a jean jacket. This stylish boutique also stocks original artwork, ceramics, books, toys, and an irresistible line of stationery. ✉ *29 rue des Gravilliers, 3e, Marais Quarter* ☎ *01–45–31–11–50* ⊕ *www.titlee.fr* Ⓜ *Arts et Métiers.*

★ WHITE bIRD

JEWELRY & WATCHES | Irresistible is the word for this shop's scintillating collection of jewels—from an assemblage of top-echelon international designers—that ranges from the daintiest of diamond rings, bracelets, and necklaces to

brilliantly colored stones in edgy settings. This spare boutique, a stone's throw from concept store Merci, may be tiny, but it's had a big impact on fashion jewelry in Paris. If you're looking for a piece to be worn every day or a statement piece that goes from day to night, this is your place. Trunk shows and openings are held at WHITE bIRD's first and larger boutique at 38 rue du Mont Thabor, just off the Rue St-Honoré. ✉ *7 bd. des Filles du Calvaire, 3e, Marais Quarter* ☎ *01–40–24–27–17* ⊕ *www.whitebirdjewellery.com* Ⓜ *Filles du Calvaire.*

SHOES, HANDBAGS, AND LEATHER GOODS

★ Isaac Reina

HANDBAGS | It takes up to several days of painstaking work to create one of Isaac Reina's refined handbags, satchels, totes, backpacks, or small leather goods. Meticulous detailing and gorgeous finishes are just some of the trademarks of this Barcelona native's elegant designs, all handcrafted in Paris in his sleek boutique near the Musée Picasso. These luxury bags are for people who appreciate superlative quality but don't care to flash a logo. ✉ *12 rue de Thorigny, 3e, Marais Quarter* ☎ *01–42–78–81–95* ⊕ *www.isaacreina.com* Ⓜ *St-Paul, Chemin Vert.*

Mademoiselle Chapeau

HATS & GLOVES | This is the only hatmaker in Paris where you can see jaunty cloches, fedoras, and flat-topped straw boaters being made with centuries-old techniques in an on-site atelier. Classic models in straw, wool, rabbit felt, or silk in a huge range of colors come in a dozen styles, from a charming pillbox to an elegant wide-brim model so light and graceful it could easily pair with an evening suit or wedding gown. ✉ *15 rue des Tournelles, 4e, Marais Quarter* ☎ *01–72–60–77–68* ⊕ *www.mademoisellechapeaux.com* Ⓜ *Bastille, St-Paul.*

Chapter 10

EASTERN PARIS

Updated by
Jennifer Ladonne

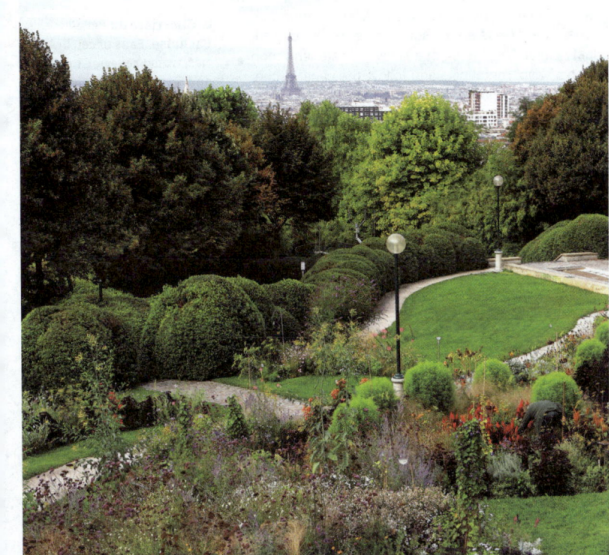

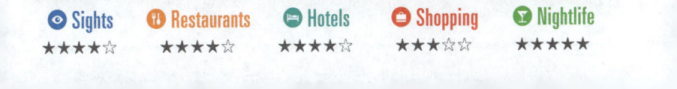

NEIGHBORHOOD SNAPSHOT

GETTING HERE

Eastern Paris includes the 10e, 11e, 12e, 19e, and 20e arrondissements. The Bastille *métro* stop, on Lines 1, 5, and 8, is a good place to start. For the Canal St-Martin, use the Place de la République stop (Lines 3, 5, 8, 9, and 11) and walk along Rue Faubourg du Temple; use the Gare de l'Est stop (Lines 4, 5, and 7) and walk along Rue des Récollets; or choose the Jaurès stop (Lines 2, 5, and 7 bis), take the Boulevard de Villette exit, and walk a mere 80 feet south. For the Cimetière du Père-Lachaise, take Line 2 or 3 to the eponymous stop.

MAKING THE MOST OF YOUR TIME

The Canal St-Martin is one of the most popular destinations in the city, particularly on Sunday afternoon, when the streets are closed to cars. Walk along the leafy canal, have lunch in a sidewalk café, and then grab a Vélib' rental bike and follow the canal all the way to Parc de la Villette. A Sunday morning trip to the picturesque Marché d'Aligre, which includes the covered Marché Beauvau, is also recommended, even if you're not buying (it's open every morning but Monday). The heaps of fresh produce and colorful flowers sold by spirited vendors are worth seeing. On any day Place de la Bastille is a lively spot to stop for drinks or lunch. If time is limited, save this neighborhood for after dark, when the streets around Place de la Bastille and Oberkampf really come to life.

PAUSE HERE

One of the oldest and prettiest parks in Paris, the towering Parc de Belleville is also its highest, affording spectacular panoramas of the city. Its winding *allées*, sprawling lawns, and shady lanes lead to fountains, woods, and gardens, with lovely spots for picnicking along the way. Famous for its taverns since the 14th century, it is now home to one of Paris's 10 wine-producing vineyards.

TOP REASONS TO GO

■ **Canal St-Martin.** This scenic canal, built by Napoléon Bonaparte, is now one of the city's hottest, hippest hangouts—it's great for strolling, with plenty of galleries, shops, and cafés.

■ **Place de la Bastille.** The flashpoint of the French Revolution still draws unruly crowds, but not so much agitators as partiers. It's also home to the Opéra Bastille.

■ **Cimetière du Père-Lachaise.** Fans of celebrities, from Frédéric Chopin and Oscar Wilde to Gertrude Stein and Jim Morrison, come to pay tribute at their final resting place.

■ **Parc de la Villette.** As the site of the city's esteemed science museum and planetarium, this is a great destination for curious kids and grown-up science buffs. For music lovers, it's also the site of the Cité de la Musique and the stunning Philharmonie de Paris.

■ **Coulée Verte René-Dumont/Promenade Plantée (Viaduc des Arts).** This abandoned railway extending 5 km (3 miles), from Bastille all the way to the Bois de Vincennes, was transformed into a beautiful tree-lined walkway perched atop a brick viaduct.

This vast slice of Paris is full of attractions, from the thrilling bistronomic dining in the 11th arrondissement and boutique-hopping on the Rue de Charonne to a leisurely stroll along the Canal St-Martin's cobbled walkways or Père Lachaise Cemetery's leafy *allées*. The Bastille's buzzy nightlife scene gives way to world-class performances at the Opéra Bastille, and the Parc de la Villette hosts the Paris Jazz Festival and the silvery silhouette of the Philharmonie de Paris.

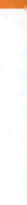

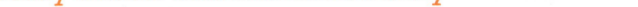

There are also noteworthy attractions, like the nearby **Coulée Verte René-Dumont (Viaduc des Arts)**, an urban-renewal project that transformed an old elevated rail line into arcaded, design-focused studios and shops. Along the top, the Promenade Plantée makes for a lovely stroll through the 12e arrondissement, which includes stately apartment buildings and pretty Square Trousseau, gateway to the **Marché d'Aligre**.

The **Canal St-Martin**, once the down-and-out cousin on the northern border, is now trend-spotting central, brimming with funky bars, cafés, bistros, art galleries, and boutiques. The scene is similar on Rues Oberkampf, St-Maur, Folie Méricourt, and Jean-Pierre-Timbaud, where artists, small designers, and gastronomic bistros have set up shop, and where a substantial slice of the city's *bobo* (bourgeois-bohemian) contingent is buying up the no-longer-so-affordable apartments.

Continuing east, you'll find the city's largest and most scenic cemetery, **Père-Lachaise**, with a roster of famous tenants lining its winding, cobbled streets. Heading north, the impressively wild **Parc Buttes-Chaumont**, with grassy fields, a small Greek-style temple, and sweeping hilltop views of Paris, is a perennial favorite. It's the perfect place to take a picnic lunch and let museum-weary kids blow off some steam. The eastern section is also home to three other popular parks: the **Parc de la Villette**, which contains a pair of engaging museums and the monumental Philharmonie de Paris to the northeast; the sky-high **Parc de Belleville**; and the **Bois de Vincennes**, home to the Château de Vincennes, the

Parc Floral, and the city's largest zoo to the southeast.

South of the Bastille, the old wine warehouses at **Bercy** have become a veritable village of shops and restaurants bordering Parc de Bercy. Directly across the Seine is the **Bibliothèque Nationale François Mitterrand**, the National Library of France, and the **Piscine Joséphine Baker**, the only swimming pool in the Seine.

Bastille, Bercy, Nation, and Around

The cafés and clubs of bustling Bastille give way to a less-touristed area around the Gare de Lyon and Bercy. You'll find fascinating Art Deco remnants of the 1931 Paris Colonial Exposition in the stunning Palais de la Port Dorée, which houses the Musée Nationale de l'Histoire de l'Immigration and Paris's most charming aquarium. Right nearby these sights are the many riches of the Bois de Vincennes.

Sights

Bercy

NEIGHBORHOOD | FAMILY | Tucked away south of the Gare de Lyon in the 12e arrondissement, blocks of stone warehouses that once stored wine are now home to **Bercy Village** (✉ *28 rue François Truffaut*), a collection of boutiques and eateries that stay open unusually late for Paris. Adjacent to the shops is the tranquil **Parc de Bercy**, with lawns, ponds, and flower beds crisscrossed by gravel paths, and the Jardin Yitzhak Rabin, a garden named for the late Nobel Peace Prize winner. Nearby, at 51 rue de Bercy, a Cubist building by Frank Gehry houses the **Cinémathèque Française**, a film buff's paradise, showing classic films, many in English; there are frequent homages to directors and actors, plus a cinema

bookshop and museum. ✉ *Bastille* Ⓜ *Cour St-Émilion, Bercy.*

Bercy Village

OTHER ATTRACTION | The cobbled streets and picturesque stone that once housed Paris's thriving 19th-century wine trade were restored in the 1990s and repurposed as a charming shopping and dining district. Brimming with unique and French chain boutiques and lively cafés, bars, and a multiplex Pathé cinema, this is a great place to spend a few hours strolling, snacking, shopping, and lingering till evening for dinner and a movie, especially since shops and bars stay open late. Check out the website for seasonal activities for kids. ✉ *28 rue François Truffaut, 12e, Bastille* ☎ *01–40–02–90–80* 🌐 *www.bercyvillage.com* Ⓜ *Cour St-Émilion.*

Bibliothèque Nationale François Mitterrand

LIBRARY | The National Library of France, across the sleek Simone de Beauvoir footbridge from Bercy Park, is a stark complex comprising four 22-story L-shape buildings representing open books. Commissioned by President Mitterrand, the €1-billion library was said to be the world's most modern when it opened in 1998—a reputation quickly sullied when it was discovered that miles of books and rare documents were baking in the glass towers, unprotected from the sun (movable shutters were eventually installed). Some of the most important printed treasures of France are stored here, though the majority of them are available only to researchers. Visitors can see the impressive 17th-century Globes of Coronelli, a pair of 2-ton orbs made for Louis XIV. There's a sunken center garden with tall trees (open to the public the first weekend in June) ringed by low-ceilinged reading rooms, which are nothing special. A first-floor gallery hosts popular temporary exhibitions. Enter through the easternmost tower. ✉ *Quai François Mauriac, 13e, Bastille* ☎ *01–53–79–59–59* 🌐 *www.bnf.fr* ✉ *Globes gallery free; all* other entries from €9 ©) Closed Mon. Ⓜ Bibliothèque, Quai de la Gare.

★ Bois de Vincennes

CITY PARK | FAMILY | Like the Bois de Boulogne to the west, this much-loved retreat on the city's eastern border was landscaped by Napoléon III. Its roots, however, reach back to the 13th century, when Philippe Auguste created a hunting preserve in the shadow of the royal Château de Vincennes, which once ranked as the largest château in Europe. In 1731 Louis XV created a public park here, and the *bois* (or woods) now features a Japanese garden, La Grande Pagode (a Buddhist temple containing the largest golden statue of the Buddha in Europe), and the exquisite Parc Floral, with acres of flower gardens, a huge kids' park, and summertime jazz and classical concerts. Horse races at the restored Vincennes Hippodrome de Paris are an event for the whole family, but perhaps not the Espace Naturiste, Paris's first area for nudists, opened in 2017. Rowboats are for rent at a pair of lakes: Lac Daumesnil, which has two islands, and Lac des Minimes, which has three. For the kids, there are pony rides, a miniature train, and numerous play areas. Here, too, you'll find the stunning Palais de la Porte Dorée, home to an immigration museum and tropical aquarium. Through late summer, the Parc Floral hosts two beloved music festivals, the Paris Jazz Festival and the Festival Classique au Vert. Grab a picnic and a blanket and enjoy classical music or jazz in the amphitheater or on the lawn in Paris's prettiest park. ✉ *Bois de Vincennes, 12e, Bastille* Ⓜ *Château de Vincennes, Porte Dorée.*

★ Château de Vincennes

CASTLE/PALACE | This imposing high-walled château, on the northern edge of the Bois de Vincennes, was France's medieval version of Versailles. Built and expanded by various kings between the 12th and 14th centuries, it is now surrounded by a dry moat and dominated

by a 170-foot keep, the last of nine original towers. The royal residence eventually became a prison holding, notably, convicts of both sexes—and "the doors did not always remain closed between them," as one tour guide coyly put it. Inmates included the philosopher Diderot and the Marquis de Sade, and the alleged spy Mata Hari was executed in its dry moat bed. Both the château and its cathedral, Sainte-Chapelle—designed in the style of the Paris church of the same name—have been restored to their previous glory. If you speak French, the free 90-minute tour is worthwhile; otherwise, consider spending €3 for the English audioguide. The entrance to the lovely Parc Floral de Paris is just behind the château. ✉ *Av. de Paris, 12e, Bastille* ☎ *01–43–28–15–48* ⊕ *www.chateau-vincennes.fr* ✉ *€13* Ⓜ *Château de Vincennes.*

★ Coulée Verte René-Dumont/Promenade Plantée (*La Coulée Verte*)

CITY PARK | Once a train line from the Paris suburbs to Bastille, this redbrick viaduct (often referred to as Le Viaduc des Arts) is now one of the park highlights of the unpretentious 12e arrondissement. The rails have been transformed into a $4\frac{1}{2}$-km (3-mile) walkway lined with trees, bamboo, and flower gardens, offering a bird's-eye view of the stately Haussmannian buildings along Avenue Daumesnil. Below, the *voûtes* (arcades) have been transformed by the city into artisan boutiques, many focused on decor and design. There are also temporary galleries showcasing art and photography. The Promenade, which gained fame as a setting in the 2004 film *Before Sunset,* was the inspiration for New York's High Line. It ends at the Bastille. From there, you can continue your walk to the Bois de Vincennes. If you're hungry, grab a bite at L'Arrosoir, a cozy café under the viaduct (✉ *75 av. Daumesnil*). ✉ *1–129 av. Daumesnil, 12e, Bastille* ☎ *01–86–95–95–07* ⊕ *www.leviaducdesarts.com* Ⓜ *Bastille, Gare de Lyon.*

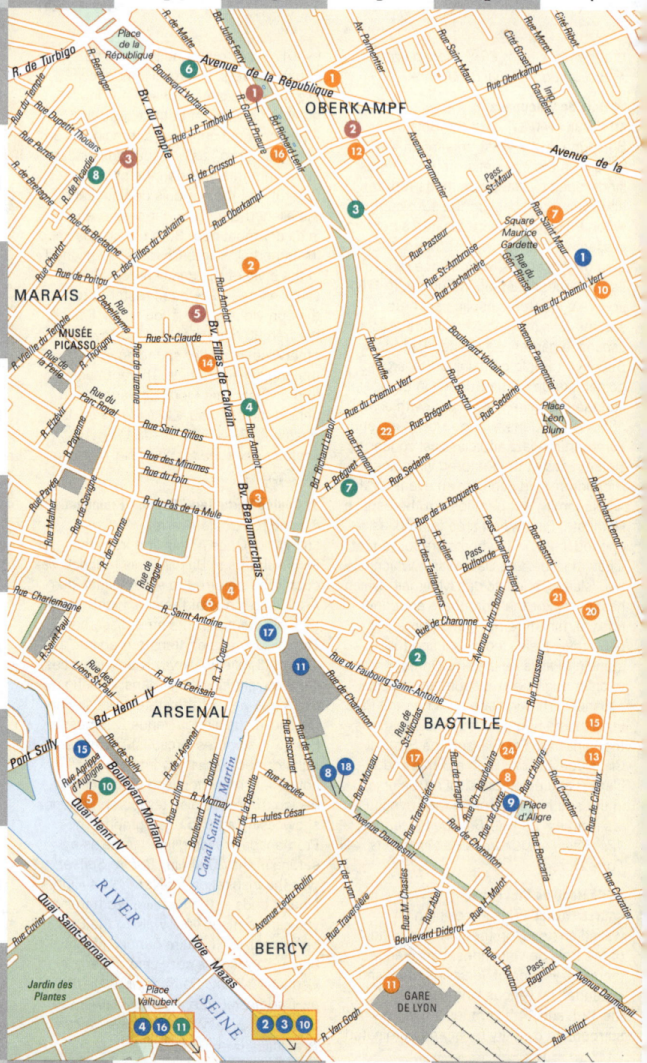

Bastille, Bercy, Nation, Oberkampf, and Charonne

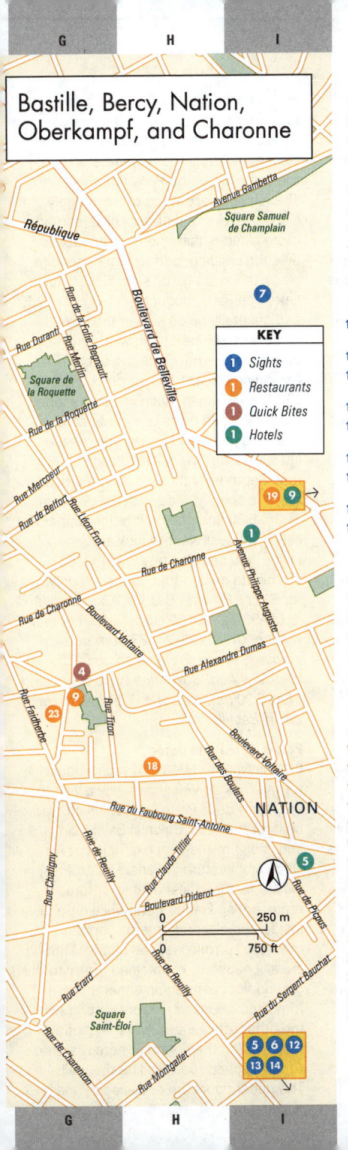

Sights ▼

1	Atelier des Lumières	F3
2	Bercy........................	C9
3	Bercy Village	C9
4	Bibliothèque National François Mitterand	B9
5	Bois de Vincennes..........	I9
6	Château de Vincennes ...	I9
7	Cimetière du Père-Lachaise	I3
8	Coulée Verte René-Dumont/ Promenade Plantée	D7
9	Marché d'Aligre	E7
10	Musée des Arts Forains	C9
11	Opéra Bastille	C6
12	Palais de la Porte Dorée	I9
13	Parc Floral de Paris......	I9
14	Parc Zoologique de Paris..........................	I9
15	Pavillon de l'Arsenal....	A7
16	Piscine Josephine Baker........	B9
17	Place de la Bastille	C6
18	Viaduc des Arts..........	D7

Restaurants ▼

1	Astier........................	D1
2	Au Passage..................	C3
3	Back in Black Coffee....	C5
4	Bistrot des Tournelles...	C6
5	Bonnie	A7
6	Bubar......................	B6
7	Double Dragon............	F2
8	Le Baron Rouge...........	E7
9	Le Bistrot Paul Bert.....	G6
10	Le Servan..................	F3
11	Le Train Bleu	D9
12	Le Villaret..................	D2
13	L'Ébauchoir	F7
14	Maison Plisson...........	B4
15	Mokonuts...................	F7
16	Ober Mamma	C2
17	Passerini...................	D7
18	Reyna	H7
19	Sadarnac	I4
20	Septime	F6
21	Septime La Cave..........	F6
22	Ten Belles Bread	D4
23	Unico........................	G6
24	Virtus.......................	E7

Quick Bites ▼

1	Folderol	C1
2	The French Bastards – Oberkampf...............	D2
3	Jacques Genin Salon de Thé	B2
4	La Chocolaterie Cyril Lignac	G6
5	The Used Book Café...	B3

Hotels ▼

1	Eden Lodge.................	I5
2	Hôtel Antoine..............	D6
3	Hôtel Fabric	D2
4	Hôtel Marais de Launay.................	C4
5	Hotel Paradiso	I7
6	Le Général Hôtel.........	B1
7	Maison Bréguet...........	D5
8	Maison Proust	A2
9	Mama Shelter Paris East..................	I4
10	SO/Paris	A7
11	TOO Hotel..................	B9

★ Marché d'Aligre

MARKET | Place d'Aligre has two of Paris's best markets: the lively outdoor Marché d'Aligre and the covered Marché Beauvau. Open every day but Monday, both are great places to pick up picnic essentials, which you can enjoy nearby in the small park at Square Trousseau or on the Promenade Plantée. The picturesque outdoor market has dozens of boisterous vendors, their stands laden with fresh fruits and vegetables, flower bouquets, and regional products such as jam, honey, and dried sausage. Many vendors are happy to give you a taste of whatever they're selling. The covered Marché Beauvau stocks everything from cheeses and olive oil to brewed-in-Paris craft beer. Sunday morning, when the accompanying flea market is in full swing, is the liveliest time to visit. Stop for a plate of fresh oysters, charcuterie, and a glass of *rouge* (even on Sunday morning) at one of the city's quirkiest wine bars, Le Baron Rouge (✉ *1 rue Théophile Roussel*), or one of the many chic cafés in the neighborhood. ✉ *Pl. d'Aligre, 12e, Bastille* ⊘ *Closed Mon.* Ⓜ *Ledru-Rollin, Bastille.*

Musée des Arts Forains

SPECIALTY MUSEUM | This unique museum in the historic Pavillons de Bercy in the Bercy Village shopping district chronicles Paris's Belle Époque heyday of carnivals and the fairground arts. Visitors discover a world of colorful, fantastical objects that conveyed all the romance and whimsy of 19th- and early 20th-century funfairs, culminating in a ride on a vintage carousel. ■ **TIP→ The museum is open by reservation only.** ✉ *53 av. des Terroirs de France, 12e, Bastille* ☎ *01–43–40–16–22* ⊕ *arts-forains.com* ✉ *90-min guided tours (French only) €18.80* ⊘ *Closed Mon.–Tues., Thurs.–Fri.* ☞ *Museum open by advance reservation only* Ⓜ *Cour St-Émilion.*

★ Opéra Bastille

PERFORMANCE VENUE | Designed by architect Carlos Ott and inaugurated in 1989, this mammoth ultramodern facility long ago took over the role of Paris's main opera house from the Opéra Garnier (although both operate under the same Opéra de Paris umbrella). The fabulous acoustics of the steeply sloping, stylish auditorium have earned more plaudits than the modern facade. Like the building, performances tend to be on the avant-garde side. Tickets for Opéra de Paris productions run €15–€230 and generally go on sale at the box office a month before shows, earlier by phone and online. Once the doors open, "standing places" can be purchased for €10 from vending machines in the lobby, but you'll need coins or a credit card (no bills) and patience to snag one, as the lines are long. The opera season usually runs September through July; the box office is open Monday through Saturday 11:30–6:30 and one hour before curtain call. If you just want to look around inside, you can also buy tickets for a 90-minute guided tour (in French only) for €17. ✉ *Pl. de la Bastille, 12e, Bastille* ☎ *08–92–89–90–90 tickets and tour information, 01–71–25–24–23 from outside France* ⊕ *www.operadeparis.fr* ⊘ *Closed mid-July–Aug. Box office closed Sun. and after 6:30 pm, except 1 hr before curtain call* Ⓜ *Bastille.*

Palais de la Porte Dorée

HISTORIC SIGHT | FAMILY | If you're bound for the Bois de Vincennes, pay a visit to the Palais de la Porte Dorée, which was built for the 1931 Colonial Exhibition and is one of the best examples of Art Deco architecture in Paris. The ornate facade features bas-relief sculptures representing France's erstwhile empire. Inside, the elaborate marble, ornate metalwork, frescoes, and original lighting are all beautifully maintained. Entry to the ground floor is free. On either end are furnished salons, one representing Asia, the other Africa; peek into the central room, called the Forum, where restored Africa-inspired mosaics line the walls. The upper floors are occupied by the

Musée Nationale de l'Historie de l'Immigration, a fascinating modern museum tracing the history of immigration in France through photographs, artworks, and first-person accounts. The basement contains **L'Aquarium Tropical,** a favorite among generations of Parisians, who all visited as kids, with a pair of rare albino alligators, plus 300 species of exotic marine life. ■ TIP→ **Be sure to check out the Palais's excellent temporary exhibitions.** ✉ *293 av. Daumesnil, 12e, Bastille* ☎ *01–53–59–58–60* ⊕ *www.palais-portedoree.fr* ✿ *Ground floor free; museum €10; aquarium €10; combined ticket €14* ◷ *Closed Mon.* Ⓜ *Porte Dorée.*

★ Parc Floral de Paris

CITY PARK | FAMILY | A lake, a butterfly garden, a bonsai pavillion, and seasonal displays of blooms make the Bois de Vincennes's 70-acre floral park a lovely place to spend a warm afternoon. Kids will also enjoy the extensive playgrounds and the marionette (*guignol*) theater. A café and a sit-down tea salon make dining easy, but picnicking under the trees is highly recommended, especially when the park hosts jazz and classical concerts (most weekends from June through September). In winter months, some attractions may be closed. ✉ *Rte. de la Pyramide, 12e, Bastille* ☎ *01–49–57–24–81* ⊕ *www.parcfloraldeparis.com* ✿ *€2.50 Apr.–Sept.; free Oct.–Mar.* Ⓜ *Château de Vincennes.*

Parc Zoologique de Paris

ZOO | FAMILY | The 35-acre zoo in the Bois de Vincennes is France's largest, with 1,000 or so animals housed in cleverly designed environments (aka "biozones") that mix species as Mother Nature intended. These include a free-range aviary you can walk through and a greenhouse that re-creates a slice of the rain forest. ✉ *53 av. de St-Maurice, 12e, Bastille* ⊕ *Entrance at intersection of Av. Daumesnil and Rte. de Ceinture du Lac Daumesnil* ☎ *08–11–22–41–22* ⊕ *www.parczoologiquedeparis.fr* ✿ *€22* ◷ *Closed 3 wks in Jan.* Ⓜ *Porte Dorée.*

Pavillon de l'Arsenal

HISTORY MUSEUM | FAMILY | If your knowledge of Paris history is *nul* (nil), stop here for an entertaining free tutorial. Built in 1879 as a private museum, the Pavillon today is a restored structure of glass and iron that showcases the city's urban development through the ages. A giant model of Paris traces its evolution (with information in English). There are photos, maps, and videos, plus a giant digital interactive model detailing what Paris is predicted to look like in the future. Reconstruction plans—called Grand Paris—are vast and take into account the 2024 Olympics and beyond. The Pavillon also has a café-bookstore and hosts frequent architecture-theme temporary exhibits. ✉ *21 bd. Morland, 4e, Bastille* ☎ *01–42–76–33–97* ⊕ *www.pavillon-arsenal.com* ✿ *Free* ◷ *Closed Mon.* Ⓜ *Sully-Morland, Bastille.*

Piscine Josephine Baker

POOL | FAMILY | This modern aquatic center, which floats on the Seine and is named after the much-beloved American-born entertainer, features a pool with a retractable glass roof, two solariums, a steam room, Jacuzzis, and a gym. Check the opening hours and schedule of classes online. ✉ *Porte de la Gare, 21 quai François Mauriac, 13e, Bastille* ☎ *01–56–61–96–50* ⊕ *www.piscine-baker.fr* ✿ *Pool €3.50 (€6.50 in summer); fees may apply for other activities* Ⓜ *Quai de la Gare, Bibilothèque.*

Place de la Bastille

HISTORIC SIGHT | Almost nothing remains of the infamous Bastille prison, destroyed in 1789, though tourists still ask bemused Parisians where to find it. Until the late 1980s, there was little more to see here than a busy traffic circle ringing the Colonne de Juillet (July Column), a memorial to the victims of later uprisings in 1830 and 1848. The opening of the Opéra Bastille in 1989 rejuvenated the area, however, drawing art galleries, bars, and restaurants to the narrow streets, notably along Rue de Lappe—once a haunt of Edith Piaf—and Rue de la Roquette.

Before it became a prison, the Bastille St-Antoine was a defensive fortress with eight immense towers and a wide moat. It was built by Charles V in the late 14th century and transformed into a prison during the reign of Louis XIII (1610–43). Famous occupants included Voltaire, the Marquis de Sade, and the Man in the Iron Mask. On July 14, 1789, it was stormed by an angry mob that dramatically freed all of the remaining prisoners (there were only seven), thereby launching the French Revolution. The roots of the revolt ran deep. Resentment toward Louis XVI and Marie-Antoinette had been building amid a severe financial crisis. There was a crippling bread shortage, and the free-spending monarch was blamed. When the king dismissed the popular finance minister, Jacques Necker, enraged Parisians took to the streets. They marched to Les Invalides, helping themselves to stocks of arms, then continued on to the Bastille. A few months later, what was left of the prison was razed—and 83 of its stones were carved into miniature Bastilles and sent to the provinces as a memento (you can see one of them in the Musée Carnavalet). The key to the prison was given to George Washington by Lafayette and has remained at Mount Vernon ever since. Today, nearly every major street demonstration in Paris—and there are many—passes through this square. ✉ *4e, Bastille* Ⓜ *Bastille.*

Viaduc des Arts

STORE/MALL | Since before medieval times, the Bastille area has been Paris's historic center for artisans' ateliers. Continuing that tradition, more than 40 craftspeople, designers, and gourmets work and sell their handicrafts to the public in the elegant (vaulting) underpinning the Coulée Verte René-Dumont promenade. From the wares of

goldsmiths and silversmiths, brewers and distillers, clothing designers, and perfumers to such items as handmade musical instruments, bespoke shoes, and artisanal chocolate and jams, a world of fine crafts awaits under the soaring ceilings of a place utterly unique in Paris. ✉ *1–127 av. Daumesnil, 12e, Bastille* 🌐 *www.leviaducdesarts.com* Ⓜ *Bastille, Gare de Lyon.*

🍴 Restaurants

★ Back in Black Coffee

$ | **FRENCH** | An easy walk from Place de la Bastille and the Marais, this sleek 2,000-square-foot café is a favorite spot for breakfast, veggie-centric nibbles, and exceptional scones, breads, and sweet rolls served all day, seven days a week. Mornings are a good time to enjoy the fragrance of fresh roasting coffee, performed in full view. **Known for:** famous scones; some of the best café food around; excellent brunch (reserve ahead of time). **§** *Average main: €6* ✉ *25 rue Amelot, 11e, Bastille* 🌐 *backinblackcoffee.com* ♡ *No dinner* Ⓜ *Bastille, Chemin Vert.*

Bistrot des Tournelles

$$$ | **BISTRO** | Tile floors, mercury mirrors, bentwood chairs, and a menu of classic French comfort foods proffered by talented young chef Édouart Vermynck take you back to a charming Paris of old (the bistrot was first opened in 1922). Start with homey *oeufs*-mayo (eggs) or croque-monsieur with *jambon* de Paris (a type of cooked ham) followed by golden Landes hen with morel cream or tender scallops in a delicate beurre blanc. **Known for:** charming ambience and warm service; outstanding takes on the classics; reservations are essential. **§** *Average main: €30* ✉ *6 rue des Tournelles, 4e, Bastille* ☎ *01–57–40–99–96* 🌐 *www.bistrotdestournelles.com* ♡ *Closed Mon. No lunch* Ⓜ *Bastille.*

Bonnie
$$$$ | **FRENCH** | Spectacular doesn't even begin to describe the views from the cocktail bar and restaurant *du jour* on the 15th and 16th floors of the SO/Paris hotel—the tallest building in the lower Marais. The panoramic vistas of Paris from the all-glass bar, dining room, and wraparound terrace are easily some of the best in the city, and in a brilliant sleight of decor, the terrace's mirrored overhang—by artist Olafur Eliasson—give diners an upside-down view of the Seine's rippling water and boats passing both above and below. **Known for:** gorgeous outdoor terrace in warm weather; lobster roll and cod beignets; reservations essential, though the food doesn't always match the excellence of the views. **§** *Average main: €40* ✉ *SO/Paris, 10 rue Agrippa d'Aubigné, 4e, Bastille* ☎ *01–78–90–74–74* ⊕ *www.bonnie-restaurant.com* **Ⓜ** *Sully-Morland.*

Bubar
$ | **WINE BAR** | In summer, look for the crowd spilling out the front of this signless wine bar named for Jean-Louis, the bartender (*bubar* or *barbu* is French slang for "bearded"). The wine menu—with many selections available by the glass—features French wines and small-batch vintages from South Africa, Chile, and Argentina. **Known for:** low-lit, almost clandestine atmosphere; wines to discover, guided by a knowledgeable and generous owner; bring-your-own snacks option as well as small-plate menu. **§** *Average main: €13* ✉ *3 rue des Tournelles, 4e, Bastille* ☎ *01–40–29–97–72* ⊘ *No lunch* **Ⓜ** *Bastille.*

★ Le Baron Rouge
$ | **WINE BAR** | This laid-back, no-reservation wine bar near the Place d'Aligre market is a throwback to another era, with just a few tables plus giant wine barrels along the walls for filling and refilling your take-home bottles. A fun time to come is Sunday morning (yes, morning) when it's packed with locals who have just been to

the market and want to linger over good food and that first *petit blanc* of the day. **Known for:** wine by the barrel; authentic neighborhood atmosphere; oysters on a winter evening. **§** *Average main: €12* ✉ *1 rue Théophile Roussel, 12e, Bastille* ☎ *01–43–43–14–32* ⊕ *www.lebaronrouge.net* ⊘ *No dinner Sun. No lunch Mon.* **Ⓜ** *Ledru-Rollin.*

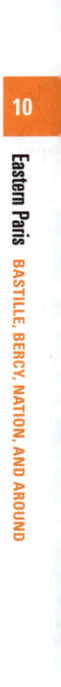

L'Ébauchoir
$$$ | **BISTRO** | From its traditional bentwood bistro chairs to its well-priced menu of contemporary French classics, this is the kind of neighborhood bistro we dream about when we think of Paris. Friendly service, a convivial atmosphere, a top-notch wine list, and delicious market-fresh fare all add up to the kind of place you want to keep all to yourself. **Known for:** warm and welcoming service (in English); a local favorite; reliably excellent food. **§** *Average main: €25* ✉ *43–45 Rue de Cîteaux, 12e, Bastille* ☎ *01–43–42–49–31* ⊕ *lebauchoir.com* ⊘ *Closed Sun. No lunch Mon.* **Ⓜ** *Faidherbe-Chaligny, Reuilly-Diderot.*

★ Le Train Bleu
$$$$ | **FRENCH** | Paris's grandest Belle Époque beauty, hidden within the Gare de Lyon train station, has been fully restored to a culinary status almost befitting its eye-popping decor. The menu of French classics is not cheap, though the €49 "travelers menu" for lunch assures you'll be wined, dined, and on your train in 45 minutes. **Known for:** unique historic atmosphere; gorgeous setting including frescoes; tasty and creative cocktails. **§** *Average main: €38* ✉ *Pl. Louis-Armand, 12e, Bastille* ☎ *01–43–43–09–06* ⊕ *www.le-train-bleu.com/en* **Ⓜ** *Gare de Lyon.*

★ Maison Plisson
$ | **MODERN FRENCH** | The deep sidewalk terrace at this three-in-one gourmet grocer, restaurant, and café is a great place to linger over lunch and a glass of wine, or an early (for France) dinner. The daily menu of hot dishes, soups, and salads

complements a wide selection of tasty pastries and classic sandwiches made with top-notch ingredients. **Known for:** French specialties from every corner of the country; good sandwiches to stay or take away; snob appeal. [$] *Average main: €12* ✉ *93 bd. Beaumarchais, 3e, Bastille* ☎ *01–71–18–19–09* ⊕ *www.lamaisonplisson.com* Ⓜ *St-Sébastien–Froissart, Chemin Vert.*

★ Passerini

$$$ | ITALIAN | Chef Giovanni Passerini, a favorite Parisian chef, has done it again with this wine-focused spot, the companion to his wildly popular Italian restaurant just a few steps away. It's a wine bar, gastro-bistro, and pasta factory all in one, and the oh-so-good plates of high-brow Italian comfort food are served with his typically masterful selection of well-priced French and Italian wines. **Known for:** always excellent Italian classics; tons of finds on the wine list; fun, laid-back atmosphere. [$] *Average main: €28* ✉ *44 rue Traversière, 12e, Bastille* ☎ *01–43–42–27–56* ⊕ *www.passerini.paris* ♡ *Closed Sun. and Mon. No lunch Tues.–Fri.* Ⓜ *Ledru-Rollin.*

Ten Belles Bread

$ | CAFÉ | The two British chefs behind this bustling café in an industrial-style loft on an up-and-coming corner of the 11e are known around town for their gourmet take on healthy foods. Here the emphasis is on breakfast, lunch, and brunch, with a range of salads, savory pies, and pastries all made in the on-site bakery. **Known for:** rustic whole-grain breads made fresh throughout the day; gourmet take-out lunches; top-notch coffee. [$] *Average main: €7* ✉ *17–19 rue Breguet, 11e, Bastille* ☎ *01–47–00–08–19* ⊕ *tenbelles.com* ♡ *No dinner* Ⓜ *Bréguet-Sabin, Richard Lenoir, Chemin Vert.*

★ Virtus

$$$$ | FRENCH | Two young chefs bring their heritage (Argentine and Japanese) and impressive cooking credentials to bear in their beautiful restaurant, steps from the Marché d'Aligre, that's almost worth a visit for the decor alone. But it's the food that has earned them a passionate following among Parisians, for its range, imagination, quality, and sheer deliciousness. **Known for:** prix-fixe menus only, with exquisite pairings of seafood and vegetables; vegetarian and gluten-free friendly, and great wine list; reservations are required. [$] *Average main: €125* ✉ *29 rue de Cotte, 12e, Bastille* ☎ *09–80–68–08–08* ⊕ *www.virtus-paris.com* ♡ *Closed Sun. and Mon. No lunch except Fri.* Ⓜ *Ledru-Rollin.*

Hotels

★ Hôtel Antoine

$$ | HOTEL | If you want designer digs in a well-located boutique lodging that won't break the budget, this hotel designed by Christian Lacroix is a great spot for you. **Pros:** location on the area's best fashion shopping street; quiet, cozy lobby with complimentary coffee; spacious suites. **Cons:** double rooms on the smaller side; gym is minuscule; breakfast not always complimentary. [$] *Rooms from: €207* ✉ *12 rue de Charonne, 11e, Bastille* ☎ *01–55–28–30–11* ⊕ *www.hotelantoineparis.com* ↝ *38 rooms* 🍽 *No Meals* Ⓜ *Bastille, Ledru-Rollin.*

Hôtel Marais de Launay

$$ | HOTEL | The no-frills decor might seem spartan at first, but this tidy boutique hotel also offers modern amenities like free Wi-Fi, a perfect location a few blocks from the regal Place des Vosges, and outstanding prices for the area. **Pros:** homey touches; attentive service; reasonably spacious for the neighborhood. **Cons:** tiny elevator; some small rooms; basic bathrooms. [$] *Rooms from: €215* ✉ *42 rue Amelot, 11e, Bastille* ☎ *01–47–00–88–11* ⊕ *www.hotelmaraisdelaunayparis.com* ↝ *35 rooms* 🍽 *No Meals* Ⓜ *Chemin Vert.*

Hotel Paradiso

$$ | HOTEL | Film buffs might opt to forego the light of day at MK2 Cinema's hotel,

where each of the 36 cozy rooms comes with an overhead projector and giant screen. **Pros:** superb design and lighting; plush private cinema; 2,500 DVDs to choose from. **Cons:** smallish rooms; limited bar menu; technology can be complicated. $$$ *Rooms from: €330* ✉ *135 bd. Diderot, 12e, Bastille* ☎ *01–88–59–20–01* ⊕ *www.mk2hotelparadiso.com* ↝ *34 rooms* 🍴 No Meals Ⓜ Ledru-Rollin.

★ Maison Bréguet

$$$ | **HOTEL** | Tucked away on a quiet street so close and yet far enough from the bustling Bastille, this is one of Paris's more elegant boutique lodgings. **Pros:** beautiful rooms with plenty of light; lovely hammam and pool on-site; five-minute walk to Bastille. **Cons:** not as good a deal as it used to be; pool could be bigger; some rooms on the small side. $$$ *Rooms from: €384* ✉ *8 rue Bréguet, 11e, Bastille* ☎ *01–58–30–32–31* ⊕ *www.maison-breguet.com* ↝ *53 rooms* 🍴 No Meals Ⓜ Bréguet-Sabin, Bastille.

★ Maison Proust

$$$$ | **HOTEL** | Scrupulously devoted to the legacy of Marcel Proust, what this gorgeous hotel lacks in space it makes up for in sheer opulence. **Pros:** incredibly romantic atmosphere; reservation comes with private one-hour session for two at the luxury pool; fabulous location. **Cons:** quite expensive; intimate spaces not for everyone; rooms and suites are minuscule. $$$ *Rooms from: €600* ✉ *26 rue de Picardie, 3e, Bastille* ☎ *01–86–54–55–55* ⊕ *www.maison-proust.com/en/maison-proust* ↝ *22 rooms* 🍴 No Meals Ⓜ Oberkampf, Filles du Calvaire.

★ SO/ Paris

$$$$ | **HOTEL** | A behemoth 1960s administrative building has become one of Paris's hottest hotels, sought after for its glam interiors, fashion credentials, and show-stealing views that are second only to the Eiffel Tower. **Pros:** excellent on-site restaurant; unprecedented views; great spa, fitness room, and big pool. **Cons:** a pricey option for the area; oh-so-chic bar can get crowded; restaurant doesn't prioritize hotel guests. $$$ *Rooms from: €600* ✉ *10 rue Agrippa d'Aubigné, 4e, Bastille* ☎ *01–78–90–74–00* ⊕ *so-hotels.com/en/paris* ↝ *162 rooms* 🍴 No Meals Ⓜ Sully-Morland.

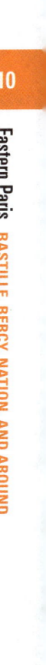

★ TOO Hotel

$$ | **HOTEL** | In this hotel on the top floors of one of architect Jean Nouvel's shimmering Duo Towers, guests get an unprecedented view of Paris from one of the city's tallest buildings and its second-tallest hotel. **Pros:** tramway a 30-second walk away; tremendous views (each room comes with binoculars); five-star amenities at four-star prices. **Cons:** bar sometimes closed for private parties; not centrally located; no lobby for hanging out. $$$ *Rooms from: €270* ✉ *65 rue Bruneseau, 13e, Bastille* ☎ *01–78–90–79–90* ⊕ *www.toohotel.com/en* ↝ *139 rooms* 🍴 No Meals Ⓜ Bibliothèque François Mitterrand.

 Nightlife

BARS

★ Calbar

BARS | This off-the-beaten-path watering hole, where the drinks are so good, the music so cool, and the atmosphere so right, is a big draw for a laid-back but knowing crowd. Relax on the big leather sofa while sipping a well-priced craft cocktail that pairs perfectly with your plate of Iberian ham or cheese and charcuterie. ✉ *82 rue de Charenton, 12e, Bastille* ☎ *01–84–06–18–90* ⊕ *lecalbar-cocktail.com* Ⓜ Ledru-Rollin.

Moonshiner

BARS | In true Prohibition-era fashion, this 1920s-style speakeasy is reached through a freezer door in the depths of a pizzeria, so don't be alarmed at first glance (it's quite obvious when you're there). House cocktails are imaginative and delicious, but the friendly bartenders are equally adept at the classics—and the pizza's good, too. ✉ *5 rue Sedaine,*

11e, Bastille ☎ *09-50-73-12-99* ⊕ *www.moonshinerbar.fr* Ⓜ *Bastille, Bréguet-Sabin.*

Performing Arts

 **Cinémathèque Française**

FILM | This mecca for cinephiles brought up on Federico Fellini, Ingmar Bergman, and Alain Resnais is known for its superb, and exhaustive, retrospectives of world cinema past and present. Its spectacular home—in the former American Center, designed by Frank Gehry—includes elaborate museum exhibitions plus three cinemas and a video library. British and American films are always screened in the original language with French subtitles. ✉ *51 rue de Bercy, 12e, Bastille* ☎ *01-71-19-33-33* ⊕ *www.cinematheque.fr* Ⓜ *Bercy.*

Théâtre de la Bastille

MODERN DANCE | An example of the innovative activity in the Bastille area, Théâtre de la Bastille has an enviable record as a launchpad for tomorrow's modern-dance stars. ✉ *76 rue de la Roquette, 11e, Bastille* ☎ *01-43-57-42-14* ⊕ *www.theatre-bastille.com* Ⓜ *Bastille.*

Shopping

Confiture Parisienne

FOOD | Customers swoon over the 50-some wildly delicious jam flavors at this artisan shop specializing in homemade (jams) that change with the seasons: black currant-jasmine or apricot-lavender in summer; in winter, chestnut-pear-tonka bean or carrot-passion fruit; and spring strawberry-cherry blossom or raspberry-violet. You'll also find jellies to accompany cheeses (Champagne-rosé; port wine), and sublime caramel, nut, and chocolate spreads. Design-your-own gift boxes are the perfect way to bestow these beautifully packaged gourmet, oh-so-Parisian flavors. All products are made on the premises in the Viaduc des Arts, and you can watch the chefs in action in the glassed-in kitchens. ✉ *17 av. Daumesnil, 12e, Bastille* ☎ *01-44-68-28-81* ⊕ *www.confiture-parisienne.com* Ⓜ *Ledru-Rollin, Gare de Lyon.*

Laura Puntillo

SHOES | Working in the vaults of the Viaduc des Arts, this artisan shoemaker crafts fully shoes in the age-old Parisian tradition for discerning buyers. Customers meet with the artisan-designer to decide exactly what they're looking for and to choose the skins, colors, laces, and other features of their dream shoe. There's also a selection of ready-to-wear shoes you can try on and take with you. ✉ *53 av. Daumesnil, 12e, Bastille* ☎ *01-46-28-98-41* ⊕ *www.laurapuntillo.com* Ⓜ *Ledru-Rollin, Gare de Lyon.*

Marché Bastille

MARKET | Paris's largest market is as much an event as a place to shop. Blocks of specialized stalls—including ones devoted to rare wines, regional cheeses, game, seafood, and flowers—cater to scores of Parisian chefs and epicures. It's open Thursday and Sunday 8:30 am to 1:30 pm. ✉ *Bd. Richard Lenoir, between Rues Amelot and St-Sabin, 11e, Bastille* Ⓜ *Ledru-Rollin.*

Oberkampf and Charonne

Paris's hip Oberkampf and Charonne neighborhoods form a rectangle between Nation and République, extending from the eastern border of the Marais all the way to Père Lachaise cemetery. In this central area—popular with Parisians but sometimes overlooked by visitors—you'll find some of the city's most exciting dining and shopping opportunities, not to mention chic boutique hotels and irresistible cocktail bars.

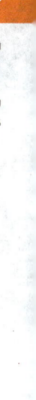

 Sights

 **Atelier des Lumières**

ARTS CENTER | An abandoned iron foundry in the hip 11e arrondissement is the soaring backdrop for Culturespace's feast for the eyes and the senses, where visitors are invited to actually step into the midst of some of the great masterpieces of 19th- and 20th-century painting (many found in famous Parisian museums). More than 100 video projectors cast vivid scenes of gorgeously colored artwork on the walls, ceilings, and floors, accompanied by a dynamic soundtrack for total immersion into a 30-minute explosion of color and sound. ✉ *38–40 rue St-Maur, 11e, Père Lachaise* ☎ *01–80–98–46–00* ⊕ *www.atelier-lumieres.com* ✉ *€17* Ⓜ *Voltaire, Rue St-Maur, Père Lachaise.*

 **Cimetière du Père-Lachaise**

CEMETERY | Bring a red rose for "the Little Sparrow" Edith Piaf when you visit the cobblestone avenues and towering trees that make this 118-acre oasis of green perhaps the world's most famous cemetery. Named for Père François de la Chaise, Louis XIV's confessor, Père-Lachaise is more than just a who's who of celebrities. The Paris Commune's final battle took place here on May 28, 1871, when 147 rebels were lined up and shot against the Mur des Fédérés (Federalists' Wall) in the southeast corner. Aside from the sheer aesthetic beauty of the cemetery, the main attraction is what (or who, more accurately) is belowground.

Two of the biggest draws are Jim Morrison's grave (with its own guard to keep Doors fans under control) and the life-size bronze figure of French journalist Victor Noir, whose alleged fertility-enhancing power accounts for the patches of bronze rubbed smooth by hopeful hands. Other significant grave sites include those of 12th-century French philosopher Pierre Abélard and his lover Héloïse; French writers Colette, Honoré de Balzac, and Marcel Proust; American writers Richard Wright, Gertrude Stein, and Alice B. Toklas; Irish writer Oscar Wilde; French actress Sarah Bernhardt; French composer Georges Bizet; Greek American opera singer Maria Callas; Franco-Polish composer Frédéric Chopin; painters of various nationalities including Georges-Pierre Seurat, Camille Pissaro, Jean-Auguste-Dominique Ingres, Jacques-Louis David, Eugène Delacroix, Théodore Géricault, Amedeo Clemente Modigliani, and Max Ernst; French jazz violinist Stephane Grappelli; French civic planner Baron Haussmann; French playwright and actor Molière; and French singer Edith Piaf. (To visit the grave sites of a few other famous French men and women, head south to Cimetière du Montparnasse, north to Cimetière de Montmartre, or west to Passy Cemetery.)

■ **TIP→ Pinpoint grave sites on the website before you come, but buy a map anyway outside the entrances—you'll still get lost, but that's part of the fun.**

One of the best days to visit is on All Saints' Day (November 1), when Parisians bring flowers to adorn the graves of loved ones or favorite celebrities. ✉ *Entrances on Rue des Rondeaux, Bd. de Ménilmontant, and Rue de la Réunion, 20e, Père Lachaise* ☎ *01–55–25–82–10* ⊕ *pere-lachaise.com* ✉ *Free* Ⓜ *Gambetta, Philippe-Auguste, Père-Lachaise.*

 Restaurants

Astier

$$$ | BISTRO | FAMILY | There are three good reasons to go to Astier: the generous cheese platter plunked on your table atop a help-yourself wicker tray, the exceptional wine cellar with bottles dating back to the 1970s, and the French bistro fare (even if portions seem to have diminished over the years). Dishes like marinated herring with warm potato salad, sausage with lentils, and baba au rhum

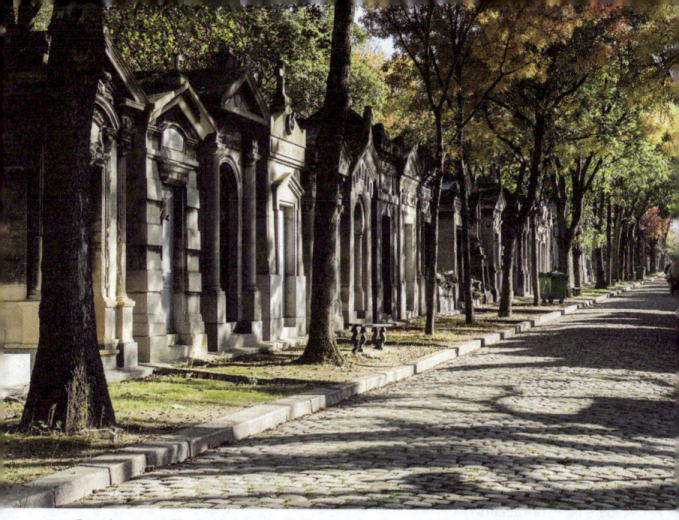

Famed cemetery Père-Lachaise is the final resting place for artists like Edith Piaf, Jim Morrison, Marcel Proust, Oscar Wilde, and many more.

are classics on the frequently changing set menu, which includes a selection of no less than 20 cheeses. **Known for:** same-day reservations possible (but good to reserve ahead); traditional atmosphere; excellent choice for authentic French cooking. **§** *Average main: €29* ✉ *44 rue Jean-Pierre Timbaud, 11e, République* ☎ *01–43–57–16–35* 🌐 *www.restaurant-astier.com* Ⓜ *Parmentier.*

Au Passage

$$ | **WINE BAR** | This *bistrot à vins* has the lived-in look of a longtime neighborhood hangout—which it was until two veterans of the raging Paris wine-bar scene reinvented the place, keeping the vintage, laid-back atmosphere and adding a serious foodie menu that's one of the best deals in town. A blackboard lists a selection of tapas, including several house-made pâtés, fresh tomato or beet salads, a superb seafood carpaccio, and artisanal charcuterie and cheeses. **Known for:** gastronomy on a budget, with a friendly vibe; roasted lamb haunch to

share; reservations essential. **§** *Average main: €20* ✉ *1 bis, passage St-Sébastien, 11e, République* ☎ *01–43–55–07–52* 🌐 *www.restaurant-aupassage.fr* ⊘ *Closed Sun. and Mon. No lunch* Ⓜ *St-Ambroise, St-Sébastien–Froissart, Richard Lenoir.*

★ Double Dragon

$ | **CHINESE** | Anyone with a hankering for enticing, well-priced, gourmet-inflected Chinese fare in a chic setting need look no further. Friendly to both carnivores and herbivores alike, the fried tofu filled with Comté cheese, the cold noodles, and the cucumber salad are just as good as the perfectly crisp caramelized pork or fried chicken. **Known for:** affordable lunch menu; local beers and natural wines; Chinese classics with a French flair. **§** *Average main: €16* ✉ *52 rue St-Maur, 11e, Oberkampf* ☎ *0–71–32–41–95* 🌐 *www.doubledragonparis.com* ⊘ *Closed Sun. and Mon. No lunch Tues.* Ⓜ *St-Ambroise, Rue St-Maur.*

★ **Le Bistrot Paul Bert**
$$$ | **BISTRO** | The Paul Bert delivers everything you could want from a traditional Paris bistro (faded 1930s decor, thick steak with real frites, and good value), so it's no wonder its two dining rooms fill every night with a cosmopolitan crowd. The impressively stocked wine cellar helps, as do the laid-back yet efficient staff, excellent and abundant cheese trolley, and hearty dishes such as monkfish with white beans and duck with pears. **Known for:** delicious dessert soufflés; sidewalk seating in summer; reservations are essential. § *Average main: €25* ✉ *18 rue Paul Bert, 11e, Charonne* ☎ *01–43–72–24–01* ⊕ *www.bistrotpaulbert.fr* ♡ *Closed Sun. and Mon.* Ⓜ *Rue des Boulets.*

★ **Le Servan**
$$ | **MODERN FRENCH** | The impressive but unfussy gastronomic menu here features Asian-inflected dishes that express the food's far-flung influences. A starter of "zakouskis," several small dishes that may include deep-fried giblets, fresh radishes with anchovy butter, or herb-infused cockles, warms you up for a sublime entrée of whole lacquered quail, cod with spicy black-bean reduction, or crispy melt-in-your mouth pork on a bed of braised leeks. **Known for:** great-value lunch menu; accommodating to vegetarians; reservations essential at this lovely, intimate place. § *Average main: €24* ✉ *32 rue St-Maur, 11e, Père Lachaise* ☎ *01–55–28–51–82* ⊕ *www.leservan.fr* ♡ *Closed Sun. No lunch Sat.* Ⓜ *Voltaire, Rue St-Maur, Parmentier.*

★ **Le Villaret**
$$$ | **BISTRO** | Classic bistros are making a comeback in Paris, and this neighborhood favorite embodies everything people love about this French institution. Here, traditional fare is lovingly prepared with top-quality ingredients and paired with a wine list that's so good it's a draw unto itself. **Known for:** wonderful service; generous portions of always reliable

food; relaxed but cool vibe. § *Average main: €32* ✉ *13 rue Ternaux, 11e, Oberkampf* ☎ *01–43–57–89–76* ⊕ *www.levillaret-restaurant.fr/en* ♡ *Closed Sun. and Mon.* Ⓜ *St-Ambroise.*

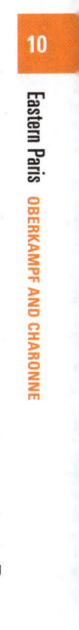

★ **Mokonuts**
$ | **CONTEMPORARY** | One of the city's best examples of the casual gourmet cafés popping up around Paris, Mokonuts is run by a talented husband-and-wife team who create delicious dishes and pastries that are as pleasing to the eye as they are to the palate. Prepare for crowds at breakfast and teatime, when you can choose from chunky multigrain cookies, sweet or savory muffins, tarts, and other sweet goodies. **Known for:** excellent coffee; late hours for a café (open until 6 pm); small space means it gets crowded fast, but you can reserve at lunch. § *Average main: €13* ✉ *5 rue St-Bernard, 11e, Oberkampf* ☎ *09–80–81–82–85* ⊕ *www.mokonuts.com* ♡ *No dinner* Ⓜ *Faidherbe-Chaligny, Ledru-Rollin.*

Ober Mamma
$ | **ITALIAN** | **FAMILY** | This chic trattoria draws an enthusiastic local crowd for its fabulous wood-oven-fired pizzas, copious pasta dishes, and refreshing craft cocktails. You can sit in the soaring dining room or relax with a plate of Italian charcuterie and a drink at the very popular, and often crowded, cocktail bar. **Known for:** good price-to-quality ratio; large pizzas; lively atmosphere. § *Average main: €16* ✉ *107 bd. Richard Lenoir, 11e, Oberkampf* ☎ *01–58–30–62–78* ⊕ *www.bigmammagroup.com* Ⓜ *Oberkampf, République.*

★ **Reyna**
$ | **FILIPINO** | **FAMILY** | Cotton-candy-color walls, comfy banquettes, and giant mirrors belie the fact that this cozy eatery is one of the city's top destinations to experience the flavors of the Philippines. Meals are served family-style with one plate for each diner to sample from a succession of dishes, each more

delicious than the next, including Hainan soy-glazed burrata flecked with ginger; fried chicken wings with black coffee sauce; and a fish of the day in coconut milk with truffle. **Known for:** great prices; warm and welcoming atmosphere; some good desserts. **ⓘ** *Average main: €16* ✉ *41 rue de Montreuil, 11e, Oberkampf* ☎ *01–40–09–06–82* 🌐 *www.reyna.paris* ⓒ *Closed Mon. and Tues. No lunch except Sun. No dinner Sun.* Ⓜ *Rue des Boulets.*

Sadarnac

$$$$ | **FRENCH** | If you love to discover Paris's authentic corners and hidden culinary gems, this is a place for you. In a pretty dining room set on a charming cobbled street five minutes from Père-Lachaise, chef Lise Deveix crafts memorable dishes that mix her passion for healthy local ingredients with an outsized talent that has won her a following from the four corners of the city. **Known for:** award-winning young chef; prix-fixe menus only, with excellent prices; reservations required. **ⓘ** *Average main: €57* ✉ *17 rue St-Blaise, 20e, Père Lachaise* ☎ *01–72–60–72–06* 🌐 *restaurantsadarnac.fr* ⓒ *Closed Sun. and Mon. No lunch Tues. and Wed.* Ⓜ *Alexandre Dumas, Porte de Bagnolet.*

 **Septime**

$$$$ | **BISTRO** | With amazing food and a convivial, unpretentious atmosphere, Septime has become one of the hottest tables in town. Seasonal ingredients, inventive pairings, and excellent natural wines bring in diners ready for exciting and sophisticated dishes like creamy gnochetti in an orange-rind-flecked Gouda sauce sprinkled with coriander flowers. **Known for:** exceptional Parisian bistro with prix-fixe menu only; one Michelin star; reservations needed far in advance. **ⓘ** *Average main: €120* ✉ *80 rue de Charonne, 11e, Charonne* ☎ *01–43–67–38–29* 🌐 *www.septime-charonne.fr* ⓒ *Closed weekends* Ⓜ *Ledru-Rollin, Charonne.*

Septime La Cave

$$ | **WINE BAR** | This minuscule wine bar and boutique serves as a first stop for those lucky enough to have snagged a sought-after reservation at Septime restaurant or the ideal place to taste handpicked wines by the glass from small producers you won't find stateside. Early opening hours make it the perfect spot for an apéro accompanied by gourmet snacks before dinner at the restaurant or elsewhere in this gastronomically rich neighborhood. **Known for:** intimate atmosphere; great for wine discoveries; close to the mother ship (Septime). **ⓘ** *Average main: €18* ✉ *3 rue Basfroi, 11e, Oberkampf* ☎ *01–43–67–14–87* 🌐 *www.septime-lacave.fr* Ⓜ *Ledru-Rollin, Charonne.*

Unico

$$$ | **MODERN ARGENTINE** | An architect and a photographer, both Parisians born in Argentina, teamed up to open one of Bastille's hottest restaurants—literally hot, too, because the Argentinean meat served here is grilled over charcoal. Whichever cut of beef you choose (the ultimate being *lomo*, or fillet), it's so melt-in-your-mouth that the sauces served on the side seem almost superfluous. **Known for:** tender Argentinean beef, aged and grilled; chic retro atmosphere; excellent value prix-fixe menus. **ⓘ** *Average main: €30* ✉ *15 rue Paul-Bert, 11e, Charonne* ☎ *01–43–67–68–08* 🌐 *www.resto-unico.com* ⓒ *Closed Sun. and Mon.* Ⓜ *Faidherbe-Chaligny.*

 Coffee and Quick Bites

Folderol

$ | **ICE CREAM** | In a city where we all scream for ice cream (and wine), thank goodness for Folderol, where delicious handmade ice creams in flavors like nectarine hibiscus, jasmine-blood orange, spicy watermelon, pecan pie, or chocolate wedding cake are savored

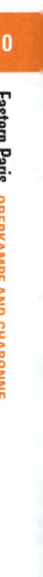

like the natural wines you can sip by the glass or bottle along with a plate of fine charcuterie and other small plates. **Known for:** insanely inventive ice creams and sorbets; great small plates menu; hard-to-find wines. ⓘ *Average main: €7* ✉ *10 rue du Grand-Prieuré, 11e, Oberkampf* ☎ *01–43–55–02–57* 🌐 *www.folderol.com* ⊘ *Closed Mon. and Tues. No lunch* Ⓜ *Oberkampf.*

The French Bastards – Oberkampf

$ | **BAKERY** | This place is irreverent in every way except about what goes in the product. From the flours to the chocolates, everything is meticulously sourced for the team's "food porn," pastries that delight every sense, whether it's the chocolate and pistachio babka, almond croissants, praline brioches, fudge brownies, or "cruffins," a melt-in-your-mouth croissant-style brioche dusted with cocoa or sugar. **Known for:** strong focus on sustainability; seasonal offerings; delicious breads. ⓘ *Average main: €5* ✉ *61 rue Oberkampf, 11e, Oberkampf* 🌐 *thefrenchbastards.fr* Ⓜ *Parmentier.*

★ Jacques Genin Salon de Thé

$ | **BAKERY** | Master chocolatier Jacques Genin's sophisticated *carrés* are like small jewels, perfumed with ganaches of exquisite subtlety in seasonal flavors like rosemary, Szechuan pepper, or bergamot. The glorious pastries served in this tearoom and chocolate boutique (one of the loveliest in Paris) are no longer available for takeaway but rather are assembled to order, to be eaten fresh on the premises. **Known for:** sinful hot chocolate; some of the city's best chocolates and pastries; melt-in-your-mouth caramels. ⓘ *Average main: €10* ✉ *133 rue de Turenne, 3e, Marais Quarter* ☎ *01–45–77–29–01* 🌐 *www.jacquesgenin.fr* ⊘ *Closed Mon.* Ⓜ *Filles du Calvaire.*

★ La Chocolaterie Cyril Lignac

$ | **MODERN FRENCH** | You don't have to be a chocoholic to appreciate this cozy little nook of a café focused on all things derived from the cocoa bean: decadent cakes and pastries, chocolates and *tablettes* (bars of chocolate), and a most sinful *chocolat chaud.* There are also coffee and other beverages to linger over inside or at a sidewalk table. **Known for:** top-notch chocolate in every form; good spot for coffee; classic Parisian hot chocolate. ⓘ *Average main: €8* ✉ *25 rue Chanzy, 11e, Charonne* ☎ *01–55–87–21–40* 🌐 *www.lachocolateriecyrillignac.com* ⊘ *Closed Mon.* Ⓜ *Rue des Boulets.*

The Used Book Café

$$ | **CAFÉ** | At the entrance of Merci, a chic concept store, you'll find the perfect spot for a quick lunch or snack (or a place to catch up on the latest French novels) among rows of books and comfy chairs. Highlights include a small soup menu, a risotto of the day, and hearty vegetarian salads. **Known for:** quick lunchtime spot; fresh juices and mint iced tea; rosé by the glass. ⓘ *Average main: €19* ✉ *111 bd. Beaumarchais, 3e, Marais Quarter* ☎ *01–42–77–79–28* 🌐 *www.merci-merci.com* ⊘ *Closed Sun. No dinner* Ⓜ *St-Sébastien–Froissart.*

 Hotels

★ Eden Lodge

$$ | **B&B/INN** | **FAMILY** | With a location in a hidden, tree-shaded courtyard off a nondescript street minutes from Père-Lachaise cemetery, no lodging in the capital is quite as unobtrusively fabulous as this trailblazing, 100% sustainable, five-room eco-lodge. **Pros:** chic contemporary decor; tons of great restaurants in the neighborhood; spacious terraces in all rooms. **Cons:** low-key neighborhood; no in-house bar; not on the prettiest street. ⓘ *Rooms from: €235* ✉ *175 rue de Charonne, 11e, Père Lachaise* ☎ *01–43–56–73–24* 🌐 *www.edenlodge-paris.net* ↝ *5 rooms* 🍴 *Free Breakfast* Ⓜ *Père Lachaise, Charonne.*

 **Hôtel Fabric**

$$ | HOTEL | This urban-chic hotel tucked away on an old artisan street is fully in tune with the pulse of the lively Oberkampf neighborhood and close to fabulous nightlife, cocktail bars, restaurants, bakeries, and shopping (and the Marais and Canal St-Martin). **Pros:** all-you-can-eat breakfast for €20; lots of great sightseeing within walking distance; warm and helpful staff. **Cons:** rooms can be noisy; very popular, so book well in advance; might be too party-focused for some. **[§]** *Rooms from: €240* ✉ *31 rue de la Folie Méricourt, 11e, Oberkampf* ☎ *01–43–57–27–00* ⊕ *www.hotelfabric.com* ↝ *33 rooms* 🍴 *No Meals* Ⓜ *St-Ambroise, Oberkampf.*

Le Général Hôtel

$$ | HOTEL | Designer Jean-Philippe Nuel applied his sleek styling to Le Général, one of Paris's first affordable, high-design hotels. **Pros:** friendly service; smart design; in popular nightlife district. **Cons:** noisy neighborhood; not within easy walking distance of major tourist attractions; basic breakfast (not included). **[§]** *Rooms from: €260* ✉ *5–7 rue Rampon, 11e, République* ☎ *01–47–00–41–57* ⊕ *www.legeneralhotel.com* ↝ *46 rooms* 🍴 *No Meals* Ⓜ *République, Oberkampf.*

 **Mama Shelter Paris East**

$ | HOTEL | Close to Père-Lachaise in the up-and-coming 20e arrondissement, this large hotel is an experiment in quirky postmodern countercultural cool, with a fun and funky interior designed by Philippe Starck. **Pros:** trendy design without designer prices; fun vibe with hip bar on-site; entertainment center in each room. **Cons:** 10-minute walk to métro; nearby club can be noisy; small rooms. **[§]** *Rooms from: €169* ✉ *109 rue de Bagnolet, 20e, Père Lachaise* ☎ *01–43–48–48–48* ⊕ *www.mamashelter.com* ↝ *172 rooms* 🍴 *No Meals* Ⓜ *Gambetta.*

 **Nightlife**

BARS

Bar Principal

BARS | For well-priced Brazilian-inspired cocktails (try the delicious caipirinha, pisco sour, or spicy rosé margarita), check out Bar Principal. Here you can also enjoy the menu of delicious South American–inspired nibbles in the streamlined interior or outdoors on a pretty leafy square. ✉ *5 rue du Général-Renault, 11e, Oberkampf* ⊕ *www.instagram.com/bar-principalparis* Ⓜ *Voltaire, Rue St-Maur.*

Bluebird

COCKTAIL BARS | Its swank Mad Men–meets–tiki bar atmosphere and dynamic gin-centric cocktails have earned this dusky cocktail den an avid following. ✉ *12 rue St-Bernard, 11e, Charonne* Ⓜ *Faidherbe-Chaligny, Rue des Boulets.*

 **Dirty Lemon**

COCKTAIL BARS | When Palestinian chef Ruba Khoury (a veteran of several Michelin-starred kitchens) struck out on her own, she surprised everyone by opening a cocktail bar, "made by women for women." But no one's complaining: along with some of the city's most splendid cocktails and mocktails, highlighting fresh fruit and veggie juices, her accompanying menu of scintillating finger food makes settling in for the evening a pleasure. ✉ *24 rue de la Folie Méricourt, 11e, Charonne* ☎ *01–43–38–77–02* ⊕ *www.dirtylemonbar.com* Ⓜ *St-Ambroise.*

CLUBS

Le Nouveau Casino

DANCE CLUB | You'll find this concert hall and club tucked behind the Café Charbon. Pop and rock concerts prevail during the week, and the revelry continues on Friday and Saturday from midnight until dawn. House, minimal, and techno DJs are the standard. ✉ *109 rue Oberkampf, 11e, Oberkampf* ☎ *01–43–57–57–40* ⊕ *www.nouveaucasino.fr* Ⓜ *Parmentier.*

 Performing Arts

Cirque d'Hiver Bouglione

CIRCUSES | FAMILY | This circus brings together two famous institutions: the beautiful Cirque d'Hiver hall, constructed in 1852, and the Bouglione troupe, known for its rousing assembly of acrobats, jugglers, clowns, trapeze artists, tigers, and house cats that leap through rings of fire. Shows run mid-October to early March, with a new production each season. ✉ *110 rue Amelot, 11e, République* ☎ *01-47-00-28-81* ⊕ *www.cirquedhiver.com* Ⓜ *Filles du Calvaire.*

 Shopping

CLOTHING

★ FrenchTrotters

CLOTHING | A handpicked selection of the best in French and European fashion for men and women (hard to find outside Europe) is gathered in this sleek duplex boutique. There's also a small selection of accessories, including scarves, bags and leather goods, outerwear, jewelry, perfume, and scented candles. ✉ *30 rue de Charonne, 11e, Charonne* ☎ *01-47-00-84-35* ⊕ *frenchtrotters.fr* Ⓜ *Bastille.*

Sessùn

CLOTHING | Designer Emma François's main inspiration is traveling to faraway places, where she picks up ideas for the textures, prints, and colors of her versatile collection of fashion staples for women. Separates range from neutral basics—a lace inset top or camisole, a wraparound jumpsuit, a knitted cape—to brilliantly colored or natty print sweaters, trousers, blouses, and blazers. The collection is completed with a gently priced line of shoes, boots, scarves, and accessories. The Rue de Charonne concept store, the largest of her Paris shops, also has a gallery featuring the work of French artists and artisans and a selection of handmade textiles, housewares, and

jewelry. ✉ *34 rue de Charonne, 11e, Charonne* ☎ *01-48-06-55-66* ⊕ *boutique.sessun.com* Ⓜ *Bastille.*

HOME DECOR

★ Borgo delle Tovaglie

HOUSEWARES | This Naples-based label's soaring concept store eschews sterile minimalism for an opulence well suited to its lavish Italian linen sheets and pillows. Crafted by hand in yummy colors that change with the seasons, they can be paired with a chic array of dishes, candles, and other treasures for the home. Linger at the stylish bistro—a neighborhood hipster hangout—for an espresso, a glass of wine, or a plate of Italian charcuterie. ✉ *4 rue du Grand Prieuré, 11e, Oberkampf* ☎ *09-82-33-64-81* ⊕ *www.borgodelletovaglie.com* Ⓜ *Oberkampf.*

JEWELRY AND WATCHES

★ Yves Gratas

JEWELRY & WATCHES | With a knack for pairing gems of varying sizes, brilliance, and texture, Yves Gratas allows each stone to influence the design. Whether it's a spectacular necklace of sapphire beads to be worn long or doubled, or a simple agate sphere tipped in gold and dangling like a tiny planet, these stellar jewels feel like one organic whole. ✉ *9 rue Oberkampf, 11e, Oberkampf* ☎ *01-49-29-00-53* ⊕ *www.yvesgratas.com* Ⓜ *Filles du Calvaire, Oberkampf.*

SHOES

★ La Botte Gardiane

SHOES | Craftsmanship and style that won't wreck your budget—that's the trademark of this artisan bootmaker from the Camargue, a wild area of Provence where cowboys require durable boots to rustle the wild horses. That doesn't mean the boutique is short on chic. La Botte Gardiane has impeccably designed and beautifully classic full-length boots, slouchy booties, chukkas, espadrilles, and strappy sandals in suede, python, shearling, and the supplest calf leather from the tanner that supplies Hermès. Look for styles for men, women, and kids. ✉ *25 rue de Charonne, 11e, Charonne* ☎ *09–51–11–05–15* 🌐 *www.labottegardiane.com* Ⓜ *Bastille, Charonne.*

Canal St-Martin and République

The Place de la République stands as a crossroads between the upper Marais and Oberkampf neighborhoods and as a gateway to the 10e arrondissement and the Canal St-Martin. This lively, fashionable area was once overlooked but is now a big draw for its chic, offbeat boutiques and many top-notch cafés, restaurants, and cocktail bars along with its scenic walks by the leafy canal.

 **Sights**

★ Canal St-Martin

HISTORIC SIGHT | The once-forgotten canal has morphed into one of the city's trendiest places to wander. A good time to come is Sunday afternoon, when the Quai de Valmy is closed to cars and some of the shops are open. Rent a bike at any of the many Vélib' stations, stroll along the banks, or go local and cuddle quai-side in the sunshine with someone special.

In 1802 Napoléon ordered the 4.3-km (2.7-mile) canal dug as a source of clean drinking water after cholera and other epidemics swept the city. When it finally opened 23 years later, it extended north from the Seine at Place de la Bastille to the Canal de l'Ourcq, near La Villette. Baron Haussmann later covered a 1.6-km (1-mile) stretch of it, along today's Boulevard Richard Lenoir. It nearly became a highway in the 1970s, before the city's urban planners regained their senses. These days you can take a boat tour from end to end through the canal's nine locks: along the way, the bridges

swing or lift open. The drawbridge with four giant pulleys at Rue de Crimée, near La Villette, was a technological marvel when it debuted in 1885. In recent years gentrification has transformed the once-dodgy canal, with artists taking over former industrial spaces and creating studios and galleries. The bar and restaurant scene is hipster central, and small designers have arrived, fleeing expensive rents in the Marais. Canauxrama (🌐 *www.canauxrama.com*) offers 2½-hour boat cruises through the locks (€25). Embarkation is at each end of the canal: at Bassin de la Villette or Port de l'Arsenal.

✉ *10e, Canal St-Martin* Ⓜ *Jaurès (north end), République (south end), Gare de l'Est (middle).*

La Gaîté Lyrique

ARTS CENTER | One of Paris's younger contemporary-art venues (it opened in 2011) combines innovative exhibits with live musical performances and a multimedia space that features a library, movies, and free video games. Think of it as a smaller, more interactive Centre Pompidou. La Gaîté Lyrique occupies three floors of a 19th-century theater—remnants of which are visible in the café upstairs. ✉ *3 bis, rue Papin, 3e, Canal St-Martin* ☎ *01–53–01–52–00* 🌐 *www.gaite-lyrique.net* 💰 *Free; €7–€14 for temporary exhibitions; concert prices vary* ⊘ *Closed Mon.* Ⓜ *Réaumur-Sébastopol.*

Musée des Arts et Métiers

SCIENCE MUSEUM | FAMILY | Science buffs should not miss this fascinating place, Europe's oldest museum dedicated to invention and technology. It's a treasure trove of wonkiness with 80,000 instruments, machines, and gadgets—including 16th-century astrolabes, Pascal's first mechanical calculator, and film-camera prototypes by the Lumière Brothers, fathers of modern cinema. You can watch video simulations of groundbreaking architectural achievements, like the cast-iron dome, or see how

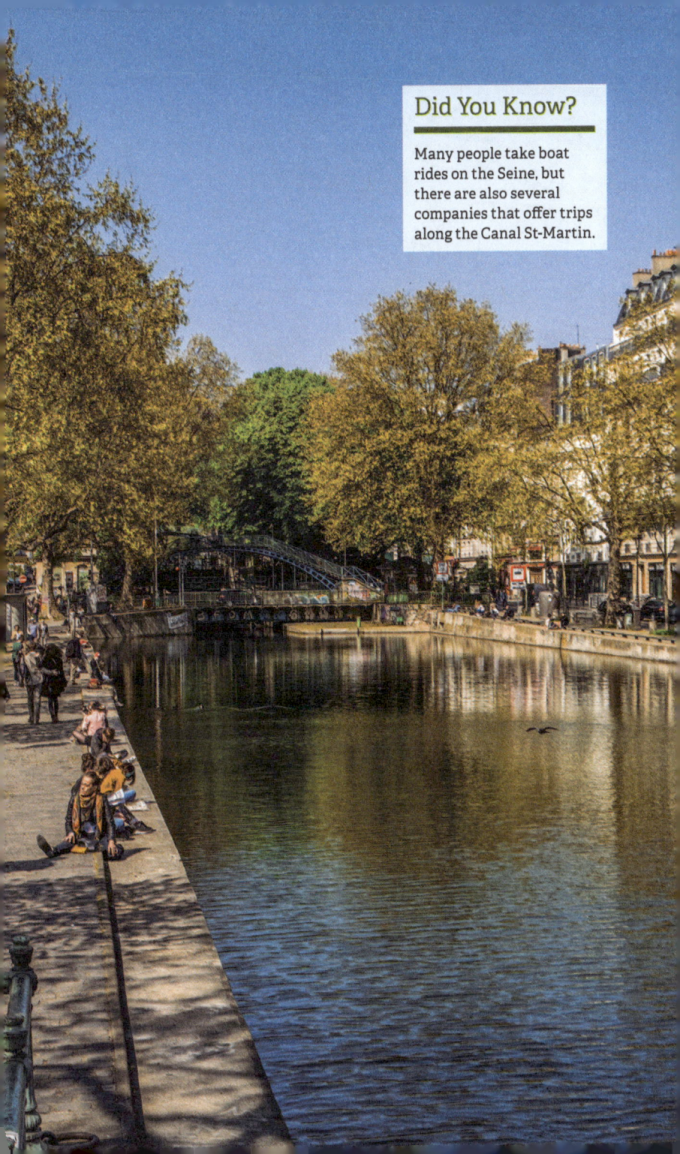

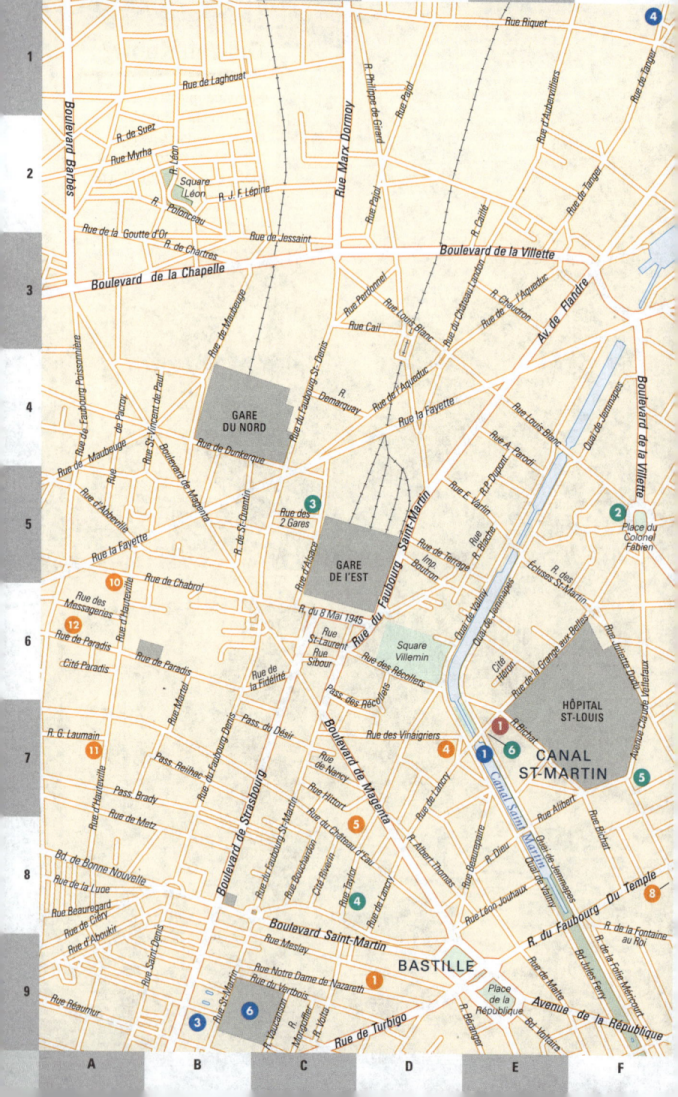

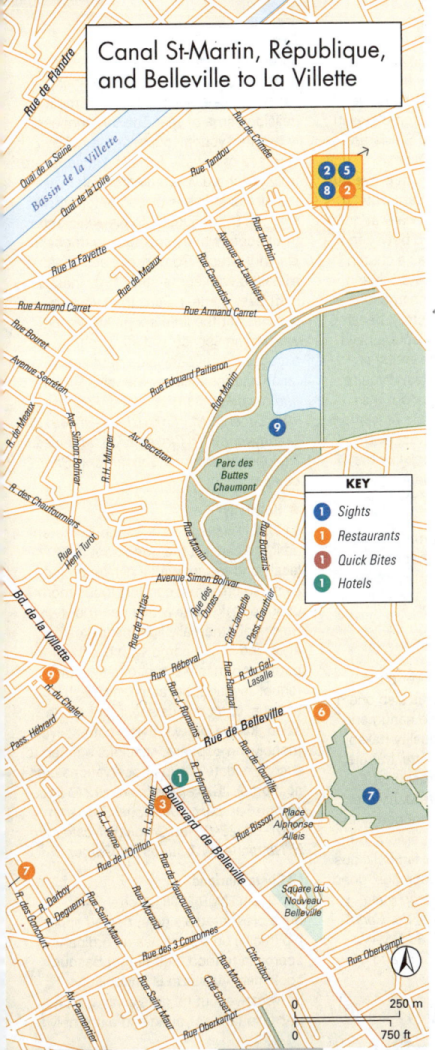